"GOLDEN TIMES"

Human Documents of the
Victorian Age

By the same Author

"HARD TIMES": HUMAN DOCUMENTS OF THE
  INDUSTRIAL REVOLUTION
PIONEERS OF SOCIAL CHANGE
POLITICAL PARTIES AND POLICIES
ADAM SMITH
CHARLES DARWIN
ETHICS OF THE GREAT RELIGIONS
ENCYCLOPAEDIA OF RELIGION AND RELIGIONS
THE WORLD'S STRANGEST CUSTOMS

Editor

ENCYCLOPAEDIA OF MODERN KNOWLEDGE
NEW POPULAR EDUCATOR
TWENTIETH CENTURY ENCYCLOPAEDIA
WONDERS OF THE PAST

"GOLDEN TIMES"

HUMAN DOCUMENTS
OF THE VICTORIAN AGE

E. ROYSTON PIKE

SCHOCKEN BOOKS · NEW YORK

INTRODUCTION

Since it was a Victorian Mamma who taught me my letters—as a young girl she had worn a crinoline, and earlier still little lace-trimmed drawers or pantalettes had frilled around her ankles—I have always had a soft spot for the Victorians. They have always interested me—and what better reason can there be for writing a book about them?

Oh, you say, that's not good enough. There are heaps of books about the Victorians already, and you must really think of a better reason than that for adding another to the tremendous pile.

Admitted, there are books about them without number; but (at least, so it appears to me) the picture all too many of them paint is not only incomplete—that is inevitable in the circumstances—but it is a picture reflected in a distorting mirror. *This* book will I hope be different. It is no nostalgic excursion into the Britain of country-house parties or even the drawing-room 'at homes' of the leisured classes. It is concerned with the ordinary people (although, as we shall soon see, some of them were by no means 'ordinary'). But more important, what we are about to read in these pages is not what historians and biographers and essayists have written about the Victorians in the calmer and clearer light of a much later time, but what they *themselves* wrote *about themselves* in what was a hot and urgent present. The story is, then, authentic to an exceptional degree, in that it is told by the people who knew it best, the people who had lived through it, who had lived in it and indeed made it what it is.

There is still something more that should be said. In this collection of 'documents' are more than a hundred and fifty items, drawn from a vastly greater mass of available material. How have I made my selection? What principle has guided me as, for instance, I have waded through the hundreds of volumes of Government reports in the State Paper Office at the British Museum? The answer is easy. What I have looked for throughout is the *human*. All these documents reveal the 'human side of life': if they didn't, they wouldn't be here.

Now this is something that so many books about 'the Victorians' leave out. Only too often the Victorians are represented as dour and drab and depressing, when in fact they were, many of them, quite cheerful fellows, and the women, some of them, even though they did wear 'their stays too tight' were 'soft, giddy things'. (If you doubt it, read the chapter on 'Queen Victoria's Sisters'). Economic historians, all too many of them, seem to be oblivious of the fact that their graphs and statistics stand for human beings who were as much flesh and blood as we are, of the same brain and brawn; while as for the social historians, they seem to think that the people of Victorian Britain, especially in the 'Golden Age' of the mid-century, spent their lives in a round of sophisticated pleasure. This book is, then, an attempt to put the matter right. All the people we are about to meet are *human*, very much so . . .

Time and place are the next things to be considered. The Victorian Age was a very long one, and the Victorians were pretty thick on the ground. So far as 'time' is concerned, I have concentrated on the twenty-five years from, say, 1850 to 1875, which, by comparison with what had gone before and what came after, have been commonly referred to as the 'Golden Age'. These were the years when British capitalism may be said to have come of age. Business organization was still built around small private companies, often disdaining the 'limited liability' allowed them by law, and financed out of the savings of individual investors. Compared with the great firms of today they were insignificant, and yet in that short period of time Britain established herself as the world's workshop, the world's carrier, the world's clearing-house, the world's banker, and a good deal else. Furthermore there were great advances in political representation, public education, sanitary improvements, the provision of housing accommodation, the emancipation of women, and social matters generally.

As for 'place', nearly all the people we are about to meet come from what have been superciliously denominated the 'lower orders'. Very seldom shall we encounter one of the 'great' Victorians. Why, the dumpy little lady in black silk, who gave her name to the age—we shall see her only once, in the box at the opera (and then screened behind curtains). But what does that matter? There are chances innumerable of meeting Gladstone and Disraeli and Darwin and Tennyson, and all the rest of them—but it is unlikely that you will meet elsewhere than in these pages Mary Ann the Match-box Maker, and the other little Ann who wanted to be an angel, Miss Matilda Davis whose crinoline was the death of her, Mr Bryant and Mr May, Mr Marshall and Mr Snelgrove, the girls in the brickyards who were always singing the latest songs, those naughty hussies the Evesham gloveresses, the working-men who first made trade unionism a power in the land and the 'poor weavers' of Rochdale who founded the 'Co-op', and—who else shall we mention when there are so many to choose from?—the London prostitute who wrote to *The Times*.

Make no mistake about it, these were real people, all of them, and they are real people still. They come alive, and we may listen to what they have to say, and on our ear will strike the distinctive accents of

Brummagem and Tyneside, the boors of Somerset and the sturdy
peasantry of the Border country and the Lowlands. Yes, they come
alive, these people: they pluck at our sleeves, perhaps our heartstrings
may feel a jerk . . .

As in the case of my previous volume, *"Hard Times": Human Documents
of the Industrial Revolution*, a large number of the 'documents' have
been drawn from official publications of the period. Most of these may
be seen only in our very largest libraries, and few if any have ever been
reprinted. As source material of the deepest human interest they are
invaluable. I have also chosen a number of articles from the great
reviews and periodicals of what was the greatest age of that form of
public instruction and entertainment—the *Quarterly* and *Cornhill* (here
I would express appreciation of the courtesy of Sir John Murray), the
Edinburgh and the *Fortnightly*. From *The Economist* have come several
articles of exceptional interest. For the rest, the selections have come
from books published during the years under review, and pamphlets,
some of them from Edwin Chadwick's collection and others that Karl
Marx may have handled when he was writing *Das Kapital* in the
Reading Room at the British Museum.

As will be seen, the material has been arranged in eight main chapters,
most of which have subdivisions. The first chapter has for its subject
The Great Exhibition of 1851. This was indeed what Thomas Hardy
calls it in one of his short tales, 'a precipice in time', and no one can hope
to understand the Victorians who does not realize the extent to which
the Crystal Palace symbolized their pride in present achievement and
boundless hope for the future. This is followed by *Life and Labour*, a
series of picturesquely detailed description of London and the great
industrial regions, a farm labourers' saga, and an account of railway
life when trains were still hand-signalled into the London termini.
Young England is concerned with the juvenile workers in factory and
workshop, and there are independent sections on the Climbing Boys
who cleaned Victorian chimneys, and the Juvenile Delinquents, who
were even more of a problem then than they are now. Next we have the
longest chapter in the book. *Queen Victoria's Sisters* contains a number
of documents describing the life of women in Domestic Service, the
London Dress Trades, Factories and Workshops, Pit-banks and
Brickfields, and in Agriculture. The length of this chapter reflects the
deep human interest and importance of the subject. Closely connected
with this is the chapter that follows, called (a little ironically perhaps)
Home Sweet Home. Much that is revealed here will come as a surprise to
those who have been led to suppose that the 'stately home' was typical
of Victorian domestic arrangements. In the chapter on *The Sanitary
Idea* we are brought up against the horrible conditions in which the

mass of the people lived and moved and had their being, and we are privileged to meet Dr John Simon, whose scathing indictments of what he found and tried to remedy are not only history but literature. *Workers Unite!* echoes Karl Marx, but it has to do with the British working-men who founded the modern Trade Union and Co-operative movements. Finally, in '*Sex*' *and the Victorians* we explore a field of human activity which has but seldom attracted the notice of historians. Probably this chapter more than any other will surprise those readers who have been brought up to believe that 'the Victorians' were a set of more or less unconscious prigs and humbugs. In Chapter 1 we have seen that they were not afraid to mention in an Official Report water-closets and urinals; and now, in Chapter 8, we find them discussing and describing in the frankest and most matter-of-fact way the prostitute and her clients and the various environments in which her trade was carried on. Just as surprising is the last document of all. For here we have instructions in the matter of family limitation which, there is good reason to believe, were carefully followed in innumerable Victorian bedrooms.

Each chapter, and some of the sub-sections, have been given an Editorial Introduction, designed to put the reader 'in the picture' so far as the respective author and background are concerned. The headings to the documents are mine, and in some of the longer pieces I have inserted subsidiary headings. Editorial additions or amendments, etc. are placed within square brackets. No other alterations have been made in the text. Full details as to source are appended to each document.

The illustrations are an essential part of the whole. They have been chosen for their documentary value, and I gratefully acknowledge the assistance rendered in this connection by the Editor of *Punch* and the Photographic Service of the British Museum. So in conclusion, here is a collection of 'documents,' textual and pictorial and *human*, illustrating and describing one of the most vigorous, vital, fertile periods in the history of the modern world.

CONTENTS

(P.P. = Parliamentary Papers)

page

INTRODUCTION

1. THE GOLDEN AGE   7

(*a*) THE GREAT EXHIBITION   21

1. *'A most gorgeous sight.'* Lord Macaulay   26
2. *Mr Punch's Own Report.* Punch   27
3. *'Shilling Day' at the Crystal Palace.* Henry Mayhew   29
4. *What They Ate at the Exhibition.* P.P. 1852, vol. 26   33
5. *'Ladies' and 'Gents'.* P.P. 1852, vol. 26   34

(*b*) WHAT MADE THE VICTORIANS SO PROUD?   36

6. *Past and Present.* The Economist   38
7. *'Man's sacred mission.'* H.R.H. Prince Albert   43
8. *'Endless progression.'* The Economist   45

2. LIFE AND LABOUR   47

1. *Round the Clock in Victorian London.* Geo. Augustus Sala   49
2. *Food and Drink for London's Millions.* Quarterly Review   57
3. *Pit-people of Tyneside.* Cornhill Magazine   64
4. *Social Condition of Lancashire Factory People.*   72
   Fortnightly Review
5. *The Black Country.* Edinburgh Review   78
6. *Birmingham, 'City of a Thousand Trades.'* P.P. 1864,   85
   vol. 22
7. *'The Social and Provident Proclivities of Potters.'*   90
   P.P. 1865, vol. 20
8. *People on the London & North-Western.*   95
   Sir Francis Bond Head
9. *The Life of a Farm Labourer.* Cornhill Magazine   102

3. YOUNG ENGLAND

(*a*) CHILDREN'S EMPLOYMENT COMMISSION (1862)   109

1. *Why Little Children Are Sent out to Work.*   111
   P.P. 1852/3, vol. 90

CONTENTS

page

2. *The Young Potters.* P.P. 1863, vol. 18   112
3. *Wretched Places, Match Factories.* P.P. 1863, vol. 18   115
4. *'Nothing unpleasant' at Bryant & May's.* P.P. 1863,   117
   vol. 18
5. *Why Young George 'goggled'.* P.P. 1863, vol. 22   118
6. *Mary Ann the Match-box Maker.* P.P. 1863, vol. 18   119
7. *A Stab in the Eye.* P.P. 1864, vol. 18   120
8. *Going to School in the Straw Plait Country.* P.P. 1864,   120
   vol. 22
9. *'White Slavery' in Manchester.* P.P. 1864, vol. 22   123
10. *What They Didn't Know in Brummagem.* P.P. 1864,   124
    vol. 22
11. *Smelly Work in the Steel-pen Factory.* P.P. 1864,   125
    vol. 22
12. *The Three Sisters in the Button Factory.* P.P. 1864,   126
    vol. 22
13. *'My sister—her swears awful.'* P.P. 1864, vol. 22   127
14. *'The nailers are coming!'* P.P. 1864, vol. 22   128
15. *Oh, To Be a Nailer's Boy.* P.P. 1864, vol. 22   129
16. *Little Ann Wants to be an Angel.* P.P. 1864, vol. 22   131
17. *Sheffield's Child of Doom.* P.P. 1865, vol. 20   132
18. *The Boys at John Brown's.* P.P. 1865, vol. 25   133
19. *'Awful brutes' in the Glass-house.* P.P. 1865, vol. 25   135
20. *'A good many as wash dirty.'* P.P. 1865, vol. 25   136
21. *A Brick in His Mouth.* P.P. 1966, vol. 24   137
22. *Scaring Crows.* P.P. 1867, vol. 16   137

(*b*) THE LONG AGONY OF THE CLIMBING-BOYS   138
23. *The Nottingham Master-sweep's Story.* P.P. 1863,   140
    vol. 18
24. *'As bad as the Negro slavery.'* P.P. 1863, vol. 18   142
25. *'Sleeping black.'* P.P. 1863, vol. 18   143

(*c*) JUVENILE DELINQUENTS   145
26. *'City Arabs.'* P.P. 1852, vol. 7   146
27. *A Little Boy's First Crime.* P.P. 1852, vol. 7   147
28. *Ten and Eleven: Brothers in 'Crime'.* P.P. 1852, vol. 7   148
29. *'Ragged Schools' to the Rescue.* P.P. 1852, vol. 7   150

page

4. QUEEN VICTORIA'S SISTERS

(*a*) THE INDUSTRY OF A MILLION WOMEN   155

  1. *Domestic Service in the 1860s.* Edinburgh Review   157
  2. *'Hardest worked women.'* Englishwoman's Review   162
  3. *'Early closing' for Servant Girls!* Comic Almanack   164
  4. *'Drat the little minx!'* Brothers Mayhew   164

(*b*) LONDON DRESSMAKERS   169

  5. *The Sanitary Circumstances of London Dressmakers.*   170
     P.P. 1864, vol. 28
  6. *Meet Mr Marshall and Mr Snelgrove.* P.P. 1864,   175
     vol. 22
  7. *At Swan & Edgar's.* P.P. 1864, vol. 22   176
  8. *Stout and Sherry for Mr Jay's Young Ladies.*   177
     P.P. 1864, vol. 22
  9. *'Letters with coronets.'* P.P. 1864, vol. 22   178
  10. *Ladies Are to Blame.* P.P. 1864, vol. 22   179
  11. *'Their stays are too tight.'* P.P. 1864, vol. 22   180
  12. *Miss Bramwell's Revelations.* P.P. 1864, vol. 22   181
  13. *The Girls Who Were Told to Leave.* P.P. 1864, vol. 22   182
  14. *'They chuck the bottles over the roof.'* P.P. 1864, vol. 22   183
  15. *Wonderful Stuff, Cod-liver Oil!* P.P. 1864, vol. 22   184
  16. *Penal Shirt-making.* Punch   185

(*c*) FEMALE LABOUR IN FACTORY AND WORKSHOP   187

  17. *Messrs Fry's Factory a Pleasure to Visit.* P.P. 1866,   188
     vol. 24
  18. *The Best Nottingham Could Show?* P.P. 1863, vol. 18   189
  19. *The Lace-Girl's Letter.* P.P. 1863, vol. 18   190
  20. *What Made Mr Chamberlain's Girls Scream.* P.P. 1864,   191
     vol. 22
  21. *Matilda Davis's Crinoline.* P.P. 1864, vol. 22   192
  22. *'Girls are soft, giddy things.'* P.P. 1865, vol. 20   193
  23. *'Curse and swear like troopers.'* P.P. 1865, vol. 20   194
  24. *The Girls Who Make Cigars.* P.P. 1865, vol. 20   195
  25. *Night and Day in the Paper Mills.* P.P. 1865, vol. 20   197
  26. *Girls in Pickle.* Henry Mayhew   199
  27. *A Job behind the Counter?* Emily Faithfull   200

CONTENTS

		page
28.	*Mr Bennett Had to Sack His Young Ladies.* Dr A. Wynter	201
29.	*When Married Women Work in Factories.* P.P. 1861, vol. 16	202
30.	*Cold Feet and Round Shoulders.* P.P. 1861, vol. 16	203
31.	*Evesham's Gloveresses.* P.P. 1864, vol. 22	204

(*d*) WOMEN OF THE PIT-BANKS AND BRICKFIELDS · 207

32.	*'Degrading employment of females.'* P.P. 1865, vol. 18	207
33.	*Good-looking Welsh Women.* P.P. 1867/8, vol. 39	208
34.	*Jolly Breaks in the Pit-girls' Life.* Edinburgh Review	209
35.	*Clay-splashed Females in the Brickyards.* P.P. 1865, vol. 20	211
36.	*'Anything new in the way of a song.'* P.P. 1864, vol. 22	213
37.	*'Foul-mouthed boys before they are women.'* P.P. 1866, vol. 24	213
38.	*'They have to stoop down.'* P.P. 1866, vol. 24	214
39.	*'The girl's virtue is gone.'* P.P. 1866, vol. 24	214

(*e*) WOMEN IN AGRICULTURE · 216

40.	*Women and Girls of the 'Gangs'.* P.P. 1867, vol. 16	217
41.	*'All dripping wet.'* P.P. 1867, vol. 16	220
42.	*'The girl was calling out.'* P.P. 1867, vol. 16	221
43.	*'The gangmaster pulled me down.'* P.P. 1867, vol. 16	221
44.	*What 8d a Day Does to a Woman.* P.P. 1868/9, vol. 13	222
45.	*'Looked over like cattle.'* P.P. 1868/9, vol. 13	223
46.	*Northumbria's Women Bondagers.* P.P. 1867/8, vol. 17	224
47.	*Criminal Mothers of the Marshlands.* P.P. 1864, vol. 28	228

5. HOME SWEET HOME · 233

1.	*'Every man's house is his castle.'* P.P. 1852/3, vol. 85	234
2.	*A Carpet in the Sitting-room.* G. R. Porter	236
3.	*A Londoner's Home.* George Godwin	237
4.	*Miss Octavia Hill's Housing Venture.* Octavia Hill	239
5.	*Prince Albert's Model Cottages.* The Great Exhibition Catalogue	242
6.	*England's 'Show' Villages.* P.P. 1865, vol. 26	245
7.	*The Shame of 'Cottage Herding'.* P.P. 1867/8, vol. 17	246

page

8. *The Leicestershire Lad's Bride.* P.P. 1865, vol. 26   248
9. *The Home of a Somersetshire Peasant.* F. G. Heath   249
10. *As Bad as the Black Hole of Calcutta.* P.P. 1865,   251
    vol. 26
11. *Duck and Green Peas.* P.P. 1850, vol. 23   252
12. *What the Miners Read.* P.P. 1850, vol. 23   254
13. *The Nailers' Wash-basin.* P.P. 1868/9, vol. 14   255
14. *Halstead Weaver.* Mary Merryweather   257
15. *'Diabolic odour' of Welsh Cottages.* P.P. 1865, vol. 26   259
16. *Cardiganshire's Wretched Hovels.* P.P. 1870, vol. 13   260
17. *'But-and-Ben' Cottages of the Scotch Peasantry.*   262
    P.P. 1870, vol. 13
18. *Seen from a Bus-top.* Chas. M. Smith   263
19. *Saturday Afternoon to Sunday Dinner.* A Journeyman   264
    Engineer
20. *Chit-Chat over the Wash-tub.* Henry Mayhew   269

6. THE SANITARY IDEA

(*a*) LONDON THE INSANITARY CITY   271

1. *Sanitary Neglect.* Dr John Simon   273
2. *Social Condition of the Poor.* Dr John Simon   274
3. *'Pestilential heaping of human beings.'* Dr John Simon   276
4. *The 'Cesspool city' beneath the City.* Dr John Simon   278
5. *Scuffling at a Standcock.* Dr John Simon   279
6. *What's in London Water.* Dr John Simon   281
7. *'Gigantic poison bed.'* Dr John Simon   282
8. *London Smoke.* Dr John Simon   284
9. *'Grievious nuisance' of Slaughter-houses.* Dr John Simon   286
10. *The Corpse amid the Living.* Dr John Simon   286
11. *The Horrors of the Graveyards.* Dr John Simon   288
12. *Plea for a Ministry of Health.* Dr John Simon   290
13. *'Unfit for human habitation.'* Dr John Simon   292
14. *The Shocking Truth about London Bakehouses.*   293
    P.P. 1862, vol. 47
15. *Much Worse Things than Water in the Milk!*   295
    P.P. 1854/5, vol. 8
16. *Deadly Gas at Westminster.* P.P. 1857/8, vol. 48   297
17. *A Bed for the Night.* Westminster Review   298

page

18. *Cleaning Up the Lodging Houses.* P.P. 1857, vol. 16   300

(*b*) KING CHOLERA   302

19. *When Mr G. Got Cholera.* Dr John Simon   303
20. *A Visit to the 'Capital of Cholera'.* Henry Mayhew   306
21. *Lord Palmerston's Advice.* H. T. Buckle   309

7. WORKERS UNITE!

(*a*) TRADE UNIONS   313

1. *Trade Unionism in the 1860s.* Thomas Hughes and   315
   Frederic Harrison
2. *Joining the Union.* P.P. 1867, vol. 32   320
3. *'Rattening' Explained.* P.P. 1867, vol. 32   321
4. *Pickets on the Gate.* P.P. 1867, vol. 32   322
5. *'Stinking hussies!'* P.P. 1867/8, vol. 31   324
6. *The Strike at Trollope's.* P.P. 1867, vol. 32   324
7. *Letters from America.* P.P. 1867/8, vol. 39   328

(*b*) CO-OPERATION   330

8. *Rochdale's 'Equitable Pioneers'.* G. J. Holyoake   331
9. *Even the Cocks Crowed 'Co-operation'!* G. J. Holyoake   335

8. 'SEX' AND THE VICTORIANS   337

1. *The London Prostitute who wrote to* The Times   339
2. *'A revelation', says the Editor.* The Times   346
3. *A Plain Guide to London's Harlotry.* Dr Wm. Acton   347
4. *The Sixteen-year-old Streetwalker.* Henry Mayhew   353
5. *'Kiss me quick' Bonnets.* The Times   355
6. *Welsh 'Laxity'.* P.P. 1870, vol. 13   356
7. *Courting Customs of the Lowland Scotch.* P.P. 1870,   356
   vol. 13
8. *Unpalatable Facts about the 'Concubinage Market'.*   358
   Dr John Simon
9. *Mrs Josephine Butler to the Rescue.* P.P. 1871, vol. 19   361
10. *Victorian Methods of Family Limitation.*   362
    Dr George Drysdale

EPILOGUE   367

INDEX   369

ILLUSTRATIONS

PLATES

facing page

1. Specimens from Mr Punch's Industrial Exhibition   32
   Exhibition Refreshment Room Scene   32

2. Over London, by rail   33

3. Pride of Beauty! The Ladies' Mile in Hyde Park   64

4. Disgrace of Destitution: Under the Arches   65
   Found in the Street   65

5. The Haunted Lady, or 'The Ghost' in the Looking Glass   224
   What Will Become of the Servant-gals?   224

6. Dudley Street, Seven Dials, London   225
   A Stranger Clean from the Country   225

7. The Dead and the Living   256
   A Londoner's Home   256

8. A Weaver's Garret in Spitalfields   257
   John P— and his Cottage   257

LINE DRAWINGS

page

1. Her Majesty as She Appeared on the First of May   20

2. The Crystal Palace in Hyde Park   23
   Messrs Osler's Fountain   23

3. 'Machinery—the grand focus of attraction'   30

4. Getting home from the Crystal Palace on a Fête Day   31
   London traffic in 1862   31

5. A London Dairy   61

6. Up-to-date equipment for British farms, as shown at the
   Great Exhibition   105

7. Northumbrian 'Bondagers'   227

8. Prince Albert's Model Cottages   243

9. The Cottage   247

10. Father Thames introducing his offspring to the Fair City
    of London   263

11. Water in the milk . . .   294

12. A Court for King Cholera   305

13. 'Black-leg!'   323

		page
14.	Effects of a Strike	325
15.	The Great Social Evil	341
16.	Over Population: George Cruikshank's vision of 'things to come!'	363

The Cartoons from *Punch* are reproduced by courtesy of the Editor

Plates No. 2, 3, 4, 6, 7, 8 and Line Drawing No. 5 are from British Museum Photographs

The Gustave Doré drawings are from Blanchard Jerrold's *London* (1872)

"GOLDEN TIMES"

HER MAJESTY, as She Appeared on the FIRST of MAY, Surrounded by "**Horrible Conspirators and Assassins.**"

1. John Leech in *Punch*, 1851

CHAPTER I

THE GOLDEN AGE

(a) THE GREAT EXHIBITION

> Look yonder where the engines toil:
> These England's arms of conquest are,
> The trophies of her bloodless war:
> Brave weapons these.
>
> Victorious over wave and soil,
> With these she sails, she weaves, she tills,
> Pierces the everlasting hills
> And spans the seas.

Thackeray's *May-Day Ode*, written on the occasion of the opening of the Great Exhibition of 1851, is surely an altogether appropriate choice with which to open this selection of 'documents' illustrating the social and economic life of that 'golden age'. Perhaps as poetry it is hardly of Tennysonian quality, and it may not even be very good verse. But—no doubt about it—it is a genuine recapturing of the mood of the vast crowds of people, of every class and of most nations, who on that rain-into-sunshine morning thronged all the ways that led to the Crystal Palace in Hyde Park.

> But yesterday a naked sod
> The dandies sneered from Rotten Row,
> And cantered o'er it to and fro:
> And see 'tis done!
>
> As though 'twere by a wizard's rod
> A blazing arch of lucid glass
> Leaps like a fountain from the grass
> To meet the sun!

Yes, it was *done*, and Britain (Thackeray wrote *England*, but since his time we have become more considerate of the susceptibilities of Scots and Welsh and Irish) had done it. British brains had conceived what had seemed at first a fantastic project. British capitalists had dipped their hands in their pockets—no Government grants, not even a Government guarantee—and put up the money; and such was their excellent business management, that they showed a substantial profit at the end. British architects and designers had drawn up the plans, British engineers and building contractors had transferred the plans from the drawing-board on to the hard ground of reality, British working-men—two thousand of them at the maximum—had laid the foundations, manœuvred the 4,000 tons of iron work into position, raised the 2,300 cast-iron girders, the 3,300 pillars, the 30 miles of rainwater guttering, the 202 miles of sash-bars, and the 800,000 superficial feet of glass. And (so much for our pride in our prefabricating methods) most of the materials had been prepared and put together away from the site, and taken there in horse-drawn carts and waggons.

The tender for the great structure—a structure such as had never been seen before, so that those responsible had no accumulated wealth of experience to go by—was not accepted by the Royal Commissioners who had charge of the project until July 26, 1850. (It was put in by Messrs Fox, Henderson & Co., and the amount was £79,800). Possession of the site was obtained four days later. They had to get a move on. The first column was fixed on September 26th, and work was continued without a break. Without any of the modern aids to speed in construction, they kept at it day and night, and, so far as we are informed, there were no demarcation disputes, no labour troubles, no hold-ups worth the mention. On April 28, 1851, the painters—who had been following hard on the heels of the glaziers as they moved in their little covered carriages along the miles of guttering—were out, the scaffolding was coming down, and men were fitting the blinds in hopeful anticipation of the sun which in fact did put in an impressive appearance. On May 1st the Crystal Palace (as it had been christened by *Punch* in a moment of the happiest inspiration) was opened by the Queen, dead on time.

What a splendid advertisement for British enterprise and skill and organizing ability! But this was not all. So confident were those who planned and prepared the Exhibition, that British inventors and designers, manufacturers and industrialists of every description, had nothing to fear from foreign competition, that an invitation had been extended to all the countries of the civilized world to send their choicest products to be displayed with Britain's in the many miles of stands. 'Let them all come! We can do everything that they can do—and do it cheaper, and better!' And although France had perhaps the advantage in some of the finer textiles and fancy goods, and the influence of continental furniture-designers was all too horribly obvious, it was generally allowed that the Exhibition was a massive demonstration of British supremacy in the industrial fields.

'One of the wonders of the world', is how Queen Victoria described it in her 'Exhibition Journal', after she had returned to Buckingham Palace from one of the numerous visits she paid to the great building, just to see how things were getting along—'which we English may

2. The Crystal Palace in Hyde Park.

A great centre of attraction was Messrs. Osler's Fountain in cut crystal glass.

Official Catalogue of the Great Exhibition (1851)

indeed be proud of . . . It made me feel proud and happy.' And on the evening of May 1st she wrote:

'The tremendous cheering, the joy expressed on every face, the vastness of the building, with all its decorations and exhibits, the sound of the organ (with 200 instruments and 600 voices, which seemed nothing) and my beloved husband, the creator of this peace festival, "uniting the industry and art of all nations of the earth", all this was indeed moving, and a day to live for ever. God bless my dearest Albert, and my dear Country, which has shown itself so great to-day.'

*   *   *

Among those who walked across the Park on that ecstatic morning was Macaulay (he was not 'Lord' till 1857), and that evening, on his return to his flat in 'Albany', he wrote down his impressions in the entry that is the first of our 'documents'. It is a typically Victorian piece, breathing an air of complacent confidence in the solid virtues, the honest good sense, of the common people. To think that there were persons—persons, too, who considered themselves to be well-informed—who feared that these well-fed, well-dressed, and well-behaved men and women could ever be so foolish as to go in for revolutions and such like! The very idea was preposterous. But Macaulay didn't care for crowds; and, dazzled by the gorgeousness of what he had seen, he was glad to get back to Jane Austen.

*   *   *

Another 'eminent Victorian' has put his name to No. 2. Having, 'with our usual good fortune', managed to secure a front place, 'Mr Punch' was able to give an account of the 'most gratifying incident of the day', when the Queen and Prince Albert, holding by the hand their two eldest children (Victoria the Princess Royal, and the future King Edward VII), moved slowly through the crush of spectators. We know how they appeared, for in the same number of *Punch, or the London Charivari*, to give that inimitable mirror of the Victorian social scene its full title, there was published the drawing reproduced on page 20, of 'Her Majesty, as she appeared on the 1st of May, surrounded by "Horrible Conspirators and Assassins",'—a sly dig, this, at those people whose fears Macaulay had so rightly scoffed at.

Between that opening day and Saturday, October 11th, when the Exhibition closed its doors, it had received over six million visitors. The maximum was on the last Tuesday, when 92,000 persons were assembled together at one time under the 'arch of lucid glass', and the total for the day was 109,915. The admission charge was half a crown on Fridays and five shillings on Saturdays, but from Monday to Thursday it was only a shilling.

The Sandboys seem to have gone there on one of the shilling days. And who (you may ask) were the Sandboys? Well, according to that celebrated journalist Henry Mayhew, Mr Christopher Sandboys, 'who after the old Cumberland fashion was called Cursty', was one of those small landed proprietors in the Lake District known as 'statesmen', and he had never been farther from his farm at Buttermere than Keswick until the fame of the Great Exhibition drew him, as it drew so many others from even more remote places. So he and his wife and their children—their son Jobby and their daughter Eley—set out for London, and what happened to them is described in Mayhew's *1851: or, The Adventures of Mr and Mrs Sandboys, and Family, who came up to London 'to enjoy themselves', and to see the Great Exhibition.* Our No. 3 is taken from this little book, and it is just as accurate a piece of reportage as anything in Mayhew's most famous production, *London Labour and the London Poor,* the first version of which was appearing at about this time.

Now for a couple of 'documents' of a different character, dealing with matters that are seldom mentioned in official reports.

A careful account was kept of what visitors to the Great Exhibition ate, and this is reproduced in No. 4. The privilege of supplying refreshments to the visitors was put out to tender, and Messrs Schweppe secured the contract for the sum of £5,500. Judging from what we are told here, the firm must have done quite well out of it. Nearly two million buns—and, what is more to the point, over a million bottles of the 'minerals' for which Schweppe was even then famous. But the Commissioners had ordained that 'No wines, spirits, beer, or intoxicating drinks are permitted to be sold to the visitors', an injunction which provided John Leech with a subject for one of his most celebrated *Punch* cartoons. No, you can't have a pint o' beer, says the attractive little piece of feminine assurance behind the counter, but you can have 'a strawberry ice and a wafer'.

Official notice was also taken of the fact that visitors might want to 'go to the lavatory'—although that was not the phrase that was used (No. 5). As the Commissioners reported in due course, it was 'a somewhat novel step to provide these conveniences for the public on a large scale, and at the same time'—true Victorian business instinct this!—'to derive a revenue from them'. As will be seen from the statement, the 'waiting rooms' more than paid for themselves.

Do these references to water-closets and urinals seem out of place in a historical record? If they do, they ought not to. The fact that in 1851 it was considered a startling novelty to make public provision for the convenience of the tens of thousands of visitors of both sexes is of definite historical importance. Clearly this was the view of the Commissioners, who through their secretary, Henry (later Sir Henry) Cole, expressed concern for 'the sufferings which must be endured by all, but more especially by females'. This should be borne in mind by those who think that the Victorians were too prudish for words.

Many other little details worth retrieving may be found in the newspapers of the time. This, for instance, that the total number of charges made at the police-station at the Prince of Wales's Gate relating to offences within the Crystal Palace was twenty-five, of which nine were for picking pockets, six for attempts to do so, and ten for petty larcenies from stalls. Then there were the 'mishaps'. Across more than a century comes the joke, that 'when the teetotallers appeared in force, all the fountains suddenly ceased to play, owing to an accidental obstruction in the water-pipes'. Of course, not a few children got separated from their parents, and were duly cared for by the police. Then the lost-property office was kept busy. Pocket-handkerchiefs, parasols, bracelets, brooches, and shawl-pins by the hundred . . . and one petticoat, which was never claimed . . .

So the days passed, until that Saturday in October when, as *The Times* put it in an editorial on the following Monday morning, 'the Great Exhibition closed its wonderful career, and the public took a last farewell of its splendours. After being open for five months and eleven days and concentrating in that time a larger amount of admiration than has probably ever been given within the same period to the works of man, the pageant terminates . . .'

I

'A most gorgeous sight'

Thursday, May 1, 1851.—A fine day for the opening of the Exhibition. A little cloudy in the morning, but generally sunny and pleasant. I was struck by the number of foreigners in the streets. All, however, were respectable and decent people. I saw none of the men of action with whom the Socialists were threatening us. I went to the Park and along the Serpentine. There were immense crowds on both sides of the water. I should think there must have been near three hundred thousand people in Hyde Park at once. The sight among the green boughs was delightful. The boats, and little frigates, darting across the lake; the flags; the music; the guns;—everything was exhilarating, and the temper of the multitude the best possible.

I fell in with Punch Greville, and walked with him for an hour. He, like me, thought the outside spectacle better worth seeing than the pageant under cover. He showed me a letter from Madame de Lieven, foolish, with an affectation of cleverness and profundity, just like herself. She calls this Exhibition a bold, a rash, experiment. She apprehends a horrible explosion. 'You may get through it safe; and, if you do, you will give yourself more airs than ever.' And this woman is thought a political oracle in some circles! There is just as much chance of a revolution in England as of the falling of the moon.

I made my way into the building; a most gorgeous sight; vast; graceful; beyond the dreams of the Arabian romances. I cannot think that the Caesars ever exhibited a more splendid spectacle. I was quite dazzled . . . I wandered about, and elbowed my way through the crowd which filled the nave, admiring the general effect, but not attending much to details . . . Home, and finished *Persuasion* . . .

Life and Letters of Lord Macaulay (1876).

2

Mr Punch's 'Own Report'

————

May has often belied its character for merriment by occasional fits of gloom, but the first of May in the present year has sufficed to retrieve all former faults of that frequently fickle month, and render it for ever famous in the annals of glorious sunshine and cheerfulness.

We had intended to get up with the lark, but there being no local lark to regulate our movements, we accepted as a substitute those well-known London black-birds, the sweeps, whose cry was the signal for our rising. Everything seemed auspicious. Even our razor was in excellent temper, which was fortunate, for had it been obstinate, we should have had a terribly close shave to join in the line of equipages, which already, before eight o'clock, extended in one rank—a rank in which no aristocratic distinctions were observed—from the doors of the Crystal Palace to the very centre of the Metropolis. The proudest equipage of the peer was obliged to fall in behind the humblest fly [cab] or the ugliest Hansom; there being no privileged order, but the order of arrival . . .

During the time of waiting for the opening of the doors, good humour kept up the spirits of all, except some of those who, being driven impatiently by the side of the line, found themselves obliged to retrace their steps on arriving at the park gates, and take their places at the back of the whole string, which had lengthened a mile or so since they had foolishly quitted it ... Nevertheless, the arrangements were so excellent, and every foot of ground was so well apportioned, that scarcely any one had room for complaint ...

The doors were at length opened, and the crowd awaiting the arrival of Her Majesty, furnished an exhibition of various kinds of industry not represented within the doors of the Crystal Palace. Every available place for catching a sight of the procession had been taken possession of in every available manner ... The trees opposite the principal door seemed to have burst out suddenly into a crop of eager boys, who, in spite of the warnings of the police ... seemed to think every tree a legitimate tree of knowledge, if anything could be learned or seen by climbing it. In vain did the constable look up at the trees and threaten the juvenile branches ... Here and there an adventurous policeman would climb after the contumacious urchin; but the latter, with provoking levity, would scramble on to some bough too slender to bear the weight of the civil authority, who, however, on this occasion, seldom lost his temper, though sometimes losing his balance.

We now entered the building, and with our usual good fortune, secured a front place ... At length a cheer without, and a flourish of trumpets within, announced the arrival of the Queen—and the Prince, who, by the idea of this Exhibition, has given to Royal Consortship a new glory ... Prince Albert has done a grand service to humanity, and earned imperishable fame for himself by an idea, the greatness of which, instead of becoming less, will appear still greater as it recedes from us ...

During the ceremonial, which was of a solemn and imposing nature, it was not surprising that several eyes, including the Royal one, were slightly crystallized in graceful harmony with the Crystal Palace ...

At the conclusion of the ceremonial, a Chinese, carried away, or rather pushed forward, by his enthusiasm, performed suddenly, before Her Majesty, an elaborate salaam, consisting of a sudden act of prostration on his face ...

Beyond comparison, the most gratifying incident of the day was the promenade of the Queen and Prince, holding by the hand their two eldest children, through the whole of the lower range of the building. It was a magnificent lesson for foreigners—and especially for the Prussian princes, who cannot stir abroad without an armed escort— to see how securely and confidently a young female Sovereign and her family could walk in the closest possible contact, near enough to be touched by almost everyone, with five-and-twenty thousand people, selected from no class, and requiring only the sum of forty-two shillings as a qualification for the nearest proximity with royalty.

Here was a splendid example of that real freedom on the one hand, and perfect security on the other, which are the result of our constitutional monarchy, and which all the despotism and republicanism of the world cannot obtain elsewhere, let them go on as long as they may, executing each other in the name of order, or cutting each other's throats in the name of liberty.

It was delightful to see the smiling confidence of the Queen, as— leaning on her husband's arm, the father and the mother each holding by the hand one of the royal children—she acknowledged the heartfelt cheerings of the enthusiastic but perfectly orderly multitude ...

'Punch's own report of the Opening of the Great Exhibition'; *Punch*, 1851.

3

'*Shilling Day*' at the Crystal Palace

For the first week or two, the road within a mile of the 'Glass Hive' was blocked with carriages. From the Prince of Wales' Gate to Apsley House there stretched one long line of cabs, omnibuses, carriages, 'broughams', 'flies', now moving for a few minutes, and now stopping for double the time, while the impatient visitors within let down the blinds and thrust their heads out to see how far the line extended ...

Now, there is scarcely a carriage or a Hansom cab to be seen. The great stream of carriage visitors has ceased (except on the most expensive days) ... The southern entrance is no longer beset with broughams, but gathered round it are groups of gazers, too poor or too 'prudent' to pay for admission within. The public-houses along the road are now filled to overflowing, for outside them are ranged long benches, on which sit visitors in their holiday attire, resting on their way. Almost all the pedestrians, too, have baskets on their arms, evidently filled with the day's stock of provisions.

The ladies are all 'got up' in their brightest-coloured bonnets and polkas [jackets], and as they haste along, they 'step out' till their faces are seen to glow again with their eagerness to get to the Grand Show, while the gentlemen in green or brown felt 'wide-awakes', or fluffy beaver hats, and with the cuffs of their best coats, and the bottoms of

3. 'Machinery—the grand focus of attraction.' (Official Catalogue of the Great Exhibition)

their best trousers turned up, are marching heavily on—some with babies in their arms, others with baskets, and others carrying corpulent cotton umbrellas.

And inside the Great Exhibition the scene is equally different from that of the first week or two. The nave is no longer filled with elegant and inert loungers—lolling on seats, and evidently come there to be seen rather than to see. Those who are now to be found there, have come to look at the Exhibition, and not to make an exhibition of themselves. There is no air of display about them—no social falsity—all is plain unvarnished truth. The jewels and the tapestry, and the Lyons silks, are now the sole objects of attraction. The shilling folk may be an 'inferior' class of visitors, but at least, they know something about the works of industry, and what they do not know, they have come to learn.

Here you see a railway guard, with the silver letters on his collar, and his japan pouch by his side, hurrying, with his family, towards the locomotive department. Next, you come to a carpenter, in his yellow fluffy flannel jacket, descanting on the beauties of a huge top, formed of

4. Getting home from the Crystal Palace (after its removal to Sydenham in 1854) on a fête day in the 1860s. The lady on the right has burst her crinoline in the crush!

London traffic in 1862, when a second International Exhibition was in progress at South Kensington. (Drawings by William M'Connell)

one section of a mahogany tree. Then may be seen a hatless and yellow-legged Blue-coat boy mounting the steps of one of the huge pneumatic lighthouses, to have a glance at the arrangements of the interior. Peeping into the model of the Italian Opera are several short-red-bodied and long-blacked-legged Life Guardsmen; while, among the agricultural implements, saunter clusters of countrymen in smockfrocks.

On the steps of the crimson-covered pedestals are seated small groups of tired women and children, some munching thick slices of bread and meat, the edges of which are yellow with the oozing mustard. Around the fountain are gathered other families, drinking out of small mugs, inscribed as 'presents for Charles or Mary'; while all over the floor, walk where you will—are strewn the greasy papers of devoured sandwiches.

The minute and extensive model of Liverpool, with its long strip of looking-glass sea and thousands of cardboard vessels, is blocked round with wondering artisans, some, more familiar with the place, pointing out particular streets and houses. And as you pass by the elaborate representation, in plaster, of Underdown Cliff, you may hear a young sailor—the gloss upon whose jacket indicates that he has but recently returned from sea—tell how he went round the Needles last voyage in a gale of wind. Most of the young men have catalogues or small guide-books in their hands, and have evidently, from the earnest manner in which they now gaze on the object, and now refer to the book, come there to study the details of the whole building.

But if the other parts of the Great Exhibition are curious and instructive, the machinery, which has been from first to last the grand focus of attraction, is, on the 'shilling days', the most peculiar sight of the whole. Here every other man you rub against is habited in a corduroy jacket, or a blouse, or leathern gaiters; and round every object more wonderful than the rest, the people press, two or three deep, with their heads stretched out, watching intently the operations of the moving mechanism.

You see the farmers, their dusty hats telling of the distance they have come, with their mouths wide agape, leaning over the bars to see the self-acting mills at work, and smiling as they behold the frame spontaneously draw itself out, and then spontaneously run back again. Some, with great smockfrocks, are gazing at the girls in their long pinafores engaged at the doubling-machines.

But the chief centres of curiosity are the power-looms, and in front of these are gathered small groups of artisans, and labourers, and young men whose coarse red hands tell you they do something for their living, all eagerly listening to the attendant, as he explains the operations, after stopping the loom.

Here, too, as you pass along, you meet, now a member of the National

SPECIMENS FROM MR. PUNCH'S INDUSTRIAL EXHIBITION OF 1850.

(TO BE IMPROVED IN 1851).

1. John Leech in *Punch*, 1850

SCENE—EXHIBITION REFRESHMENT ROOM.

Visitor. "Pint o' Beer, Miss, Please."
Miss. "Don't keep it. You can have a Strawberry Ice and a Wafer!"

John Leech in *Punch*, 1851

2. Over London, by rail. Gustave Doré

Guard, in his peculiar conical hat, with its little ball on top, and horizontal peak, and his red worsted epaulettes and full-plaited trowsers; then you come to a long, thin, and bilious-looking Quaker, with his tidy and clean-looking Quakeress by his side; and the next minute, may be, you encounter a school of charity girls, in their large white collars and straw bonnets, with the teacher at their head, instructing the children as she goes.

Round the electro-plating and the model diving-bell are crowds jostling one another for a foremost place. At the steam brewery, crowds of men and women are continually ascending and descending the stairs; youths are watching the model carriages moving along the new pneumatic railway; young girls are waiting to see the hemispherical lamp-shades made out of a flat sheet of paper; indeed, whether it be the noisy flax-crushing machine, or the splashing centrifugal pump, or the clatter of the Jacquard lace machine, or the bewildering whirling of the cylindrical steam-press—round each and all these are anxious, intelligent, and simple-minded artisans, and farmers, and servants, and youths, and children clustered, endeavouring to solve the mystery of the complex operations.

For many days before the 'shilling people' were admitted to the building, the great topic of conversation was the probable behaviour of the people. Would they come sober? Will they destroy things? Will they want to cut their initials, or scratch their names on the panes of the glass lighthouses? But they have surpassed in decorum the hopes of their wellwishers. The fact is, the Great Exhibition is to them more of a school than a show . . .

From HENRY MAYHEW'S *1851; or, The Adventures of Mr and Mrs Sandboys, and Family, who came up to London to 'enjoy themselves' and to see the Great Exhibition* (1851); pp. 159–161.

4

What They Ate at the Great Exhibition

Bread, quarterns	52,094	Savoury Patties	23,040 lbs
„ cottage loaves	60,698	Italian cakes	11,797
„ French rolls	7,617	Biscuits	37,300 lbs
Pound cakes	68,428	Bath buns	934,691
do at 3d	36,950	Plain buns	870,027
Savoury cakes	20,415	Banbury cakes	34,070
„ Pies	33,456 lbs	Sausage rolls	28,046

Victoria biscuits	73,280	Mustard	1,120 lbs
Macaroons	1,500 lbs	Jellies	2,400 quarts
Rich cakes	2,280 lbs	Coffee	14,299 lbs
Pastry at 2d	36,000	Tea	1,015 lbs
Schoolcakes	4,800	Chocolate	4,836 lbs
Preserved cherries, etc.	4,840 lbs	Milk	33,432 quarts
Pine apples	2,000	Cream	32,049 quarts
Pickles	1,046 gallons	Schweppe's Soda	
Meat	113 tons	Water, Lemonade,	
Potted meat,		& Ginger beer	1,092,337 bottles
tongues, etc.	36,130 lbs	Masters' Pear Syrup	5,350 bottles
Hams	33 tons	Rough ice	363 tons
Potatoes	36 tons	Salt	37 tons

1st Report of the Commissioners of the Exhibition of 1851: P.P. 1852, vol. 26, Appendix 29.

5

'Ladies' and 'Gents'

————

Waiting Rooms and Washing Rooms. It being a somewhat novel step to provide these conveniences for the public on a large scale, and at the same time to derive a revenue from them, the following particulars are given:

The Waiting-rooms were situated near the Refreshment-courts, those in the Transept being most frequented; the price was made higher, in order to induce the public to go to those which were not so central. No difference was made in the mode of fitting them up, or in the attendance. The total amount expended in constructing and fitting up the Water-closets and Washing-places was about £1600.

The Urinals for gentlemen were not charged for; 54 of the latter were provided. It would have been convenient if more accommodation had been provided in the Ladies Waiting-rooms, especially in the Transept. The following was the number of *Waiting-rooms* provided for each locality:

	Gentlemen	Ladies	Total	Charge
Transept	6	24	30	1d
Eastern Refreshment-court	6	11	17	½d
Western do	10	12	22	½d
	—	—	—	
	22	47	69	

The current expenditure (Superintendent, 6 male attendants, 10 female) was £671. 17. 3; current receipts, £2441. 15. 9. Excess of receipts over expenditure, £1769. 18. 6.

Washing-places. Expenditure (Superintendent, 3 male attendants, female attendants, 532 lbs soap, towels, etc.) £281. 4. 8; deduct value of towels, etc. £8. 10s. Receipts, £443. 17. 6. Excess of receipts over expenditure, £171. 2. 10.

It would appear that the use of the Washing-places fell off as the weather got colder.

The largest receipt from the Waiting-rooms on any one day was on the 8th October, and amounted to £32. 16. 3, on which day 11,171 persons made use of the Waiting-rooms. The number of visitors on that day was 109,760.

On that day each of the 1d. waiting-rooms must have been used by 229 persons, and the ½d. by 169 persons, during the 8 hours the building was open to the public.

It will appear that 827,820 persons paid for the use of these conveniences during the time of the Exhibition, or 14 per cent of the visitors, in addition to an equal if not larger proportion of gentlemen who made use of the urinals, of which no account was kept.

No apology is needed for publishing these facts, which, throughout the whole time of the Exhibition, strongly impressed all concerned in the management with the necessity of making similar provisions for the public wherever large numbers are congregated, and with the sufferings which must be endured by all, but more especially by females, on account of the want of them. These statements will also show that in England, as well as in France, such establishments may be made perfectly remunerative.

1st Report of the Commissioners of the Exhibition of 1851: P.P. 1852, vol. 26, Appendix 30.

(b) WHAT MADE THE VICTORIANS SO PROUD?

No doubt about it, on that May morning in 1851 Britain seemed to be on top of the world. The Crystal Palace shone in the sun as a symbol of something new and hopeful. There was a hint of spring in the air. Taking them as a whole, the people were as bouncey as the women's skirts.

All fears of a foreign war had receded, since the revolutionary fires of 1848 had burned themselves out. At home the Chartist agitation of only a few years back, that had sent such shivers down the middle-class man's spine, had fizzled into a fiasco. The bad old days of the 'hungry forties', though so recent, were so much a thing of the past that those who had lived through them found it hard to believe that there really had been a time when they had 'clemmed', when they had often not had enough to eat and had gone about in rags and patched shoes.

Since the repeal of the Corn Laws in 1846 Britain had been a Free Trade country, or very near it. Food was reasonably cheap and few people went short. There was generally a job for everybody who was able and not too lazy to work. Wages were on the upgrade, and on the whole kept slightly ahead of prices. Capitalists found plenty of openings for profitable investment. New factories were going up. Houses by the thousand and tens of thousand were being run up for a population which was growing at the rate of 200,000 a year. The railways were still in their impetuous youth, but they had enlarged the mobility and broadened the horizon of millions. The land was bearing heavier crops than ever before, what with the new machinery and artificial manures and the better deployment of labour; and though the farmers grumbled —well, was there ever a time when they didn't? British ships were carrying British manufactures to every land and people, and bringing back from the four corners of the world the foodstuffs and raw materials which made all this industrial and social activity possible.

But, even so, is all this sufficient to entitle us to speak of the 'Golden Age'?

36

Think of the other side of the picture. Our eyes are offended by the horrible squalors of the new towns, our nostrils quiver as they are assailed by noisome stinks. We are staggered by the public unconcern for the working conditions of men, women, and little children. We shudder when we read of hospitals that were compared with slaughter-houses, of the prisons that were the biggest manufactories of crime, of the proud vessels that were rightly denominated 'coffin ships'. And if there were many new openings for employment, the national income was still insufficient, even if it had been fairly distributed, to provide a standard of living above subsistence level for those who did the hard and dirty work of the community.

Why, then, we may well ask, were the Victorians so proud? What made them so confident, so generally pleased with themselves?

The answer lies, of course, on what they, in the middle of the century, were looking back upon, the way they had come. As *we* see *them*, it is from the vantage-point created by a hundred years of humanitarian effort and applied science. But when they looked back . . . Suppose we place ourselves at the elbow of Mr James Wilson as he edits *The Economist*, the weekly financial and commercial review that he had founded in 1843? Early in 1851 there appeared in its columns a series of articles in which the writer compared the state of things in 1851 with what they had been fifty years earlier. What a difference! 'Too many of us are disposed to place our Golden Age in the past', he writes, but it is to the future that he looks with the most happy confidence. These articles are drawn upon for our No. 6, and this, then, is how things looked to the business man of 1851.

Another reason may be advanced for Victorian optimism, one that may be not inappropriately described as religious. The Victorians, especially those of the early and middle periods, were nothing like so 'religious' as they are sometimes stated to have been—regular church-going, for instance, was largely confined to the upper classes (who went to set a good example to the 'lower orders') and the middle and lower middle (who went because it was 'the thing to do')—but they took themselves seriously, and in their addiction to business and making money there was a strain of the ancient puritanism. This attitude was evidenced, almost we may say personified in Prince Albert, as will be clear from the speech that he delivered in the City in 1849, on the occasion of the Banquet given by the Lord Mayor of London to the municipal authorities of the United Kingdom with a view to launching the Great Exhibition project. Here we have Man represented as co-worker with God in the establishment of a world-order of peace, brotherhood, and mutual prosperity.

6

Past and Present

Too many of us are disposed to place our Golden Age in the past ...
Nearly everybody agrees by common consent to undervalue and abuse
the present. We confess that we cannot share their disappointment, nor
echo their complaints. We look upon the past with respect and affection
as a series of stepping-stones to that high and advanced position which
we actually hold, and from the Future we hope for the realization of
those dreams, almost of perfectibility, which a comparison of the Past
with the Present entitles us to indulge in. But we see no reason to be
discontented either with our rate of progress or with the actual stage
which we have reached ...

Perhaps the best way of realizing ... the actual progress of the last
half-century would be to fancy ourselves suddenly transferred to the
year 1800, with all our habits, expectations, requirements, and standard
of living formed upon the luxuries and appliances collected round us
in 1850.

In the first year of the century we should find ourselves eating bread
at 1s. 10½d. the quartern loaf, and those who could not afford this price
driven to short commons, to entire abstinence, or to some miserable
substitute. We should find ourselves grumbling at heavy taxes laid on
nearly all the necessaries and luxuries of life—even upon salt; blas-
pheming at the high price of coffee, tea, and sugar, which confined these
articles, in any adequate abundance, to the rich and easy classes of
society; paying fourfold for our linen shirts, threefold for our flannel
petticoats, and above fivefold for our cotton handkerchiefs and stockings;
receiving our newspapers seldom ... and some days after date;
receiving our Edinburgh letters in London a week after they were
written, and paying thirteen pence-halfpenny for them when delivered;
exchanging the instantaneous telegraph for the slow and costly express
by chaise and pair; travelling with soreness and fatigue by the 'old
heavy' [coach] at the rate of seven miles an hour, instead of by the
Great Western [railway] at fifty; and relapsing from the blaze of light
which gas now pours along our streets, into a perilous and uncomfor-
table darkness made visible by a few wretched oil lamps scattered at
distant intervals.

But these would by no means comprise the sum total, nor the worst
part of the descent into barbarism. We should find our criminal law in a

state worthy of Draco; executions taking place by the dozen; the stealing of five shillings punishable and punished as severely as rape or murder; slavery and the slave trade flourishing in their palmiest atrocity. We should find the liberty of the subject at the lowest ebb; freedom of discussion and writing always in fear and frequently in jeopardy; religious rights trampled under foot; Catholics, slaves and not citizens; Dissenters still disabled and despised. Parliament was unreformed; public jobbing flagrant and shameless; gentlemen drank a bottle where they now drink a glass, and measured their capacity by their cups; and the temperance medal was a thing undreamed of. Finally, the *people* in those days were little thought of, where they are now the main topic of discourse and statesmanship; steamboats were unknown, and a voyage to America occupied eight weeks instead of ten days; and while in 1850, a population of nearly 30,000,000 paid £50,000,000 of taxes, in 1801 a population of 15,000,000 paid no less than £63,000,000.

'Increased command over the comforts and essentials of life'

Let us now collect together a few facts showing the increase in the consumption of those articles of necessity, or luxury, which are used indiscriminately *among all classes.*

We have no means of comparing the amount of butchers' meat consumed now with that consumed at the beginning of the century, but the price we know has fallen from 5s. 8d. to 3s. 4d. a stone . . . During the latter part of the 18th century rye and barley bread were very extensively used in many parts of England, the former being . . . the habitual food of one-seventh of the population; it is now unknown, except in Durham, while the use of wheaten bread is almost universal among the poorer classes.

In the use of coffee, tea, and sugar also, a marked advance has taken place. The consumption of coffee has risen from 1 1-10th oz. per head in 1801 to 1¾ lb. in 1849; that of tea from 19 oz. to 23 oz. per head; while that of sugar, which was 22½ lb. in 1801, and had fallen as low as 15 lb. in 1821, owing to the high prices, has now again risen since the reduction of the duty to 24 lb. per head. The bushels of malt used [for beer] in 1801 were 19,000,000; in 1849, 38,000,000 . . . The quartern loaf which in 1801 was selling at 1s. 10½d. is now at 6d. . . . Coffee has fallen from 200s. to 117s. per cwt.; tea from 5s. to 3s. 4d. per lb.; sugar from 80s. to 41s. per cwt; while a piece of calico, 28 yards long, and of 72 reed quality, has, even since 1814, fallen from 28s. to 6s. 6d., and was sold in 1848 as low as 5s.

If we except the excise on soap, it may be said that no tax now remains on a single one of the strict necessaries of life. If a poor man is content to live, as wise and great men have often thought it well to live, in health and comfort, but with strict frugality . . . he may escape taxation almost entirely . . .

To this enumeration of our increased command over the comforts and essentials of life must be added one more item, not the least important in its influence. In 1800 the poor man paid from 6d. to a shilling for each letter he received; it now costs him only one penny.

On the novel and extraordinary attention which is now being paid to sanitary matters, we can look with far more unmingled satisfaction . . . Even in these respects, however, our progress since 1800 has been far from contemptible. The population is less crowded than it was, and roomier dwellings are constantly in process of erection. The average number of individuals to a house which was 5·67 in 1801 had fallen to 5·44 in 1841 . . . Many removable causes of premature death yet remain, but the four or five years which the last half-century has added to the average duration of life . . . are a hopeful earnest of what may yet be done to prolong it, now that the subject has awakened public interest, and that administrative exertions are conducted under the guidance of scientific skill.

'All classes have participated in the blessings'

We hope we [have] succeeded in satisfying those who [have] followed our facts and figures that the national advance in wealth and all the material appliances of civilization . . . has not been turned solely to the benefit of the more favoured children of fortune, but that all classes of the community, the humbler as well as the richer, have participated in the blessings of the change . . . The only way in which our conclusion could be shown to be erroneous, would be by proving that the wages of labour had fallen to an equal or a greater ratio; but this, it is well known, is far from having been generally the case . . . While unquestionably wages have fallen considerably in a few departments of industry, this fall has been confined to those departments in which a change in the machinery employed has taken place, and in which the artisans have obstinately refused to accommodate themselves to the new state of things, and have continued to overstock an impoverished and doomed employment, as in the case of plain hand-loom weaving; or to those where senseless *strikes* have introduced supernumerary hands or new mechanism into the trade, as in the cases of coarse cotton spinners and of the London tailors; or to those where the easiness and collateral conveniences of the occupation have attacted to it excessive numbers, as in the case of needlework. In these branches wages have undoubtedly fallen, and the hours of work have become in some instances longer; but the general tendency in most departments of industry has been the reverse;—a desire for shorter hours has been of late rapidly spreading.

The hours of labour in factories have been reduced for adults from 74 to 60 a week, and for children from 72 to 40; shops are beginning to be closed much earlier, and great, and in some cases already successful, efforts are making to secure a weekly half-holiday for the generality of tradespeople. All these, where not pursued by illegitimate means, are steps in the right direction . . .

'*Stupendous progress in locomotion*'

The progress of scientific discovery has been magnificent, and its application to the arts of life more remarkable still . . . The first steamship constructed in the British Empire carried passengers upon the Clyde in 1811: in 1816 we had 15 steamboats with a burden of 2,612 tons; in 1848, we had 1,253, registered at 168,078 tons. Many of these are ocean steamers, and ply between England and America at an average speed of ten miles an hour. Between Holyhead and Dublin we have attained a speed of 15 miles an hour.

But this advance is nothing compared to that which has taken place in *locomotion by land* within the last twenty years. It is here that our progress has been most stupendous—surpassing all previous steps since the creation of the human race. In 1829 the first railway for the transport of passengers was opened between Liverpool and Manchester;—it opened at the modest speed of 20 miles an hour. At the period at which we write, the whole of England is traversed by almost countless railways in every direction . . . In the days of Adam the average speed of travel, if Adam ever did such things, was four miles an hour . . . in the year 1828, or *4,000 years afterwards, it was still only ten miles,* and sensible and scientific men were ready to affirm and eager to prove that this rate could never be materially exceeded;—in 1850, it is habitually forty miles an hour, and *seventy* for those who like it. We have reached in a single bound from the speed of a horse's canter, to the utmost speed comparable with the known strength and coherence of brass and iron.

Now, who have specially benefited by this vast invention? The rich, whose horses and carriages carried them in comfort over the known world?—the middle classes to whom stage coaches and mails were an accessible mode of conveyance?—or the poor, whom the cost of locomotion condemned often to an almost vegetable existence? Clearly the latter. The railroad is the Magna Carta of their motive freedom. How few among the last generation ever stirred beyond their own village? How few among the present will die without visiting London? . . . The number who left Manchester by cheap trips in one week of holiday time last year exceeded 202,000; against 150,000 in 1849, and 116,000 in 1848.

But even the rapid augmentation of our locomotive speed shrinks into nothing when compared to that which has taken place in the last five years in the transmission of intelligence. If Abraham had wished to communicate to Lot some important tidings by express, he must have sent a man on horseback with the news, and even then he could not have transmitted it much faster than 10 miles an hour ... In the year 1800, the case was exactly the same; the most important expresses could seldom average more than ten miles an hour. The same was the case in 1830 and 1840, except where the old signal telegraphs enabled Governments to transmit their orders in fine weather, by the raising and lowering of certain clumsy arms attached to a high tower. But now in 1850, for a sum varying from 5s. to 12s. 6d., any private individual may send a message or summon a friend, the distance of many hundred miles in a space of time reckoned by seconds rather than by minutes ...

More schools, purer morality, better taste

Economists as we are, we should be little satisfied with even these signs of astounding progress ... were there not ample reason to believe that a corresponding improvement has taken place in *Education, Social Morals*, and *Public Principle* ...

When we remember that it is only within our own recollection that the propriety or wisdom of educating the lower orders at all was seriously and very generally questioned; that before 1800 the only provision for popular instruction was to be found in grammar and other endowed schools (the funds for the support of a large proportion of which had been scandalously jobbed away or misapplied), together with a few dame schools in towns, and a few squires' and ladies' schools in the rural districts; and that now not only is the paramount necessity of general education universally insisted upon, but every sect vies with every other in the number and excellence of its schools; that even pauper schools are systematically good; that even ragged schools for the most desolate and depraved of our town population have been established with great success in many localities ... that Lancasterian schools, National schools, model schools, and normal schools, are all the product of this century; that a Committee on Education now forms a recognized department of the Government; and finally, that Parliament, which in 1833 could with difficulty be persuaded to vote £20,000 for educational purposes in aid of private munificence, now votes liberally and ungrudgingly £150,000 a year:—when we remember all those things, we shall scarcely be disposed to deem our national progress under this head unsatisfactory or slow.

The general tone of morals in the middle and higher classes has unquestionably become much higher and purer in the last generation. Language which was common in our fathers' days would not be tolerated now. A higher sense, both of duty and of decency, has taken possession of all ranks.

Debt, which used to be considered as an indispensable characteristic of a man of fashion, is now almost everywhere scouted as disreputable; and reckless extravagance is no longer regarded as an indication of cleverness and spirit . . . Within the memory of men still in middle life, excess in wine was the rule, not the exception; few left the dinner-table without having taken more than was good for them; many got drunk every day . . . *Now*, intemperance is as disreputable as any other kind of low debauchery, and, except in Ireland and at the Universities, a drunken gentleman is one of the rarest sights in society . . .

'The Bees more considered than the Butterflies'

Labour is ceased to be looked down upon—exertion is no longer regarded as derogatory, nor a life of languid indolence as the supreme felicity. The Bees are more considered than the Butterflies of society; wealth is valued less as an exemption from toil, than as a call to effort, and an instrument of influence and power; the duties of property are, far less than formerly, forgotten in its rights; if the poor do not yet work less, the rich certainly work more; and while Carlyle preaches the 'Evangel of Labour' to the frivolous and idle, [John Stuart] Mill preaches the 'Evangel of Leisure' to the toil-worn and heavy-laden.

From leading articles in *The Economist*, January 18, January 25, and February 1, 1851.

7

Prince Albert on 'Man's sacred mission'

It must, indeed, be most gratifying to me, to find that a suggestion which I had thrown out, as appearing to me of importance at this time, should have met with such universal concurrence and approbation; for this has proved to me that the view I took of the peculiar character and requirements of our age was in accordance with the feelings and opinions of the country.

Gentlemen, I conceive it to be the duty of every educated person closely to watch and study the time in which he lives; and, as far as in him lies, to add his humble mite of individual exertion to further the accomplishment of what he believes Providence to have ordained.

Nobody, however, who has paid any attention to the particular features of our present era, will doubt for a moment that we are living at a period of most wonderful transition, which tends rapidly to the accomplishment of that great end to which, indeed, all history points— the realization of the unity of mankind. Not a unity which breaks down the limits, and levels the peculiar characteristics of the different nations of the earth, but rather a unity the result and product of those very national varieties and antagonistic qualities.

The distances which separated the different nations and parts of the globe are gradually vanishing before the achievements of modern invention, and we can traverse them with incredible ease; the languages of all nations are known, and their acquirements placed within the reach of everybody; thought is communicated with the rapidity and even by the power of lightning.

On the other hand, the great principle of division of labour, which may be called the moving power of civilization, is being extended to all branches of science, industry, and art. Whilst formerly the greatest mental energies strove at universal knowledge, and that knowledge was confined to the few, now they are directed to specialities, and in these again even to the minutest points; but the knowledge acquired becomes at once the property of the community at large. Whilst formerly discovery was wrapped in secrecy, the publicity of the present day causes that no sooner is a discovery or invention made, than it is already improved upon and surpassed by competing efforts; the products of all quarters of the globe are placed at our disposal, and we have only to choose which is the best and cheapest for our purposes, and the powers of production are intrusted to the stimulus of competition and capital.

So man is approaching a more complete fulfilment of that great and sacred mission which he has to perform in this world. His reason being created after the image of God, he has to use it to discover the laws by which the Almighty governs his creation, and, by making those laws his standard of action, to conquer Nature to his use—himself a divine instrument. Science discovers these laws of power, motion, and transformation; industry applies them to the raw matter, which the earth yields us in abundance, but which becomes valuable only by knowledge: art teaches us the immutable laws of beauty and symmetry, and gives to our productions forms in accordance with them.

Gentlemen,—The Exhibition of 1851 is to give us a true test and a living picture of the point of development at which the whole of mankind has arrived in this great task, and a new starting point from which all nations will be able to direct their further exertions. I confidently hope the first impression which the view of this vast collection will produce upon the spectator will be that of deep thankfulness to the

Almighty for the blessings which He has bestowed upon us already here below; and the second, the conviction that they can only be realized in proportion to the help which we are prepared to render to each other—therefore, only by peace, love, and ready assistance, not only between individuals, but between the nations of the earth.

H.R.H. Prince Albert, Prince Consort: speech·at the Guildhall, London' 1849; Official Catalogue of the Great Exhibition of 1851, page 3.

8

'Endless progression'

When we refer to a few only of the extraordinary improvements of the half-century just elapsed ... we become convinced that it is more full of wonders than any other on record.

Of that wonderful half-century the Great Exhibition is both a fitting close and a fitting commencement of the new half century, which will, no doubt, surpass its predecessor as much as that surpassed all that went before it ... All who have read, and can think, must now have full confidence that the 'endless progression', ever increasing in rapidity, of which the poet sang, is the destined lot of the human race.

From an article on 'The Great Exhibition' in *The Economist*, January 4, 1851.

CHAPTER 2

LIFE AND LABOUR

When the Census was taken in 1851, Britain's population was shown to be just under twenty-one millions, just about double what it had been when the first census was taken, fifty years earlier. Excluding those children under ten years of age—although even in those days there were numbers of children of that age, and even younger, employed in industry —there was a potential labour force of rather more than seven and a half million males and more than eight million females. The majority— probably the great majority—of these were employed for wages, more or less regularly, in some job or other. What kind of job? What were they all 'up to'?

An interesting question, as indeed the Commissioners thought. So they published long and detailed lists of occupations, filling many a column of small type. Furthermore, under their direction, 'Her Majesty's Geographer', Augustus Peterman, produced a map purporting to show the Distribution of the Occupations of the People, which was issued with the text. It is a large folded map, and on unfolding it one gets the impression that the British Isles in those days were a rather muddy green—which is probably not far from the truth. But closer examination reveals much of extraordinary interest and value, for Peterman covered the whole area with signs and symbols as ingenious as they are illuminating.

With the Census Tables before him and Peterman's map at his elbow, a man in the middle of the last century would be able to form a very fair idea of what he and his fellows were 'up to'. But we want something more than this. We feel that the skeleton of industrial geography needs to be filled out with the flesh and bones and blood of human experience. And it is with this in view that the documents in this chapter have been chosen, even while we realize that in the nature of things anything like a really comprehensive pictorial anatomy is quite out of the question.

As is only fitting, No. 1 shows us something of London, the metropolis, the capital city of Country and Empire, the seat of Royalty and Government, of money power and commercial enterprise and the great organs of public opinion. Its author, George Augustus Sala, was a Londoner born and bred, and for forty years up to his death in 1895 he was one of the most versatile and justly appreciated journalists of his day. His book *Twice Round the Clock* was published in 1859, and it provides a

47

wonderfully vivid picture of London life of the period. No. 2 is also about London and Londoners, describing as it does how the millions were fed—a subject which is all too seldom dealt with in our economic histories. It comes from the *Quarterly Review*, which then as now was published by the famous house of John Murray. It is well to be reminded that all through the Victorian Age such magazines and periodicals were in the forefront of popular enlightenment. With No. 3 we are transported to Tyneside in an article from the *Cornhill*, another famous journal of the time. No. 4 takes us across the Pennines, to make the intimate acquaintance of those employed in the cotton manufactures of Manchester. This is drawn from the *Fortnightly*, and in No. 5 we have an article from yet another of the great organs of public entertainment and instruction, the *Edinburgh Review*. From the Black Country we move only a little way to Birmingham, 'city of a thousand trades' as it has been proudly and not inaccurately called. This is an 'official' document, since it comes from that invaluable and inexhaustible source of information on the life of the period, the reports of the Children's Employment Commission that was appointed in 1862. But it will be soon understood that Mr White, its author, was no severe collector of economic facts, any more than was his colleague Mr Baker, who writes (No. 7) so understandingly of the people of the Potteries.

After this we are given the opportunity of taking a trip on the London & North Western Railway under the guidance of the enterprising and entertaining Sir Francis Head (Waterloo veteran, miner on the River Plate, Canadian governor). *Stokers and Pokers* (No. 8) is quaintly named, but not so quaint as some of the methods adopted by the railwaymen in getting their trains in and out of Euston. Railways were in those days still in their hectic youth, but already there were bright young ladies behind the counter in the station buffets.

So much for the industrial scene. But while, to quote Sir John Clapham's *Economic History of Modern Britain*, 'Britain had turned her face towards the new industry—the wheels of iron and the shriek of the escaping steam', since 'in them lay for the future not only her power and wealth but her very existence', agriculture was still by far the greatest of her industries, the one in which the largest number of her workers were engaged. What sort of a life it was for the farm labourer and his wife will be gathered from the clergyman's description (No. 9), taken from the *Cornhill Magazine*.

I

'Round the Clock' in Victorian London

As 8 o'clock chimes from the smoky-faced clock of the Horse Guards . . .
the magnificent promenade of the park, on which look the stately
mansions of the nobles, is pervaded by figures very mean, very poor and
forlorn in appearance. Little troops of girls and young women are coming
from the direction of Buckingham Palace and the Birdcage Walk, but all
converging towards the Duke of York's column: that beacon to the
great shores of Vanity Fair. These are sempstresses and milliners'
workwomen, and are bound for the great Dress Factories of the West
End. Pinched faces, pale faces, eager faces, sullen faces, peer from under
the bonnets as they pass along and up the steps. There are faces with
large mild eyes, that seem to wonder at the world and at its strange
doings, and at the existence of a Necessity (it must be a Necessity, you
know), for Jane or Ellen to work twelve hours a day; nay, in the full
London season, work at her needle not unfrequently all night, in
order that the Countess or the Marchioness may have her ball dress
ready.

Taking down the shutters

There is another ceremony performed with much clattering solemnity
of wooden panels, and iron bars, and stanchions, which occurs at eight
o'clock in the morning. 'Tis then that the shop-shutters are taken down.
The great 'stores' and 'magazines' of the principal thoroughfares
gradually open their eyes; apprentices, light-porters, and where the
staff of assistants is not very numerous, the shopmen, release the
imprisoned wares, and bid the sun shine on good family 'souchong',
'fresh Epping sausages', 'Beaufort collars', 'guinea capes', 'Eureka
shirts', and 'Alexandre harmoniums'.

In the magnificent linen drapery establishments of Oxford and
Regent Streets, the vast shop-fronts, museums of fashion in plate-glass
cases, offer a series of animated *tableaux* of *poses plastiques* in the shape
of young ladies in morning costume, and young gentlemen in whiskers
and white neckcloths, faultlessly complete as to costume, with the
exception that they are yet in their shirt sleeves, who are accomplishing
the difficult and mysterious feat known as 'dressing' the shop window.
By their nimble and practised hands the rich piled velvet mantles are
displayed, the *moire* and *glacé* silks arranged in artful folds, the laces and

gauzes, the innumerable whim-whams and fribble-frabble of fashion, elaborately shown, and to their best advantage.

The morning rush hour

Nine o'clock . . . If the morning be fine, the pavement of the Strand and Fleet Street looks quite radiant with the spruce clerks walking down to their offices governmental, financial, and commercial . . . You may, as a general rule, distinguish government from commercial clerks by the stern repudiation of the razor, as applied to the beard and moustaches, by the former . . . You may know the cashiers in the private banking houses by their white hats and buff waist-coats; you may know the stock-brokers by their careering up Ludgate Hill in dog-carts, and occasionally tandems, and by the pervading sporting appearance of their costume; you may know the Jewish commission-agents by their flashy broughams, with lapdogs and ladies in crinoline beside them; you may know the sugar-bakers and the soap-boilers by the comfortable double-bodied carriages with fat horses in which they roll along; you may know the Manchester warehousemen by their wearing gaiters, always carrying their hands in their pockets, and frequently slipping into recondite city taverns up darksome alleys, on their way to Cheapside, to make a quiet bet or so on the Chester Cup or the Liverpool Steeplechase; you may know, finally, the men with a million of money, or thereabouts, by their being ordinarily very shabby, and by thus wearing shocking bad hats, which have seemingly never been brushed, on the backs of their heads.

'Every road', says the proverb, 'leads to Rome'; every commercial way leads to the Bank of England. And there, in the midst of that heterogeneous architectural jumble between the Bank of England itself, the Royal Exchange, the Poultry, Cornhill, and the Globe Insurance Office, the vast train of omnibuses, that have come from the West and have come from the East . . . with another great army of clerk martyrs outside and inside, their knees drawn up to their chins, and their chins resting on their umbrella handles, set down their loads of cash-book and ledger-fillers. What an incalculable mass of figures must there be collected in those commercial heads! . . . They file off to their several avocations, to spin money for others, often, poor fellows, while they themselves are blest with but meagre stipends.

So the omnibuses meet at the Bank and disgorge the clerks by hundreds; repeating this operation scores of times between nine and ten o'clock. But you are not to delude yourself, that either by wheeled vehicle or by the humbler conveyances known as 'Shanks's mare', and the 'Marrowbone stage'—in more refined language, walking—have all those who have business in the city reached their destination. No; the

Silent Highway has been their travelling route. On the broad—would that I could add the silvery and sparkling—bosom of Father Thames, they have been borne in swift, grimy little steamboats, crowded with living freights from Chelsea, and Pimlico, and Vauxhall piers, from Hungerford, Waterloo, Temple, Blackfriars, and Southwark—to the Old Shades Pier, hard by London Bridge. Then for an instant, Thames Street, Upper and Lower, is invaded by an ant-hill swarm of spruce clerks, who mingle strangely with the fish-women and the dock-porters. But the insatiable counting-houses soon swallow them up . . .

Lunch-hour in the City

It is one o'clock in the afternoon . . . With just one thought at the vast number of merchants', brokers', shipping agents', warehousemen's, wholesale dealers' counting houses that exist in London city, you will be able to form an idea of the legions of clerks, juniors and seniors, who, invariably early-breakfasting men, must get seriously hungry at one p.m.

Some I know are too proud to dine at this patriarchal hour. They dine, after office hours, at Simpson's, at the Albion, at the London, or, save us, at the Wellington. They go even further west, and patronize Feetum's, or the Scotch Stores in Regent Street, merely skating out, as it were, for a few minutes at noon, for a snack at the Bay Tree . . . Many, and they are the married clerks, bring neat parcels with them, containing sandwiches or bread-and-cheese, consuming these refreshments in the counting-house. In the very great houses, it is not considered etiquette to dine during office-hours, save on foreign-post nights.

As to the extremely junior clerks, or office-boys, as they are irreverently termed, they eat whatever they can get, and wherever they can get it, very frequently getting nothing at all. But there are yet hundreds upon hundreds of clerks who consume an orthodox dinner of meat, vegetables, and cheese—and on high days and holidays pudding—at one p.m. Their numbers are sufficient to cram almost to suffocation the eating-houses of Cheapside, the Poultry, Mark Lane, Cornhill, and especially Bucklersbury . . . Of late years there has been an attempt to change the eating-houses of Cheapside into pseudo 'restaurants'. Seductive announcements . . . have been hung up, relating to 'turtle' and 'venison'; salmon, with wide waddling mouths, have gaped in the windows; and insinuating mural inscriptions have hinted at the existence of 'Private dining-rooms for ladies'. Now, whatever can ladies want to come and dine in Cheapside for? At these restaurants they give you things with French names, charge you a stated sum for attendance, provide the pale ale in silver tankards, and take care of your hat and coat;

but I like them not—neither, I believe, do my friends, the one-o'clock-dining clerks . . .

Most fashionable street in the World

Regent Street at 2 p.m. Not without reason do I declare it the most fashionable street in the world. I call it not so for the aristocratic mansions it might possess; for the lower parts of the houses are occupied as shops, and the furnished apartments are let, either to music or operatic celebrities or to unostentatious old bachelors. But the shops themselves are innately fashionable . . . Regent Street is indeed an avenue of superfluities—a great trunk-road in Vanity Fair. Fancy watchmakers, haberdashers, and photographers; fancy stationers, fancy hosiers, and fancy staymakers; music shops, shawl shops, jewellers, French glove shops, perfumery, and point lace shops, confectioners and milliners . . .

Beautiful women on horseback

Four p.m. Leaning over the wooden rails in Hyde Park, I contemplate the horsemen and horsewomen caracoling along the spongy road of Rotten Row with admiration, not unmixed with a little envy . . . For once in a day I see gentlemen dressed in the exact similitude of the emblazoned cartoons in the *Monthly Magazine of Fashion*. Such peg-top trousers! such astounding waistcoat patterns! such lofty heels to the varnished boots! such Brobdingnagian moustaches and whiskers! such ponderous watch-chains . . . such bewildering varieties of starched, choking all-round collars! such breezy neckties and alarming scarves!

Ladies, too—real ladies—promenade in an amplitude of crinoline difficult to imagine and impossible to describe; some of them with stalwart footmen following them, whose looks beam forth with conscious pride at the superlative toilettes of their distinguished proprietresses; some escorted by their bedized beaux. Little foot-pages . . . gambolling children . . . severe duennas . . . wicked old bucks, leering furtively under the bonnets—what a scene of more than 'Arabian Nights' delight and gaiety! And the blessed sun is in the heavens, and rains gold upon the beauteous Danaes, who prance and amble, canter and career, on their graceful steeds throughout the length of Rotten Row.

The Danaes! The Amazons! the lady cavaliers! the horsewomen! can any scene in the world equal Rotten Row at four in the afternoon, and in the full tide of the season? . . . Rotten Row is a very Peri's garden for beautiful women on horseback. The Cliff at Brighton offers, to be sure, just as entrancing a sight towards the end of December; but what is Brighton, after all, but London-super-Mare?

Watch the sylphides as they fly or float past in their ravishing riding-habits and intoxicatingly delightful hats: some with the orthodox cylindrical beaver, with the flowing veil; others with rogueish wide-awakes, or pertly cocked cavaliers' hats and green plumes. And as the joyous cavalcade streams past ... from time to time the naughty wind will flutter the skirt of a habit, and display a tiny, coquettish, brilliant little boot, with a military heel, and tightly strapped over it the Amazonian riding-trouser.

Only, from time to time, while you gaze upon these fair young daughters of the aristocracy disporting themselves on their fleet coursers, you may chance to have with you a grim town Diogenes ... who, pointing with the fingers of a hard buckskin glove will say: 'Those are not all countesses' or earls' daughters, my son. She on the bay, yonder, is Lais. Yonder goes Aspasia, with Jack Alcibiades on his black mare Timon: see, they have stopped at the end of the ride to talk to Phryne in her brougham. Some of those dashing delightful creatures have covered themselves with shame, and their mothers with grief, and have brought their fathers' gray hair with sorrow to the grave. All is not gold that glitters, my son.'

The Queen at the Opera

Ladies and gentlemen, we are going to the Opera—to Her Majesty's Theatre in the Haymarket; and by 8 o'clock it behoves us all to be in our seats ... Look around you, in the vast arena ... look around, and around again, the enormous horseshoe, at this magnificent theatre, glorious with beauties and with riches. Here are gathered the mighty, and noble, and wealthy, the venerable and wise, the young and beauteous of the realm ... Mark yonder, that roomy box on the grand tier, which a quiet, plainly dressed party has just entered. There is a matronly lady in black with a few bugle ornaments in her *coiffure*. She ensconces herself in a corner, her back towards the audience, screens herself with a curtain, and then calmly proceeds to take a review of the front rows of the stalls, and the occupants of the proscenium boxes. It is not considered etiquette to take more than a cursory glance of the matronly lady in black through *your* opera-glass. Presently there sits down by the matronly lady's side, a handsome, portly, middle-aged gentleman, in plain sober evening dress, and with a very high forehead ... In the opposite angle of the box sits a demure young lady—sometimes a couple of demure ones—who doesn't move much or speak much; and at the back of the *loge* are two gentlemen in white waistcoats, who never sit down ... Now, take the hat of your heart off ... and with your spirit salaam three times, for the matronly lady is Victoria Queen of England, and the middle-aged gentleman, inclined to corpulence and baldness, is His Royal Highness the Prince Consort ...

I should be wilfully deceiving you, and unworthy the name I have been always striving to gain—that of a faithful chronicler—if I were to lead you to imagine that the brilliant theatre is full only of rank, fashion, wealth and happiness. There are many aching hearts, doubtless, beneath all this jewellery and embroidery; many titled folks who are thinking of pawning their plate on the morrow, many dashing young scions of aristocracy who, between the bars of the overture, are racking their brains as to how on earth they are to meet Mephibosheth's bill ... And in the great equality that dress-coats, bare shoulders, white neckcloths, and opera-cloaks make among men and women, how much dross and alloy might we not find among the gold and silver! ... There is lately come to town, at least within these latter years, an Italian gentleman by the name of Verdi, to whose brassy screeds, and tinkling cymbalics, it is expected that all *habitués* of the opera must listen ... I have brought you to Her Majesty's Theatre, and this is unfortunately a Verdi night. You may listen to him, but I won't ...

Blood-and-thunder at the 'Vic'

There is a transpontine theatre, situated laterally towards the Waterloo Road, and having a northern front towards an anomalous thoroughfare that runs from Lambeth to Blackfriars, for which I have had, during a long period of years, a great esteem and affection. This is the Royal Victoria Theatre ... Come with me, and sit on the coarse deal benches in the coarsely and tawdrily-decorated cheap theatre, and listen to the sorrily-dressed actors and actresses—periwigged-pated fellows and slatternly wenches, if you like—tearing their passion to tatters, mouthing and ranting, and splitting the ears of the groundlings. But in what description of pieces? In dramas, I declare and maintain, in which, for all the jargon, silliness, and buffoonery, the immutable principles of right and justice are asserted; in which virtue, in the end, is always triumphant, and vice is punished; in which cowardice and falsehood are hissed ... in which, were we to sift away the bad grammar, and the extravagant action, we should find the dictates of the purest and highest morality. These poor people can't help misplacing their h's ... They haven't been to the university of Cambridge; they can't compete for the middle-class examinations; they don't subscribe to the *Saturday Review*; they have never taken dancing lessons ... they can't even afford to purchase a *Shilling Handbook of Etiquette*. Which is best? That they should gamble in low coffee-shops, break each other's heads with pewter pots in public-houses, fight and wrangle at street corners, or lie in wait in doorways and blind alleys to rob and murder, or that they should pay their threepence for admission to the gallery of the 'Vic.'?

Beer, glorious Beer!

Here we are, at the corner of the New Cut. It is nine o'clock precisely, and while the half-price is pouring into the Victoria Theatre, the whole-price (there is no half-price in the gallery, mind, the charge for the evening's entertainment being only threepence) is pouring out and deluging the New Cut. Whither, you may ask, are they bound? They are in quest of their Beer.

The English have been a beer-loving people for very many ages. It gives them their masculine, sturdy, truculent character ... Beer and beef have built railways all over the world. Our troops in the Crimea languished, even on beef (it was but hard corned junk, to be sure) till the authorities sent them beer ... The authorities of the Victoria Theatre have preserved, I am glad to say, a wholesome reverence for the provisions of the Strong Beer Act, and it is, I believe, a clause in the Magna Carta of the management, that the performance on Saturday evenings shall invariably terminate within a few minutes of midnight, in order to afford the audience due and sufficient time to pour out their final libations at the shrine of Beer, before the law compels the licensed victuallers to close ...

There may be a few cheap dandies—Cornwall Road exquisites and Elephant-and-Castle bucks—who prefer to do the 'grand' in the saloon attached to the theatre; there may be some dozens of couples sweet-hearting, who are content to consume oranges, ginger beer, and Abernethy biscuits within the walls of the house; but the great pressure is outwards ... towards a gigantic 'public' opposite the *Victoria* which continually drives a roaring trade.

Eleven o'clock, and thousands are yet in the streets, tens of thousands still in pursuit of the avocations by which they earn their daily (or nightly) bread, hundreds of thousands awake, busy, and stirring. The children of the aristocracy and some sections of the middle classes have gone to bed ... but the children of the poor do not dream of bed. They are toddling in and out of chandlers' shops in quest of ounces of ham and fragments of Dutch cheese for father's supper; they are carrying the baskets of linen—mother takes in washing—to the residences of clients; they are fetching the beer and the 'clean pipe' from the public house; nay—not unfrequently, alas!—they are fetching father himself home from the too-seductive establishment of the licensed victualler. Eleven o'clock at night is the great supper-time of the working class; then, by the steady and industrious mechanic, the final pipe is smoked, the borrowed newspaper read, the topics of the day, the prospects of the coming week, discussed with the cheery and hard-working helpmate who sits by the side of her horny-handed lord, fills his pipe, pours out his beer, and darns the little children's hose ...

At eleven o'clock close the majority of the coffee, chop-houses, and reading rooms. There are some that will remain open all night, but they are not of the most reputable description. At eleven the cheap grocer, the cheesemonger, and the linen-draper, in low-priced neighbourhoods, begin to think of putting up the shutters; and by half-past eleven, the only symposia of merchandise open will be the taverns and cigar-shops, the supper-rooms and shell-fish warehouses, the night coffee-houses, and the chemists . . .

Eleven o'clock at the West-end is, morally speaking, broad daylight. Midnight will be high noon. Fashionable life's current riots through the veins of West-end streets; mirth, and gaiety, and intrigue, are heard on staircases and at street corners.

Phantoms in satin and lace

Midnight: an awful sound . . . A new life for London begins. Strange shapes appear of men and women who have lain-a-bed all the day and evening, or have remained torpid in holes and corners. They come out in strange and fantastic garments, and in glaringly gas-lit rooms screech and gabble in wild revelry. The street corners are beset by night prowlers. Phantoms arrayed in satin and lace flit upon the sight. The devil puts a diamond ring on his taloned finger, sticks a pin in his shirt, and takes his walks abroad . . . Supper is now the great cry, and the abundant eating and drinking resources of the Haymarket are forthwith called into requisition. You may sup in the Haymarket as your taste would lead, or as the state of your finances would counsel . . .

Past, long past two in the morning. The much-suffering House of Commons is at last shut up . . . the last cabs in Palace Yard driven away . . . And now, for the first time since this clock was set in motion, something like a deep sleep falleth over London. There are night revellers abroad, night prowlers a-foot. There is houseless wretchedness knowing not where to lay its head; there is furtive crime stalking about, and seeking whom it may devour. Yet all has a solemn, ghastly, un-earthly aspect; the gas-lamps flicker like corpse candles; and the distant scream of a profligate, in conflict with the police, courses up and down the streets in weird and shuddering echoes . . .

From GEORGE AUGUSTUS SALA: *Twice Round the Clock; or, the Hours of the Day and Night in London* (1859).

2

Food and Drink for London's Millions

If, early on a summer's morning before the smoke of countless fires had narrowed the horizon of the metropolis, a spectator were to ascend to the top of St. Paul's, and take his stand upon the balcony, he would see sleeping beneath his feet the greatest camp of men upon which the sun has ever risen ... As he gazed upon this extraordinary prospect, the first stir of the awakening city would gradually steal upon his ear. The rumbling of wheels, the clang of hammers, the clear call of the human voice, all deepening by degrees into a confused hum, would proclaim that the mighty city was once more resuming the labour of the day, and the blue columns of smoke climbing up to heaven that the morning meal was at hand. At such a moment the thought would naturally arise in his mind—In what manner is such an assemblage victualled?

If our spectator will now descend from his giddy height, and will accompany us among the busy haunts of men, we will attempt to point out to him whence the innumerable commodities ... pouring into the town have been obtained, the chief marts to which they are consigned, and the manner in which they are distributed from house to house ... Let us begin with fish, and that unrivalled fish-market which all the world is aware rears its head by London Bridge ...

'They are not polite at Billingsgate'

The busy scene within the market, between the hours of 5 and 7 in the morning, is one of the marvels of the metropolis. Billingsgate is the only wholesale fish-market in London, and it may therefore be imagined how great must be the business transacted within its walls. Of old nine-tenths of the supply came by way of the river ... now the railways are day by day supplanting smacks, and in many cases steamers ... Nearly one-half in fact of the fish-supply of London is hurried in the dead of night across the length and breadth of the land to Billingsgate, and, before the large consumers in Tyburnia and Belgravia have left their beds, may be seen lying on the marble slabs of the fishmongers, or penetrating on the barrow of the costermonger into the dismal lanes and alleys inhabited by 'London Labour and the London Poor'.

Let the visitor beware how he enters the market in a good coat, for, as sure as he goes in in broad cloth, he will come out in *scale* armour.

They are not polite at Billingsgate, as all the world knows, and 'by your leave' is only a preliminary to your hat being knocked off your head by a bushel of oysters or a basket of crabs . . .

Busiest among the busy is seen the 'Bommeree', or middle-man. The province of this individual is to purchase the fish as it comes into the market, and divide it into lots to suit large and small buyers, separating the qualities as they are designed for St. James's or St. Giles's . . . After the 'trade' has been supplied, and the serge-aproned 'regulars' have loaded their light spring carts, there comes an eruption of purchasers of a totally different character—the costermongers of the streets. This nomade tribe, which wanders in thousands from market to market, performs a most important part in the distribution of food. They are for the most part the tradesmen of the poor, and by their energy and enterprise secure to our working-classes many of the fruits of both sea and land, which they would never taste but for them . . .

Smithfield's 'hideous nightmare'

London has always been celebrated for the excellence of its meat, and her sons do justice to it; at least, it has become the universal impression that they consume more, man for man, than any other town population in the world. The visitor accustomed to the markets of our large provincial towns would doubtless expect to find the emporium of the livestock trade for so large a population of an imposing size. The foreigner, after seeing the magnificence of our docks—the solidity and span of our bridges—might naturally look for a national exposition of our greatness in the chief market dedicated to that British beef which is the boast of John Bull. What they do see in reality, if they have courage to wend their way along any of the narrow tumble-down streets approaching to Smithfield, which the Great Fire unfortunately spared, is an irregular space bounded by dirty houses and the ragged party-walls of demolished habitations, which give it the appearance of the site of a recent conflagration—the whole space comprising just six acres, fifteen perches, roads and public thoroughfares included.

Into this narrow area, surrounded with slaughter-houses, triperies, bone-boiling houses, gut-scraperies, etc., the mutton-chops, scrags, saddles, legs, sirloins, and rounds, which grace the smiling boards of our noble imperial capital throughout the year, have, for the major part, been goaded and contused for the benefit of the civic corporation installed at Guildhall.

The best time to see this enormous aggregation of edible quadrupeds . . . is early in the morning—say, at one or two o'clock of the 'great day', as the last market before Christmas-day is called. On this occasion, not only the space—calculated to hold 4,100 oxen and 30,000 sheep, besides calves and pigs—is crammed, but the approaches around it overflow with live stock for many hundred feet...

If the stranger can make his way through the crowd ... and can manage to raise himself a few feet above the general level, he sees before him in one direction, by the dim light of hundreds of torches, a writhing party-coloured mass, surmounted by twisting horns, some in rows, tied to rails which run along the whole length of the open space, some gathered in one struggling knot. In another quarter, the moving torches reveal to him, now and then, through the misty light, a couple of acres of living wool, or roods of pigs' skins. If he ventures into this closely wedged and labouring mass, he is enabled to watch more narrowly the reason of the universal ferment among the beasts. The drover with his goad is forcing the cattle into the smallest possible compass, and a little further on half a dozen men are making desperate efforts to drag refractory oxen up to the rails with ropes ... The sheep, squeezed into hurdles like figs into a drum, lie down upon each other, 'and make no sign'; the pigs, on the other hand, cry out before they are hurt.

This scene, which has more the appearance of a hideous nightmare than a weekly exhibition in a civilized country, is accompanied by the barking of dogs, the bellowing of cattle, the cursing of men, and the dull blow of sticks ... The hubbub generally abates from 12 o'clock at night, the time of opening, to its close at 3 p.m. the next day, although during the whole period as fresh lots are 'headed up', individual acts of cruelty continue ... Many of the drovers we doubt not are ruffians, but we believe the greater part of the cruelty is to be ascribed to the market-place itself, which, considering the immense amount of business to be got through on Mondays and Fridays, is absurdly and disgracefully confined ...

A considerable proportion of the pork consumed in London is 'town made', or at least is the produce of the immediate suburbs. Shepherd's Bush might perhaps be termed *the* pigsty of the metropolis; for here every house has its piggery, and the air is sonorous with the grunting of porkers. Again, in those portions of the outskirts, such as Kensington, the Celtic population does not forget its old habits or companions, especially that all-important 'jintleman who pays the rint' ...

Country slaughtering will in time, we have little doubt, deliver the capital from the nuisances which grow out of this horrible trade ... Twenty years ago 80 miles was the farthest distance from which carcases came; now the Great Northern and North Western railways, during the winter months, bring hundreds of tons from as far north as Aberdeen ... Aberdeen is in fact becoming little else than a London abattoir. The style in which the butchers of that place dress and pack the carcasses leaves nothing to be desired, and in the course of the year mountains of beef, mutton, pork, and veal arrive the night after it is slaughtered in perfect condition . . .

The great receptacle of country-killed meat brought up to town by the railways is Newgate market . . . Every precaution is taken by the railways to keep the meat sweet. When, in spite of care, it turns out to be tainted, the salesman to whom it is consigned calls the officer of the market, by whom it is forthwith sent to Cow Cross, and there burnt in the nacker's yard. According, however, to a competent witness, bad meat in any quantity can be disposed of in the metropolis to butchers living in low neighbourhoods, who impose it upon the poor at night . . .

Grouse from the Scottish moors

Leadenhall and Newgate are the great metropolitan markets for game and poultry. The quantities of game and wild birds consigned to some of the large salesmen almost exceeds belief. After a few successful battues in the Highlands, it is not at all unusual for one firm to receive 5000 head of game, and as many as 20,000 to 30,000 larks are often sent up to the market together . . . The Highlands and Yorkshire send up nearly all the grouse; and scores of noblemen, members of Parliament, and other wealthy or enthusiastic sportsmen, who are at this present moment beating over the Moors, and walking for their pleasure twenty-five miles a day, assist to furnish this delicacy to the London public at a moderate rate.

Pheasants and partridges come mainly from Norfolk and Suffolk; snipes from the marshy lowlands of Holland, which also provides our entire supply of teal, widgeon, and other kinds of wild fowl, with the exception of those caught in the 'decoys' of Cambridgeshire and Lincolnshire. From Ostend there are annually transmitted to London 600,000 tame rabbits, which are reared for the purpose on the neighbouring sand dunes. We are indebted to Ireland for flocks of plovers, and quails are brought from Egypt and the south of Europe . . . Of the 2,000,000 of fowls that every year find a resting-place vis-à-vis to boiled tongues on our London tables, by far the greatest quantities are drawn from the counties of Surrey and Sussex, where the Dorking breed is in favour. Ireland also sends much poultry . . . The bulk of the geese, ducks, and turkeys, however, come from Norfolk, Cambridge, Essex, and Suffolk—four fat counties, which do much to supply the London commissariat . . . How many eggs we get from across the Channel we scarcely like to say. Mr. McCulloch considers that the capital receives from 70 to 75 million—a number which we think must be much below the mark, seeing that the Brighton and South Coast line brings annually 2600 tons, the produce of Belgium and France . . .

London's dairies

In taking leave of the poultry-yard we are reminded of the dairy, and of the large establishments required to fill the milk-jugs of London. There are at the present moment, as near as we can learn, 20,000 cows in the metropolitan and suburban dairies, some of which number 500 cows apiece ... The larger dairies of the metropolis are on the whole admirably managed, and the cows luxuriate in airy outhouses, but the smaller owners are often confined for space, and the animals are sometimes cooped in sheds, placed in tiers one above another ... It must be

5. A London Dairy. (Geo. Godwin, *Town Swamps and Social Bridges*, 1859)

evident that the London and suburban dairies alone could not supply the metropolis ... Here, again, the railway, which in some cases brings milk from as far as eighty miles, makes up the deficiency ... The milk is collected from the farmers by agents in the country, who sell it to the milkmen, of whom there are 1347, to distribute it over the town ... The milk which comes by railway has, however, this disadvantage, that it will not keep nearly so long as the indigenous produce of the metropolitan dairies. The different companies have constructed waggons lightly hung on springs, but the churning effect of sudden joltings cannot be altogether got rid of.

What makes the cabbages grow

Of the vegetables and fruit that are brought into the various markets of the capital, but especially to Covent Garden, a very large quantity is grown in the immediate neighbourhood ... The far-famed market-gardens are principally situated in the long level tracts of land that must once have been overflowed by the Thames—such as the flat alluvial soil known as the Jerusalem Land, extending between London Bridge and Greenwich—and the grounds about Fulham, Battersea, Chelsea, Putney, and Brentford ... Four and sometimes five crops are extracted from the land in the course of the year ... After every clearance the ground is deeply trenched, and its powers restored with a load of manure to every thirty square feet of ground. This is the secret of the splendid return, and it could be effected nowhere but in the neighbourhood of such cities as London, where the produce of the fertilizer is sufficiently great to keep down its price. And here we have a striking example of town and country reciprocation. The same waggon that in the morning brings a load of cabbages, is seen returning a few hours later filled with dung. An exact balance as far as it goes is thus kept up, and the manure, instead of remaining to fester among human beings, is carted away to make vegetables ...

The coarser kinds of vegetables are but sparingly grown in these valuable grounds, but come up in large quantities from all parts of the country; and some of the choice kinds are now reared far away in Devonshire and Cornwall, where they are favoured by the climate ...

Before dawn at Covent Garden

As early as two o'clock in the morning, a person looking down the dip of Piccadilly will perceive the first influx of the daily supply of vegetables and fruit to Covent-Garden market: waggons of cabbages ... light spring-vans fragrant with strawberries ... milk-white loads of turnips which slowly roll along the great western road ... Different portions of the market are dedicated to distinct classes. The finest of the delicate soft fruits, such as strawberries, peaches, &c., are lodged in the central alley. On the large covered space to the north is the wholesale fruit-station, fragrant with apples, pears, greengages, or whatever is in season. The southern open space is dedicated to cabbages and other vegetables; and the extreme south front is wholly occupied by potato-salesmen. Around the whole quadrangle, during a busy morning, there is a party-coloured fringe of waggons backed in towards the central space, in which the light green of cabbages forms the prevailing colour, inter-rupted here and there with the white of turnips, or the deep orange of carrots; and as the spectator watches, the whole mass is gradually absorbed into the centre of the market. Meanwhile the space dedicated to wholesale fruit sales is all alive. Columns of empty baskets twelve feet high seem progressing through the crowd 'of their own motion'. The vans have arrived from the railways, and rural England, side by side with the Continent, pours in its supplies . . .

The busiest time at the market is about six o'clock, when the coster-mongers surround Covent Garden with their barrows, and hundreds of street hawkers, with their hand-baskets and trays, come for their day's supply. The regular street vendor who keeps his barrow, drawn by a donkey or pony, looks down with a certain contempt upon the inferior hawkers, principally Irish. They only deal in a certain class of vege-tables, such as peas, young potatoes, broccoli, or cauliflowers, and have nothing to do with *mere greens*.

Another class of purchasers are the little girls who vend watercresses. Such is the demand for cresses, that they are now largely cultivated for the market . . . The best come from Camden Town. Most people fancy that clear purling streams are necessary for their production, but the Camden Town beds are planted in an old brick-field, watered by the Fleet Ditch; and though the stream at this point is comparatively pure, they owe their unusually luxuriant appearances to a certain admixture of the sewerage . . .

Oranges and lemons

The foreign-fruit trade has its head-quarters in the city. The pedestrian who walks down Fish Street Hill would assuredly never surmise that at certain seasons a regular fruit exhibition is kept up within those dull brick houses, before which the tall column lifts its head . . . The pine-apple market is of modern date. The first cargo was brought over about twelve years ago, and since that time the traffic has rapidly increased, and at the present moment 200,000 pines come yearly into the port of London . . . principally from the Bahamas in the West Indies . . . There are five clippers appropriated to the carriage across the sea of this single fruit. The melons come from Spain, Portugal, and Holland . . . The largest foreign fruit-trade, however, is that in oranges. We shall perhaps astonish our readers when we tell them that upwards of 60,000,000 are imported for the use of London alone, accompanied by not less than 15,000,000 lemons . . . Any time between December and May the orange clippers from the Azores and Lisbon may be seen unloading their cargoes in the neighbourhood of the great stores in Pudding and Botolph Lanes . . .

Of the amount of bread consumed in London we have no specific information, but there are data which enable us to approximate to the truth. Porter, in his *Progress of the Nation*, gives us the returns of eight schools, familes and institutions, containing 1902 men, women, and children, each of whom ate on the average 331 lbs. of bread per annum. Now if we multiply this quantity by the number of the inhabitants of the metropolis—2,500,000 or thereabouts—we have a total of 413,750,000 half-quartern loaves of 2 lbs. each ... Some of this bread is a contribution from the country, and one Railway—the Eastern Counties—brought last year 237 tons 12 cwts. to town.

Rivers of Beer

Now let us see how much sack goes to all this quantity of bread—with what rivers of stout, etc., we wash down such mountains of flesh. According to the excise returns, there were 747,050 quarters of malt consumed in London in the year 1853 by the seventeen great brewers. As each quarter of malt, with its proportionate allowance of hops, produces three and a half barrels of beer, we get as the total brew of last year 2,614,675, or pretty nearly a thousand million tumblers of ale and porter ... Of the seventeen great London breweries, the house of Truman, Hanbury, Buxton, & Co. stood last year at the top of the list, having consumed 140,000 quarters of malt, and paid to the excise £180,000, or enough to build two ninety-gun ships ...

Such, then, is a slight sketch of the great London larder ...

From an article by DR ANDREW WYNTER on 'The London Commissariat' in the *Quarterly Review*, No. cxc, vol. xcv (1854).

3

Pit-people of Tyneside

The great northern coal-field lying round the rivers Tyne and Wear is the best known and the most deeply and extensively wrought coal-field in the world at this time. Lying under Northumberland and Durham, it has an area of about four hundred and sixty square miles of known coal formation. The rate at which this great deposit of fuel has been, and is now being drawn upon, is indeed astonishing. No less than sixteen millions of tons were extracted in 1859, and it is not improbable that the annual yield of the entire field will in a few years amount to twenty millions of tons. Should only the present rate of mining continue, the whole attainable coal might be exhausted in less than five hundred years from this time ... Meanwhile it has supplied half the world with coal for open grates; and 'Wallsend' has become a household word.

No one, perhaps, would dream of making an excursion for pleasure to this great district of subterranean darkness and superficial blackness;

3. The Pride of Beauty: 'The Ladies' Mile' in Hyde Park.   Gustave Doré

4. The Disgrace of Destitution: Under the Arches beside the Thames. Gustave Doré

Found in the Street: Applying for admission to a 'refuge'. Gustave Doré

yet few places in our country, and certainly not in any other, are so full of real interest. To wander amongst one hundred and eighty-three collieries congregated in two counties; to witness the extraordinary mechanisms and erections for the extraction of coal and its delivery to collier vessels; to note the hundreds of tall chimneys, the streaming black barriers of smoke fuming away in the breeze, and the perplexed network of colliery railways and tramways, which run along and across in such confusion to the eye of the visitor that hourly collisions of coal trains seem inevitable; to stand at a pit's mouth and watch the ceaseless arrival of coaly cargoes and their despatch to the screens; to listen to the fearful clattering of all these coals against the strong, sounding wires, or rather bars, of the large screens themselves; and to take note of the rough and begrimed human beings who throng all around and seem to belie the appellation of 'white men'—all this affords a source of interest and excitement which cannot be adequately conceived until it is experienced . . .

'Metropolis of Coal'

Approaching Newcastle, the true metropolis of coal, from the Durham side, the dingy town of Gateshead stands before us on one side of the Tyne, dense with houses which swarm with population, and clouded with the soot and smoke of many a manufactory. On the other side of the Tyne, which we reach by the High Level Bridge—an imposing structure—rises Newcastle on its half-hidden hills; and deep down between the two towns rolls the broad black river, with its ships and boats, its 'keels and keelmen' . . . Passing over the bridge, we enter Newcastle by one of its least promising approaches. If we keep to the banks of the Tyne, we are in a labyrinth of lanes and 'stairs', as the old narrow streets are named, amidst a crowd of unwashed and clamorous natives; but if we ascend to Grey Street, a splendid curvilinear range of buildings opens upon us for a length of four hundred yards. The West Hill consists of three ranges of buildings in the Corinthian style . . . the third compartment including a large central Exchange, conspicuous in situation, magnificent in design, and rich in ornament.

Its chief interest to us at present arises from the assemblage of coal-agents and mine-managers and owners under one roof . . . Here are congregated the agents and managers, or, as they are locally termed, the 'viewers', of most of the principal Newcastle and Durham pits, discussing the probabilities of a rise of sixpence or a shilling per ton in coal.

There is one sprucely got-up viewer, jauntily swinging a riding-whip, and rather aspiring to the exterior of a jockey than a gentleman, whom we have seen in very different attire and under very different circumstances—more than a thousand feet under ground; his blue-spotted handkerchief, gaudy waistcoat, trebly-crossed gold guard-chain, fashionable hat, and glossy cloth coat, replace the old black leather cap, turned-up corduroy trousers, short jacket, flannel vest, clay candlestick, and tough ash walking-stick, which marked this jaunty gentleman in the darkness of the pit. Then he was a viewer, a first workman among working pitmen; now he is not a whit behind the best of gentlemen in his own esteem, and desirous of chatting with you about the Italian opera or the Prince of Wales, rather than anything that concerns the Tyne and the mine.

Yonder, amongst that knot of older, stouter, and sturdier men, is one of the most eminent viewers in this district. Portly in person, ruddy to look upon, and affable to converse with, he is deferentially regarded by all under-viewers and inferior officers of mines; yet he himself was once a 'pit-lad', and has risen up to his present pre-eminence as a mining engineer; he was a working man in the pits with George Stephenson, although he held at that time a position superior to him . . .

That short, rather stout, but benevolent-looking man hard by yonder pillar, is now a partner in one of the principal iron-works near the Tyne, and has risen to his present position from the lowest grade of pit life— that of a trapper-boy, earning sixpence a day. He will describe to you, after dinner, all the phases and misfortunes of a pit-lad's life some fifty years ago, bringing tears into your eyes as he depicts in homely yet striking language the hardships which he himself has suffered in boyhood and youth, while sitting in the deep darkness to open a door for ten or twelve hours a day, or dragging a full coal-basket, like an unfortunate donkey, harnessed with ropes and cut by cords. While among the viewers we will make an appointment for a visit to one of the principal pits . . . and in a few hours we start in the viewer's carriage . . .

The larger collieries in the vicinity of the three navigable rivers—the-Tyne, the Wear, and the Tees—which so fortunately intersect the coal-field, have railways or tramways of their own running in the most direct line they can obtain down to the nearest river's bank . . . Descending from the carriage, and following one of these lines, we find that it leads us close to the banks of the blackened waters, and here, on a ballast-heap, we may take our stand aside, while we watch the course of coal embarkation.

At the end of the railway stands a huge shed-like erection, covering a platform of wood. Upon this platform, or 'staith', the fast-running coal waggons are suddenly brought to a stand; their number is checked by a clerk, and they are placed, one at a time, upon an open square frame in the middle of the platform, which frame, upon the withdrawal of a bolt, is lowered from the staith by curious machinery until it becomes sus-

pended over the hatchway of the vessel below. A man descends with
the waggon, but outside of it; unfastens a latch at its bottom, which,
turning upon a hinge like a trap-door, permits the whole of the laden
coal to descend, but little broken, into the hold of the ship . . .

Yonder on the left, across the half green and half black grass, is a
gloomy engine-house and a tall chimney; that is the colliery station, and
the nearer we approach it the more audible are the whistlings, groanings,
crackings, and clashings that issue from certain pulleys or 'gins',
waggons and 'breaks', boys and men, engaged in transporting the
upsent coal. The engine-beam protruding from the upper part of the
engine-house, alternately elevating and depressing itself in measured
motion, has attached to it the rod and bucket of a pump, which, at the
depth of perhaps a thousand feet, is lifting water from the pit, and
enabling the men to labour in dry galleries, which otherwise would be
speedily flooded . . .

Dressing ourselves in rough pilot-jackets, vests, and trowsers, a
round, hard, leather cap, a stout stick, a pound of pit candles, and a clay
candle-stick, complete our preparations. The obliging under-viewer
awaits us at the door: he knows more than we shall learn, and is
capable of instructing us in everything that concerns this pit, for he
perambulates it twice a week . . .

Long rows of blackened sheds appear in the lingering dusk; and
groups of yawning pitmen assemble upon the brink of the shaft,
arrayed like ourselves, pale in visage, somewhat short in stature, half
bowed in the legs, gently rounded in the back; half-suspicious and half-
sagacious in their glances, they eye us askance, joking with the overman,
and complaining to the wasteman of 'bad air' down the pit: they are
awaiting their turn to descend.

Gradually life and bustle begin to be observable: the engine for winding up the first load begins to steam, and the 'banksman'—a constant
attendant at the pit's mouth—prepares for all comers. Two huge arms
rise inclining over the shaft, supporting a couple of large pulleys, over
which rolls the double pit rope of plaited wire, flat, tough, and entirely
metallic: a pair of such ropes may cost £500. Hemp will hang a man;
but wire will alone, after a twelvemonth's wear-and-tear, preserve him
from breaking his neck in a great coal shaft.

The descent and ascent of these shafts have of late years lost half of
their interest, because they have lost all their romance. Now, a vertical
pair of 'guides' supplies an upright railway for iron cages, which are not
unlike third-class railway carriages on English lines. Into these cages
the men creep, and the coal waggons are wheeled. You cannot fall out,
nor can the cages fall down; only a carelessly protruding arm or finger
may be lopped off. When we were boys, pitmen either descended in

swinging, banging, and bounding baskets, or, with true professional dignity, inserting one leg in a loop at the end of the rope and winding their arms round it, 'rode down', defiant of danger and a thousand feet of darkness!

Down among the 'human moles'

Embarking with the first passengers, we creep into the iron compartment, and crouch in the cage, taking special care to draw in elbows, hands, and fingers. The word is given and down we go. Four minutes are enough to land us at the bottom, one minute to disembark us, and five to adapt our eyes to the darkness and equip us for the interior. Timidly, yet trustfully, we walk along the mainway of the mine—the Cheapside or the Regent Street of this underground town . . .

Not a few lads and boys have passed us, the latter as charioteers of the trains of coal waggons. Bigger boys now appear in corners and side passages; and into one of these side passages we now diverge, for the main line would lead us a mile or two onward in the same order of blank excavation. The side-passages, however, take us to the working places, the coal-getting localities, the scenes of suffering, and the sources of pay and wages.

The entire mine is excavated upon the panel-work plan: a few leading streets are intersected by dozens of cross streets, less in height, breadth, and length, and themselves intersected again by longitudinal passages parallel to the leading paths of the pit. The solid pillars left standing by this mode of excavation serve to uphold the roof, and form a reserve of coal. But they themselves may ultimately be, and often are, trenched upon; and when entirely exhausted, the wooden props which help to support the roofs are knocked out and drawn away, by daring and agile 'deputies' or 'wastemen'; then down come the unsupported shales and cones with a tremendous clash . . .

Penetrating farther into these holes and corners of the vast excavation, we ever and anon come upon the bigger lads at their several occupations; the *putters*, or, more plainly, pushers; *marrows* and *half marrows*, and little *foals*. All of these are engaged in propelling or dragging the laden baskets of coal, which must first be brought under a crane before they can be hoisted on to a *rolley* for the horses. This is the hardest and most distressing labour of the pit for these boys; who do work which ponies cannot do, because they can creep, and drag, and push where the smallest of the equine race cannot set a hoof . . .

The real getters of the coal are the so-called *hewers*—the strong and able men of the mine; and their work is the most peculiar we have ever witnessed. In a small corner-like recess, full of floating coal-dust, foul and noisome with bad air and miscellaneous refuse and garbage, glimmer three or four candles, stuck in clay which adheres to wall and roof, or there may be only a couple of Davy lamps. Close and deliberate scrutiny will discover one hewer nearly naked, lying upon his back, elevating his small sharp pickaxe a little above his nose, and picking into the coal-seam with might and main; another is squatting down and using his pick like a common labourer; a third is cutting a small channel in the seam, and preparing to drive in wedges. By one or other kind of application the coal is broken down; but if too hardly embedded, gunpowder is employed, and the mineral blasted; the dull, muffled, roof-shaking boom that follows each blast startling the ear of the novice, who commonly concludes that the whole mine has exploded and that his last minute is near at hand . . .

At the busiest hours of the day here are in all some four hundred living human beings in the different parts of the vast mine we are visiting. You would not think so, as you meet them only in threes or fours or fives . . . There is only one time in the twenty-four hours when we can see all these people together and in working trim, and that is the hour of 'loosening' or stopping work. At that hour let us take our stand at the bottom of the shaft.

The long-wished-for minute arrives, and is signalled, not by clock or bell, but by one long, shrill, resonant cry, coming from the top of the shaft and the banksman's lips. 'Loose; l-o-o-s-e; l-o-o-s-e—' is the one word thrice repeated, but drawled and drawn out into vocal lengths of some seconds' duration. The cry is taken up by men below, and rings from mouth to mouth and gallery to gallery, until the remotest corners of the pit are echoing with the welcome sound. Down fall picks from the hands of hewers, and implements of all kinds are left by human beings of all ages. Every five or ten minutes shows us gang after gang winding their dim and perilous way to the base of the shaft; to that little circle of light which, like a fairy ring, lies brightly upon the black coal floor. On it stands the empty cage; into that get the men and boys as they arrive, and up they go, black and weary . . .

Ascending with the last freight of human moles, what a congregation of dusky workpeople do we find at the pit's mouth! Here are a dozen middle-aged hewers awaiting our arrival, peering at us with glimmering eyes, deep-set in begrimed visages; and twenty or thirty stout lads—the *fretters*—showing white teeth in darkest lips, as they broadly grin at our awkwardness in landing. Behind them are groups of little boys, some of whom have been lugging coal-baskets for eight or nine hours, and others, as *trappers*, who have sat for twelve hours behind wooden doors erected in the mainways of the mine for ventilating purposes, pulling a string to open the door when any coal-waggons come up for passage: weary work. We enter the nearest house, put off our pitmen's dresses, resume our customary habiliments, and make the best of our way to the neigh-bouring pit village.

Files of pitmen and groups of pit-lads are now dotting all the roads converging towards the village. Yonder come two more upright and rather better dressed men, who seem to be a grade above the com-monalty; these are the subordinate officers of the pit: they have rather better wages, and the best of the cottages; where they reside the set of houses is nicknamed 'Quality Row'. Going with them to their cottages, we see them enter and close the door; and although we shall accept their invitations to drop in for a 'bit of talk' at tea-time, we leave them now to their retirement and ablutions: the latter being a most indispensable performance, and one that claims precedence of every other domestic duty.

Meanwhile let us walk across and down the side lane till we come upon the lads and boys. A rough, roystering, laughing, chattering, song-singing company they are, even though their subterranean fatigues might have subdued all their superfluous vigour: when free, they will be funny and frolicsome; playing leap-frog, or hop, step, and jump, and it is as well to keep out of their way when they are bowling huge stones before them. There are a couple of them turning aside to settle by might of fists some underground quarrel: arms so brawny, and fists so knotty, are seldom observable in town artisans; and a blow from one of those burly lads is no trifle. The fight is done, the ring is re-opened into rank and file, and on they proceed into the village, down 'Quality Row', along 'Shiney Row', and finally disappear one by one in cottage doors. What ablutions and detergent scrubbings will go on there for the next half-hour! . . .

Pit villages, like that in which we find ourselves, vary much in their character for cleanliness and neatness in proportion to their age; the majority of the older pit villages being very unsightly and unsavoury. If unluckily detained in one on a wet day you will see a stream of Acheron-tic blackness pouring down the lanes and along the backs of the houses, and the effluvia arising from the rubbish heaps is disgusting. Little gardens, or fields, divided into culturable patches, lie all around; but the plants appear to maintain a mere reminiscence of green under a prevailing shroud of coaly blackness. The interiors of the cottages, however, present a much more agreeable appearance . . .

'The pride of the pit-man's wife'

In nearly all the cottages, and especially in all those tenanted by respectable families, the furniture is of a superior order: the bedstead is pretty sure to be a mahogany four-poster, with imposing pillars, clean white furniture, and a quilted coverlet; it is placed in the best room as an ornamental piece of furniture, and beside it will frequently stand a mahogany chest of drawers, well polished, and filled with linen and clothes. An old-fashioned eight-day clock, in a good case, usually flanks the four-poster. In the best ordered pit dwellings I have often seen also good chairs, china, bright brass candlesticks, and chimney ornaments; every one of these items being kept scrupulously clean, for cleanliness is the pride of the pitman's wife. Herself probably the daughter of a pitman, she cherishes all the old associations of a similar home, and what constituted her mother's pride stimulates hers: things must indeed be in a bad state when the four-poster, the eight-day clock, the little ornaments of the chimney-piece, and the chest of drawers are poor or neglected.

Pitmen have been charged with not a few vices and faults, but there is an increasing body of them opposed to all profligacy and intemperance. They become religious, and they exhort, preach and teach after their own fashion; and if that be not the fashion of others, it is nevertheless to be respected and honoured. Men who may at any hour be buried alive in a dark pit which shall prove their tomb, may well think of that other world into which two hundred of them entered recently without warning. There is one virtue for which the pitmen of the North of England are distinguished, viz. their deep sympathy for their brothers in misfortune, and their courageous conduct in aiding to rescue them, if rescue be possible, in any case of a colliery calamity. In the recent accident at Hartley, the men of all orders manifested a courage and a perseverance in seeking to reach the buried victims of misfortune which has elicited universal admiration. Nor is this a solitary instance of the kind . . . If all such instances were collected and published, they would illustrate to an extraordinary degree the annals of herosim in humble life, and show that the human heart can feel as warmly a thousand feet underground as in the most refined and cultivated circle of society.

From an article by J. R. LEIFCHILD, 'Life and Labour in the Coal-fields', in *The Cornhill Magazine* for March 1862.

4

Social Condition of the Lancashire Factory People

My first recollections of the factory people of Lancashire date from the year 1843, when I was resident in a manufacturing village on the eastern border of the county. I have often watched the factories 'loosing' to use a local phrase, towards eight o'clock in the evening, and noticed how the poor jaded wretches—men, women, and children, who had been kept incessantly at work, with the briefest intervals for meals devoured hastily in the rooms, from five o'clock in the morning— dragged their limbs wearily up the steep hill to their homes.

These miserable objects, many of them grievously deformed in frame, their skins and clothing smeared with oil and grime, the young among them sickly and wan, the middle-aged prematurely broken-down and decrepit, and all so evidently dejected in spirit, seemed to my young eyes the very embodiments of hopelessness. The common bodily deformity was partially due to the practice of setting children to heavy work before their limbs had become set, and partly to the propulsion of machinery in certain departments of the manufacture by the knees of the operative. It was no wonder if these disagreeable impressions led one to consider the old factory system as a system of galling and grinding slavery.

The Hours of Labour in Factories Act, passed in 1844, and materially amended in 1847 and 1856, worked a thorough reform. Its beneficial effects upon the population cannot be exaggerated. The excessive hours of labour (twelve to thirteen hours daily for adults and children alike) have been legally reduced to ten hours per day, and females and young persons of both sexes are protected against the pernicious encroachments upon their meal-times which were formerly so flagrant. The Saturday half-holiday is now universal. Wages, so far from being diminished by the shortening of the period of labour, have—thanks mainly to accelerated machinery and improved methods of working—largely increased. Moreover, the short-time system of juvenile labour guarantees a certain elementary education to the operative's child.

In many other directions marked progress has been made. The low, dark, noisome rooms in which manufacturing processes were formerly carried on, have been replaced by vast sheds, lighted from the roof, for the weaving branch, and by lofty, large, and well-ventilated chambers for spinning and the preparatory processes. A new cotton mill of the first class is a model of spaciousness and convenience. Outside the mill, too, the operative is not uncared for. The lavish provision of public parks, pleasure grounds, baths, and free libraries in all the larger Lancashire towns, testifies that the corporate authorities are not unmindful of their obligations to promote the health, happiness, and culture of the industrial orders.

The effect of these changes upon both the moral and physical condition of the operatives is most apparent. Far seldomer than of yore do we hear the murmur of popular discontent. Sickness and mortality have been reduced to an extent that is almost incredible. Deformity of body is now a rare exception among the younger operatives. A few old men still exhibit the rounded backs and twisted limbs induced by a bygone system. The young men and maidens employed in the mills are as robust as the families of the indolent classes. The homes of the more thrifty of the work-people are moderately comfortable.

A piano in the parlour

The dwellings of the operatives are mostly long rows of two-storied buildings, with a couple of rooms upon each floor, the rental of which varies according to size and situation, from half-a-crown to four shillings and sixpence per week. the landlord generally paying the rates. The furniture of the living room may consist of a dresser, an eight-day clock, kitchen sofa, and a couple of rocking-chairs on either side of the fire-place. The walls are usually adorned with two or three framed engravings or coloured lithographs. The better-paid workmen improve upon this a little. Their front apartment on the ground-floor is dubbed a parlour, and its furniture includes a small book-case if the man be studious, or if, as is not infrequent, he has a taste for music, a piano.

The exclusive possession of a house, though ever so small, is no slight advantage to the artisan, and places the operative in these districts in a superior position for securing domestic comfort to the workman of London or Glasgow, who is fain to lodge his family in a portion of a tenement, often in the attic, and to whom privacy is a thing unknown and unattainable. I believe there is no operative population in the world so well and cheaply housed as are the factory workers in a Lancashire manufacturing town of the second or third magnitude.

The Career of a Factory Hand

Let us turn from their houses to the life-experiences of the cotton craftsmen and craftswomen. To describe them in the bulk or in groups would not, perhaps, produce so vivid a picture as if were to take a single typical factory-hand, and trace his career from infancy to age.

The strength of children is very early utilised in this province. Too brief is the period of immunity from manual toil enjoyed by the operative's child. Let us suppose that our selected urchin is permitted to disport in the street, or to frolic upon the hill-slopes with his fellows, during the absence of both his parents at the mill, until the age of eight; then he is sent to the factory, and enrolled a 'short-timer'. The next five years are rife with trials. For several hours in the morning he works behind the loom, or beneath the 'mule', acquiring the handicraft which is to bring him bread. In the afternoon he is sent, by legal stipulation and at the charge of his employers, to the factory school. Thus, from the age of eight to that of thirteen, it is expected that the factory-boy will complete both his general education and his trade-apprenticeship . . . At thirteen the boy 'passes the doctor' (i.e. obtains a medical certificate of age), and becomes a 'full-timer'. Henceforth he is amenable to the same rules, and subject to the same hours of labour, as the adult operative.

No very alluring prospect for a boy, one might imagine; yet the eagerness of some of these children to cheat the doctor, and to anticipate the important epoch, is notorious. All manner of tricks are devised to mislead the medical examiner, and the lad who chances to be rejected as under age regards his fellow who has passed as the object of cruel favouritism. It is hardly necessary to say that this singular anxiety to become a full-blown labourer is attributable to the constant promptings of avaricious parents, impatient to seize the proceeds of the child's industry, and who thus impress him with the notion that to become a full-worker will be a happy change in his condition. The wages of a half-timer are about 2s. 6d. per week; those of a 'full-timer', on his promotion, from 4s. to 5s.

If the youth be put to weaving, he begins his working life as a 'tenter', and his duties are to assist some adult weaver in watching his looms, and to call his attention to any disarrangements in the weaving process. A forward and diligent 'tenter' is no small help to the weaver, from whose earnings his wages are deducted. Two or three years suffice to familiarize our neophyte with the mechanism and working of the power-loom, and at the age of fifteen or sixteen he is entrusted with the control of a pair of looms, and is paid by a fixed scale for all the cloth he can produce. Ten to twelve shillings weekly will now be his income; and by-and-by he will get a third loom, and so add another 5s. to that. An expert hand, by the time he attains his majority, may have the sole management of four looms, and earn with good work, from 22s. to 25s. per week . . .

I have chosen my sample workman from the class of weavers because that is by far the most numerous class of factory workers, outnumbering the operative spinners in the proportion of perhaps six to one. The spinner rises by very similar gradations, beginning as a 'piecer', or 'creeler', and, on reaching adolescence, is entrusted with more or fewer spindles, according to his skill and activity. Other subsidiary processes (the carding preparations for spinning, and the winding, warping and sizing preliminaries to the weaving) also engage a limited number of persons. The females in a cotton mill are employed as weavers, winders, and warpers, and the less fastidious of them (chiefly Irish girls) as carders.

We have accompanied our workman to manhood, and the occupation of two pair of power-looms, but before this, in all likelihood, he has changed his social condition. From the age of eighteen to twenty many of the operatives marry. The weaver usually takes a weaver to wife; and, in such cases, the newly-married couple contrive, if possible, to work alongside. Between them they may superintend six looms, and earn 30s. or more per week. This remuneration is not small for persons who learn their handicraft so early, and with such facility.

For the first wedded year or two a thrifty pair will save something or at least provide themselves with many household requisities which they have failed to procure before they ventured to marry. Afterwards, the usual concomitants of matrimony will frequently call away the help-meet from her toil, and sorely diminish the family income at the very periods when expenditure is heaviest. The operative blessed with a numerous progeny will, therefore, often find his impoverishment steadily going on, despite his utmost efforts, for the first fifteen years of married life. Then the tide of his fortunes begin to turn; his children get successively into work, and, for the next dozen years, there may be some chance of pecuniary accumulation.

Finally, as his sons and daughters marry off, which they may be trusted to do at the first feasible opportunity, the operative, if still alive, lapses into penury—perhaps, if his children prove ingrates, falls to the parochial officers, and so ends the story. A minority of the class, more fortunate, or having taken full advantage of such means of advancement as their lot affords, finish their days in frugal independence.

The chances a spinner or weaver have of going a-head are not, to be sure, particularly splendid. The more energetic and capable of them rise to be overlookers or 'tacklers',—men whose duty it is to superintend a given number of workmen and machines; and here and there an opera-tive is promoted to the responsible post of departmental manager. Overlookers' wages range from 30s. to 40s. weekly, and an under-manager will be paid 50s. or so. The first qualification for these places is not superior education or exceptional intelligence, but a rough force of character and activity of habit, which enable the man to keep in check the heterogeneous and at times mutinous mass of a mill-population.

Should our typical workman close his career as the manager of a loom-shed, he may set himself down as the favourite of the gods. For one who reaches that elevation fifty superannuated weavers are relegated to the duties of odd-men, messengers, casual labourers, and the like, until death rescues them from the buffeting and contumely of circumstance.

'Indomitable striving'

The operatives of Lancashire are not, as a rule, deficient in ambition. The aspirations of thousands of them are deep and strong in their vigorous youth. There is very little of that shocking mental stupor and grovelling inertia so observable in the rural labourer, which more than his actual destitution makes his case appear hopeless. An unsatisfied, aggressive, acquisitive spirit is often to be met with in the toilers of the factory, developing in some instances into an indomitable striving which presages better things. Only a limited sediment is sunk in utter sottishness and abasement. But the impulse to progress is not in itself sufficient. In multitudes whose aspirations are high enough, the qualities of persistence and self-denial which might give them practical realization are wanting, and after one or two spasmodic efforts to alleviate their fate the majority become dispirited.

Why this 'inveterate repugnance'?

The omnipresent and probably the strongest sentiment of this people is an inveterate repugnance to factory-work, and a constant desire to get away from it. We shall not wonder much at this if we consider the irksomeness of the employment and the rigidity of its regulations.

First, there is the strict punctuality of mill-life. Every morning the factory-bell rings at half-past five o'clock, and work commences at six. Five minutes after that hour the entrance-gate is shut, and the laggard has the mortification of waiting for admission until breakfast-time, and of losing a quarter of a day. Half an hour is allowed for breakfast, but before that brief interlude is gone the machinery is again in motion. The dinner hour is also curtailed considerably when the Government inspector is thought to be out of the way, and then the ponderous engine swings its indefatigable arms for five hours longer, the day's work ceasing at six p.m.

To be tied down to such inexorable fixity and routine for years at a stretch would, I fancy, be found a trial to most of my readers.

Within the mill the worker is chafed and worried by the stipulations of an oppressive task system. A given quantum of work is fixed as the minimum production of each machine; and any operative who drops frequently behind must expect to be discharged. Whether the default arises from lack of application and industry, or from physical inability to compete with his fellow-workmen, the penalty is generally the same; and I have been told that feeble persons of both sexes, sooner than endure the stigma of incompetency, superadded to the loss of employment, have been known literally to work themselves into their graves.

Again, the piece-worker in a cotton mill suffers serious drawbacks, and has to contend with many difficulties arising from the badness of material. Inferior cotton makes inferior yarn, and is liable to incessant breakages in the manufacturing processes, involving so many stoppages of the machinery and great additional labour to the manipulator. The harder, in fact, the operative has to work the smaller are his earnings at the week's end ... Contending with such obstacles, the wages of some weavers within my own cognizance were reduced so low that when they had wrought a full week their winnings were scarcely sufficient to discharge the house-rent due to the landlord-employer.

The worker is also liable to fines and abatements for blemishes in his work, so that his lot, notwithstanding the many alleviations of late years to which I have alluded, is still far from being one of extreme felicity ... A Lancashire mill-hand said to me the other day, 'I often hear the operatives say that eighteen shillings a week out of the mill is preferable to twenty-five shillings in it'.

Faith and Morals

Now let me devote a sentence or two to the morals and religion of the Lancashire operatives. Our average of morality is not, I think, low. The Lancashire operative is little versed in the great world's refinements of sin. The consummate profligacy of more polished communities is unknown to this coarse but unsophisticated populace. The early and strict hours of labour at the mill compel the work-people to a-bed early, and after eleven o'clock at night the absolute quietude of a manufacturing town is in strange contrast with the midnight din of London or Liverpool. Saturday night is an exception, however, being devoted by the baser sort to a weekly carousal. The weakest point in the moral panoply of these operatives is intemperance. We have singularly little crime of the more heinous kind. Professional crime is almost unheard of. The garotter, the pickpocket, the burglar, are only seen in imported samples. The streets by night are wonderfully safe. The commonest charge at the police-courts is that of domestic brutality, arising for the most part out of drunkenness. A very limited number of the people of these districts can be said to be intrinsically vicious.

The religious instinct among the Lancashire peasantry is neither weak nor inactive. The most successful forms of religion here are those which are most stimulative. Methodism, Congregationalism, and other forms of dissent are largely distributed. The National Church, at all events in the towns, exhibits an activity which does not always distinguish it elsewhere. Roman Catholicism, too, is alert and vigorous, gathering around it all the Irish and some portion of the English inhabitants. The strenuous Lancashire mind has little faith in theological dilutions and compromises. Here Episcopacy generally takes the line of downright, almost savage Evangelicalism . . . Of active scepticism there is very little among the operatives, but oblivion of religion is widely prevalent . . .

From an article by w. A. ABRAM, 'Social Condition and Political Prospects of the Lancashire Workmen', in *The Fortnightly Review*, October 1868

5

The Black Country

The 'Black Country' has points of interest which no one can dispute. Not the pyramids of Egypt, nor the dikes of Holland, bear more conspicuous testimony to human energy and perseverance.

The natural aspect of the country is changed by countless mounds, as large as good-sized hills, which have been gradually formed round the pits, by the accumulation of 'spoil' or rubbish which has been brought up from below . . . Near the furnaces are huge mounds of different and perfectly sterile material. This is the 'cinder' of the furnace, a kind of artificial lava formed chiefly by the combination of flux and the clay of the limestone. It accumulates very rapidly—probably at the rate of two to every ton of iron made; and somewhere it must remain to cumber the ground, for no extensive use has yet been found for it, except to supply materials for the roads, and ballast for the railways . . .

In convenient proximity to the furnaces is the coke-hearth, with its blazing fires and black stream of driving smoke, while hard by, in heavier eddies, curls a yellow earthy volume, which proceeds from huge heaps of ironstone undergoing the process of calcining. The very ground seems on fire, like the representations of Pandemonium, in an old edition of *Paradise Lost*. Far and near the surface is studded with buildings. Every pit has its winding apparatus, its engine-house, and tall chimney. But nothing looks neat, nothing is in perfect repair. Houses—even those of some importance—are girded and cramped together with iron; sheds, stables, cottages, seen stuck into the ground like pins into a pin-cushion . . .

The smelting furnaces are the centre of activity, and to them tramways and railways converge, bearing strings of trucks loaded with materials; and the 'bridge-house'—as it has been called, because it connects the top of the furnace with the furnace yard—is full of men breaking the limestone which serves for flux, and wheeling the calcined limestone to the 'filling holes'.

Under the furnace-manager the charge of the upper part of the furnaces belongs to a contractor called the Bridge-Stocker. He employs a gang of men, women, and boys, and also keeps horses, for the purpose of supplying the furnaces with the necessary materials; and as much depends on his care and regularity, it is found best to give him an interest in the work by paying him so much per ton on the produce. The office of the 'fillers' who work under him, requires watchfulness. They relieve each other by turns; night and day, with unremitting regularity, the furnaces must be fed. The work is hard, but ought to be unattended with danger. The 'filling holes' or orifices by which the materials are poured down the throat of the furnace are not larger than is necessary for the purpose; a man who was 'in liquor' would not be suffered to remain at the post, but man is ever making danger for himself where none exists.

'Precipitated into the furnace'

One dark night at a Shropshire ironwork, a 'filler' found a barrow improperly left in his way, and, in a moment of passion, he seized it with violence, supposing it to be full; but being empty, it gave way with unexpected facility, and by the force of his own movement he was precipitated into the furnace. The charge was within four feet of the 'filling hole', and two of his comrades, one of whom nearly sacrificed his life in the effort, succeeded in pulling him out with very little delay. The surgeon was immediately in attendance—but hope or help there was none. The poor man presented a spectacle fearful to behold, but it is believed he suffered little pain. He retained his senses to the last, and during the greater part of the hour for which his life was prolonged his voice was heard in low, rapid, and fervent prayer.

The lower part of the furnace is in the charge of the keepers and the 'stock-taker'. They prepare the sand, form the moulds, superintend the casting, weigh the pigs [of iron], and remove 'the cinder'. At casting-time their situation seems full of peril, but they rarely receive any injury, though they may be seen skipping about among rivulets of molten metal with more indifference than a tidy housemaid shows to the water with which she is washing the door-step; and they flit about among sparks and burning fragments of fuel as unconcernedly as a harlequin jumps through a blaze of squibs. It might be supposed that their eyes must be affected by the heat and the glare of the iron fluid; but we cannot find, on inquiry, that they are subject to blindness, or even to premature decay of sight.

Sometimes, indeed, accidents occur: the sand at the tapping-hole gives way, and the molten metal unexpectedly bursts forth. Or it may happen that the 'charge' of the furnace sinks irregularly, arching over, and leaving a hollow such as is often seen at the bottom of an ordinary grate. The vast mass then collapses, and falling suddenly upon the molten cinder, projects it together with no small portion of the blazing contents of the furnace into the 'casting-house'. On such occasions, if anyone happened to be standing near, he would be in imminent peril . . .

In a colliery and ironwork the distribution of the coal is usually made subservient to the manufacture of the iron. The 'sweetest' kinds of coal (the freest from sulphur) are reserved for the smelting furnace, and when it is intended to make the best quality of iron they are further purified by coking. The superior coals less suited to the smelting furnace are sold for household purposes. The inferior kinds are used at the engines, at the pits, and to supply the workman with his allowance of a ton per month. They are also sold to the workhouses and to the poor. But there is nothing in this to alarm the sensibility of the philanthropist. He is probably burning worse coal in his own London study, unless he is very particular in selecting, and also in scolding, his coal merchant . . .

It is not surprising that the deep mines of modern days have hitherto been preferred for description. In them everything is on a colossal scale, and their every detail is astonishing. They have further acquired a melancholy notoriety by those wholesale catastrophes which can occur only in works of such magnitude. But it is for this reason the more necessary to turn our attention to the less known, but not less important, mines of the older districts which still produce some of the most valuable materials for the iron trade . . .

In one particular, the danger to the workmen, the resemblance is only too strong. The world will not dispense with coal and iron; and were the risk of getting them infinitely greater, men would be found in abundance who would brave them all . . . The annual aggregate of accidents, which used to be estimated at 1,000, now averages about 800. The causes of death are classified under five heads, and the mortality assignable to each is in round numbers as follows:—Accidents in the shaft, 150; explosions, 70; falls of the roof or of minerals, 400; miscellaneous below ground, 130; above ground, 50.

As the minerals in the old ironstone district lie near the surface, the shafts are not deep, and their diameter does not exceed six or seven feet. The areas of the pits are comparatively small, the workmen few, and the 'winding' very slow. The minerals are raised in 'skips' or baskets, and so at first were the men; but another method is now universally employed. They insert their legs in certain loops of chain, which they call 'doubles', and, holding on with their hands to the main chain, they are drawn up to the bank in a cluster, like a swarm of bees . . . It is wisely regulated by law that not more than eight men shall go up or down the shaft at once, and in going down this restriction is endured patiently enough; but in coming up the greatest firmness on the part of the 'hooker-on' is necessary to prevent more than the legal number obtaining a place . . .

In spite of many regulations for fencing the pits' mouths, deaths by falling down the shafts are frequent. Many years ago, we remember to have seen the men, at an unusual hour, issuing slowly from a pit, and moodily straggling homewards. After a fatal accident, it is their invariable custom to abandon the pits for the remainder of the day. On this occasion a poor girl had incautiously come too near the pit's mouth, and, losing her balance, had fallen down the shaft. And sometimes a tragedy occurs which no precaution can prevent. A few months ago, a worthless drunkard ran off deserting his infant child and a wife who only loved him the more for all his ill-usage. The poor woman made no complaint—she pined in grief and want till one morning, with her remaining strength, she clambered over the fence of a closed pit. She deliberately threw down her famine-struck child. A charter-master saw her and rushed forward, but came up in time only to hear the rushing sound of her fall down the shaft.

Under the head of Explosions all their fatal consequences are also comprehended. The bad air which assails the miner's life in the pit is of two kinds . . . carbonic acid gas, or 'choke-damp' . . . and carburetted hydrogen, or 'fire-damp'. These two gases league together against the collier. When an explosion has done its work of destruction, the 'choke-damp' rises to suffocate those whom the fire has spared, and with such deadly effect, that, in general, the deaths by suffocation greatly exceed those by fire . . . The only defence against these noxious gases is a sufficient current of pure air, and the art of ventilation becomes a matter of first-rate importance . . .

Accidents from falls of the minerals or the roof equal the aggregate of casualties from all other causes whatever . . . But to dangers of this class the men seem singularly indifferent, in spite of all the pressure that can be put upon them, and their own dearly bought experience . . . 'Not yet' seems to be the delusion which keeps men working on, moment after moment, in situations of peril, till at last they stay one moment too long—and all is over . . .

Death comes to a 'noble spirit'

In a Shropshire pit, not long ago, an accident occurred which occasioned very general sorrow. Three men, who were working without the usual precautions, were struck down by a mass of earth and stone. Their fellow-workmen rushed up to them, and in the first instance turned to the man who seemed most to need help. He was lying beneath a huge fragment of rock. 'No,' he said, 'go to those other men first.' They hesitated. 'Go to those other men first, I say; I am "doggie" of this pit; you must do as I tell you. GO!' The two men were liberated, and ultimately recovered. The lacerated 'doggie' was with difficulty raised to the bank. The surgeon prepared to do what he could, and tied up the femoral artery which was severed, but it was too late. Suddenly a change came over the countenance of the wounded man. 'Let me turn on my face, lads', he said. The surgeon paused, and raised his hand with a meaning which could not be misunderstood. The noble spirit had fled.

But it is not enough that air, earth, and fire combine against the poor miner; among his worst foes we must reckon water. Not only does the water rise so suddenly in many pits that an accident which has stopped the pumps might occasion serious risk, but sometimes in the course of the workings the men come upon some powerful spring of subterraneous reservoir, which bursts upon them with fatal force . . .

Strong sense of kin

The ties of kinship are felt in the Black Country with the force of Highland clanship. It is common for families descended from a common stock severally to assume, in addition to their patronymic and often in lieu of it, some uncouth nickname . . . On all occasions they cling together, and for right or wrong—more especially the latter—they are ready to stand by each other to the uttermost.

The inhabitants of the Black Country have warm feelings, and show great kindness to each other in times of difficulty and distress. In one poor-looking cottage, perhaps, may be found an orphan child, adopted by a kind neighbour, on whom it had no claim but its helplessness; in another a poor woman, whose sick husband is occupying their only bed, and who has been taken in by a kind friend for her approaching confinement. For the most part they have little intercourse with their superiors, but their manners are plain rather than rude. They have the substance of true courtesy, if not its external forms. They have a quick sense of kindness. They are acutely alive to neglect and injustice . . .

We do not deny the existence of the brutalized being who is often set up as the type of the workman of the mines, but we admit it as the exception only . . . When the moral degradation of the miner is inferred from the dirtiness of his habits, we deny both the fact and the inference.

His white woollen jacket or blouse is frequently washed, and when he gets to his cottage he takes infinite pains to scrub off the grime of the pits. It was on observing this that a proprietor in the Midland district established baths, which were supplied with a perpetual stream of hot water from the blast-engine; but the experiment has not as yet succeeded. Old habit still prevails, and the tub at home is preferred . . .

The rate of wages is high, but is liable to considerable fluctuations; and the miner glories in his power of maintaining it by the combinations and strikes, which form so important a feature in the history of mining . .

[Those] misunderstand the feelings of the black population [who] assume that their reckless disregard of danger proceeds from indifference to an existence so little worth preserving. On the contrary, their relish for enjoyment is keen; their passion for excitement is strong; and their aversions to self-control they mistake for dignity and independence. A prize-fight, or a poaching adventure, has a charm for them that is irresistible. A wake, a fair, or a race empties the pits of all but the steadiest hands. The great difficulty of the employers is to induce their men to go regularly to their work, especially when they are most wanted, when the trade is good and wages rise. Every Monday after pay-day is devoted by many to jollity. On such occasions the pit is said to be at 'play' . . .

A bottle of port on pay-day

It is a curious fact that by far the largest part of the deposits at the savings-banks are contributed by the classes who are in receipt of low wages. Self-indulgence increases with the means of gratifying it, and improvidence is the besetting sin of the highly paid workman. Immediately after pay-day many a man will feast on rump steaks for breakfast, without considering on what he must fast before pay-day comes round again. When wages are high, it is one of the miner's chief triumphs to call at the bar of some large inn for a bottle of port. He rejoices in the glow of the full-bodied, heady, liquor which he feels to his fingers' ends; but the chief source of his satisfaction is the consciousness that he walks off with five shillings' worth under his belt, and 'what could my Lord Duke do more?'

In the Black Country drunkenness is the direct cause of nine-tenths of all the crimes that are committed. Many a man, who in his sober moments is reasonable, industrious, docile, and kind, is changed by drink into something worse than a wild beast; he quarrels with his equals, insults his superiors, and maltreats his family . . .

It is no doubt with the idea that men *must* be amused, that in some collieries the officials encourage, or at least we may presume do not discourage, horse-racing; for we have seen on the walls, in bills six feet long, the 'charter-masters' stakes' advertised. It is for the purpose of diverting the men from these amusements, which lead to every species of disorder and riot, that Mr Tremenheere [the Government Commissioner appointed to enquire into the state of the Mining Districts in 1859] recommends that all manly games, such as cricket, all humanizing and refined tastes, should be encouraged as much as possible. Music is often cultivated with much zeal and some success. The advice, that a small plot of garden should be assigned, if possible, to each cottage, is excellent. A passion for gardening under difficulties is very common, and it is touching to see the pride and pleasure with which some self-taught horticultural genius will exhibit the first flowers, or the earliest vegetables of his own growing. We have seen a pigstye converted with infinite ingenuity into a conservatory; and we remember on one occasion to have been offered a picotee carnation by an enthusiast, who after a hard day's work had sat up all the previous night to catch the sound of the first pattering drops of rain, which, on the wind's changing from E.N.E. to S.W., he fondly hoped would come at last to refresh his parched garden . . .

Sunday amusements

The observance of Sunday is much what might be expected . . . To many it is a day of rest and nothing more. The toil of the week makes mere physical repose an enjoyment. To many it is a day of household cares . . . To some, and those not a few, it is a day of riot and debauchery. In many cottages a suspicious-looking dog, who slinks away on meeting a stranger's eye, as if conscious of his guilty complicity, sufficiently indicates the nature of the morning's amusement. If no other excitement offers itself, drinking and gambling fill up the day; but, if the weather is fine, pigeon-flying is the favourite diversion. This sport is pursued in various ways; sometimes the bet turns on which of a rival pair of 'tumblers' makes the greatest number of summersets in the air; sometimes it is a race between two pigeons, turned out to fly to their usual feeding-place; or several are let loose at once, and the owner of the bird which arrives at a designated spot pockets the stakes. Their flight is followed by their owners and a rabble on foot. Disputes and quarrels ensue, and all is riot and disorder . . .

The miner is more fortunate than many other classes of operatives inasmuch as he is less affected by the vicissitudes of trade. The fluctuations of the iron-market are notorious; but the pressure, in the first instance, falls on the employers. If the depression is long continued, wages fall; but the workman can live, and the iron-master has not the power of dismissing his hands to any great extent. It is not safe to let his men disperse; it is ruinous to let his pits fall in. He is obliged to hold out to the last moment. If, in spite of all his efforts, and all the help he can obtain, he sinks at last, then, indeed, the distress is fearful to contemplate. The cottages deserted by their starving inhabitants, who roam about, seeking work and finding none, or throng the thoroughfares of the neighbouring towns in listless groups—the furnaces cold, the engines silent, and all that used to speak of life and bustle standing motionless and meaningless—all this presents an image of desolation and despair which can only be surpassed by the real wretchedness of which it is the outward sign . . .

From an article on 'The Black Country' in *The Edinburgh Review*, April 1863.

6

Birmingham, 'City of a Thousand Trades'

The manufactures [of the Birmingham district] are so various, and, with few exceptions, so intermingled, that it is difficult to classify them fairly by distinction either of processes used, or of articles produced, or of the importance of the manufactures themselves. They are, however, generally spoken of as included under the head of 'Hardware', and are most, though not all of them, concerned with the production of metallic or earthern wares.

As long ago as the year 1841 it was ascertained, on an inquiry made for an official purpose, that there were at that date in Birmingham 97 trades not common to all large towns, and 2,100 firms in those trades. Since that time many new trades, some of great importance, employing a large number of persons, have been established in the town, and the population of the town has increased in the succeeding 20 years from 183,000 to 296,000, or, with the suburbs, 310,000 . . . Though the number and size of large factories has grown, it is probable that the number of employers of all kinds, small as well as large, has grown also. In one trade alone, which has received its chief development within the last 15 years, viz. jewellery, the number of masters, employing on the average from 3 to 50 persons, was in 1862 upwards of 250 . . .

Some of the more important manufactures of the town and district are,—glass; brass and other metal foundry; guns, military and sporting; jewellery; electro-plate; metallic bedsteads; buttons and screws; and, principally in the Stourbridge neighbourhood, bricks . . .

The number of factories employing large numbers is undoubtedly increasing with the improvements of machinery and the increase of capital, and the forest of tall chimneys which meets the eye in every direction in Birmingham, and the large new works in all parts of the town . . . with the actual returns obtained from many of these factories . . . show that the numbers of children, young persons, and women employed in large works alone must be very considerable. It has, however, been already remarked that Birmingham is probably unequalled in its number of smaller masters, employing numbers of all amounts, ranging from one upwards . . .

Many work-places, including some of the establishments of the highest standing in Birmingham, are in one or more parts very deficient in space, ventilation, light, and perhaps in consequence of this, in cleanliness. The passages are sometimes almost entirely dark, and the ladder steps, by which the shops are reached, often steep and dangerous. This arises, no doubt, chiefly from factories having grown from small beginnings in crowded places, where adequate extension on the spot is impossible or difficult, and removal may, for several reasons, be inconvenient . . . Some of the new places, those of jewellers especially, have been described to me as objectionably small in proportion to the numbers employed in them . . . But in some of the larger old work-places, as some kinds of button manufactories, the rooms are low and ill arranged, and the crowding is extreme, being reduced almost to the minimum of possible sitting space, the work not requiring more than hand motion, with narrow passages between for reaching the seats. But even such spaces for passage are not always found, the girls creeping in under the women's legs and the benches. I have found rows of little girls sitting back to back on common benches so close that their backs actually touch, with rows of women, sitting as close as they can be packed, fronting them across work-benches only 18 inches wide. In these and like places fresh air can be admitted through the windows, only at the expense of the youngest girls, who often sit in rows along the sides of the room with their backs to the windows.

The gloominess of some of the work-places is extreme. In some, as casting and many stamping shops, good light is not essential to the work. Where it is essential it is generally got by working close in front of the windows. Some of the stamping shops, placed on the ground floor on account probably of the shocks of the stamps, are half cellars, and most are extremely dark and untidy, and seem likely to be damp in winter, at least in the pits which are often sunk for the workers to stand in, as a means of gaining height for the fall of the stamp; the soil, however, of Birmingham is dry, and in great measure drains itself. Some places depend for much of their light upon the furnaces, and after dark the nailers have no light but that of the forge and the hot iron . . .

'Vast number of small workshops'

But in addition to the larger distinct work-places which may be more properly called 'factories', and many of which are named 'Works', there are in the yards in which Birmingham abounds ... a vast number of small workshops, forming either separate floors or parts of floors in the same block of buildings, and in some of these cases renting the steam power needed for the work, as gun or plate polishing, &c., or standing alone or attached to houses. In some of these men alone work, in others women, girls, and boys also. I have visited many of these shops, but have found the space in nearly all cases sufficient for the small numbers employed. The yards, however, in which they stand, are often offensive to the eye or nose, and probably injurious to health, from their neglected condition. There are commonly surface drains running or stagnant with dirty water, and often heaps of refuse or decaying matter, loaded ashpits, or privies abominably close to or under parts of the shops, and the cleanliness of the inside of the shops corresponds to that of the approach.

It may not be immaterial to refer to the general state of the atmosphere, which is full of dust and smoke from the number of factories and shops, and which it seems probable is affected in other less apparent ways by the amount of metallic fumes. At the late meeting of the British Association at Newcastle ... it was stated that some of the medical men of Birmingham 'attributed the remarkable freedom of that town from cholera to the minute presence of arsenious acid in the atmosphere of that district derived from the metal works'.

Birmingham is said to be a very healthy town, and one covering a very large amount of space in proportion to its population ... with broad streets, and scarcely any cellars, and 5 persons to each house against $5\frac{1}{2}$ at Manchester and 7 in Liverpool, a considerable number of the houses being the property of the occupiers, and also with great natural advantages from the nature and general slope of the soil. These advantages may probably counteract some of the natural effects of the state of the yards, and of other causes just referred to. Bowel complaints, however, were stated at the General Hospital, at the time of my inquiry there, to be extremely prevalent. The rate of infant mortality, which had attracted the attention of the Medical Officer of the Privy Council, is referred by him mainly to the employment of married women in factories leading to neglect of their infants.

Birmingham, however, notwithstanding its great size, importance, and general activity, is without a Medical Officer of Health. Were an efficient person appointed to discharge these duties the greater part of the present objections to the yard workshops would probably in a short time be removed ...

Steam power is used in one or more parts of a large number of occupations, and in the smallest separate shop, where it can be rented, as well as in the largest factory . . . Many of the machines . . . are fed, attended, and cleaned by boys, girls, and women, one person sometimes attending a considerable number; and in processes involving cutting and hammering cause an intolerable noise, often so loud as to drown the loudest voice . . . While I was in one of the nail-cutting factories the pace of the machinery from some cause or other was increased to such a degree as to become positively painful, and to cause the workpeople to stop their work till it moderated. The floors and benches also sometimes vibrate from the force and pace of the machinery—in one case, indeed, not of a metal, but of a skin and parchment factory, the floor shook so violently that I found it as difficult to write as in a carriage in a jolting train . . .

Though many of the employments are very dirty, dusty, or greasy, and some noxious, the means of cleanliness are very scantily, if at all, provided in such places, and where water may be had it often is not used. Boys may be seen at work, or in the streets plainly coming from work, who, from their grimed faces and general appearance, might not unnaturally be mistaken for sweeps, as was indeed the case with a boy taken to a hospital here. He was, however, only one of the 'cobbers', amongst whom dirtiness is not necessarily caused by the work, though it prevails largely from neglect and probably also from the gloom of the stamping shops. The faces of foundry boys are grimed with the dust caused by their work. These causes, with burns from molten or flying metal and powerful acids, which are common, act in some cases as obstacles to attendance at schools or places of religious worship; and in extreme cases produce destruction of clothing, too apt to end in an entire discontinuance of such attendance, and so probably work serious moral injury, in addition to the loss of the self-respect of which personal cleanliness seems a natural condition.

In Birmingham the stated hours of work in the majority of trades are short, viz. from 8 till 7. In certain trades, especially the heavier, they are longer, but in very few cases exceeding 12 hours . . .

'Saint Monday'

In Birmingham, however, and more or less throughout the district, an enormous amount of time is lost, not only by want of punctuality in coming to work in the morning and beginning again after meals, but still more by the general observance of 'Saint Monday', which is shown in the late attendance or entire absence of large numbers on that day. One employer has on Monday only about 40 or 50 out of 300 or 400, and the day is recognized by many masters as an hour shorter than others at each end . . .

The actual holidays, whether allowed or not, are ample. In addition to the extensive appropriation of Monday to this purpose already referred to, and to certain seasons, there are many other occasions, as those of local *fêtes*, on which holidays are given or taken; and many employers give their workpeople an annual trip to Malvern or elsewhere, which seems to be beneficial in more ways than the most obvious. It is, at least, highly enjoyed and gratefully remembered. One or two fix the date of their coming to work from a 'gipsy party' a year or two back. The practice of a half day on Saturday prevails in many factories, though in several it is made good by extra work during the earlier part of the week. Sometimes, it seems, no holiday is recognized . . .

Toll of accidents

Considering the amount of machinery used in Birmingham, accidents resulting in loss of life or limb by the young are rare, but not to such a degree as to show that there is no danger to them. Children are brought but little in contact with the more dangerous parts, but young persons are often engaged in the same way as adults; and it is a mere chance when accidents have happened to females over 18 that they did not happen to girls working at machinery of precisely the same kind beside them, the risk from dress being the same, and from thoughtlessness probably greater. The principal sources of serious danger are shafts and bands used for turning lathes and wheels, especially in screw factories, in which by far the greater proportion employed are females. A woman lately killed in a screw factory from being entangled in the shaft had been caught in the same way at least four times, and in another factory of the same kind three females were thus entangled in one day. The same sources of danger exist in button and other factories in which lathes, wheels, drills, &c., are used for turning, grinding, boring, and polishing materials of various kinds. Even where no harm is done, the skirts are often torn off, and even a boy was stripped to the skin all but his boots and stockings.

Accidents, however, of a slighter kind, chiefly from stamps and presses, causing mutilation or injury of the thumbs and fingers, are extremely common, as appears not only from the experience of hospitals and medical men, but also from a personal observation of the hands of girls at work, of whom a great number indeed bear marks of injuries which, though in numerous cases not of sufficient importance to send them to the hospital, must have been extremely painful, and interfere more or less with the free and dexterous use of their fingers for general purposes, though not actually incapacitating them from labour. Sometimes, however, the injury to hands is more serious. A mere thumb 'pinch' has kept a little girl at home three months . . .

On the whole the condition of the working classes in this district, except in cases in which their own conduct is in fault, is one of considerable independence and comfort, more so probably, as generally represented, than in many other manufacturing districts; more so certainly than that of the persons engaged in the other occupations and districts with which I have become acquainted ... I cannot, however, help observing in conclusion that I have found not only very defective workplaces, but in some cases severe overwork, in others very young children in a wretchedly squalid and forlorn condition in the factories of large employers of liberal minds and most kindly feelings, shown not only in their expression of their views, but in their kindness of manner and evident regret that the mental and bodily condition of many of the young, perhaps only indirectly, in their charge should be so far as it is from being cultivated, bright, and happy.

From MR J. EDWARD WHITE'S report upon the Metal Manufactures of the Birmingham District; Children's Employment Commission, Appendix to 3rd Report (1864), pp. 51–63; P.P. 1864, vol. 22.

7

'The Social and Provident Proclivities of Potters'

In any consideration of the social state of the Potteries, the question of wages must take precedence, for without some knowledge of the sources of income, we can form but an indifferent estimate of the expenditure. It has been shown that the potters in the Potteries proper amount to 11,323 men, 6,332 women, 3,561 young men, 2,749 young women, and 3,913 children; and from reliable information, I believe in ordinary times, that the aggregate amount of wages distributed among them weekly amount to £21,264. 7s., or about 15s. 3d. per person, young and old ... This rate is considerably above any textile average that I am aware of, and many other averages also; and for various reasons a comparison with the wages of other trades will not be without interest. Thus, for example, not very long ago, the average weekly rate of wages in the following other trades was as follows:—

	s.	d.
In the Iron Trades	18	—
In Dyeing	17	8
In Fire-clay	17	2½

	s.	d.
On Railways	16	11
(In China and Porcelain)	15	3
In Paper	14	8¼
In Silk (spinning)	12	8¼
In the Woollen manufacture	11	7¾
In the Cotton manufacture the average wages per person per week was about	10	6
In common Earthenware	9	10¼
In Flax	8	—

So we find, notwithstanding the number of children and females employed in the pottery trade, it stands fifth on the list of twelve occupations such as these; and that the wages are so large as to constitute an element of considerable social importance to the class amongst whom they are distributed.

With 15s 3d per head per week, there ought to be some very prominent economical and educational features amongst the Pottery population; since high wages are a vast power for good or evil, according as they are the property of educated or uneducated recipients. And it is satisfactory to find that, persons have been found considerate enough, and interested enough in the welfare of their neighbours, to endeavour to direct the distribution of these receipts into a proper channel, and that these endeavours have met with considerable success. Thus Mr Palmer, of Longton, writes:—

'The provident institutions established in the town have contributed largely to its improvement. Some of the earliest of these institutions were identified with the Sabbath school system, and were called "The Children's Saving Fund", established for the laudable object of enabling parents to provide for the clothing of their children, and to secure other household comforts. In this fund, parents and children were allowed to accumulate their savings without interest. And to show the extent to which they were made use of, from one of these funds, £400 was invested in one year by upwards of 700 depositors. Since savings banks and other facilities for depositing money at interest have arisen in the town, these societies have diminished in extent and importance. They continue to exist, however . . . In addition to these savings banks, there are insurance societies, and sick and friendly societies, eminently calculated to benefit the working classes. Last, though not least, I would notice another institution which has yielded a giant power for good, and borne a very important share in improving re-organizing, and remodelling the town and in elevating its social status: I allude to building societies . . . These have effected reforms in character, improved positions, elevated and enlarged conceptions, and with many, have changed the very objects of life. A man can place his foot on his own little spot of earth, and with honest pride, call it his own . . .

'The extent of these building society operations may be guessed at from the following statistics:—

They have advanced upon mortgage securities	£211,640.	16.	3
Paid on completion or withdrawn shares	40,925.	18.	1
	252,566.	14.	4

'The number of shareholders by whom this amount has been paid is 1,914, and the number of shares 77,898½ . . . There are now more than 1,400 subscribing members to building societies, in the town, anxiously looking forward to the day when their own homes will repay their prudence and economy.'

'The simple fact of these savings being effected, and of these houses being erected, by the will of the working men, is an immensely significant one. All these owners of houses are freeholders; and every man has earned his own freehold from a desire to possess it. Whilst in the same locality, employed at the same work, earning the same wages, and without any extraordinary drawback, a vast number of those who possess no such properties, live on from day to day, regardless of every enjoyment that is not sensual . . .'

Then Mr Palmer, after presenting the bright side of the picture, very fairly shows the other side also. 'To attempt to set up the dogma that we are all provident people, would be a glaring fallacy. Wherever there is excess of any kind, there will be found improvidence; and in Longton, it must be honestly admitted, that improvidence develops itself in many forms. Amongst a large class of men, whose facilities for personal, domestic, and social elevation are great, there is a strong vitiated tendency. Whilst their weekly means hold out, they revel in excess. They freely eat, drink, and take their pleasures. Very often they earn their money like slaves, and spend it in the most lavish manner. When they get hold of it, they are in an intense hurry to dispose of it. They appear to have no conception of its value, except so far as it may secure their present gratifications, and never dream of providing for future contingencies. They neither understand the theory nor the practice of economy. Their lifelong creed is 'sufficient unto the day is the evil thereof'. So there exists a class of men, of whose virtues we can say but little, but of whose want of virtue, volumes might be spoken. The tattered, sallow, begrimed aspect of these men, the forlorn condition of their poorly-clad wives and half-naked and half-starved children, and the abject wretchedness of their filthy and ill-furnished homes, are features peculiar to this type of humanity, which excites both pity and disgust.

'Towards these deplorable evils, it is to be feared, that a portion of the female community contributes. Amongst the class to which we refer, there is a glaring neglect or ignorance of home duties, and utter incapacity to manage well their household affairs. Dirt, disorder, and discord are everywhere present. The husband finds no comfort in his home, and little or nothing to enlist his sympathies, and accordingly seeks pleasure and comfort elsewhere. Home becomes gradually neglected, forsaken, hated. Excesses creep upon him, and, at last, an odious reputation attaches to him, which shuts him out from the companionship of respectable associates . . .

'Drunkenness is at other times, perhaps, the most generally demoralizing form of Longton depravity. From robbery and violence we are well protected by a vigilant police, under most excellent management and supervision. Prostitution, as compared with some other places, is scarcely known here, for it is stated by one very well informed on the subject, that there are but sixteen known prostitutes among us, and some of these not wholly dependent upon their nefarious trade for a living.'

This is what Mr Palmer writes of Longton in 1864, and . . . much of what has been written of Longton applies not only to the Potteries, but to much of South Staffordshire also, of which I shall say a few words before I close my report.

What strikes one most forcibly, is the great lack of any middle class of workmen, between those who appear utterly unprovident and wasteful, and the 'careful', provident, and energetic men of whom Mr Palmer has spoken with such force, who thrive well in business, and to whose thrift is owing mainly the great number of freeholds round about. The men appear to be all thriving and saving, or else in want, except immediately on the receipt of their wages; and it is to this latter class to which a considerable number of the wage population belongs. To use the expressive language of a workman, to whom I was speaking on the subject, 'there is no set of workmen among the potters who will wash and dress themselves after a day's labour, go out and smoke a pipe, have one glass and no more, and then go home. They are all thoroughly for home, or against home.'

How many excuses do the drunkards make for the holydays which they keep! Saint Monday has hitherto been a very patron amongst them, and is, by some, absolutely idolized. On his day occur all the weekly rabbit races, dog races, and hop-step-and-jump matches, for sums which, to an agricultural labourer, would be a year's maintenance for his whole family. If they hire at Martinmas, an old-fashioned condition of labour which is still retained in the Potteries, they 'wet the bargain' till it is drenched through and through. If there is a 'wake' they keep it up for a week. In short, whatever can be converted into an excuse for a break-off, is adopted as a matter of course.

Under these circumstances, the homes of the people, what are they ?

'What I should call a comfortable and well-furnished house,' says an informant who is in the habit of visiting them regularly, 'is scarcely ever to be found amongst this class. The furniture above and below stairs is, generally, of the poorest kind. The women, from going early to work, have had but few opportunities afforded them of becoming acquainted with home duties before they marry; and in consequence, their homes are deserted by the men for the public house. In those parts of England with which I am familiar, I have never met with girls and women who knew so little of the common use of the needle, as in Longton. Hence the rags which disgrace the children, and the great waste of money which is caused by the want of a few stitches in time. Even the children's under-clothing is often bought ready made, and worn till it will no longer hold together.

'The same waste and extravagance goes on with the food. At the beginning of the week I have seen often, meat, fish, spirits and beer, where, three days afterwards, there was only bread and water. A full stomach during the early part of the week, and an empty one at the end of it, is a very common rule.

'Education, I consider, to be at a very low ebb amongst them; rather better amongst the women than the men. But, in most cases, even the simplest reading and writing is most imperfect . . .

'Unchastity, so far as I can judge, is not a common vice amongst the potters. Drunkenness and ignorance, which latter is more a misfortune than a fault, are the present great evils of which society has to complain, for neither of these are considered a disgrace, even in these days of progress . . .'

Rags and comfortless homes certainly stand everywhere in prominent relief, in many of the wealthiest districts, of both North and South Staffordshire, where the wages of the family often amount to £3, £4, or £5 a week. I have been told of an instance, in South Staffordshire, where the family wages were as high as £6 a week, and where a prepayment of them was necessary, in consequence of extravagance, before the Saturday night . . .

I will make no further comment on this fact, otherwise than to observe, that if the state of society is moulded by surrounding circumstances, as undoubtedly it is, some idea may be gathered of the condition of a population where so large a percentage is ignorant of the merest elements of learning. That it is so is undoubted, the misfortune being, that it is only a type of a vast class; and that the remedy now applied can be only very partial in its operation, and very slow of producing results. Nevertheless, I thoroughly believe that the present state of things is quite remediable; that thousands need but the opportunity of education and social influence to raise themselves to the height reached by so many of their fellow-workers ... All that they want is instruction, guidance, example, and sympathy. They must be educated, and healthily amused; the beer house must be exchanged for the public park, and athletic games for dog-fighting and rabbit-hunting, ignorance and rags must be made to give place to schools and clothing-clubs, gluttony and the burial clubs, to the savings bank and the building society. We must in fact teach them to provide for life, that they may live as men, and feel the responsibilities which belong to manhood. If all this is done, the next generation of potters will no more resemble the present than the present do their Saxon ancestors ...

ROBERT BAKER, factory inspector; Factory Inspectors' Reports for half-year to October 31, 1864; pp. 90-96, 112; P.P. 1865, vol. 20.

8

People on the London & North-Western

On the great covered platform at Euston Square Station ... are congregated persons of all countries, of all religions, and of all languages. People of high character, of low character, and of no character at all. Infants just beginning life—old people just ending it. Many desirous to be noticed—many, from innumerable reasons, good, bad, and indifferent, anxious to escape notice. Some are looking for their friends—some, suddenly turning upon their heels, are evidently avoiding their acquaintance.

Contrasted with that variety of free-and-easy costumes in which quiet-minded people usually travel, are occasionally to be seen a young couple—each, like a new-born baby, dressed from head to foot in everything perfectly new—hurrying towards a coupé, on whose door there negligently hangs a black board, upon which there is printed, in white bridal letters, the word 'Engaged'.

Across this mass of human beings a number of porters are to be seen carrying and tortuously wheeling baggage and property of all shapes and sizes ... Within the long and apparently endless straight line of railway carriages which bound the platform are soon seen the faces and caps of various travellers, especially the old ones, who with due precaution have taken possession of their seats; and while most of these, each of them with their newspapers unfolded on their knees, are slowly wiping their spectacles, several of the younger inmates are either talking to other idlers leaning on their carriage-windows, or, half kissing and half waving their hands, are bidding farewell to the kind friends who had accompanied them to the station . . .

The driver's whistle announces the immediate departure of the train. . . . In a very short time it has attained its full speed, and men of business are then intently reading the 'City news', and men of pleasure the leading article of their newspapers, when this runaway street of passengers—men, women, and children—unexpectedly find themselves in sudden darkness, visible only by a feeble lamp which modestly shines over their head . . .

By this time the boarded platform at Euston Station, but a few minutes ago so densely thronged with passengers, is completely deserted. The lonely guard on duty, every footstep resounding as he walks, paces along it like a sentinel. The newspaper vendors are indolently reclining in their stalls; even the boy who sells *Punch* is half asleep; there is nothing to break the sober dulness of the scene but a few clerks and messengers, who, like rabbits popping from one hole of their warren into another, enter upon the platform from the door of one office to hurry into that of the next. In a few minutes, however, the loud puffing of an engine announces the approach towards the platform of a string of empty carriages, which are formed into the next departure train . . .

'A melancholy whine'

The out train having been despatched, we must now beg our readers to be so good as to walk, or rather to scramble, with us from the scene of its departure across five sets of rails, on which are lying crowds of railway-carriages preparing to depart, to the opposite platform, in order to witness the arrival of an incoming train. This platform is infinitely longer than that for the departure trains. It is a curve 900 feet in length, lighted by day from above with plate-glass, and at night by 67 large gas-lamps suspended from above, or affixed to the iron pillars that support the metallic net-worked roof.

Upon this extensive platform scarcely a human being is now to be seen; nevertheless along its whole length it is bounded on the off-side by a line of cabs, intermixed with private carriages of all shapes, gigs, dog-carts, and omnibuses, the latter standing opposite little ugly black-faced boards which are always exclaiming, 'Holborn—Fleet Street —and Cheapside!'—'Oxford Street—Regent Street—and Charing

Cross!' In this motley range of vehicles, smart coachmen, tall pale powdered footmen, and splendid horses are strangely contrasted with the humble but infinitely faster conveyance—the common cab. Most of the drivers of these useful machines are absent; the remainder are either lolling on benches or dozing on their boxes. Their horses stand ruminating with a piece of sacking across their loins, or with nosebags, often empty, until for some reason a carriage before them leaves the line, in which case, notwithstanding the absence of their drivers, they quietly advance along the edge of the little precipice which bounds the rails. They know quite well what they are waiting for . . .

As soon as the reeking engine-funnel of an up-train is seen darting out of the tunnel at Primrose Hill, one of the Company's servants stationed there, who deals solely in compressed air—or rather, who has an hydraulic machine for condensing it—allows a portion to rush through an inch iron pipe; and he thus instantaneously produces in the little signal-office on the up platform at Euston Station, where there is always a signal-man watching by night as well as by day, a loud melancholy whine, which will continue uninterruptedly for five minutes . . . The moment this doleful intimation arrives, the signal-man, emerging from his little office, touches the trigger of a bell outside his door, which immediately in two loud hurried notes announces the arrival at Camden Station of the expected up-train; and at this moment it is interesting to watch the poor cab-horses, who, by various muscular movements, clearly indicate that they are perfectly sensible of what has just occurred . . .

As soon as the green signal-man has created this sensation among bipeds and quadrupeds, taking with him the three flags, of danger (red), caution (green), and security (white), he proceeds down the line a few yards to a point from which he can clearly see his brother signal-man stationed at the mouth of the Euston tunnel. If any obstruction exists in that direction, the waving of the red flag informs him of it; and it is not until the white one from the tunnel as well as that from the station-master on the platform have reported to him that 'all is clear' that he returns to his office to announce, by means of his compressed-air apparatus, this intelligence to the ticket-collector at Camden Station . . .

About four minutes after the up-train has been authorised by the air-pipe to leave Camden Station, the guard who stands listening for it at the Euston tunnel . . . announces by his flag its immediate approach; on which the signal-man at the little office on Euston platform again touches his trigger, which violently convulsing his bell as before, the cab-horses begin to move their feet, raise their jaded heads, prick up their ears, and champ their bits; the servants in livery turn their powdered heads round; the Company's porters, emerging from various points, quickly advance to their respective stations; and this suspense continues until in a second or two there is seen darting out of the tunnel, like a serpent from its hole, the long dark-coloured train, which by a tortuous movement is apparently advancing at full speed . . . But the breaks . . . soon slacken its speed, until the Company's porters at a brisk walk are preparing to unfasten one after another the doors of all the carriages . . .

Pity the poor Engine-driver!

The duties which the engine-driver has to perform are not only of vital importance, but of a nature which peculiarly illustrates the calm, unpretending, bull-dog courage, indigenous to the moist healthy climate of the British Isles. Even in bright sunshine to stand—like the figure-head of a ship—foremost on a train of enormous weight, which, with fearful momentum, is rushing forward faster than any racehorse can gallop, requires a cool head and a calm heart; but to proceed at this pace in dark or foggy weather into tunnels, along embankments, and through deep cuttings, where it is impossible to foresee any obstruction, is an amount of responsibility which scarcely any other situation in life can exceed; for not only is a driver severely, and occasionally without mercy, punished for any negligence he himself may commit, but he is invariably sentenced personally to suffer on the spot for any accident that from the negligence of others may suddenly befall the road along which he travels, but over which he has not the smallest control.

The greatest hardship he has to endure, however, is from cold, especially that produced in winter by evaporation from his drenched clothes passing rapidly through the air. Indeed, when a gale of wind and rain from the north-west, triumphantly sweeping over the surface of the earth at its ordinary rate of say sixty miles an hour, suddenly meets the driver of the London and North-Western, who has not only to withstand such an antagonist, but to dash through him, and in spite of him to proceed in an opposite direction at the rate of say forty miles an hour—the conflict between the wet Englishman and Aeolus, tilting by each other at the combined speed of a hundred miles an hour, forms a tournament of extraordinary interest.

As the engine is proceeding, the driver, who has not very many inches of standing-room, remains upon its narrow platform, while his fireman, on about the same space, stands close beside him on the tender. We tried the position. Everything, however, proved to be so hard, excepting the engine, which was both hard and hot, that we found it necessary to travel with one foot on the tender and the other on the engine, and, as the motion of each was very different, we felt as if each leg were galloping at a different stride. Nevertheless the Company's drivers and firemen usually travel from 100 to 120 miles per day, performing six of these trips per week; nay, a few run 166 miles per day—for which they are paid eight days' wages for six trips.

As soon as an engine has safely dragged a passenger-train to the top of the incline at Camden Station, at which point the coupling-chains which connect it with its load are instantly unhooked, it is enabled by the switchman to get from the main line upon a pair of almost parallel side rails, along which, while the tickets are being collected, it may be seen and heard retrograding and hissing past its train. After a difficult and intricate passage from one set of rails to another, advancing or 'shunting' backwards as occasion may require, it proceeds to the fire-pit, over which it stops. The fireman here opens the door of his furnace, which by a very curious process is made to void the red-hot contents of its stomach into the pit purposely constructed to receive them, where the fire is instantly extinguished by cold water ready laid on by the side . . .

After dropping his fire, the driver conducts his engine into an immense shed or engine-stable 400 feet in length by 90 in breadth, generally half full of locomotives, where he examines it all over, reporting in a book what repairs are wanting, or, if none (which is not often the case), he reports it 'correct'. He then takes his lamps to the lamp-house to be cleaned and trimmed by workmen solely employed to do so, after which he fetches them away himself. Being now off duty, he and his satellite fireman go either to their own homes or to a sort of club-room containing a fire to keep them warm, a series of cupboards to hold their clothes, and wooden benches on which they may sit, or ruminate until their services are again required; and here it is pleasing to see these fine fellows in various attitudes enjoying rest and stillness after the incessant noise, excitement, and occasional tempests of wind and rain, to which—we will say nothing of greater dangers—they have been exposed . . .

Don't forget the Pointsman!

Among the servants of a railway company, or rather we should say of the public, there is no one who, in his secluded station, has more important duties to attend to than 'the pointsman' in charge of the switches for diverting a train from one set of rails to another.

As it is of course necessary that these switches should be carefully worked and guarded by night as well as by day, there are usually appointed to each station two pointsmen, each of whom remains on duty twelve hours at a time, taking the night and day work week about. At Camden Station one of these men has fourteen switches to attend to, and at Wolverton thirteen pairs . . . At Crewe Station, from whence radiate three important lines of rails, namely, on the right to Manchester, straight on to Liverpool, and on the left to Chester, there are constantly on duty three pointsmen, one of whom has seventeen pairs of points to attend to . . .

Nothing can apparently be more cheerless than the existence of these poor fellows, who, cut off from society, in all weathers and in all seasons have, in solitude, to perform duties for which no passing traveller ever thanks them, and which he probably does not even know that they perform. It is, however, providentially decreed that the human heart warms under almost every description of responsibility; and, accordingly, we invariably found these pointsmen not only contented but apparently intently interested in their important duties; indeed the flowers which we observed blooming around their little wooden habitations were not, we felt, unappropriate emblems of the happiness which naturally springs up in the heart of every man who will honestly perform the duties of his station.

The Company's pointsmen have nominally not very high wages:—a gratuity, however, every twelve months is given to them, provided they cause no accident; but should one occur from their switches, no matter how small, they forfeit it . . .

*   *   *

Flying by rail through green fields below Harrow Hill and thence to Watford . . . we will now conduct our readers to the Station and town of Wolverton . . . It is a little red-brick town composed of 242 little red-brick houses . . . three or four tall red-brick engine-chimneys, a number of very large red-brick workshops, six red houses for officers, one red beer-shop, two red public-houses, and, we are glad to add, a substantial red schoolroom and neat stone church, the whole lately built by order of a Railway Board, at a railway station, by a railway contractor, for railway men, railway women, and railway children; in short, the round cast-iron plate over the door of every house, bearing the letters L.N.W.R., is the generic symbol of the town.

The population is 1405, of whom 638 are below sixteen years of age; indeed, at Wolverton are to be observed an extraordinary number of young couples, young children, young widows, also a considerable number of men who have lost a finger, hand, arm, or leg. All, however, whether whole or mutilated, look for support to 'the Company'. . . At Wolverton the progress of time itself is marked by the hissing of the various arrival and departure trains. The driver's wife, with a sleeping infant at her side, lies watchful in her bed until she has blessed the passing whistle of 'the down mail'. With equal anxiety her daughter long before daylight listens for the rumbling of 'the $3\frac{1}{2}$ a.m. goods up', on the tender of which lives the ruddy but smutty-faced young fireman to whom she is engaged . . .

The girls in the station buffet

The refreshment establishment at Wolverton is composed of: A matron, seven very young ladies to wait upon the passengers, four men and three boys do., one man-cook, his kitchen-maid, and his two scullery-maids; two housemaids; one still-room maid, employed solely in the liquid duty of making tea and coffee; two laundry-maids and one baker's boy, one garden boy. And lastly, 'an odd man'.

Very early in the morning—in cold winter long before sunrise—the 'odd man' wakens the two housemaids, to one of whom is entrusted the confidential duty of awakening the young ladies exactly at 7 o'clock, in order that their *première toilette* may be concluded in time for them to receive the passengers of the first train, which reaches Wolverton at 7.30 a.m. From that time until the departure of the York Mail train, which arrives opposite to the refreshment-room at about 11 o'clock at night, these young persons remain on duty, continually vibrating, at the ringing of a bell, across the rails (they have a covered passage high above them, but they never use it) from the North refreshment-room for down passengers to the South refreshment-room constructed for hungry up-ones. By about midnight . . . they are all enabled once again to lay their heads on their pillows with the exception of one who, in her turn, assisted by one man and one boy of the establishment, remains on duty receiving the money, etc. till four in the morning for the up-mail. This young person, however, is allowed to sleep on till noon . . .

In the refreshment-room at Wolverton, these youthful handmaidens stand in a row behind silver urns, silver coffee-pots, silver tea-pots, cups, saucers, cakes, sugar, milk with other delicacies . . . On the arrival of a train, the confused crowd of passengers simultaneously liberated hurry towards them with a velocity exactly proportionate to their appetites . . . Considering that the row of young persons have among them only seven right hands, with but very little fingers at the end of each, it is really astonishing how they can in the short space of a few minutes manage to extend and withdraw them so often—sometimes to give a cup of tea—sometimes to receive half-a-crown, of which they have to return two shillings—then to give an old gentleman a plate of warm soup—then to drop another lump of sugar into his nephew's coffee-cup—then to receive a penny for a bun, and then again threepence for four 'lady's fingers'.

It is their rule as well as their desire never, if they can possibly prevent it, to speak to any one; and although sometimes, when thunder has turned the milk, or the kitchen-maid over-peppered the soup, it may occasionally be necessary to soothe the fastidious complaints of some beardless ensign by ... the hundred thousandth part of a smile—yet they endeavour on no account ever to exceed that harmless dose. But while they are so occupied at the centre of the refreshment table, at its two ends, each close to a warm stove, a very plain matter-of-fact business is going on, which consists of the rapid uncorking of, and then emptying into large tumblers, innumerable black bottles of what is not inappropriately called 'Stout', inasmuch as all the persons who are drinking the dark foaming mixture wear heavy great-coats, with large wrappers round their necks—in fact, are *very* stout. We regret to have to add, that among these thirsty customers are to be seen, quite in the corner, several silently tossing off glasses of brandy, rum, and gin ...

Having partially detailed, at some length, the duties of the seven young persons at Wolverton, we feel it due to them, as well as to those of our readers who, we perceive, have not yet quite finished their tea, by a very few words to complete their history. Considering, then, the difficult duties which our seven young attendants have to perform—considering the temptations to which they are constantly exposed, in offering to the public attentions which are ever to simmer and yet never to boil—it might be expected that our inquiries should considerably go no further than the arrival at 11 p.m. of the 'the York up-mail'. The excellent matron, however, who has charge of these young people, who always dine and live at her table, with honest pride declares that the breath of slander has never ventured to sully the reputation of any of those who have been committed to her charge.

(*Postscript.* We quite forgot to mention that, notwithstanding the everlasting hurry at this establishment, four of the young attendants have managed to make excellent marriages, and are now very well off in the world.)

From *Stokers and Pokers; or, The London & North-Western Railway* (1850), by SIR FRANCIS BOND HEAD, Bt.

9

The Life of a Farm Labourer

In order to enable the reader more readily to possess himself of the particulars of the actual state of the case, an average specimen of the respectable farm labourer will be taken ...

Unless the education of the farm labourer be commenced early, and diligently prosecuted in the fields, he will not learn it well. For this purpose the young labourer is taken from school as soon as he can earn 4d. or 6d. a day on the farm. He forgets all he has learnt at school as fast as boys do, and has few opportunities of doing more than just retain what he was taught before 10 years of age.

As my specimen grows bigger he is worth more money. He leaves home and goes into service as a mate or lad to help the waggoner with the team. He boards with a respectable waggoner, whose wife takes care of his clothes, etc. But he soon is ambitious of all the distinctions of early manhood, and after passing through the half-dozen violent attachments which matrons denominate calf love, he is seen some fine morning, before he is two-and-twenty, on his way from church, with his bride, who is seventeen . . .

If they cannot be accommodated under the roof of the parents, they lodge themselves in a couple of rooms already furnished, in a noisy row of cottages. They hire the furniture of a broker, and, for a time, all goes on smoothly. Work is plentiful, she is a managing girl, he is hard-working, and by the time there are a couple of children, they are in a cottage. One thing has been a trouble, and that is the broker's bill. As that wary dealer saw opportunity, he would sell them some useful article of furniture which they had hitherto rented. So by slow degrees the bed they sleep on, the table, the chairs, and household clock, in due time, are all their own. Still they have not bought cheap, and while they owed him a bill for furniture-hire had a cogent reason for not disputing his price-list.

The doctor's bill proves a heavy item, but the doctor is kind, and will wait till they can pay him, and will have a tolerable test of his kindness, I fear. In addition is the monthly call of the bagman-clothier for contribution for a dress nearly worn out, but not nearly paid for; also of the bagman shoemaker for boots in the same predicament; so that what with rent, and occasional outgoings, as well as fixed ones, the wife has looked trouble in the face, and trouble has returned the gaze, and stamped upon her countenance a careworn expression before she is one-and-twenty.

There is also another confinement approaching, and this time there will be less scruple in obtaining [Poor Law] Union relief, for the ice was broken on a former occasion; and if their case was good then, it is better now.

In the meantime my specimen has joined his sick and benefit club. He had heard of several which offered various advantages, but nothing so good, he thinks,—and so also thinks the landlord of the Black Bear, who manages the club, which holds its meetings in the tap-room every other Saturday night.

The club night furnishes him with the opportunity of spending a social hour or two with his neighbours. His wife is pleased rather than otherwise with his account of the evening's amusement, and it is a little change for a hard-working man—not unreasonable—for he never comes home the worse for what he has drunken, but the better. Altogether, the 5d. a week in the club, with the extra 6d. a fortnight for beer and use of room, is, they think, not badly laid out. The landlord, and a good many of his friends, are of the same opinion. And if the first Monday in May is fine, as it ought to be, the annual festival of the club has attractions for both husband and wife. The one has a dinner and tobacco, and the other lemonade, wine negus, cakes, almonds and raisins, and nuts; so that the dance which winds up the proceedings is, in one sense, an excellent institution; for there is no telling what might happen if, after so many good things, they were debarred three or four hours' exercise so violent as the jumping, stamping, screaming and laughter, which go to make up the sinful catalogue of poor folks' pleasures.

At this festival two or three of the old club members are turned over to the 2s. 6d. a week from the parish, but they had had enough of the club-money, and were fast becoming unpopular with the members; and my specimen is not sorry to get rid of such troublesome customers. He forgets the turn which he may have by-and-by, when grey hairs and rheumatism begin to make his closer acquaintance.

Meanwhile, if he is ill, there is 10s. a week secure, and as much more as the Board of Guardians, which is a liberal body, will allow. If my specimen dies, there is enough to ornament the nine-and-sixpenny elm coffin which the Guardians order, with black nails and plate, with an inscription on it in bright yellow letters, which is 'ever so much more respectable than a common pauper's coffin'. Again, there is enough money to console both father and mother a little in the loss of a delicate child, removed to a happier state . . .

The cottage he lives in is not so bad, after all, but the rent is high—3s. a week—but others are ready to take it over his head at 3s. 6d., so that little need be complained of. He might get a hovel for 1s., and a very moderate sort of tenement for 2s. 6d. He takes in a lodger or two, but what with an increasing family of little ones, and the unavoidable work thrown on his wife in cooking and caring for the family, and trying to keep things tidy, she looks faded and worn at five-and-twenty, while he is becoming rather difficult at times, neighbours say.

Still they are a respectable couple, and that at a time when there is the greatest pressure, many mouths to feed, and no child yet old enough to earn as much as 4d. a day on the farm.

The children go to school on Sundays, and to church as well; and the mother is glad to get them out of the way morning and afternoon. Both

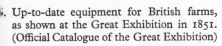

Up-to-date equipment for British farms, as shown at the Great Exhibition in 1851. (Official Catalogue of the Great Exhibition)

parents go generally in the afternoon to church. And thus time passes on, and sees the family of six or seven children; the oldest boy working like a man at a shilling a day, and eating like two men; and the second, only nine years old, occasionally employed in seed time, etc., as a perambulating scarecrow; at other times as sheep-boy, etc. at 6d. a day. Here are the average earnings of the family for a week, and their expenses:—

Income	s.	d.	Expenses	s.	d.
Father (average)	14	—	House-rent	3.	—
Mother „	2	—	Club		9
Eldest boy „	7	—	Food (say 8 in family)	15.	6
Second boy „	2	—	Beer (at home) at 1s. 4d.		
			a gallon	1.	—
			Schooling for 3 children		6
			Fuel	2	—
	25s.			22s.	9d.

There remains a balance of 2s. 3d. for the bagmen, and—save the mark! —for clothing father, mother, and children, for bedding, for accidents and repairs to domestic furniture and other incidental expenses, which will arise and must be met . . .

But if the good couple are blessed with health and strength, and cheerful tempers, they continue to struggle on, while, as the children become older, they will be worth more money. But no man can count on a single day's health. Illness comes at times, and now take the dark side of the picture:—

Income	
Father ill—on the club	10s.
Mother's average [work in fields]	2s.
Boys' „	9s.
	21s.
From Union, 4 children dependent on medical relief	4s. (viz. 4 galls of flour at 1s. per gallon)
	25s.

Expenses are the same as before, excepting that the club fee is no more than 5d., as he does not attend the meetings, and, being ill, is not fined for his absence . . .

Pass on half-a-dozen years and examine my specimen again, and his maintenance. He has been married over twenty years, and the family are growing up. Two sons, out as lodgers, are conducting themselves on the approved system, as their father before them; two daughters out at service, one boy at 7s. a week; one girl still at school.

Earnings		Expenses		
Father	14s.	Rent	3s.	—
Mother	2s.	Club		9d.
Boy	7s.	Food	9s.	—
	———	Beer	1s.	—
	23s.	Schooling, one child		3d.
		Fuel	2s.	—
			———	
			16s.	—

It will be seen that whereas in the former period there remained but 2s. 3d. for clothes and other out goings, there is now 7s., and the easier state is perceptible in the improved condition of parents and home, and they begin to be freer agents in the world—not in debt to broker, and punctual in their payments to bagmen—and keep a better table.

The age of the husband is now about 43 in years and 53 in constitution. He is, however, a good workman, and a steady, honest man. But he might now begin to save money, and has heard a good deal about savings' banks and better benefit clubs than the United Order . . . He only wishes he had known of the better society before he joined the Black Bear club . . .

Pass over another decade, and take another peep at the family. Sons and daughters are married and settled, and have families of their own to provide for, and nothing but good wishes for the 'old folks', as they are now called, and who begin to look cheerlessly upon the lot to which they are nearing rapidly. She is still worth her shilling a day on the farm. He is not worth his 2s. 6d. The younger ones would strike for a rise in their rates of payment if he were not reduced, and so our old friend, whose life is here sketched, submits to the necessary reduction to 2s. a day for a time, and soon makes the best of it at 1s. 6d. He is as civil and well-conducted a man as any in the parish, and has been blessed, as he says frequently, with capital health and spirits, better than nineteen men out of twenty. Still he does not like to look ahead much, for he is conscious of bodily ailments, the hints of which are unmistakeable and stronger each winter. He and the 'old lady', once the blooming bride of sweet seventeen, get enough to live on pretty comfortably; and so they wear out the time, till the limbs become unequal to earn the body's maintenance, and then comes out-door relief—none too soon . . .

A shock of illness comes; it is advisable to nurse him in the 'house'; and thus the Union opens its doors to receive the old couple, for the wife must go too. They give up the world, sell or give the furniture of their cottage among their children, and retire, separated, for the rest of their lives, and doomed to meet no more as man and wife, but once a week for a short half-hour.

The old woman is the first to go. She has taken to fretting at being parted from home and husband, and in six months dies, of no disease in particular. Then he is left for the first time in his life desolate in the world; a feeble old man among feeble old men; brought under restraint for the first time since boyhood, and not allowed the indulgences which had become in a manner necessary to him. I will kill my specimen and bury him, though his funeral will cost nobody much when it comes ...

From an article by REV. J. Y. STRATTON in *The Cornhill Magazine*, February 1864.

CHAPTER 3

YOUNG ENGLAND

Mention 'Young England', and there comes to mind the group of young Tories who, early in Queen Victoria's reign, rallied round Benjamin Disraeli in support of those principles of antique aristocratic benevolence that are expressed in his socio-political novels *Coningsby* and *Sybil*. Here, however, we are about to give a different meaning to the term. The 'Young England' displayed to view in the following collection of 'documents' are dressed in nondescript garments, they are generally dirty and unkempt, they are pulled out of bed and kicked out to work at an ungodly hour in the morning and, after ten or twelve or more hours of labour in a stifling atmosphere and subject often to harsh treatment, return at night to the crowded tenements that they call 'home'. These little children and young people—these boys and girls, these youths and young women—are the raw material of British industry, the up-and-coming generation on whose labour so much of the country's industrial advance may be said to depend.

As a matter of history, the condition of the young workers of both sexes was the first to arouse humanitarian concern. Even before the eighteenth century had run its course, the child slaves of the factory system had attracted public notice, and as the years passed various committees and commissions inquired into the matter, and attempts were made to give the young workers some measure of legislative protection. The most comprehensive of these was the Children's Employment Commission of 1842–1843, which investigated the condition of children and young people (and incidentally of women) in mines and in trades and manufactures. What the Commission's reports revealed was so painful that it shocked the Victorian conscience. Parliament was prodded into action. Something was done, but that something was confined to begin with to juvenile workers in mines and textile factories, since these were the places in which the conditions had been shown to be, if not the worst, then the most obvious and perhaps the most easily remedied.

Such as it was, it was sufficient to put the public conscience to sleep for another generation. Then in 1861, the Earl of Shaftesbury (who, as Lord Ashley, had played a most honourable and effective part in the earlier agitation), moved in the House of Lords that a fresh inquiry should be instituted into the 'Employment of Children and Young Persons in Trades and Manufacturers not already regulated by law'.

Clearly the time was ripe for such a move, since both Houses of Parliament agreed to the setting up of the proposed Royal Commission. In the name of Her Majesty, three 'trusty and well beloved' gentlemen,—Hugh Seymour Tremenheere, Richard Dugard Grainger, and Edward Carleton Tufnell—were entrusted with the work, and these three forthwith appointed a further three—Messrs F. D. Longe, J. E. White, and H. W. Lord—to do the actual work of investigating those 'places of work' in which 'Young England' went about their daily (and often their nightly) toil.

No time was wasted. The first of a series of six Reports was signed by the Commissioners on June 1, 1863, and published soon after. It covered a number of trades which were held to be most in need of regulation (pottery manufacture, the manufacture of lucifer matches, percussion-cap and cartridge manufacture, paper-staining, the employment of finishers and hookers in the bleaching and dyeing industries, and fustian-cutting). 'If Parliament should think fit to adopt our recommendations with regard to the above-mentioned manufactures,' stated the Commissioners, 'the considerable number of upwards of 17,000 more children and young persons will be placed under the protection, and be benefited by the privileges of the Factory Act.'

Parliament *did* so decide, when in the very next year (1864) the Factory Acts Extension Act was put on the Statute Book.

From the material contained in the Report we include here selections from Mr Longe's report on the Pottery Manufacture in Staffordshire, and Mr White's on the manufacture of lucifer matches in the East End of London. In the latter, it is interesting to note, we meet in person the Mr Bryant and the Mr May whose names have been made so familiar on countless millions of matchboxes.

The Commissioners also included in their first Report a special 'Report on the Violation of the Law regulating the Employment of Climbing Boys', and this is quoted from in (*b*) of this chapter. Then in 1864 they issued two Reports. The outstanding feature of the 2nd is the report on the Manufacture of Wearing Apparel made by Mr Lord and Mr White, from which extensive extracts are given in Chapter 4. From the remainder of the Report we take what a Bedfordshire postmaster had to say about the Strawplaiting industry in his district. He speaks of 'schools', but these were not schools in the ordinary sense of the word but domestic factories in which children were put to work under a 'teacher' whose job it was to get as much straw plait out of them as possible, which was then disposed of by the parents.

The 3rd Report contains a detailed account of the Metal Trades of the Birmingham District (*see* Chapter 2, No. 6), for which Mr White was responsible. By way of preface we have his disclosures concerning the state of education of the young workers of both sexes. We read of his astonishment that a child should think a primrose was red like a rose. But much worse in his opinion was the ignorance they displayed in religious matters. He was shocked to discover that they only knew of 'Christ' as a swear-word, and that some of them faced death with a pagan resignation.

A 4th Report appeared in 1865 and a 5th in 1866, and such was the strength of the case that the Commission had made out, another Factory Act was passed in 1867, bringing under control all premises in which fifty or more persons were employed in any manufacturing process. This was followed by a Workshops Act covering establishments in which fewer than fifty were employed.

Finally, in 1867 there was published a 6th Report, which was concerned entirely with the Gang system in Agriculture (*see* Chapter 4). So the Children's Employment Commission of the 1860s reached its conclusion, and it may surely be claimed on behalf of all those responsible that they had deserved well of their country, and of 'Young England' in particular.

I

Why Little Children Are Sent out to Work

Children of the labouring classes are employed at an early age—some permanently, others temporarily—at a rate of recompense which, though apparently but trifling, is sufficient for their maintenance, and more than sufficient to induce their parents to remove them from school. It is evident that even the lowest amount of wages which the child of a labouring man will receive (from 1s 6d to 2s per week) must be so great a relief to the parents as to render it almost hopeless that they can withstand the inducement, and retain the child at school in face of such temptation. And this inducement will be almost equally powerful whether or not the school be one where payments from the children are required. It is not for the sake of *saving a penny* per week that a child is transferred from the school to the factory or the fields, but for the sake of *gaining a shilling or eighteen pence* per week; and the mere opportunity of saving the penny by sending the child to a *free* school would not restrain the parents from making a positive addition to their weekly income if the absence of the child from school could ensure it.

Many children obtain permanent employment as early as the age of nine, and all from that age upwards are considered capable of certain kinds of agricultural labour. Indeed, some persons qualified to judge are of opinion that the business of a farm labourer cannot be thoroughly acquired if work be not commenced before eleven or twelve. In mechanical employments labour begins at even an earlier age. Children begin to be employed in needle making, in button making, as errand boys, and in various other capacities, some as early as six, others at any time from 6 to 10.

Among the middle classes, children remain longer at school, and the boys become apprentices, &c, at the age of fourteen or fifteen. In very few cases—excepting those where the sons are destined for professional pursuits, are placed by fortune beyond the necessity of labour, or proceed to college—is the period of education protracted beyond 15.

HORACE MANN, in Census Report (1851), page xxiii; P.P. 1852/3, vol. 90.

2

The Young Potters

The average age at which 58 children in the [pottery] manufactories in Stoke had commenced work was 9 years 3 months . . . 62 children in the manufactories in Hanley 8 years one month . . . In most cases, upon enquiring into the circumstances of those children who had begun work at the earliest ages, I found that they were either the children of widows, or that their fathers were incapable of working, or of drunken habits. Many of the younger children were the children of colliers.

These boys are employed:—(1) In turning the 'jigger', a simple machine for turning the wheel or whirler on which the workman forms the ware. (2) In carrying the moulds with the moist ware pressed upon them into an adjoining drying room or 'stove', and placing them upon shelves to dry. (3) In assisting the workman in 'wedging' the clay, 'batting out,' and cleaning the ware when dry. (4) In sweeping out the shops and stoves, lighting fires, etc.

The youngest children are generally employed in turning the jigger. This operation, though not requiring much strength, is very hard work for children to be engaged in the whole day . . .

The flatpressers form one of the most numerous branches. It includes dishmakers, platemakers, saucermakers, and cup and bowl makers. A great number of very young boys are employed by these men. The dish-maker generally employs one boy; the platemaker two; the saucermaker three; and the cupmaker three and sometimes four.

Close at hand to the flatpresser's bench is the 'stove'. These 'stoves' are little rooms, or rather ovens, about 13 feet square, and from 8 to 12 feet high, partitioned off from the shop. They are fitted inside with shelves, on which the moulds with the moist ware upon them are placed in order that the ware may be dried sufficiently to be removed. In the centre is the stove, which I have often observed red hot. I tested the heat of three of these drying rooms or 'stoves'. In one the thermometer rose to 120°, in one to 130°, and in the third to 148°. As the potter forms the plate or saucer on the mould, the mould runner runs off with it into the 'stove' . . .

These boys are generally required to come before the men in the morning to light the fires in the stoves, and to stay after the men have done work to sweep out the shops and stoves . . . It is still too frequent a practice among the flatpressers, as with other potters, to waste the first days of the week in idleness or the beerhouse, and then work them-selves and their boys until 8 or 9 o'clock on Thursday and Friday to recover their lost time . . . These workmen, except the young appren-tices, are all paid on the piecework system, while they hire the boys for the day or week, as they may require their assistance. The average weekly earnings of these boys are about 3s. or 3s. 6d. Boys of 9 to 11 years of age get from 1s. 6d. to 2s. 6d.; boys of from 12 to 14 get from 3s. to 5s. In a few instances boys of 14 or 15 years earn as much as 6s.

The means of the workman with respect to the wages he can afford to pay to his assistants may be thus shown. The price for the ordinary kind of full-sized plates is 3s. per score dozen. A good workman can make two score dozen of these plates per day. His earnings, therefore, for a full week's work would be 36s.; out of this he would pay about 8s. to his two boys. Saucermakers and cupmakers, employing three or four boys, would pay them about 9s. or 10s. . . .

Many of the medical men whose evidence I have obtained speak in very strong terms of the injuries caused to the constitutions of these boys by their employment; though . . . I have myself . . . found very few who had suffered from any ailment which seemed attributable to their work. They generally appeared brisk and happy, notwithstanding their dirty and ragged appearance. It would seem that the injurious effects of their employment do not show themselves in youth, further than by impeding growth. When the mould runner has become a young journeyman the serious effects of many years' work in these shops and stoves becomes more palpable ...

The operation of dipping the ware is a specially injurious employment, owing to the poisonous nature of the lead which generally forms a large ingredient in the glaze. Boys of a very young age are employed in carrying the ware to the dipper, and are thus compelled to spend much of their time in the poisoned atmosphere of the dipping house. The injurious effects of the dipping tub are well known. Few dippers continue many years at their work without suffering from painter's colic or paralysis; many become crippled at an early age. Boys of about 14 or 15 years of age are employed to 'gather' the ware from the dipper; they are brought more in contact with the glaze than the other boys ... The boys employed in the dipping house are generally a better class than the flatpressers' assistants. Their wages are much higher and the work is less laborious.

The employments in the finishing department, in which children are engaged, are Printing, Painting, Gilding and burnishing. Printers employ two women or girls as 'transferrers', and one young girl as a 'paper cutter'. These paper cutters are generally very young; many of them begin work at 8 years of age; their regular work is cutting into pieces the paper on which the pattern has been impressed by the printer; these pieces are then applied to the ware by the transferrers. They are also employed in lighting the printer's fire, fetching water, etc. Next to that of the flatpressers' boys, the condition of these children most demands consideration, on account of the very young age at which they are employed, their liability to be overworked, and the great heat of the rooms in which they work ...

Painters

This branch includes persons of both sexes and every age, from the talented artist, who paints flowers and landscapes on the most costly porcelain, to the little girls of nine or ten, who are employed in painting cheap earthenware and ornaments. A great number of young girls are employed in this work; their occupation is for the most part refined and agreeable and not necessarily injurious to their health. The children and young persons of different sexes generally work in different rooms, under the superintendence of respectable over-lookers, or of the adults who are engaged in the same employment. I have entered several paintresses rooms in different manufactories, and always found them well dressed, well behaved, and apparently enjoying their occupation. Medical evidence, however, shows that they are liable to be seriously injured by being kept for so many hours at this sedentary work in crowded and badly-ventilated rooms . . .

Children's Employment Commission, 1st Report (1863); report of MR F. D. LONGE, assistant commissioner, on the Pottery Manufacture, pp. 2–5; P.P. 1863, vol. 18.

3

Wretched Places, Match Factories

Match manufacture embraces many branches, including the making of the box as well as of the match itself . . . Again, there are many distinct classes of match, such as the wax taper match, the common wood match, and fusees for tobacco, as well as many varieties within these large classes. There are likewise many varieties of boxes . . . At one large factory, where the whole work was completed on the premises, I counted as many as twenty distinct processes through which every match has to pass, and as many in the case of the boxes . . .

Lewis Waite's, Wharf Road, Bethnal Green . . . is a very small place, employing about six men and eighteen boys. It consists of two small sheds, one a mere lean-to, the other a cart hovel. The latter is, I should say, judging by the eye, about 20 by 11 feet only, with no ventilation whatever. The door is at one end, and the only window close by it. This place serves for both dipping room and drying room, as well as for mixing and heating the sulphur and the phosphorous composition. The dipper is helped in mixing by a small boy whom I saw beside him paddling the mixture, actually leaning over the dipping stone. The smell on entering this place is quite suffocating, and one would think unendurable for any length of time. The other shed . . . is much of the same kind, without any ventilation, and is perhaps 30 by 10 feet. In this all the remaining processes are carried on. A white vapour may be seen constantly rising from the matches. Of course, places for washing, etc. could not be looked for here . . .

Lewis Waite has carried on this business for seven years. Has worked himself for 17 or 18 years, as a dipper for 10 or 12 years. It never caught hold of his teeth. It does of some people. The dipping is the worst part. Never finds the work hurt his people. 'It's not in these places that the harm is done; it is in those great places. They make more in an hour than we do in a day.' Can always get workers when he wants.

Could get a hundred every day if he could employ them. 'They come bothering your life out all day pretty near.'

William Lovell has dipped for six years. Is about here all day. Of course, does not dip all the time; that would be too hard work. Brings his meals with him, and eats them in here sometimes. It is too far to go home. Always goes out to dinner. Cooks on that stove (pointing to that used for heating the mixture and also the dipping stone). Goes home as he is. Keeps no change [of clothes]. Only changes if he wishes to be tidy. Can see his dress shine in the dark. 'Mine often shines.' Has had no toothache for seven or eight years. Has had one or two out because they ached. (*Note*. This witness is not a healthy looking man.)

Halsey's, Belle Isle, York Road, King's Cross. A wretched place, the entrance to which is through a perfectly dark room, much like a cow-house, and after this through one end of a room stored with lucifers in small boxes, there being at the other end an open hearth with a fire burning. At the nearest end of the chief workshop, a long and fairly lighted but ill ventilated room, a man was preparing the materials for the composition; at the other end was the dipping slab. Between these are ranged the children at their benches. Beyond this is a room a few feet square, with a hatch opening on to the dipping slab, and also having lucifer matches stored in it, and beyond this again . . . the drying room, close and hot from the stove where the mixture is heated. Nevertheless in this small room between the workshop and drying room close by the hatch, a boy and girl fill frames.

In this drying room the late owner, Mrs Halsey's husband, was burned to death a short time since in trying to put out a fire, said to have been caused by a child out of mischief . . .

Outside at the back the arrangements are even worse. There is a water-butt with a little tub of sickly green water in it. Here, I was told, the children wash. Beyond this . . . is the yard, if that can be called so which is a passage a few feet wide, slightly broader at one end, filled in the middle with a stagnant gutter . . . Here the children eat their meals, unless it be cold or wet, when they eat them round the stove. At the end of this yard, with an open sink or cesspool in front of it, is a single privy common to all, boys and girls alike, and in a very bad state.

On one side of the yard was a little hay hovel in which a dog lived, but I could not make out that the children were allowed to eat their meals there. It would be much better than either of the other places . . .

From MR WHITE'S report on the Lucifer Match Manufacturer; *op. cit.* pp. 52–53; P.P. 1863, vol 18.

4

'Nothing unpleasant' at Bryant & May's

These are spacious, airy works [at Fairfield, Bow], with much open ground all round ... They are in fact far removed from all other buildings ... There is nothing unpleasant or objectionable here. The manufacture carried on here differs from that at other places inasmuch as no common phosphorous or other offensive ingredient is used ... The works, too, are only just established, and only partially completed.

All the processes, with the exception of mixing the composition and drying the materials when dipped, which are carried on in small rooms opening from the side, are conducted in a long shed-like building, cut into compartments by wire caging. When a larger portion of the building is ready, the boys will work in a part cut off from the girls by a party wall, and separate closets and washing places are being provided for each half ... Along the wall are pegs, each with a number on it, on which the children and others hang their bonnets, coats, etc. ...

Altogether this seems a very nicely conducted place. The children appear very happy and contented, and seem without exception much to prefer their employment here to that in other lucifer manufactories, in which most of them seem to have been engaged more or less before. They give various reasons, mostly that this work is 'not so nasty', 'has no steam', or that they can earn more or are better treated here. Just as I arrived, 1 o'clock, a bell rang, and the children rushed out as if from school; I was there when they returned at 2. The manufactory has only been at work four or five months, so that no child can have much experience of it, some had been there only a few weeks, some a few days only.

Mr William Bryant: The mode of manufacture carried on by us is, I believe, perfectly free from any injurious influence upon the health of those engaged in it. We do not use the white or common phosphorous at all. The only phosphorous used is not in the match, but applied to the outside of the surface of the box, on which the match is rubbed, and this phosphorous is of the red or amorphous kind, which is I believe perfectly harmless, and is not a poison ... We find that we can always get as many hands as we require. It is not skilled labour, though some from practice will do three times the amount of others ...

Mr Francis May. It is my own experience, and I believe that of all large employers, that the best educated workpeople are likewise the most efficient, the most economical, and the most respectful and attentive servants . . . But besides this, there is the very great advantage in a sanitary point of view in the system of schooling enforced on young children, in this manufacture in particular. The supply of fresh air, which the interval of school time gives, does much to counteract the noxious vapours inhaled during the time of work. We receive here every year a report of the progress of the school. These reports are highly satisfactory, and we believe the school does a great deal of good. . .

MR WHITE'S report; op. cit., pp. 57–58

5

Why Young George 'goggled'

———

George Gardner, overlooker at Bryant & May's.—Has worked in the business ever since he was 16. Dipped for fifteen years of this time. Used to feel it in his chest very much. Thinks that was partly because 'when I was quite young' he used to be out late and come in and lie down in the factory. That was very bad. Thinks partly too it was the sulphur dippings. That was very hot work. Used to get in a 'muck sweat', and then go out and catch cold so . . .

Has known many bad from the work. One lost his jaw. 'You could take his chin (showing) and shove it all into his mouth.' Has known several die from the 'phosphorous on their inwards'. Has known eighteen or twenty lose their jaws. But people are very different. Some are seized in four or five months. Knew one of seventeen who was. Has known his own self eleven or twelve who have died from their jaw or their lungs. Other people might die of their lungs too. But the doctors said these had it from the phosphorous.

Cleanliness is the great thing. It is very important to wash; always did so himself after dipping. Used to search his mouth with water and 'goggle' his throat out.

Some people are very dirty. One used to wash the basin for witness. Has seen him after this with his hand all plastered with the stuff eating his bread and butter, and take it all in together; this man lost his jaw after two years. When dipping witness used to blow the steam away first and then breathe; so did all the rest. Used to put a piece of tobacco in his mouth; thought that was good. Is well now except that he has a cough sometimes. Feels his chest then.

(*Note.* This witness does not look at all strong, and speaks feebly. He has all his teeth, though with many black places. He says they give no pain and thinks what looks like decay is the tobacco.)

From MR WHITE's report; *op. cit.*, pp. 59–60.

6

Mary Ann the Match-box Maker

———

Mary Ann Prancer, employed at Messrs John Baker's match factory, 2 Essex Street, Three Colt Lane, Bethnal Green.—Seems about 14, but does not know how old she is. Lives in master's house and works partly as servant and partly in here at box making. Does that for her living and a shilling a week to clothe herself. Works here and in the house till about 10 o'clock.

Never was at school in her life. Never went to church or chapel. Never heard of 'England' or 'London', or the 'sea' or 'ships'. Never heard of God. Does not know what He does. Does not know whether it is better to be good or bad.

(*Note.* This girl, though with no outward sign of stupidity, but on the contrary nice looking, seemed, as will be gathered from her answers, sunk in a state of mindless, hopeless ignorance, and to have no ideas whatever beyond her round of work, her 1s. a week, and her food and clothing. She has a mother and a home, but for some reason which I could not make out, does not even have the change of going there. It is hard to imagine how anyone born in possession of reason, can have been so utterly kept out of the reach of learning anything beyond what her animal senses might teach.)

From MR WHITE's report; *op. cit.*, page 53.

7

A Stab in the Eye

Mr F. Bostock, maker of men's boots, Northampton.—Wellington and Blucher boots are still frequently 'stabbed' by hand in Northampton. That is done at home or in small work-places; children of both sexes are sometimes employed at it . . . There must be much less pressure on the young children, even in their own homes, now and for the future, because of the sewing-machine supplying their place to a great extent; where 30 children would have been employed in stabbing, there will now be two or three operators, girls of 14 or 16, and one child of 9 or 10, to tie knots.

The stabbing was laborious, required great attention, and was even dangerous, for they often sat so close that in drawing the thread with both hands, the awl, which was always held point outwards, in the right hand, not unfrequently struck the next child in the face or eye; many have lost an eye in this way.

(Note by the Assistant Commissioner, Mr H. W. Lord: I had noticed, before seeing Mr Bostock, that several persons of both sexes, whom I met in the town, had lost an eye; but thinking it merely an odd coincidence, had not enquired about it, till Mr Bostock made the above remark.)

2nd Report, *op. cit.*, page 168; P.P. 1864, vol. 22.

8

Going to School in the Straw Plait Country

Mr William Horley, postmaster, Toddington, Bedfordshire. I am the registrar of the Toddington district, which includes six parishes lying in a line. I visit each parish once a month, so that a child may never get six weeks old unregistered, and I go constantly into the people's houses. Nearly all the females in the district, married and single alike, make straw plait, except a few who sew it; and boys plait equally up till about the age of 11, or whenever they can get other work, and when they have no work they return to plaiting again. They can't abear it, but they are obliged to do it. In some parts men plait too.

There are, I believe, in every parish one or more plaiting schools, according to the population, with much the same hours in all as in the schools here. These are from 8 a.m. till 12, and from 1 p.m. till 5, and in the winter half year again from 6 p.m. till 9. The children at the plaiting schools are most of them between the ages of 4 and 12. They are set so many yards by their mothers, and the mistresses who get the most work out of them are the most patronized. There are many unfeeling mothers, and those are said to be the hardest who have not been brought up to plaiting themselves, e.g. servants and others who settle here from a distance.

I do not hear so much complaint now as I did about the children being thrashed by the mistresses; but there used to be strange stories about it when I was a lad, and you would see boys and girls too with bumps and cuts and bruises. I think, therefore, that there is not so much of this now, though the mistresses keep a stick; but the children are made to do the work all the same, and are kept back at dinner time if they do not. When children get to be 13 or 14, they get to plait for themselves at home, and pay their friends so much a week, say 3s or 4s for board.

The rooms are small, and the children are packed as close as herrings. The commonest size is about 12 by 10 feet, and I do not know of any in this place 12 feet square. In some of the smaller villages the houses are bigger, but they are often poor old wattle and dab places. The fancy mistresses, i.e. those who are sought after because they get the most work out of the children, will have the most crowded rooms. In some places they have to sit so close into the fire-place that the fire cannot be lighted, so they have coal or wood in earthen or even tin pots, which they call 'dicky pots', and I have seen the children carrying these along. Great girls and women put them under their clothes, and children may be seen with them in their laps. These make a disagreeable smell, and I should think that the fumes must be unwholesome. The mere loss of saliva too, caused by constantly drawing the straw through the mouth, must be injurious, and it does not tend to cleanliness. Formerly each worker used to have a pot of water to dip the straw in; but now that so much double straw is used, the spittle perhaps sticks it better. Some, however, will work as dry again as others ...

I have understood that the work is carried on in just the same way all the country round, chiefly through Hertfordshire, and right across into Essex.

The work, however, is more injurious to the morals than to anything else, particularly owing to the night schools ... The bigger boys and girls are thrown indiscriminately together, even the lads after coming home from the plough, and they make such a noise about the streets, and get into a way of pulling and tearing one another about, which leads to harm. Besides this the girls and lads get out together with their plaiting into the fields, and they have no instruction or means of amusing themselves, such as newspapers, &c. This is especially the case in the smaller villages, where the proportion of illegitimate births is highest. Throughout my district it is about 10 per cent; but in one small village ... out of 12 births which I registered in one year, five were illegitimate. The plaiters are untidy women, though such fine girls in dress, and often neglect their domestic duties, such as washing, mending, &c. I see on going into their cottages that they are not the tidiest people.

Owing to the plait schools children can't be got to attend regular schools, though in this place there is a Wesleyan as well as a National school. The late minister of the parish tried to get them by only charging 1d. a week, and even allowing some to come free, and his wife gave things away to induce them to come, and he had a mistress to teach straw plait. But even so he could not keep the school up, for as other things were of course taught, the mistress could not get so much plait out of the children as a regular plait mistress ...

When trade is good, as it has been the last three or four years, children will make 6d a day, or perhaps from 3s to 4s a week, and most grown up plaiters 1s a day, though many will make more, up to 8s or 10s, and some 12s a week. A wife and children will thus earn a good deal more than the husband. Farm wages are now 9s for common labourers, and were 10s or 11s. I have a farm myself ...

Mrs Horley. I have done straw plait and am familiar with the work. Children are put to it much too early. There are not many who let their children pass 5 years without beginning, and a good many begin at 4 ... Some mothers are very brutish. I say that children ought not to be drove to school by candle light, when they ought to be in bed. Eight hours is enough for a child, and they hadn't ought to do more, poor things. But if they do not finish at school the number of yards set to them, their mothers make them do it at home, so it would be all the same. If they think that a child can earn 6d, they make it ... It's ruining the children, when they are driven so ...

Children's Employment Commission, 2nd Report (1864), pp. 203-204; P.P. 1864, vol. 22.

9

'White Slavery' in Manchester

To W. R. Coles Esq., Inspector of Factories.—Sir, I respectfully beg to call your attention to the manufactory of Mr —. He is a manufacturing milliner, and employs a large number of children and young girls, some of whom are of different ages, varying from 10 upwards.

Those children and young girls are kept at work for unreasonably long hours in rooms, that are artificially heated by steam to a very high temperature, independent of a very large number of gas-lights, thus raising the temperature to almost a suffocating point. And so largely charged is it, and impregnated with gas, that most of the young creatures complain almost continually of sore throats, loathing of the stomach, dizziness or vertigo, and headaches, &c. This pernicious effect upon their young systems, and unformed constitutions, need not be wondered at, when it is remembered that they have to breathe, and re-inhale times innumerable this pernicious atmosphere from 14 to 15 hours daily. The place is opened at 6 a.m., and never closes before 8.30 p.m. and in very many instances 9 p.m. . . .

I ask you, Sir, is it possible for either men or women, no matter how strong their constitutions may be, to withstand for any length of time the blighting effects of such a system of long hours, hard work, and poisonous atmosphere; both men and women would be broken down in a very few years, and how is it to be expected that such tender creatures can endure it . . . Sir, you may implicitly rely upon the truth of the facts in this report, although I withhold my name for obvious reasons, being related to and with some of the children at —'s. I remain, &c. *A Hater of Slavery.*

Note by Mr. Lord. From my own knowledge of the trade and of the locality of the premises . . . I consider that the statements (in the above anonymous letter) as to the hours of work and condition of the work-rooms may be not much exaggerated. H. W. L.

2nd Report, *op. cit.*, page 144.

10

What They Didn't Know in Brummagem

Considering the plentiful means of secular and religious instruction provided in Birmingham . . . it is at first sight not a little remarkable that the evidence should disclose such a low state of education or rather practical absence of it . . .

As many as 32 persons, averaging over 12 years each, and including a young man of 20 and three girls or young women, one of 18 and two of 17, could not tell the Queen's name. Some did not know of her existence; others showed a dark and lately got glimmering by such answers as that she 'is the Prince Alexandra', 'is the Prince of Wales', 'him and her got married', 'she belongs to all the world', and so on. Indeed, a question about her when put was scarcely ever answered . . .

This, however, is merely part of a wider general ignorance shown by very large numbers. Of the commonest and simplest objects of nature, flowers, birds, fishes, rivers, mountains, sea, or of places such as London, &c, in England, or other countries out of it, or how to get there, many knew little or nothing. London, however, 'is a county', but also 'is in the Exhibition'. Ireland 'is a little town'. A violet 'is a pretty bird'; lilac 'is a bird'; 'believe I would know a primrose, it's a red rose like'; 'don't know if a robin redbreast is a bird, or if it flies or sings', or 'if an eagle is a bird'; 'don't know what a river is, or where the fishes are'; 'a mountain would be on the water, I should think; don't know where the snow falls from, or whether it comes from the clouds, or sky, or where'; 'the sea is made of land, not of water'. People then may well 'go in a train to America, all the way'. Even the eye is inaccurate from want of training. A picture of a cow being milked is shown: 'he's a lion'. A map is incomprehensible to a young man of 20, who thinks that the sun 'is in the north in the middle of the day; no, it sets in the north'. Even women sometimes are unable to tell the clock.

But of very many indeed the state of mind as regards the simplest facts of religion is dark almost beyond belief. It is not too much to say that to many God, the Bible, the Saviour, a Christian, even a future state, are ideas entirely or all but unknown. God is 'a good man,' or 'the man in heaven'; 'I've heerd that (Christ), but don't know *what it* is'. Nor do others know 'where God lives', or 'about the world being made', or 'who made it', or of the Bible, 'it is not a book'. 'Have not heard of Christ: I had never done my work till so late'; 'have heard about Jesus

Christ, but it's so long since that I've forgot'; 'don't know if I'm a Christian', or 'what it is' or 'means', but all people are so. Heaven was heard of only 'when father died long ago, mother said he was going there'. Some think that bad and good go there alike, or on the other hand, that 'them as is wicked shall be worshipped, that means shall all go to hell'; or again, that when people die, 'they be buried, bain't they—their souls as well as their bodies'. 'All go in the pithole where them be buried: they never get out or live again; they have not a soul; I have not one. The soul does not live afterwards; it's quite an end of people when they die.' 'The devil is a good person; I don't know where he lives.' 'Christ was a wicked man.'

It is obvious in what a large number of cases it was useless to ask any advanced questions, such as whether he or she could write or sum, and it is impossible to give any definite idea as to the proportion that could or could not read, spell, or tell the letters, or had or had not any appreciation of figures and counting . . . Scattered through the evidence will be found numbers who did not know the letters, though in capitals, some not even great A, or could not read single figures or do the simplest counting, e.g. 'twice 11', '7 times 7', '9 and 17', '17 from 30'. A boy of eleven could not tell how many pennies there were in a shilling, or, till after much explanation, how many in sixpence; I counted 80 before a girl of 14 could tell what 3 and 2 made.

MR WHITE'S report on the Metal Manufacturers of the Birmingham District; 3rd Report, *op. cit.*, page 61; P.P. 1864, vol. 22.

II

Smelly Work in the Steel-pen Factory

John Hammond, age 17, employed at Messrs. John Mitchell's Steel Pen Factory, Newhall Street, Birmingham.—Riddle pens, and place the pans at the mouth of the muffle [oven] ready for the man to push in. Our proper work time, i.e. for the man and me, who are all that work in this place, is from 8 a.m. till 7½ p.m., but now I work from 7 a.m. till 9½ or 10 p.m., and have done so for a tidy bit now . . .

When I have got the things ready in the morning I have breakfast for about a quarter of an hour. The engine stops for an hour at dinner, and half an hour for tea. Have to bring all my day's victuals with me in the morning and keep them by me here, and eat them in here also. Bring soap with me and wash me at the tap . . .

The work don't suit me very well, and is too hard for me. Some of the things are very heavy to lift. Get 6s. a week, and 1s. 6d. for over time. Father puts it all by to buy me clothes . . . When I first came I noticed the smell [of the vitriol, or 'pickle', in which the pens are dipped] very bad, but don't at all now because I am used to it. But I can eat very little even if it be good food, and can eat nothing if it is not. Used to eat very well before I was here. Don't feel sickly, and have no pain anywhere. Used to be very strong when I came here, but ain't now. Father says I am getting as weak as ever so.

On Saturday, after leaving work, I used to wash me clean, and sit down and read my book ready for Sunday, to go to school, but can't do so now because I have forgot all my reading and can only tell the letters . . . Learned my reading at home night and morning, mother teaching me about three days a week . . .

(A thoughtful and pleasing mannered youth, and not showing in manner any wish to complain, though somewhat depressed.)

From MR WHITE'S report on Birmingham Metal Manufactures; 3rd Report, *op. cit.*, pp. 86–87.

12

The Three Sisters in the Button Factory

Messrs Dain, Watts, & Manton's, Button Manufacturers, Regent Street, Birmingham.—This is one of the principal button manufactories, and employs a large number of small children, the greater part of whom are girls who 'put in' buttons, for which the women employ and pay one child each. The buildings share the character of so many of the old Birmingham factories which have grown by degrees, by the addition of fresh workrooms; the original parts being 100 years old.

Many little girls sit with their backs right against the open side windows. In several places, however, ventilators creating an up and down current have been placed in the ceilings in places, and much regard has been shown in several ways for the well-being of the workpeople. A washing conduit is placed in each room. A night-school was established a few years back, and was well attended for a time, though it has now fallen through . . . There are also clubs for several purposes, and a committee of the workpeople also exercise control over the conduct of the people in the various rooms.

Many of the children are very young indeed, three or four being only 6. The mother of one of these, however, a boy, said that she must have him to work as she saved the value of his labour, and also the expense of his being taken care of by someone else. In another case a girl of 6, i.e. 'going 7', birthday unknown, one of three sisters working here, had worked for a woman here eight or nine months. She was a beautiful child, with bright innocent face, but looking lost and bewildered amongst so many workers. Her eldest sister, aged 12, had a sullen hardened look and manner: the middle sister seemed in the intermediate stage. So neglected, however, was their condition, both of body and of mind, as shown by their dirty appearance and tattered dress, and the want of even Sunday school instruction, and melancholy ignorance of even the eldest sister, that one of the firm who saw me talking to them was so struck and pained, that he directed the mother to be informed that they could not be received to work any more unless she showed more care for them, at least in their outward appearance. The eldest makes 2s. 6d. or 3s. a week, and the two younger 1s. each, and the father is in work as a mechanic. I have noticed this case as an illustration of the kind of care which many of the children whom I have seen in Birmingham plainly receive from their parents.

MR WHITE's report on Birmingham Metal Manufactures; 3rd Report, *op. cit.*, page 94.

13

'*My sister—her swears awful*'

Charles —, age 11; employed in a small shop in a court or yard japanning (varnishing) metal buttons.

Live at home with mother. The parish have stopped her allowance now, and my eldest sister has a very bad foot. One Sunday her was drunk and kicking up a noise, and fell off the doorstep, and her ankle fell out. Her used to bring home men with her. My next sister is about 15. Her swears awful at mother, and mother don't like to hear it, and says that some night the devil will come in the house to fetch her. Her learns it off some of the bad girls. Her goes to clean the bad girls' houses every day but Sunday, and has gone for two or three years.

I have never been at Sunday school or any other except a long time ago. They put me right through my A, B, C. I could go on with 'em now if they would tell me the next (letters), not without. I never was in church or chapel or heard any one preach or pray. Mother don't say anything about it. We had a Bible, but it had to be sold. It's a great big thing, and aint got nothing in (i.e. no pictures) ... No one told me about heaven, except when father died long ago mother said that he was going into heaven. The devil is a good person: I don't know where he lives. He puts 'em (the bad) in a great big fire.

3rd Report, op. cit., page 133.

14

'The nailers are coming!'

Hales Owen is the only town on the direct road from Birmingham to Stourbridge, and lies about half way between them. It has a few small factories for buttons, gun barrels, spades, etc ... the principal employment of the place however is the wrought nail manufacture, carried on in small forges adjoining the homes of the greater part of the cottagers, and to a great extent by women and children. These are dark, cheerless, untidy places, and sometimes unhealthy from the dampness of the ground; but the air is pure, though hot. The work seems not injurious to the young in itself, but often becomes so from the exhaustion produced by the length and irregularity of work in a hot place, with poor living.

While I was in a cottage where I found a boy with a bare foot bandaged up, lamed by a burn in a spade factory, a sound of many voices singing swelled gradually near, and the boy, limping on his stick to the door, cried, 'Oh! mother, there's the nailers coming; many a thousand of 'em', and there passed by a crowd of several hundred men, women and children, singing a hymn, of which two lines, contrasting strangely with their look and errand, were,—'And not a wave of trouble roll Across my peaceful breast'.

They were coming from the villages near Dudley to hold a meeting in Hales Owen, to see if they could 'get out' the nailers who were 'working against' them there; their strike having already lasted eleven weeks. 'It's heart-breaking work', said the woman. Amongst the many children in the crowd were two little boys, apparently six years old, or not much more, dragged along by the hand by a woman, probably their mother, foot-sore and lame from their march. To see such infants made to take part in a strike, and march miles to swell a meeting to spread it, was a sight which gave but a poor idea of the consideration which they are likely to meet with in their work at home.

3rd Report, *op. cit.*, page 135.

15

Oh, To Be a Nailer's Boy

William Tether, nailer, Hales Owen.—Began at 8 years old; am now 40. Some of my children work with me, but my 'missis' hasn't made 5s in the last 10 months. She can't stand it. It would be a very good thing if there was a law to do away with women's work. But those that are stout enough make nails; it is the most regular work for them round here, as there are scarcely any factories to take the women and children. The women with strong constitutions make big nails, and children little nails. The biggest bulk of all the people about make nails, but some men go to iron works and coal mines.

A nailer's usual day is from 5 or 6 a.m. till 9 or 10 p.m. That is many hours for a man to be stiving up (i.e. without fresh air) in a hot shop, but some work till 11 or 12, or later if busy or the master wants the work quickly. We nailers work just the same hours in winter as in summer, working by the light of the fire, from which the screen is then taken off, and of the iron as it is worked . . .

Some children begin at 8 years old, but I should say not many before 9, and most at about 10. I should not like my little boy there, now 5, to begin before 9, and he shan't if I can help it, but if I am any-ways obligated he must. He is but a little mossel, and if I were to get that little creature to work, I should have to get a scaffold for him to stand on, to reach, and with that it would be like murder-work, as you may say . . .

When children first begin work there is not one out of twenty but what knocks up, and has to stop and go out. It is like a fresh job, and don't agree with them. It is pretty healthy, but you can't stop in the shop long in the summer time, being always by the fireside, and the work being always so hot . . . If it was not for the window, and the wind coming in, we could not stand half, or a quarter, what we do; and as it is we're all of a melt and sweat, and have to go out for half an hour. But in summer the little ones, being afore the fire all the time, sweat so till it runs down their faces like anything. They they fret more with the learning, and sweat more,—fret wonderfully the little ones do. I did so myself when a little one, and even when a big one (grown person) frets he's bound to be warm and sweat.

When the children get out in the evening they're as glad as can be to get out and wash their faces, and be down the street. But plenty of times they knock up quite, and don't come back for three weeks or a month, or it may run to two months. I've often said, 'Well, you had better go out for a bit'; and when the child comes back he will perhaps be worse than ever the next time, and look so white, and have to go to bed sick bad . . . It's not much nourishment that a nailer can get. After all, it isn't the work that hurts them so much, if they had enough to put into their bellies. If I knock up, as I have done many a time, it's no use for me to go into the house to look for half a pint, because it ain't there.

My son there, 14 years old, knocked up for three weeks together. He is growing fast, and has had to work harder than many of them. He comes in at 6 in the morning and carries on till 8 at night . . . It's a great many hours in a day, and he has to work hard all that time to get 11d. or 1s., and there is the wear of the tools, the cost of firing, and something for waste iron to go out of this, which takes off altogether 2½ or 3d . . .

Besides knocking up from ill-health, the young ones sometimes knock up from being lamed or burned, and more so when they begin, as they do not know so well how to go about the work. They get a bit of red-hot iron in their shoe, and that of course will burn alarming . . . Four years ago my boy, then betwixt ten and eleven, got two pieces of iron in at the top of his trowsers, and before they could be got out they dropped and catched his leg, burning two wounds, each as big as the face of my hammer (size of a crown piece), and the scars are there now, and always will be . . .

It is quite right that the young ones should not work so long as they do, and should have some teaching. I am certain I should like my children to have an easier time of it . . . Four of my five children go to the Church Sunday-school. At the 'treat' next week, given to those who attend that school, there will be from 900 to 1000 . . . They do enjoy that day . . .

3rd Report, op. cit., pp. 136–137.

16

Little Ann Wants to be an Angel

Messrs Baker & Co.'s firebrick works, Brierly Hill: Some girls and women were engaged in 'drawing a kiln', i.e. taking out the baked bricks. A kiln is sometimes too hot to be entered at all, and the people are obliged to wait. This was warm at the door-way, and like an oven inside, where some stood, the others forming a line to hand or rather toss on the bricks, two at a time, from one to the other, to a cart outside, where they were being packed.

A small girl of 12, forming one of the line, struck me by the earnest way in which she was doing her share of a work which certainly is heavy for a child, as a slight calculation shows. The kiln, containing 17,000 bricks, of $7\frac{1}{4}$ lbs each when dry, was to be emptied by ten persons in a day and a half; i.e. this girl had to catch and toss on to her neighbour in a day of only the usual length a weight of more than 36 tons, and in so doing to make backwards and forwards 11,333 complete half turns of her body, while raised from the ground on a sloping plank. The plank is said not to be needed all the time. When called down by me she was panting.

This, however, was not her regular work; but the work which had been exacted from her at another place when 10 years old is astonishing, involving often 15 or 16 hours of heavy work daily for long periods continuously, with very scanty and few meal-times. Her energy of manner and evident love of work, and her utter absence of all tone of complaint, were remarkable; but the contrast between her hard bodily work and the pictures called up in her mind by the mention of 'angel' (see the girl's own story below) was still more striking. She was small, but healthy looking, and though ignorant very intelligent.

Ann Elizabeth Powell, age 12.—Carrying bricks is my regular work, but today I am 'drawing' a kiln. Get 6d a day. Have an hour for dinner, and eat it here. Am only just come.

Went to a red-brick yard near, at 10 years old. No girls worked there but me and their own daughter. From 6 to 6 was the regular time, but they used to make me go there by 5 a.m. and stay till 8 p.m. for a fortnight, sometimes for a month together. It used to be as the missis told us. Have worked there till 8 every night, going in the morning as early as 6, for four months together. Did not stop for tea when we worked till 8. Had a quarter of an hour for breakfast and half an hour for dinner; did not work in that time. My work was carrying bricks and heaving clay. I carried enough clay for four bricks on my head, and for two in my arms. My head used to ache, but not my back. Got 4d a day, and the same when we stayed till 8. If we had worked till 12 it would have been just the same, but I never did so late as that, though I have often worked till 9 and 9½ on the light nights in summer. Have done so for two weeks together, going at 6 in the morning. Never got beaten, and never got tired, not when staying late. I hope I shall never get tired of work. My mother always brought me up to be a good worker.

Was at a day school a little bit. Don't know all the letters. Don't know what an 'ox' is. (*Asked of* 'ship'.) Yes; about our place they keep a many of them. ('Ship' *explained not to be* 'sheep'.) No; don't know what it is, or what the sea is. Father reads the Bible out, but he only comes home once t'a week. An angel is very pretty. I wished I was an angel. They live in heaven. I hope I shall be one some day, and sit in Jesus' lap. To be one I must behave very well.

From MR WHITE'S report on the Metal Manufactures of the Birmingham District; 3rd Report, *op. cit.*, pp. 138–139.

17

Sheffield's Child of Doom

The case of a child of 8 years old, engaged in work of a specially injurious kind, needs a short notice in addition to his own statement. His pale face and squalid dress show his body to be as uncared for as from his manner and answers his mind seems to be. His father, with whom he works, was away (late on a Wednesday afternoon), and if my conductor was right in his belief, drinking; to which habit the employment of so young a child at such work was attributed. The work on which the boy was engaged when I saw him, viz. grinding cast metal scissors, is of just the same kind as cast fork grinding, the unhealthiest kind of grinding known, and he had no fan. It was mournful to feel, as from these facts, read by the light of other evidence, I could not help feeling, that this child is almost certainly doomed to much suffering and early death, probably at latest by the age of 30, perhaps much earlier; and that this sacrifice is in no way needed for the public good, but might easily be avoided by common feeling and care on the part of a parent.

William Henry Widdicombe, age 8.—Am grinding metal (i.e. cast) scissors on a dry stone. Glaze for about a couple of hours in a day, and grind dry the rest. There is no fan. Work for father, who is a grinder in this hull. Was 8 last May, and have been here now (November 2nd) six months.

Cannot read. Sometimes go to St Stephen's church. Don't know who Jesus Christ was, or if He was a man; I've never heard about Him. (This was repeated two or three times in answer to my attempts to get the knowledge out of him in other ways.—J. E.W.)

From MR WHITE'S report upon the Metal Manufactures of the Sheffield District; 4th Report, *op. cit.*, page 15; P.P. 1865, vol. 20.

18
The Boys at John Brown's

Messrs John Brown & Co.'s Steel & Iron Works, Saville Street, Sheffield. These works, with the adjoining works of Messrs C. Cammell & Co., which are of a like kind, are on a very large scale indeed, the two firms employing together upwards of 6000 persons . . . The work includes puddling, forging, rolling, casting, and other processes.

Some of the boys are exposed to considerable heat, especially some of the youngest. One, aged ten, a 'holder up', stands a few feet from the furnace, and draws up the door when the hot metal is drawn out. The flakes of hot metal, which fly many yards from the shingler's hammer, as well as hot metal or refuse lying about, require care. I noticed screens to catch such sparks put up near one hammer, and a man in another part with metal greaves to protect his legs. Masses of red hot metal, too heavy to be carried, are wheeled about, sometimes by boys. Just after my visit here, a bad accident happened to a man at some works in the neighbourhood, from a man slipping while wheeling a red hot railway wheel, which thus fell and lay on him, he, of course, being powerless to move it. Boys also drag red hot metal from the rollers; and some are 'cellar boys'.

Mr J. Ellis, one of the firm.—Our work includes the manufacture of steel and iron and heavy steel and iron goods of most kinds. We roll large quantities of armour plate, and also make railway springs and rails, shot, gun forgings, etc. We employ about 3000 men and boys, and our works cover 15 acres of ground . . . In the heavy steel work only one or two boys are employed to a score or two men. The day is from 6 a.m. to 6 p.m. and the night from 6 p.m. to 6 a.m. In the day work there are regular intervals for meals, but in the iron working branches there is no certainty as to when meals can be taken. Owing, however, to the nature of the work, there are several intervals of rest, though seldom more than half an hour at a time . . . Most of the boys are in the employment of the man, i.e. in those departments in which the work is done by the piece, which is nearly all . . . We do not think that the work hurts boys' health. It is hot, but they can often rest, and have plenty to eat and drink. We do not find them subject to colds. Nor do they suffer from accidents by machinery or burns. The worst is, say, the loss of a finger . . .

William Crompton, age 10.—Stand in front of the furnace here and hold up the door each time the metal is drawn out. It is hot work, but does not make me sweat so as to wet my clothes. Work days one week, and nights the other. When I work days I have breakfast at 5 before I come, again at 8½, and dinner about 1, as I get a chance. Sometimes stop half an hour for it, sometimes 1½. Get five bob a week, 1d for myself. Can read a bit (not well). Go to school twice on Sundays.

William Smith, age 15, moulder.—Sift on and blow off dust, etc. . . . Came three years ago to work here for my uncle, who wrote to where I live to ask me to come, as he had a place for me. Live with him. Go away an hour for dinner. Get a wash sometimes, not always.

Never was at a day school in my life, except for a week or two. I do not ever go at night, but do on Sundays, and to chapel. Heard in chapel about Samuel fighting with a lot of soldiers. Have not heard of paradise. The garden of Eden is where men goes and eats off a tree. It was not any particular men. Do not know if Adam and Eve were the first people in the world. God made man, man made woman . . .

*   *   *

I visited the Cyclops Steel and Iron Works of Messrs C. Cammell & Co., which are all on a like scale, employing between 2000 and 3000 persons . . . The answer of question 7 of the Tabular Form asking for an opinion as to the prohibition of night work by children and young persons is, 'It is impossible for us to do so: it would be tantamount to stopping our works'.

From MR WHITE'S report upon the Sheffield Metal Manufactures; 4th Report, *op. cit.*, pp. 28–29.

19

'Awful brutes' in the Glass-house

Boy, aged 17, working in a flint-glass house in the Birmingham and Stourbridge district.—The men are not very kind to you in the glass-house; they are rough brutes there. They beat you with iron things, viz. the pinchers that they handle the work with, and the iron that they blow with, and hit you about the head with them, and kick and cuff and swear at you, and they will do this for such little things, as, e.g. if you tumble down and break a glass. We do not tell the masters, they would beat us worse then. They are awful brutes and would do anything at you. I have seem them knock boys down and kick them terrible when on the ground, so as to make bruises on the body and legs.

Once I was taking in a glass and fell down and broke it, and when I came back and told the master [workman] he jumped up and ran at me and knocked me down and kicked me. There was a great bruise on my thigh for it . . . I saw a man hit a boy of about 12 on the back of his head with the blowing iron, which had some glass on the end of it, and cut his head open and made it bleed. It did not bleed much.

We all catched it sometimes. They leathered us sometimes because we did something on purpose for fun, and sometimes when we could not help it.

*　　*　　*

'A cheerful, strong-looking and nice-mannered boy, apparently one who would not complain needlessly, in a large flint-glass works in a town in the north of England': No one knows anything before he comes into a glass-house, you know a vast before you go out. You soon learn things there. Boys think it would be so pleasant and come to get money, but it would be a vast better for them to stay at school.

4th Report, *op. cit.*, pp. 258–259.

20

'A good many as wash dirty'

Thomas Compson, age 15. Taker-in at Lloyd & Summerfield's, flint-glass manufacturers, Spring Hill, Birmingham.—The work is very hot, and makes you sweaty. In summer it's awful. Wear the same shirt all through the week, but undress on going to bed ... Always wash me before going to bed, my hands, face, neck, and arms. There is a good many as wash dirty—what they call 'the glass-house wash', but father never let me do so, always made me wash over again. Can always go to sleep well if I've washed. If I haven't, I always have to get up again and do it ...

Father took me from the Bluecoat School at Dudley at ten years old to go to a glass-house. The schooling was free, and if you behaved well they reckoned to give you three new suits of clothes, one a year. I cried so not to go to work, and father and mother said I should not go, but I went.

Go to school on Sunday now, and all the nights that I am not at play (not at work). Can write a good deal better than I can read—can write my own name and letters too when mother spells the words out for me. Often do so. Never did much summing: a few, but very little ones.

(Note. Without colour—very pleasing manners.)

*　　　*　　　*

George M'Kenzie, age 14. Has worked at Carson & Warren's glass bottle warehouse, Glasgow, four years.—Get 10s. and 11s. a week with the overwork. Mother gives me 6d. for myself, and father used to give me 6d. too sometimes. I used to take it to the bank myself, and had 17s. saved, but when my little sister died they buried her with it. Father and Mother told me to draw it, and the bankman asked me 'was I going to draw it?' and I told him it was to bury my little sister. I have not put by any money since.

4th Report, *op. cit.*, pp. 227, 255.

21

A Brick in His Mouth

There is a great deal in growing up to it [i.e. brick-making]; a moulder's child is born, as the saying is, with a brick in his mouth.

Mr Ives, foreman at Mr S. Tyldesley's brickfields, near Southall, Middx.; MR LORD'S report on Brick-fields; Children's Employment Commission, 5th Report, page 136; P.P. 1866, vol. 24.

22

Scaring Crows

Sarah Gallay, Wimbotsham, Norfolk:—My eldest boy, now ten, is on a farm; sometimes he is crow-keeping. The last season . . . he had to start at 4 every morning, unless some one favoured him and took a little of his work for him, and to stay until 7 in the evening, Sundays and work-days just alike. He stays all day by himself, and takes his victuals with him, but he amuses himself somehow. He is very tired then, and will come home and almost fall down or drop asleep with the victuals in his mouth. He gets 4d. a day for this work.

At Michaelmas time the crow-keeping is not so long because the days are darker, but he has to start as soon as ever he can see, it might be 5.30 a.m. He must be there just the same, rain or shine, and if it is soaking wet. Sometimes people make a little hut for them with straw hurdles, but he had none; there were high hedgerows. One night when he came home he lay up quite stiff and cold.

Children's Employment Commission, 6th Report, page 95; P.P. 1867, vol. 16.

(b) THE LONG AGONY OF THE CLIMBING-BOYS

Although the matter hardly lay within their terms of reference, the Children's Employment Commission included in their first report in 1863 a special 'Report on the Violation of the Law regulating the Employment of "Climbing-boys".'

This was an ancient scandal. The 'climbing-boys' (sometimes there were also 'climbing-girls') were little children who were 'apprenticed' to chimney-sweeps and employed by them to force their way through the long, narrow, winding passages of domestic chimneys to clear away the accumulations of soot. What this involved will be clear from the extracts from the Report given below.

For generations this sort of thing had been going on, ever since the use of coal fires on domestic hearths had become general. One of the earliest to interest himself in the fate of the little chimney-sweeps was Jonas Hanway, who is remembered as one of the first to carry an umbrella through the streets of London, but who surely did something at least equally worthy of remembrance when in 1773 he joined with other kindly disposed persons in trying to induce the London sweeps to treat their 'apprentices' with a little more human consideration. In 1788 Parliament passed an Act forbidding sweeps to take boys under eight as apprentices, but this was just a humanitarian gesture. The climbing-boys kept on climbing.

A few years later William Blake was penning pretty little poems about chimney sweepers, as

> When my mother died I was very young,
> And my father sold me while yet my tongue
> Could scarcely cry 'weep, weep, weep, weep,'
> So your chimneys I sweep & in soot I sleep . . .

but if a tear or two was dropped by tender-hearted young ladies as they read them after dinner in the drawing-room, they had precious little effect on the lot of the miserable urchin who, long before it was light, had been forced up the chimney of that same drawing-room, with the application of a few knife-pricks on his bare soles, or wisps of lighted straw, to make him get a move on. The climbing-boys kept on climbing.

Oliver Twist would have become one of their number if he hadn't shown himself so terrified when he was taken before the magistrates to get his indentures approved. Dickens's novel was published in 1837, and may have furthered the passing of the Act of 1840, which prohibited the employment of chimney-sweeps under the age of twenty-one. This is the Act referred to in our first document, and as will be seen, it was a dead letter. The climbing-boys kept on climbing.

For thirty years their cause was championed by Lord Shaftesbury, and he was tireless in his efforts, notwithstanding a long succession of rebuffs. When the Commissioners issued their special Report in 1863, he seized the opportunity of bringing the scandal once more to public notice, and another Act was passed in the following year, making it unlawful for a master-sweep to take into a house with him an assistant under sixteen years of age, and empowering magistrates to impose sentences of imprisonment instead of a fine on masters disobeying the law. The day on which the Act was passed was hailed as 'the Chimney-sweepers' Emancipation Day'. But the rejoicings were premature. The climbing-boys kept on climbing.

So the Children's Employment Commission returned to the charge. In their 5th Report Tremenheere and Tufnell stated that there were at least 2,000 boys, nearly all between the ages of five and ten, still employed in climbing chimneys in England, that they suffered greatly physically and morally, and that the 'disgraceful scandal continues of children of tender years being sold by their parents for the purposes of this employment'. The Act of 1864, they concluded, had completely failed to answer its intended purpose.

More years passed, 'years of oppression and cruelty', as Shaftesbury called them in his Diary. In 1872 a climbing-boy was suffocated in a flue in Staffordshire. Shaftesbury wrote to *The Times* about the case, but nothing came of his letter; he raised the matter in the House of Lords, and nothing came of *that*. In 1873 he tried to interest the House of Lords in the case of 'a poor little chimney-sweeper, seven and a half years old, killed in a flue at Washington, in county of Durham'. And still the climbing-boys kept on climbing.

But in February 1875, Shaftesbury called the attention of the Government to yet one more death, a boy of 14 this time, who had died after sweeping a flue in an asylum near Cambridge. The master-sweep responsible got away with six months' hard labour, but *The Times*, bold at last, thundered that 'whoever deliberately authorized and permitted the employment of this unfortunate boy, are morally guilty of murder'.

Shaftesbury struck at once. A fresh Bill was introduced, putting teeth into the previous enactments. It was passed without demur. And so the climbing-boys didn't climb any more.

23

The Nottingham Master-sweep's Story

Mr George Ruff, of Upper Parliament Street, Nottingham, in evidence. I am a chimney-sweeper, and also own a shop here. Twenty-five years ago I was the first agent in this town of an association formed to prevent the use of climbing boys.

At one time soon after the Act (3 & 4 Vict. c. 85, 1840) their number in this town was brought very low. But lately they have very much increased. A few months ago I made out a list of 14 men here employing between them 21 boys; one employed three. The boys are, I should say, between the ages of 8 and 14, with a few perhaps of 6 and 7. I am certain that unless something is done things will soon be as bad as ever. There is a competition here between those who use boys and those who will not ... The law against climbing boys is a dead letter here. At first a paid agent was employed by some gentlemen and ladies in the town to watch the sweeps, but he was given up, as he came to neglect the duty ...

The use of boys is much encouraged by the fact that many house-holders will have their chimneys swept by boys instead of by machinery. I have myself lost a great amount of custom which I should otherwise have ... I have been sent away even from magistrates' houses, and in some cases even by ladies who have professed to pity the boys, for refusing to use them.

However, to satisfy particular customers, and in order to be able to do jobs where perhaps one chimney out of a lot would need a boy, I did for a time try to bring up one of my own children to it, but my wife and I felt that we could not stand it any longer, and that we would sooner go to the workhouse than suffer what we did from it.

No one knows the cruelty which a boy has to undergo in learning. The flesh must be hardened. This is done by rubbing it, chiefly on the elbows and knees with the strongest brine, as that got from a pork-shop, close by a hot fire. You must stand over them with a cane, or coax them by a promise of a halfpenny, etc. if they will stand a few more rubs.

At first they will come back from their work with their arms and knees streaming with blood, and the knees looking as if the caps had been pulled off. Then they must be rubbed with brine again, and perhaps go off at once to another chimney. In some boys I have found that the skin does not harden for years.

The best age for teaching boys is about six. That is thought a nice trainable age. But I have known two at least of my neighbours' children begin at the age of five. I once saw a child only 4½ years in the market-place in his sooty clothes and with his scraper in his hand. Some said, 'Look at that little fellow, he is not 4'. But one man standing by said, 'He's 4½; his father (naming him) told me his birthday, and said that he began when he was 4, and that he would make a nice little climber'.

Nottingham is famous for climbing boys. This is on account of the chimneys being so narrow. A Nottingham boy is or was worth more to sell.

A boy of about 7 or 8 was stolen from me once. As he was in the street a man seized him in his arms, carried him off to a lodging-house, and stupefied him with drugged tea. After the tea the child fell into deep sleep and lost all his appetite. An inspector and I traced him to Hull. The boy was so glad to find that 'master' had come. The man had said that if they had got him to France, they should have had £10 for him. The stealer was a sweep of Hull; letters were found on him giving orders for more boys, and these letters were read before the magistrate. The prosecution was afterwards dropped, as the magistrates said that the man must be transported for kidnapping, if it was pressed. However, he said he would not do it again, and paid more than £20 for the expenses. I would not keep any boys after that . . .

Seven or eight years ago a boy was smothered in a chimney here. The doctor (naming him) who opened his body, said that they had pulled his heart and liver all out of place in dragging him down.

Since the law would not allow of apprenticing young boys, the plan has been to give so much money down to the mother on bringing the child, and so much a quarter afterwards, say a pound or two a year. The boys are also boarded by their masters, but formerly at least, in miserable, dirty places.

Two journeymen whom I took were quite astonished at being put into a room with beds and sheets, and could not understand being obliged to wash. However, after a while they came to like it. I think that some boys near here still 'sleep black'; I hear them 'dusting' in the morning.

Formerly the sweeps, as they said themselves, had three washes a year, viz. at Whitsuntide, Goose Fair (October), and Christmas. But now they are quite different. This is owing a great deal I think to a rule which we brought about of taking no orders after twelve midday, and washing then. The object of this was to let boys go to school in the afternoon.

At first most did, but they do not now. A lady complained to me because she could not get her chimney done, and said, 'A chimney sweep, indeed, wanting education! what next?'

The day's work here generally begins at about 4 or 4½ a.m., and lasts for 12 hours, including going round for orders. A man and boy together will earn in a fair full day 6s., but perhaps one day they may sweep 20 chimneys, another half-a-dozen.

The younger boys are more valuable, as they can go up any chimney. When they get too big to climb, which in town chimneys is about 15, or 16, in the large country chimneys a few years older, they are unfitted for other employments and often do nothing. Many active young men sweeps have gone into the workhouse here after the spring cleaning is up, to spend the summer in idleness and come out again for the winter work.

Children's Employment Commission, 1st Report (1863), pp. 297–298; P.P. 1863, vol. 18.

24

'As bad as the Negro slavery'

Thomas Clarke, Goose Gate, Nottingham, in evidence: I have been a chimney-sweeper in Nottingham for 38 years; I am also a member of the Sweeps' Association here to prevent the employment of climbing boys.—The usual age at which boys begin now is from 6 upwards. I began myself at a little over five. They are generally the children of the poorest and worse-behaved parents, who want to get rid of them and make a little money by it as well, It is as bad as the Negro slavery, only it is not so known . . .

I had myself formerly boys as young as 5½ years, but I did not like them; they were too weak. I was afraid they might go off. It is no light thing having a life lost in your service. They go off just as quietly as you might fall asleep in the chair, by the fire there. It is just as if you had two or three glasses of strong drink . . .

I have known eight or nine sweeps lose their lives by the sooty cancer. The parts (private) which it seizes, are entirely eaten off. There is no cure for it once it has begun. These diseases are caused entirely by 'sleeping black', and breathing the soot in all night. I have seen a piece as big as a bean on the front teeth in the morning. What they breathe when at work they spit out . . .

The use of boys for climbing seems to harden the women more than the men. Only lately a woman who had put her child to a sweep followed me and threatened to pull my hair for speaking against having climbing boys.

Machines will do the work well, and are not dear. A common one with iron fittings may be had for 25s., a good one with brass fittings, which are much lighter, for less than £2, and the best of all with all extras complete, for £3. With yearly repairs and all I have not laid out more than equal to two new machines in twenty years, and parts of my first are still in use. There may be chimneys which cannot be swept by a machine, but I have never seen one . . .

Children's Employment Commission, 1st Report (1863), pp. 298–300.

25

'Sleeping black'

———————

Richard Stansfield, chimney-sweep of Manchester, in evidence.

Indeed, I can tell you something about sweeps, for I have been one for 35 years, and have climbed myself. Simpson, there, he had nothing of the life of hardships, for he lived with his parents, who took care of him. I went to sweep at 5 years old. I was so cruelly treated I ran away. I went to Congleton, and Newcastle, and Chester, doubling back and so to Mold, and then I thought I was safe, but my master was pursuing a day behind me all the time. I had just hired myself to a man there and was thinking that they looked kind, and his mistress was giving me some tea, when I heard my old master's voice, and the tea choked me, I couldn't take another morsel though I was very hungry. He took me off at five the next morning. There was a league then between all the masters, and the sweep at Mold could not hold me against the other; we walked the whole way here without resting; he waited till we got to the forest, and then he nearly killed me . . .

In learning a child, you can't be soft with him, you must use violence. I shudder now when I think of it. I have gone to bed with my knee and elbow scabbed and raw, and the inside of my thighs all scarified; we slept 5 or 6 boys together in a kind of cellar with the soot bags over us, sticking in the wounds sometimes; that and some straw were all our bed and bedclothes; they were the same bags we had used in the day, wet or dry. I could read, and we used sometimes to subscribe for a candle to read by when we were in bed. I have seen the steam from our bodies so thick as to obscure the light so that I couldn't read at all.

Dozens die of consumption . . . They are filthy in their habits; lads often wear one shirt right on till it is done with. I have been for fifteen months without being washed except by the rain: why I have been almost walking away with vermin! Not so now, Sir! You come with me at 9½ any night you choose to a place not 200 yards from this, and you'll see for yourself . . .

*   *   *

On a subsequent night [reported Mr H. W. Lord, making the examination] at about 10½ p.m. I accompanied the witnesses Simpson and Stansfield to some cellars where they thought we might find some boys 'sleeping black'. So far as the boys were concerned our visit was unsuccessful; my companions said that my inquiries had been heard of and the 'birds had flitted'; in one place, however, I saw what they informed me was a specimen of the habits of the ordinary journey sweep . . .

I followed Stansfield down some broken stone steps into a dirty and ill-drained area in a district of Manchester, where a dense population is closely packed in small and crowded dwellings. He entered a door, and after some delay returned and took me in with him to a low-pitched unsavoury cellar, the only occupants of which appeared at first to be a woman and two little girls in ragged clothes. After some little time I discovered by the fire-light, there being no candle, a small bedstead, which with two wooden 3-legged stools and a table constituted all the furniture of the place; on it was a mattrass, and on the mattrass a black heap, which ultimately proved to be a young man who was sleeping underneath the blanket which he used to catch the soot in his trade of chimney-sweeping; he and his blanket were both quite black, and that blanket I was told was the only bed-covering for his wife and two daughters who were then preparing to join him; I certainly could see no other.

Simpson told me that the stench there at times was enough to knock him down, and that he would never go inside, but kicked at the door and smoked his pipe outside till some one came.

Children's Employment Commission, 1st Report (1863), pp. 302–303.

(c) JUVENILE DELINQUENTS

Although there can hardly ever have been a time when society did not have its 'waifs and strays', it seems likely that there was an exceptionally large number of destitute juveniles in the middle years of the last century. The ordered family life had dissolved under the impact of changes brought about by the Industrial Revolution, and untold numbers of children of both sexes were left to fend for themselves.

The State did not concern itself with their fate. There were no social provisions for their welfare, and until 1870 there was no system of national education. True, there were the two educational societies, the National and the British, but these were not so much interested in education as in training good little Church members or good little Dissenters. The schooling provided was woefully inadequate, and a very large number of children were left out in the untutored cold. But a child was never too young to be classified as a 'juvenile delinquent', and hardly ever too young to be sent to prison, whipped, transported to the penal colonies beyond the seas. A generation earlier they might have been hanged for stealing a pocket-handkerchief . . .

Oliver Twist, with its appalling pictures of youthful depravity in the persons of the 'Artful Dodger' and the other graduates in Fagin's school of crime, must have awakened many readers to the dangers of this festering sore in London and the other great centres of population, and the publication of the successive Government reports on Children's Employment added to the anxiety. A fresh field of social rescue was opened up, in which a prominent part was played, naturally enough, by Lord Shaftesbury.

Shaftesbury did not 'invent' the Ragged School, but he threw over the movement the glamour of his great name, and to the end of his long life the fate of 'his boys' was with him a matter of the deepest and most painful concern. For forty years he was president of the Ragged School Union, whose work is described in No. 29 by its secretary, as given in evidence to the Select Committee of the House of Commons on Criminal and Destitute Juveniles, which sat in 1852 under the chairmanship of M. T. Baines, M.P. This Committee's work was continued by the S.C. on Criminal and Destitute Children, which reported in 1853. Among the latter's recommendations was the establishment of reformatories for juvenile offenders, and a beginning with these was made in 1854, when Lord Palmerston was Home Secretary. As the century wore on, voluntary efforts inspired by the Christian ethic did much to alleviate the lot of this most unfortunate class of society, but the passing of the Children Act in 1908 was a sign that, at long last, the State was awaking to its responsibilities.

26

'City Arabs'

Matthew Davenport Hill, Q.C., Recorder of Birmingham since 1839, giving evidence to the Select Committee of the House of Commons on Criminal and Destitute Juveniles.

Are there any classes of children, as far as you have observed, peculiarly liable to crime ?—Yes. The first class is the children of criminals; they are hereditary criminals; they are trained to crime; they are practically taught to think light of it, even when they are not expressly taught to consider it a merit, which they generally are, to commit offences ... Then illegitimate children: the testimony of inspectors of prisons, and of gaols, and the chaplains of gaols, is uniform to the effect that illegitimate children form a very large class of juvenile criminals. Orphans, for obvious reasons, form another class. Foundlings and stepchildren form a large class; and no doubt the children of the very poor form a class. But the result of 30 years' observations upon the subject has been to convince me that poverty, though a cause of crime, is a very much smaller cause than is usually supposed.

The character that seems to be common to all those classes appears to be that of moral destitution ?—Exactly so; and that includes the manner in which poverty works; for instance, orphans, if strangers kindly take to them and train them properly, are not more subject to crime than children who have parents, and so forth; but these children are liable to that moral destitution—that want of training ... It is training, moral, religious, and industrial, to which we are to look as the chief means of reformation.

What, according to your observation, are the chief characteristics of the class of children so brought up ?—That they have in truth all the vices and some of the virtues of savages. Sometimes they are called 'City Arabs', which is a term certainly expressive of the real state of the evidence. He is indolent, averse from a settled or steady employment, averse from restraint of any kind; on the other hand, he is patient of hunger, and thirst, and cold; and as to dirt, he rather takes delight in it than otherwise; it is by no means evil in his estimate; and he would much rather be permitted to roam about at large, even suffering at times great privations, than he would be at school or at work, under the restraints which belong to civilized society.

Are they open at all to the influences of kindness ?—After some time, but they are suspicious; they have generally been very much unused to kindness, and they suspect interested motives in those who offer it; but in a short time when they find that kindness genuine and sincere, they are often very grateful. They are open to its influence because they know what suffering is, and consequently know what it is to be relieved from suffering. But the great difficulty with them is to form the habits of steady application. Before those habits can be at all formed, it is quite clear that the nomadic habits which they have enjoyed from early childhood must be broken through; and I believe we are all of us naturally very much inclined to a wandering life. We have the advantage of early training to cure that propensity; they have not, and in them it flourishes in all its natural exuberance.

Report of the Select Committee of the House of Commons on Criminal and Destitute Juveniles, questions 389–394; P.P. 1852, vol. 7.

27

A Little Boy's First Crime

Capt. William John Williams, Inspector of Prisons, Home District: The most frequent source of crime is an instinctive love of theatrical representations; there is hardly one of these boys but begins in that way. They begin by robbing the Monday money with which they have been entrusted when going to school. In numerous cases that is the first crime committed, of running away with the penny, or twopence, or threepence, or fourpence, to go to the penny theatre with . . . There is a certain class of boys who do nothing but steal provisions, or who give themselves to stealing provisions from shop doors, and sell the provisions they get to lodging-house keepers. Then there is another class of boys who pick men's pockets, but never touch a woman's pocket; another class of boys will pick women's pockets, and give themselves up entirely to that branch of business. Then there are others who addict themselves entirely to stealing tills; drawing the damper, as it is called in the manufacturing districts.

Some of these boys rob each other?—It is a common practice as regards these boys, when children are taking money to pay their schooling at the beginning of the week, to waylay them, and persuade them to go to the penny theatres, and spend the money with which they should have paid the schooling.

Mr. Milnes. Is there any rank of society in which you could trust a young child with money to pay for the schooling, when it passed a pastry-cook's shop?—I do not know; I tell you things as they are . . .

Report of the S.C. on Criminal and Destitute Juveniles, pp. 12–13; P.P. 1852, vol. 7.

28

Ten and Eleven: Brothers in 'Crime'

Extracts from the Journal of the Chaplain of the County House of Correction, Preston, Lancs, relating to Juvenile Criminals. Saturday, March 13, 1852.—The only juvenile committed during the week is that of a child aged 10, named John Marshall, but it is his fourth committal; his offence being, 'sleeping out', and the history concerned with him is one of a truly deplorable character. Never, indeed, has a case been presented to me, showing more clearly the justice of 'visiting' the sins of the children upon the parents, when those sins are manifestly the consequences of the parents' neglect and cruelty.

This poor child is the younger brother of William M., aged 11, who was discharged on the 20th ultimo, from an 18 months' imprisonment, for robbing a shop-till, in conjunction with another boy of 14, whom it was necessary to sentence to transportation. The prison history of the two brothers is, shortly, as follows:

William Marshall, aged 11

Committed,	June 1849, under Juvenile Act, sentenced	—1 month
„	Nov. 1849, to the sessions, sentenced	—6 months
„	Aug. 1850,	ditto	—18 months

John Marshall, aged 10

Committed,	June 1849, under Juvenile Act, sentenced	—1 month
„	June 1850, for attempt at felony,	—14 days
„	Dec. 1850,	ditto	—14 days
„	March 1852, for sleeping out	—7 days

The domestic history of the children I give in William's own words.

'My father kept a jerry-shop [a low drinking-den] in Heatley Street; my father was drunk very near every night; my mother died through my father beating her; my mother sauced him for going to other jerry-shops to get drink, when we had plenty of drink in our own house; and then he punched her all up and down the house, and she was crying all day with him punching her, and shouted many a time, while he was agate, 'Murder!' She did not die all at once; she was badly two or three weeks. We was getting our breakfasts to go to school; it was on a Monday morning, and my father fetched us upstairs. My mother was dying. My father was crying, and Hannah (the youngest child) was laughing, and my father tried to make it give over. There was four children of us: James, me, John, and Hannah.

'It was not long before my father got wed again. The woman's name was Aggy Stevenson. My father then gave over drinking a bit; but he soon began again, and when he got his wages he came home drunk at 12 o'clock at night. My father was a porter at the railway station; and he came home drunk when he got paid, one Friday night; and he took James and me, and he said he would take us to the canal and drown us. He told our step-mother to reach our shoes; she said, 'If you are going to drown them, you may as well leave their shoes for Johnny'. He took us, and he threw me in; and I should have been drowned only for a boatman. There was two policemen on the bridge, with their lamps; they did not come to us then, but they came to our house after we came home; and they said they came to see about those two children; it was not a proper time to be on the canal side that time in the morning (2 o'clock). My father said it was none of their business; they had nothing to do with his children. At this time my father was as drunk as he could be, and had got knocked off his work.'

Our schoolmaster, Mr Castle, having at my request kindly made such inquiries as would lead to the confirmation of this account, if true, the result is, my conviction that substantially the poor child's statement is well founded.

It appeared that the father had kept a low beer house, 'the Black Cat', in Heatley-street, and that while there he buried his first wife; he afterwards came to Albion-street West, and while there married his present wife, who already had a child of her own, so that in a short time there were three sets of children living together. It was also stated that at the death of the first wife, her sister took the little girl, Hannah, but that the three boys remained to endure the brutal harshness of their father and stepmother.

Several of the neighbours spoke of her cruelty to the boys; how 'she locked them up in the house, tied them up to the bedposts, and "clammed" them shamefully'.

'One time,' said one of the neighbours, 'my lad heard something knocking, and he looked round, and it was one of Marshall's lads knocking the skylight out to get himself out. He had been tied up, but got loose, and then piled some things up in the room. He got out naked, and came down at the gable of one of the houses, and the neighbours gave him some clothes, and I filled his belly.' This statement relates to the younger boy, John, who had related to me the story himself.

Committee on Criminal and Destitute Juveniles; P.P. 1852, vol. 7. Appendix No. 3, pp. 427–428.

29

'Ragged Schools' to the Rescue

Mr William Locke, Hon. Sec. of the London Ragged School Union since its establishment in 1844, giving evidence:—

Ragged Schools originated a very long time ago; some think they were first begun when Mr. Raikes got ragged children out of the street into his Sunday Schools [in Gloucester, about 1780]; or when honest John Pound gathered a class of ragged children round him in his little shop at Portsmouth [for about 20 years until his death in 1839]. However, the Ragged School Union was established in 1844, when some friends and I, engaged in Sunday School teaching, found so many children excluded from the Sunday Schools in consequence of their filthy, dirty, and ragged condition, that we were very anxious indeed to have another class of schools in London at that time, and we thought it an excellent plan to have a Union so that we might arrange plans, and assist each other in carrying out so desirable an object as that of gathering in the outcast and destitute who were idling or doing mischief in the streets.

Since that time the Schools in London have increased from 16 to 110; the voluntary teachers have increased from 200 to 1600; there were no paid teachers at first, and we have now 200; the children at first were only about 2000 in number; we have now in our day and evening schools about 13,000, which does not include the Sabbath School children, who amount to about half that number. We take the children at any age, but usually from 4 to 16, and even above that; we have adult classes for some as old as 20, and even 30. About half the children are under ten years.

When they are first taken into the Schools, most of them are in a very ignorant, destitute, neglected condition... Many of them are quite homeless; many of them are entirely neglected by their parents; many are orphans, outcasts, street beggars, crossing-sweepers, and little hawkers of things about the streets; they are generally very ignorant, although in some points very quick and cunning ... We have children of convicts who have been transported; children of convicts in our prisons at home; children of thieves not in custody; children of the lowest mendicants and tramps; children of worthless drunken parents, a large class; children of stepfathers or stepmothers, often drive by neglect or cruelty to shift for themselves; children of those who, although suitable objects for a workhouse, prefer leading a vagrant life, pilfering when they can, sometimes in employment but oftener engaged in practices of a doubtful or criminal nature; children of parents who, though honest, are too poor to pay even one penny a week for a school, and who cannot clothe their children so as to obtain admission to better schools; children who have lost parents, or are deserted by them, or have run away from home, and live by begging and stealing; youths who, disliking the workhouse, have left it, and lead a vagrant life; youths who are at work during the day as ostler boys, labourers' assistants, and in other ways, or who go about selling articles in the streets, such as fish, fruit, and vegetables, and who cannot therefore attend a day school, even if free admission be offered; girls who are driven into the street by cruel and worthless parents, and live by begging and selling water-cresses, oranges, and lucifer matches; children of Roman-catholics who come in large numbers to the Ragged Schools, and do not object to reading the Bible.

The condition of admission?—Destitution. In many cases, the children are admitted by personal application; in many other cases by the teachers going round and seeking for them, and by the assistance of the City missionaries [of the London City Mission], who have been exceedingly useful to us from the first, not only in finding scholars, but in getting the good-will of parents towards us and our operations . . .

The daily routine varies according to the kind of school. Some of our schools, which are day schools, are very similar to British or National schools, assembling at 9 to 12, and then to 2 to 4, dismissing the children then for the evening. In the same building where the day school is held we have generally an evening school for boys, and also girls, who cannot attend during the day, having to work or beg in order to get food to eat.

In the day schools we have reading the Scriptures, singing, reading, writing, and arithmetic, and in some schools industrial classes; in the evening schools we have similar instruction; in many of the schools we now have industrial classes, both day and evening, for teaching the boys tailoring, shoe-making, carpentering, mat-making, brush-making, pocket-book making, and other handicrafts, and for teaching the girls to sew, knit, etc. In Liverpool and Manchester they make bags for grocers, and print reports for societies and bills for tradesmen; they have got a printing-press in the Manchester school, and in the Liverpool schools. In the latter they make clogs and also shoes, and have some garden-ground to work in . . .

In many cases, because the children are so destitute that they cannot be taught, we give food—generally soup, occasionally meat, and good wholesome bread, sometimes coffee or cocoa, and bread and cheese. In one school they feed about two hundred twice or thrice a week . . . The children who come to the schools pay nothing; all the Ragged Schools are quite free, being intended only for the destitute . . .

With regard to the results . . . We have had very many children, who were formerly very bad characters, reformed; we have many out in situations, and doing well, who were formerly quite a pest to the community . . . we have emigrated about three hundred, and from the letters which we have received from them from abroad they are all doing well—those children who, while they were here, were earning nothing; many were vagrants or pick-pockets, doing a deal of mischief, and cost the community a great deal of money by robbing tradesmen, and so on; they are now earning an honest livelihood in the colonies, and, on the average, they receive from 10s. to 20s. a week, as well as their food . . .

Would [we] consider it an objection to take a boy if he had been convicted of offences—say, four or five times ? No, we have rather from the first studied to take the worst. Boys of this description have often been of a very disorderly character; the teachers have been insulted and driven from the schools sometimes; I have myself frequently been driven out of the school, and obliged to run for the police to protect us against them; but it appears to me that nothing can withstand the influence of affection and kindness even in that very debased class, and in time we have managed to get nearly all into subjection ... Kindness, Christian love to the children, and teaching them their duty to their neighbours and to their God, and making the Bible the theme of all our instruction ...

Report of the S.C. on Criminal and Destitute Juveniles, pp. 307–313; P.P. 1852, vol. 7.

CHAPTER 4
QUEEN VICTORIA'S SISTERS

(a) THE INDUSTRY OF A MILLION WOMEN

When the Princess Victoria became Queen in 1837 she was only a few weeks over eighteen, and much was made of her youth and girlish charm and innocence. The fact that there was a young woman on the throne had little effect, however, on the circumstances of Her Majesty's female subjects—or 'sisters', as we may call them. The Queen, if not sexless (she was brought to bed nine times in the seventeen years from 1840, the year of her marriage with Prince Albert of Saxe-Coburg), was thought to be in a class by herself, a very special order of creation. The rest of the female population of the country were different. They were comprised in two main categories: (*a*) those in the upper and middle classes who were maintained by their fathers and then in due course by their husbands or some other near male relative, and (*b*) those who had to rely upon their own efforts for their livelihood.

The number of women and girls in the second category is seldom recognized. In all too many of the books that have been written about 'the Victorians' we are given a picture of Victorian women as sheltered creatures, kept safe within the walls of home from the rude buffetings of the outside world. From such books we gain the impression that all Victorian women were 'ladies', with nothing more to do than paint water-colours, strum on the piano, execute pretty embroideries, and, with their glossy heads half-turned on the antimacassars, allow themselves to become the object of some languid lovemaking. No doubt this sort of thing was true enough of the select circles envisaged by the fashionable 'lady novelists' of the period, but so far as the great majority of Victorian women are concerned, it is about as far from the truth as it is possible to get.

In the last century, as in all the centuries that went before and in the century that has led up to our own time, most women were not 'sheltered' but had to battle in a hard world to keep themselves and those dependent on them. And so far from their way being smoothed by gentlemanly esteem and consideration, it has often been roughened by economic rivalry and the age-old instincts of male domination.

Look down the Table of Occupations in the Census Report of 1851, and something like a true picture begins to emerge. In that year there

155

were some 8,155,000 females of the age of ten and upwards in the British population, as compared with 7,600,000 males. Already it will be clear that if the accepted destiny of the Victorian girl was to become a wife and mother, it was unlikely that there would be enough men to go round. (This was not exceptional: in every British census since the first in 1801 the women have outnumbered the men.) Another conclusion soon emerges, equally startling to those who hold the pretty-pretty view of Victorian womanhood, namely, that getting on for a third of all the girls and women were in some paid employment outside their own homes.

Much the most numerous of the female occupations was Domestic Service. The 1851 Census revealed that 905,000 women and girls were employed as domestic servants of one kind or another, and there were in addition 128,000 farm servant-girls. This total of well over a million was more than double the number of females employed in all the textile industries (cotton, wool, flax, silk) taken together.

A very large proportion of these were in London, where, as compared with the factory districts, there were few alternative openings for female employment. In 1851 there were in London 115,000 'females' between the ages of fifteen and twenty, and of these nearly 40,000 were paid domestic servants. It seems that there were over 100,000 'domestics' in London altogether, of whom considerably more than half were under twenty-five and not much more than a sixth over thirty-five, from which we gather that domestic service was a career that one entered as a girl and got out of as soon as might be, whether to get married or to enter some less exacting employment.

On the face of it, it must seem strange that so little is known of the working and living conditions of this great army of women. Women in factories and workshops, at pitheads and in brickfields, were approached without hesitation by assistant commissioners with pencils and note-books 'at the ready', but no 'gentleman from the Government' ever seems to have been despatched to inquire into the domestic arrange-ments of the 'Englishman's castle'. Supposing one *had* taken his stand at the head of the stairs that led down to the area or basement in which the 'skivvy' or 'slavey' passed her working day, or (even more daring) had peered into the attic where she was put to sleep—what would they have found there?

Since official reports fail us, we must seek our information elsewhere. Occasionally the periodicals found room for articles on the 'servant problem'—yes, it was already a problem, in the middle of the century, and even in London—and it would be hard to beat the article that appeared in the *Edinburgh Review* in 1862, most of which is reprinted in No. 1. The novels of the period would seem a most likely source, but on the whole they are disappointing; even Dickens failed to exploit this rich vein of human material—and in saying this we are not forgetting (who ever could forget?) the 'small slipshod girl in a dirty coarse apron' whom Dick Swiveller (in *The Old Curiosity Shop*) dubbed 'The Marchioness'. However, there is one 'novel' (it is not a novel so much as a series of journalistic sketches) which helps to fill the gap. *The Greatest Plague of Life; or, the Adventures of a Lady in Search of a Good Servant, by one who has been 'almost worried to death'*, by Henry Mayhew and his brother Augustus, must be supposed to be based on actual experience. In its lively pages we follow the fortunes of the newly-married young lady, from her honeymoon in Brighton through a succession of nerve- (and china-) shattering encounters with 'domestics' of various ages, sizes, origin and disposition, until her distracted husband decides that it would be much more comfortable, and safer, if someone else has the managing of the servants. All the characters in the book are drawn with the Mayhews' customary skill, but Rosetta, or 'plain Susan', is about the nicest of Mrs Sk-n-st-n's 'Plagues'. *'Drat her!'*

I

Domestic Service in the 1860s

There has been a great revival lately of that particular grievance which every generation laments, denounces, and perpetuates—the grievance arising out of the conditions of domestic service, and the class of domestic servants . . .

Wealthy people, at the head of large households, say that they are willing to pay any price that may be necessary to secure good service. They will make no difficulty about wages, or about the comforts or indulgences of the servants' hall. Considering that, and that the work is easy, and the comfort and freedom from care greater than in other modes of industry, they feel it hard that they cannot obtain a due return for their offers, and that they are even cheated, or bullied, or ungratefully deserted, after they have well performed their share of the compact . . .

In the next class, where two servants are kept, or three including the nurse, the mistress of the household finds that of a half-dozen cooks in succession, not one can cook a plain joint. The leg of mutton is red and raw at the bone, or the sirloin comes up in a sheath of burnt outside. The morning rolls are bitter, the potatoes have 'a bone' in them, the soup is sour—something is wrong at every dinner. Upstairs there is 'slut's wool' under the beds; and if the housemaid is reproved, she says the mistress may sweep the chambers herself . . .

If we go one step lower, we find the mistress of the maid-of-all-work in much the same state of mind as in all former times. If herself over busy, she complains that her 'help' cannot do more than is possible. If irritable, she is put out by the breakage which happens under raw hands, and by the awkwardness of mind and manners of a novice from the cottage or the workhouse; she says the girl requires more teaching than she is worth, and that she would sooner do the work herself, and so forth . . .

So much for the employers. Next—how does the question look to the employed?

When we obtain the details of the Census Returns, we shall find how far above a million the number of domestic servants in England and Wales has now risen . . . Of these nearly two-thirds come out of the rural labourer's cottage . . . and in the labourer's cottage, therefore, we shall find the source of the public opinion about domestic service which we now want to ascertain. What is the view of kitchen life which we shall find in the village alehouse, and among the gossips of the hamlet, and in the cottage itself?

When the labourer's daughter becomes a sensible burden, from her fine growing appetite and her wear and tear of clothes, something must be found for her to do, some means to support herself. The boys can get work in the field or the stockyard, and few of them, therefore, think of domestic service; but there is scarcely any other resource for the girl. If there were, she would not be a servant . . .

The reason is, that the training is one of great hardship, when it begins, as is usual, in the kitchen of the small farmer. We are told that a great number of young girls are worn out by such service before they have completed their growth. They are up early, and often late; their work is severe, their treatment coarse, and their earnings £3 a year. As soon as the girl can get away from such a place, she does; and as she is then supposed to be more or less trained, she is hired at the village shop, or as help where there are so many children that another pair of hands must be called in for the rough work. Here she gets through as she can, with nobody to teach her to do anything in the best way, no leisure for learning, and perhaps no notion of having much to learn. Always on the watch for something better, she escapes, sooner or later, into the kitchen of the curate or the half-pay officer, or the widow or single lady who can afford only a cheap servant . . .

Where only one servant is kept the position must be much the same as it always was, except (and the exception is a very large one) the public opinion of the working class has changed as to the position of domestic service.

In every village there is somebody who knows somebody else in a town, and most probably in a town where there is a staple industry ... Wherever a manufacture flourishes within a hundred miles, there will be an eager pressing into it from almost every other occupation, and especially on the part of young girls ... Mistresses of households in and near every manufacturing town can bear witness to the difficulty of obtaining good and self-respecting female servants ...

If we reflect for a moment, we shall see how natural, and even inevitable, such a state of public opinion is. The liberty which endears factory life to both lads and lasses is in strong contrast with the restraints of domestic service ... The annual or half-yearly festival—the picnic in summer, and the ball in winter—which is a conspicuous event in factory life, excites a vast sensation throughout the neighbourhood, and is an occasion of great pride or vanity to the members. Servant-girls and footboys see the vans go by in the summer morning, and hear the fiddles and the dancing in the winter evening, and feel they are 'in bondage', and 'get no pleasure'. They cannot dress as the factory lads and lasses may—buying and wearing whatever they take a fancy to. Worse still, they have not the daily stimulus and amusement of society of their own order. Beyond their kitchen mates, they seldom have any free and prolonged conversation; while the day-workers pass to and from the factory in groups, and can take walks, or spend the evenings together. The maidservant must have 'no followers', while the factory-worker can flirt to any extent. Servant-girls rarely marry, while factory-girls probably always may, whether they do or not ...

It may be very true that every freak of idleness in the day-worker entails much loss; it may be true that the liberty of one's own room may be spoiled by the stoppage of the mill and the gnawing care of subsistence; it may be that the gay dresser of the fête-day has her fine shawl in pawn from Monday morning till Saturday night; it may be that modesty and self-respect decay in the publicity of factory life, till the character becomes hard, and the mind coarse, in a large proportion of factory workers, while the burden of temptation is fearfully heavy to the rest—all these things may be true; but public opinion among the class is in favour of the independence of factory and other day-work ... In one word, it is *independence* against *dependence* ...

If popular education has improved in quality, as well as improved in extent, one consequence must be the diversion of a large number of young persons from domestic service. Of the female pupil-teachers, the greater number would now have been domestics; and when there is one of these in a family, the other members assume that the whole household have risen in rank. When once a pupil-teacher has become a certificated schoolmistress, her sisters consider it beneath them to be in service. When one girl becomes Miss A. or B., the others desire to leave off their caps, and to take rank among the educated class. If that fortunate individual has dined at the house of a school manager, and has had a footman stand behind her chair, the rest cannot be contented with the kitchen ... they look about for the chance of obtaining some post as a teacher of something—of becoming in some way, however humble, connected with a school; and if that be out of reach, they will follow any employment which exempts them from 'bondage' to authority, and enables them to call themselves 'Miss', at whatever risk of precarious subsistence, poverty, or even want.

Thus far the case seems clear. The case of domestic service is not what it was. The public opinion of the working class has changed with regard to it ... There is not much use in describing what one's grandfather's servants were, and sighing over the difference in our own day. It would be more to the purpose to inquire of ourselves what we have done to deserve to be as well treated now as our grandparents were fifty years ago. What, then, we may ask, have employers done to entitle themselves to good service in their homes?

Some of them have done a great deal, for there are certainly many thousands of good servants distributed through the country, and these must be the work of middle-class housekeepers. If the cottage girl ... ever becomes a good servant, it must be by the help of some good mistress of that class. What the task is can be understood only by those who have witnessed the bewilderment of any raw girl amidst the furniture and the methods of a middle-class home. She has to learn the use of a hundred things she has never seen before, and to take care of articles which seem made only to be broken. She does not even understand the language of educated people; she sees no meaning in their daily arrangements, and cannot remember a tithe of what she is told and must not forget ... The thing is done, however. There is a class of neat and skilful housemaids in the kingdom, and there is even a considerable number of good plain cooks ...

The change in the course of a single generation in the estimate of domestic duties is curiously shown by contrasting what they were then with the extremes of opinion and of treatment at present. One finds here and there, and particularly in Ireland, and in old-fashioned provincial towns in England, specimens of the treatment of servants as it used to be sixty years ago. In Ireland the thing is insufferable. It is enough to prevent one's accepting an invitation a second time to houses where the system prevails. One is warned on arrival to keep one's drawers and wardrobe locked, as the hostess can never answer for her servants. The hostess, or a daughter, unlocks the larder door before breakfast, gets out the loaf, butter, and eggs, brings the loaf herself to the breakfast table, where she cuts off the due number of rounds, and sends them down to be toasted. The keys are never out of sight and hearing.

When we have witnessed this method in houses where half-a-dozen or more men and women servants are kept, and when we have once seen the dens into which they are put to sleep, and the open way in which they are treated as suspected persons, we can no longer wonder at any complaints of bad servants in Ireland. The wonder is that any self-respecting man or woman should ever go into service . . .

Another form of degradation is where the mistress—'on principle' again—makes her house a nunnery to her maidservants. She will not send them to the post-office, if she can go herself; nor to church, except in her train—so painfully does she dread for them the snares of the world. We have even known her lock them into one or two back rooms, when she went out, lest anybody should speak with them at a window or door. Such mistresses cannot, of course, keep their servants, however charming their abode may look, and however liberal they may be of tracts and family-prayers, and even of entreaties to the young women to stay . . .

Servants work to earn their bread, and this of course includes their maintenance while they live. Do we pay them enough for this purpose? . . . We must remember that the class concerned does not consist of butlers at £50 a year, or cooks or lady's-maids, with about the same pay in money or gifts. We must include a million and more of general servants, housemaids, middle-class cooks, and nursery maids, whose wages lie between £18 and £8 a-year.

Maids-of-all-work in lodging-houses risk life and health for high earnings, but other 'general servants' have lower wages than any other class in service . . . Of the 400,000 maids-of-all-work few have more than £10 a-year, and many have no more than £8. It is absurd to talk of their laying by money . . . How much can the housemaid lay by out of her £10, £12, or £15 a year? or the middle-class cook out of her £12, £15, or £18? Some persons who lecture them on improvidence assume that out of £15 they might lay by £10, and so on; but any sensible housewife will say at once that this is absurd. The plainest and most economical style of dress, respectable enough for a middle-class kitchen, cannot, we are assured, be provided for less than £6 in the country, and £7 in town. Then, is the maidservant never to do a kind act to her own family, or anybody else—never to pay postage—never to buy a book or anything that is not wearable? Is she to have no taste and liking about her dress, but to determine all her purchases by the one consideration of cheapness? ... Suppose her to lay by £5 a year ... when she is settled in a good place, in health, and credit. It is a blessing to her, many a time, that she has done it. When her old mother is dying, or a young sister or she herself is out of place, her savings preserve her credit, her fortunes, and her prospects; but what can they amount to when she grows old? Certainly nothing that she can live on ... Few of the class can be expected to look forward so far ... It is more natural for them to prefer taking their chance. They may marry; they may never live to grow old; something may turn up; they will trust in Providence that they shall never have to beg their bread; and we find a large proportion of them in the workhouse at last.

'The number of old servants who are paupers in workhouses is immense', we learn from Prince Albert's address to the Servants' Provident Society on May 16, 1849 ... How can the position of the domestic servant ever be elevated if the career ends in the workhouse? ...

From an article on 'Modern Domestic Service', *Edinburgh Review*, April 1862.

2

'Hardest worked women'

The hardest worked class of women are domestic servants, especially in schools, hotels, and lodging-houses.

It was a few years ago, no uncommon thing for a lodging-house maid to be at work from six in the morning till eleven at night, getting no rest except at meal times, and even to have these short intervals broken into by the lodger's bell. No one who has habits of observation and has been often in lodgings, can have failed to remark the ceaseless activity of the unfortunate maids, and their worn and weary appearance.

Some improvement in the condition of these poor wretches is now beginning to be made. Last summer the mistress of a lodging-house complained to me that it was now necessary for lodging-house keepers to allow their maids to go to bed at ten o'clock every night, and to give them an afternoon out every other Sunday, or no servant would stay.

The cause of the improvement is not far to seek. It is simply that so many women and girls now engage in handicrafts or go into shops or factories, that what is called 'a scarcity' of servants has been produced which enables the servants to make some kind of terms for themselves with their employers.

The scarcity merely means that a healthy, honest, intelligent girl cannot now be compelled to work till her health breaks down for moderate wages. If a mistress requires an enormous amount of work she must give extra wages and get an extra strong servant, and if she will not give extra wages she must be contented with a moderate amount of work, such an amount as an average girl can do without injury to her constitution.

Even now the work of an ordinary housemaid in a gentleman's family, though not more severe than is compatible with good health, is more severe than the work of a girl in a factory or shop. Let us compare the two:—

A housemaid is usually required to begin work soon after six o'clock a.m., and goes to bed soon after ten p.m. She has for rest, half-an-hour for breakfast, an hour for dinner, and half-an-hour each for tea and supper, in all two hours and a-half for meals, and in the afternoon she is generally required to do needlework for an hour and a-half, which may fairly be regarded as rest, giving altogether four hours' rest. This leaves twelve hours of actual work, longer by two hours than the day's work of factory women, and longer than the usual day's work of a shopwoman, though in some cases a shopwoman may work equally long. The housemaid's work is besides of a more severe nature, she has to carry coals and water, and to lift heavy weights in making beds, and emptying baths, etc., but the comparatively fresh air in which she does her work may fairly be set against the greater exertion.

On Saturday, the factory-hand works two hours less than usual. The housemaid, on the contrary, works harder. On Sunday, the factory-hand and the shopwoman both rest completely; the housemaid only partially; and on Monday, in families where the washing is done at home, she is often required to rise at three or four in the morning to help the laundrymaid. It is therefore evident that even the maidservant who is fortunate enough to get a place as a housemaid in a gentleman's family, works harder than a shopwoman or a factory-hand. And it is well known that a housemaid's work is considered lighter than that of a cook, kitchenmaid, scullerymaid, or dairymaid . . .

JESSIE BOUCHERETT, 'Legislative Restrictions on Woman's Labour', in *Englishwoman's Review* (1873).

3

'Early closing' for Servant Girls!

A great domestic movement is in agitation, which, it is expected, will convulse the social fabric from the area upwards, and shake our households, not only to their centres, but to the very top of our chimney-pots, our weathercocks, and our cowls. The contemplated measure is a demand on the part of our domestic servants for a general early closing of all private houses at eight o'clock, so that after that hour the cooks, housemaids, nurserymaids, and others in our establishments may go forth in search of moral and intellectual recreation in the open air. It is argued, and with a considerable show of justice, that after cooking our dinners, and washing up our tea-things, the female servant has a right to go and get her mind cultivated, and her tastes elevated, or, as it were, put in soak in the fountain of the Muses, to be rinsed, and send forth its gushings when fitting opportunity might offer.

The Domestic Early Closing Movement will entail on the masters the necessity of limiting their wants, and allowing none to extend beyond eight p.m., which it is contended will be found quite long enough for all reasonable purposes.

The moral and intellectual training will generally be commenced by the policeman on the beat, but as boldness increases, the domestic servant may venture to improve her mind at some of the harmonic meetings in the neighbourhood of her master's residence. Adjacent barracks will be particularly sought after for the culture which it is the object of the Female Servants' Early Closing Movement to obtain.

From GEORGE CRUIKSHANK's *Comic Almanack* (2nd Series, 1844–53), page 213.

4

'Drat the little minx!'

The servant who came in after Norah was a young woman whose godfathers and godmothers (stupid people) had christened Rosetta, as if she had been a Duchess. As of course I wasn't going to have any of my menials answering to a stuck-up name like that, I gave her to understand that I should allow no such thing in *my* house, indeed, but I would take the liberty of altering pretty Rosetta into plain Susan.

She was a nice, clean-looking girl, and was—what, I dare say, some people would call—pretty, for her features were very regular; still, it was not my style of beauty. And though her complexion was certainly clear and rosy, still there was too healthy and countrified a look about it to please me . . . She had a pair of very fine blue eyes of her own; but I must confess I was never partial to eyes of that colour, for they always seem to me to want the expression of hazel ones. (Dear Edward says mine are hazel.) To do the girl justice, her mouth was the best feature she had in her face, and yet there was something about it—I can't exactly tell what—that wasn't altogether to my liking. Her figure, too, certainly did look very good for a person in *her* station of life; but all my fair readers must be as well aware as I am that things have lately come to *such* a pretty pass, and an excellent *tournure* can be had for *so* little money, that even one's maid-servants can walk into any corset-makers and buy a figure, fit for a lady of the highest respectability, for a mere trifle; and such being the case, of course there is so much imposition about a female's appearance now-a-days, that really it is impossible to tell what is natural and what is not.

When the conceited bit of goods came after the situation, she looked *so* clean and tidy, and respectable, and had on *such* a nice plain cotton gown, of only one colour—being a nice white spot on a dark green ground—and *such* a good, strong, serviceable, half-a-crown Dunstable straw bonnet, trimmed very plainly; and *such* a nice clean quilled net-cap under it; and *such* a tidy plain white muslin collar over one of the quietest black-and-white plaid shawls I think I ever saw in all my life, that I felt quite charmed at seeing her dressed *so* thoroughly like what a respectable servant ought to be; and I'm sure I was never so surprised, in all my born days, as when her late mistress (who gave her an excellent character) told me the reason why they parted with Susan was, that she was inclined to be dressy . . .

The first Sunday after she had come into the house, however, I found that her late mistress wasn't so far out in the character she had given the minx; for lo and behold! my neat, unpretending chrysalis had changed into a flaunting fal-lal butterfly. For after she had gone upstairs to clean herself that afternoon, if my lady didn't come down dressed out as fine as a sweep on a May-day. Bless us and save us! if the stuck-up thing hadn't got on a fly-a-way starched-out Balzorina gown, of a bright ultramarine, picked out with white flowers—with a double skirt, too, made like a tunic, and looking *so* grand (though one could easily see that it could not possibly have cost more than six-and-six—if that, indeed), and drat her impudence! if she hadn't on each side of her head got a bunch of long ringlets, like untwisted bell-ropes, hanging half down to her waist, and a blonde-lace cap, with cherry-coloured rosettes, and streamers flying about nearly a yard long; while on looking at her feet, if the conceited bit of goods hadn't got on patent leather shoes, with broad sandals, and open-worked cotton stockings, as I'm a living woman—and net mittens on her hands too, as true as my name's Sk-n-st-n.

I had her in the parlour pretty soon, for I wanted to ask her who the dickens she took me for. Of course, she was very much surprised that I should object to all her trumpery finery and fiddlefaddle; and she knew as well as I did that the terms I made when I engaged her were—ten pounds a year, find her own tea and sugar, and no followers, nor ringlets, nor sandals allowed; and that if, in the hurry of the moment, I had forgotten to mention the ringlets and sandals, it was an oversight on my part, for which I was very sorry; so I told her that I would thank her to go up stairs again, and take that finery off her back as quickly as she could, and never, so long as she remained under my roof, to think of appearing before me in such a disgraceful state again. When she went out that afternoon to church, the girl had made herself look something decent, and was no longer dressed out as showily as if she was the mistress instead of the maid.

Indeed, this love of dress seemed to be quite a mania with the girl; for I am sure the stupid thing must have gone spending every penny of her wages upon her back. And do what I would, I couldn't prevent the conceited peacock from poking her nasty, greasy bottles of rose hair-oil and filthy combs and brushes all among the plates and dishes over the dresser. And I declare, upon looking in the drawer of the kitchen table one morning, while she was making the beds up stairs, if I didn't stumble upon a trumpery sixpenny copy of 'The Hand-Book of the Toilet', which soon told me that the dirty messes I had been continually finding in all the saucepans, were either some pomatum, or cream, or wash, which she had been making for her face or hands. And a day or two afterwards, while I was down stairs seeing about the dinner, if the precious beauty hadn't the impudence to tell me that she wished to goodness that her 'hibrows met like mine did, for it was considered very handsome by the hancients'; and in a few minutes afterwards, the dirty puss informed me that the Hand-Book of the Toilet said that you ought to clean your teeth every morning, and that she had lately tried it, and had no hidea that it was so hagreeable; and then, with the greatest coolness imaginable, if she didn't advise *me* to rub my gums with salt water hevery night before I went to bed; for that the lady of rank and fashion who, she said, was the talented hautheress of the little work, declared that it made your gums look uncommon lovely and red . . .

But really the stupid girl's vanity carried her to such lengths, that she was silly enough to allow any man to go falling in love with her who liked, although I must say I do not think there was any harm in the minx. Still it was by no means pleasant to have a pack of single knocks continually coming and turning the poor thing's head on your door-step—so that it was really one person's time to be popping out of the parlour and calling the girl to come in directly, and not stand chatting there with the door in her hand.

But when she found that my vigilance had put an end to her court-ships on my doorstep, she soon discovered another means of corre-sponding with her admirers in the neighbourhood. For one morning, when I went into the back-bedroom to put out some clean pillow-cases, and I happened to go to the window for a minute, I was never so astonished in the whole course of my existence as when I saw that impudent monkey of a footman belonging to the S-mm-ns's (whose house is just at the bottom of our garden) holding up a tea-tray, on the back of which was written, in large chalk letters, 'Hangel, can I cum to Tee'; and I immediately saw what the fellow meant by his tricks; so I crept downstairs as gently as I could, and in the back parlour I found, just as I had expected, my precious beauty of a Susan perched on a chair, and holding up my best japanned tea-tray—that cost me I don't know what all—and on the back she had written with the same elegant writing material—'Hadoored One! You Carnt Cum—Alas! Missis will Be Hin'. So I scolded her well for carrying on those games, and daring to chalk her nasty love-letters on my tea-trays, telling her that hers were pretty goings on and fine doings indeed.

And really, if it hadn't been for Edward's aversion to changing, I do believe I should have packed her out of the house—as indeed I wish I had—then and there; for the way in which she went on towards me really was enough to make a saint swear (though I am happy to say I did not). For, in the first place the reader should know that I'm more particular about my caps than any other article of dress . . . if I can only get them *distinguée* (as we say) I don't mind what expense I go to, especially as it is so easily made up out of the housekeeping by giving my husband a few tarts less every week, and manage the house as prudently and for as little money as I possibly can. But I declare no sooner did I get a new cap to my head, and one that I flattered myself was quite out of common, than as sure as the next Sunday came round, that impudent, stuck-up bit of goods of a Miss Susan would make a point of appearing in one of the very same shape and trimming—only, of course, made of an inferior and cheaper material . . . and the consequence was, that any party who had seen either of us only once or twice, would be safe to mistake one for the other—which I suppose was her ambition, drat her.

This got me nicely insulted, indeed! For one day, after having had a very nice luncheon of two poached eggs and a basin of some delicious mutton broth, together with a glass of Guinness's bottled stout, I got up and went to look at the window; and I was standing there with my head just above the blinds, when the policeman came sauntering by, and seeing me—I declare if the barefaced monkey didn't wink at me! I never was so horrified in all my life; for of course I couldn't tell what on earth the man could mean by behaving in such a low, familiar way towards *me*; and as I remained riveted with astonishment to the spot, I saw him stop after he had gone a few paces past the house, and—I never knew such impudence in all my born days!—began kissing his hand as if he wanted to make love to me. So I shook my fists at him pretty quickly; but the jack-a-napes only grinned; and putting an inquiring look on his face, pointed down to our kitchen window, and made signs with his hands as if he was cutting something up, and putting it into his mouth, and eating it. So I very soon saw that my fine gentleman was mistaking me for that stupid, soft, fly-a-way minx of mine down stairs, and only wanted to come paying his pie-crust addresses to Miss Susan and *my* provisions.

So I determined to let him know who I was, indeed; and went to the street-door to show myself, and just take his number, and have the fellow well punished for his impertinent goings on; but no sooner did the big-whiskered puppy see me, than he went off in a hurry, like a rocket, as fast as his legs would carry him . . .

From *The Greatest Plague of Life; or, the Adventures of a Lady in Search of a Good Servant, by one who has been 'almost worried to death'*; by the BROTHERS MAYHEW (1847); pp. 85–90.

(b) LONDON DRESSMAKERS

Readers of the great Victorian novels will not need to be told that the first resort of a well-brought-up young girl, suddenly turned out into the world to earn her own living, was to try to get a position in the dress trade. To become a dressmaker or a milliner, that seemed to these disingenuous young ladies—daughters of country parsons, half-pay officers, hard-up professional men and tradesmen gone bankrupt—to be the most obvious way of keeping themselves without having to sacrifice their gentility or coming to terms with a coarse and vulgar way of life.

Dickens's novels in particular are rich in such characters. Little Dorrit, for instance, 'let herself out to do needlework, at so much a day—or so little—from 8 to 8', and Little Emily was apprenticed to a firm in the country that combined tailoring with funeral furnishing and a good deal else. More to the point, however, is Miss Kate Nickelby, seventeen and very good looking, whom her wicked old rogue of an uncle arranged should be apprenticed to Madame Mantalini's fashionable dressmaking establishment near Cavendish Square. 'Dressmakers in London', he assured her prattling fool of a mother, 'make large fortunes, keep equipages, and become persons of great wealth and fortune', and who was Kate to know any better? But she may have had her doubts when Madame Mantalini informed her that 'our hours are from nine to nine, and I should think your wages would average from five to seven shillings a week . . .' She was put to work in a large, close room at the back of the premises, where a number of other young women were employed in sewing, cutting out, making up, altering, etc., but when the dinner-hour came round she had her share of baked leg of mutton and potatoes in the kitchen. She was not at all ill-treated, having nothing much worse to put up with than the nagging of the forewoman, who was envious of her youth and beauty. So on the whole, she was one of the lucky ones. How much worse she might have fared will be apparent from our 'documents'.

Opening the selection is a detailed account of 'The Sanitary Circumstances of Dressmakers and other Needlewomen in London', that comes from the special report prepared by Dr William Ord for Dr Simon, the then Medical Officer of the Privy Council (*see* the chapter on 'The Sanitary Idea'). As for the remainder, they are nearly all taken from the 2nd Report of the Children's Employment Commission, published in 1864. The great London dress houses were investigated by Mr Lord, one of the most experienced of the assistant commissioners, and we may accompany him as he visits establishments with such still famous names as Marshall & Snelgrove and Swan & Edgar.

Following upon the accounts of the London dress houses of the superior class, we are shown something of the conditions that prevailed in less reputable establishments. But even in the best, very long hours were worked, largely because of the inconsiderate requirements of 'the ladies' (No. 10). Many a show-room might well have been haunted by a 'ghost in a looking-glass' as drawn by John Leech in the *Punch* cartoon that is reproduced facing 224. Then finally an article from *Punch* makes it clear that in 1859 those who made soldiers' clothing for the Government were not much better off (if at all) than when Thomas Hood's poem *The Song of the Shirt* appeared in its 1843 Christmas number.

5

'The Sanitary Circumstances of London Dressmakers'

The milliners and dressmakers, as far as regards social position, may be conveniently classed together. But it must be understood that they follow distinct branches of employment, and that, in some respects, they are subject to different conditions. It is difficult to estimate their numbers correctly, but it may be stated that the names of 1750 dressmaking houses are mentioned in the Post Office London Directory, and that, giving an average of ten workers to each, the number 17,500 is obtained.

The dressmakers constitute the more numerous body. They are divided into two classes; those, namely, who board and sleep in the houses of their employers, and those who, living at their own houses, go to and from the houses of business at fixed hours,—the day workers.

The latter constitute for the most part an inferior class, and are less regularly employed.

Girls enter the houses of business as apprentices, at 14 or 15 years of age. In the best houses they pay premiums ranging from £10 to £50; but in the inferior houses, recruited by girls of an inferior social position, this practice does not exist. The apprenticeship, during which they of course earn nothing for themselves, lasts two years, after which they are called improvers.

As improvers they are supposed to have mastered the drudgery of the trade, and are put to more extended and more varied work. After six months or a year spent on improving, they begin, according to their proficiency, to receive salaries of £6, £8, or £10 per annum, still living in the houses of business, and receiving the title of assistants.

The next grade is that of the second hands, who are promoted from among the assistants of two or more years' standing, and receive salaries of £20 or £25 per annum, the rapidity of promotion depending upon the skill and good taste of the girls.

The designing, cutting out, and arrangement of work, the reception of customers, and the control of the workers, are in some cases undertaken by the employers; but are more generally left to forewomen, who are called first hands, and in the large houses where there are several workrooms the first-hands are again placed under the orders of a superintendent.

In the best houses very few apprentices or improvers are to be found, their skill not being equal to the delicate work therein required; but in the inferior houses they are much more numerous; and many girls remain in such houses just long enough to enable them to be worth a salary, when they seek employment in the better establishments.

The hands living in the houses of business are of course subject to various treatment, as regards hours of work, food, and lodging, according to the liberality of their employers. With regard to the most important subject of hours of work, most extraordinary assertions are made. But without attaching too much importance to statements of extreme protraction of work hours, it may safely be said that the hours of work are generally too long, and so arranged as to give few opportunities for bodily exercise. In a considerable number of houses the arrangement appears to be as follows:—After breakfast at 8 a.m. the girls commence work at 8.30 a.m., and continue, with an interval of half an hour for dinner, and another half hour for tea, till eight or nine o'clock at night. In the season these hours are much extended; and, on the other hand, in the slack time, at the end of summer, they are shortened by one or two hours. The workrooms are in some instances closed earlier on Saturday, namely, at 4 or 5 p.m. From this account, which is carefully guarded from exaggeration, it will be seen that the ordinary hours of work are from ten to twelve hours, exclusive of meal times.

But, as before stated, the hours of work are much lengthened during the season. The London spring season commences in the end of March or the beginning of April, and lasts till about the middle of July; but there is also a shorter and less important season in the end of the year, namely, in part of November and December. In a large number of houses the earliest time of quitting work during the season, is 10 or 11 o'clock, and under the pressure of court ceremonials, the work is often carried on far into the night . . .

The food provided for in-door hands is generally good and in reasonable quantity. Complaints are occasionally but not often met with, having generally relation more to the cooking than to the food itself. Indeed it is so obviously the interest of employers to keep in good health persons from whom long hours of work are required, that one might reasonably expect them to be well fed. Meat is allowed at dinner, and, when they work late hours, at supper also. If the work be carried far on into the night coffee or tea are allowed, but beer, as tending to induce sleep, is not permitted. The time allowed for meals is generally short, and mostly so when the hours of work are longest. For then every moment becomes valuable, and the girls only leave their work to gulp down their food, and to return.

In a very few houses arrangements are made whereby the girls may get a certain amount of regular exercise, either at the beginning or end of the day. More often an understanding exists, according to which, every evening one or two girls ask and obtain leave to go out and supply themselves with necessaries; but, generally, no special provision is made for the bodily exercise essential to the health of persons engaged in sedentary employment.

In the slack time at the end of the summer the girls are allowed holidays, ranging from a fortnight to a month in duration, when they can go down into the country and see their friends.

Excepting in the large composite establishments, the work-rooms are generally nothing more than the larger rooms of ordinary dwellings, provided sometimes with special arrangements for securing ventilation, and always with increased illumination, and, consequently, increased consumption of breathing-air. In some of the larger houses ventilation by special apparatus is carefully attended to; but in the commoner work-rooms ventilation is certainly disregarded, and it is not uncommonly found that ventilators, even when provided, are obstructed either wilfully or of neglect . . . Sitting for many hours without exercise in warm rooms, the girls naturally become extremely sensitive to currents of air, and, in consequence, such obstructions of ventilators are not uncommon . . . The warming of the rooms is generally effected by open fire-places, which of course tend to assist ventilation.

The proper ventilation of bedrooms is even less regarded than that of workrooms. In a few houses special ventilatory apparatus is found, but in a very large proportion of bedrooms the fireplace is the only channel for ventilation, and even this is often purposely closed.

As far as I can learn, the bedrooms are rarely overcrowded, and altogether I have seen in the sleeping arrangements of the indoor dressmakers very few cases likely to impair the health of the workers. Independently, indeed, of the question of over-crowding, the bedrooms provided for dressmakers, resemble in most respects the bedrooms of ordinary dwellings in the metropolis. I cannot, however, refrain from observing that in matters of cleanliness and comfort, many of the bedrooms were sadly deficient.

*   *   *

The indoor milliners are subject to a great extent to similar conditions. But they differ . . . in respect of their hours, which are uniform throughout the year, averaging 11 or 12, or 15 hours, inclusive of meals.

*   *   *

The position of the out-door dressmakers and milliners differs in many important respects from the above. Their hours are limited to 12 or 13, namely, from 8 or 9 a.m. to 9 or 10 p.m., and though frequently exceeded in the season, are still practically controlled by the workers. Generally they are paid at a fixed rate, about 3d. an hour for extra work, and they are to a great extent able to refuse it if they choose. Miss Newton, the secretary to the Dressmakers Aid Association, informs us that in the case of skilled hands such refusals are not uncommon. For, at present, the demand exceeding the supply, a girl turned off from one establishment readily obtains work at another . . .

In most houses the only meal supplied to day workers is their tea. It is almost equally rare to find either that the meal is not provided, or that dinner is supplied as well. The amount of wage, comparatively unimportant in the case of the in-door hands, becomes therefore in the case of the day workers a question of the greatest importance. As far as I can learn, the general minimum wage for day workers is 9s. a week and their tea.

With these nine shillings they have to find dress, lodging, fire, and food. Girls who live with their parents or friends, casting their earnings into a common stock, and girls who club together, can manage fairly upon this wage; but for those who live alone the amount is not sufficient to provide proper food after dress and lodging are paid for. They must pay 2s. 6d. or 3s. a week for lodging, and out of the remaining 6s. or 6s. 6d. find dress and food. According to Miss Newton, the day workers get only one good meal in the day, namely, their supper, at which they try to get meat. But in some houses they are allowed to bring their food and to cook it during the dinner hour.

One large establishment provides a cook to prepare the food brought by the day workers who, here at least, earn in no instance less than 9s. a week, and generally more. The cook informed me that the food brought by the workers consisted for the most part of chops, sausages, bacon, potatoes in gallipots [small earthern glazed pots or basins] for boiling, and batter similarly prepared; that many brought animal food only on three or four days, and some even less frequently, subsisting at other times on bread with butter or pickles. The pieces of meat brought to her were often of inferior quality and even tainted.

My conclusion, after careful inquiry, is that girls living alone and without other means of support, cannot obtain proper nourishment upon 9s. a week. Many without doubt find means of increasing their earnings, mostly by taking work home, or by taking in work on their own account, or by less praiseworthy means, but in all cases by encroaching upon their hours of rest.

The position of girls going home late at night, say, 9, 10, or 11 p.m., to cold garrets, is full of discomfort. If they can afford fuel they light their fire, and cook what is often the only real meal of the day, and after that they have their own needlework to do, so that they have to stay up till 12 or 1 o'clock. But if, as has more than once been described to me, they do not or cannot light a fire, they must go to bed, even in the nights of winter, cold, supperless, and often imperfectly clothed. That under such circumstances many girls should be tempted to habits of dissipation and prostitution is not surprising.

Report by DR WILLIAM ORD on 'The Sanitary Circumstances of Dressmakers and other Needlewomen in London'; 6th Report of the Medical Officer of the Privy Council (1863), Appendix 10; P.P. 1864, vol. 28.

6

Meet Mr Marshall and Mr Snelgrove

Messrs Marshall & Snelgrove, Oxford Street, London.—Mr Marshall conducted me over the whole of the premises occupied by the firm. From conversation with him, with Mr Snelgrove, and the manager of the workroom I obtained the information which I subjoin.

At the time of my visit (November) the total number of female residents was 63; 34 were milliners and dressmakers; some of the rest were in the showrooms or shop; the carpet-stitchers, who belong to a lower class, do not live on the premises ... The hours of work were from 8.30 a.m. to 7 p.m.; in the three winter months they always left off at 4 p.m. on Saturday, and for the rest of the year at 5 p.m. In the season they are expected to be at work by 8 a.m., and do not often work after 8 p.m.... Apprentices are not taken, but young ladies go as improvers to reside in the house, without a salary, for 6 or 12 months under a verbal agreement which admits of their leaving at any time, and after that they begin with salaries of from £12 to £15 for the first year.

The health and comfort of residents of both sexes are studied here with very satisfactory results. Most of the 'young ladies' live in a separate house with an entrance in Henrietta Street, where they have sitting-rooms for their especial use; they are always allowed to go out in the evening on entering their names with the doorkeeper, but are obliged to be in by half-past ten under pain of dismissal the next morning, if they cannot account for their being out later in a proper way. If they were as late as 11 p.m. they would probably be locked out.

The kitchen and all the arrangements for feeding are very good. The young ladies are provided with a dining apartment distinct from that used by the young men of the establishment; they dine in two parties, each having half an hour. If they are detained in serving a customer, or are absent on business at the dinner hour, a separate table is always provided ...

Report by MR H. W. LORD, assistant commissioner, Children's Employment Commission, 2nd Report, page 112, P.P. 1864, vol. 22.

7

At Swan & Edgar's

Mr Macintosh.—We have, besides our resident saleswomen, from 40 to 50 young women here in our work-rooms [in Regent Street, London]; all are day-workers. Their hours are from 8 a.m. to 8 p.m., and we do not mean ever to exceed them. One hour is allowed them for dinner, and half an hour for tea. When we have as much work as we can get through in the week, we must refuse orders, or take on more hands.

I am quite sure that all philanthropic efforts, whether by individuals or associations, will end in smoke; nothing but an Act of Parliament will be of any use to restrict the hours of work . . .

Of course it would not do to have the same stringent rules applied to those who serve in the shop; on a very busy day the stock may have become so disarranged as to require some hour or two to put it in order after the shop is closed; and with respect to meals too, the overseer and others, who have to wait on ladies at their own homes or in our show-rooms, must necessarily be uncertain and irregular . . .

Miss K.—I am now the head of Messrs Swan & Edgar's work-room. I have been in several private dress-makers' houses in London. We generally considered the hours of the season to be from 8 a.m. to 11 or 12 at night. For about two months we never thought of leaving off till 12 or 1 a.m., but we did not work all night more than twice a season . . .

It certainly would be a great disadvantage to the young ladies in several ways to be obliged to live out of the house; still I must say that if I had to choose between living out of the house and working from 8 a.m. to 8 p.m., and living in the house and working from 8 a.m. to 11 p.m. I should prefer the former. As for the protection which residing in the house gives, that depends on circumstances. There are many residents who are no better in a moral point of view, than if they were wholly unprotected.

Children's Employment Commission, 2nd Report, page 111; P.P. 1864, vol. 22.

8

Stout and Sherry for Mr Jay's Young Ladies

Messrs Jay, Mourning Establishment, Regent Street, London.—*Miss L.*—I have been in this establishment as first hand or as forewoman in the work-room or the show-room for many years. We very rarely have apprentices or even improvers; they are much more in private houses. Scarcely any of ours are under 20. We have 39 in our work-room, of whom 14 sleep in the house; the rest are day-workers. Of the 14, eight are milliners and six dressmakers.

We are of course liable to sudden pressure at all times of the year, but more especially in the London season, though not to the same extent as the court milliners. From April to July we breakfast at $7\frac{1}{2}$, begin our work at $8\frac{1}{2}$, and leave off at 9 p.m., or at latest 10 p.m. At all other times our hours are from 9 a.m. to 9 p.m. .... We have not worked all night for years, except, that is, one night at the death of the Prince Consort; we had then to work for several nights till 12 or 1 ...

If those in the house have parents or friends to go to, we let them go out for Saturday and Sunday—that is to say, the younger ones. We cannot ask questions of the older ones as to where they intend to go; they have dinner and a home here on Sunday, if they prefer to stay. They can all go out for half an hour's walk in the morning before 9, if they like; some do, but it is a common fault with them to neglect exercise. Our doors are always locked at 11 every night; I could not myself get in after that time.

Our work-room here, I must admit, is not as nice as I should like to see it; but all the rooms are ill adapted for the purpose. Mr Jay has spent a good deal of money on it, but it is still very close and hot, especially on foggy days in the winter, when the gas is lit. In the summer they can have the windows open; but you see they have stuffed up the ventilators, which were over the gas jets; they said they made the gas blow about and gave them cold ...

Those that are in the house have a fortnight's holiday; they arrange so as to take it at different times. They are paid monthly. All but two or three have a salary.

Miss Mumford.—I am now the housekeeper, but I was for six years in the work-room. I never suffered in health, never fainted. My only reason for giving it up was that I liked this much better, and Mr Jay wished me to try it.

We have from 12 to 18 here dining on Sunday; they have meat and vegetables every day, and sometimes a pudding. They dine in two sets; each has 20 minutes. Sometimes the young ladies in the show-rooms are not able to come, then I always let them have a chop or steak later. They do not have beer in the middle of the day, but as much as they like at supper. When there is great pressure in the show-room, as at the time of the Prince Consort's death, we have sandwiches and sherry in an adjoining room, and they run in and get a mouthful when they can.

Note by Mr H. W. Lord, Assistant Commissioner: In answer to a question relating to the quality and amount of the food supplied to the residents in his house, Mr Jay referred me to his butcher, baker, and grocer, whom he named. At the same time he told me, in illustration of the groundlessness of complaints made on that score by the young ladies, that at one time, having thought that the porter which was then furnished for their consumption by a neightbouring public house, and was complained of, was adulterated, he arranged with a wholesale brewer to supply them with pure good stout; notwithstanding that this arrangement was properly carried out, several persisted in sending out for the previously repudiated porter, and preferred to pay for it out of their own pockets.

Children's Employment Commission, 2nd Report (1864), pp. 110–111; P.P. 1864, vol. 22.

9

'*Letters with coronets*'

Madame Elise's Dressmaking and Millinery Establishment, Regent Street, London: *Mr Isaacson.*—We have from 70 to 80 residents and about 25 day-workers in the season. We do everything we can to make those who live with us comfortable and to keep them respectable ... We pay £100 a year to a physician, that they may be attended free of cost. He calls every day, and the housekeeper informs him if any one is ill. If they are obliged to take to their bed, our rule is to send them home, or, if they have no home, to get them taken in at some hospital, or infirmary, till they recover. For trifling ailments they can be taken care of here; we have a housekeeper and five servants. They have any little thing that our doctor says they should have, when they are unwell; but we have to be on our guard against deception. Not long ago, for instance, one was taken very ill, she said, and must go home to be under the care of her own doctor; she would not let our regular medical attendant see her. Next day she was seen with a man at Hampton Court . . .

Letters come with coronets and elaborate monograms for the young ladies. Such things have but one meaning, and commonly but one end. We do not require the young ladies in our show-rooms to wear silk. If any are known to dress beyond their means, they had better go. Silk stockings and military boots are out of place with us . . .

Children's Employment Commission, 2nd Report, pp. 93–94; P.P. 1864, vol. 22.

10

Ladies Are to Blame

The great cause of these long hours [in London dressmaking establishments] is that no one will refuse an order; they make a promise for any time a lady wishes. I remember a dress ordered at 12, fitted on at 6 p.m., finished the same night, and sent home the first thing next day. The lady who ordered it said, 'I suppose you work till 11, and begin at 6 in the morning'. She did not care how long we worked. We were very much hurt at the way in which it was said.

*   *   *

When I was first hand I was several times asked by ladies, late on Saturday night, to let them have a dress home the very first thing on Monday morning. I have taken orders at tea-time—4 o'clock—for a ball-dress to be sent home that same night, 'any time before 12 would do'.

*   *   *

No doubt there are many ladies who do, and many more who are ready to give long notice, but I myself know of others who will never give their orders until the last moment for fear that other ladies should have dresses like them. This is especially the case with court dresses. There is no concealment about it, they say so to us themselves.

London dressmakers, in evidence; Children's Employment Commission, 2nd Report, pages 105, 108; P.P. 1864, vol. 22.

II

'Their stays are too tight'

———————

Madame S. Baily, Edward Street, Portman Square, London. (Dressmakers.) The late work is often caused by the French girls, in houses like ours, where both French and English are employed. The French girls like to work late, and will not be got to begin early in the morning. They detain the rest, because there are perhaps five or six girls working on one dress, and though any one may have finished the particular part, on which she was busy, she will then have to help the others, until the whole is done . . .

The girls are not unhealthy, but still they want looking after, and we have to give them medicine for indigestion and pains in the chest; their appetite fails now and then; that may be for want of exercise, they only walk on Sunday. Their stays are often too tight, and too long-waisted for persons who have to sit and stoop.

They have a good dinner on Sunday if they like. We always give good food and plenty of it; joints three or four times a week at dinner, and stews or made dishes for a change. We generally give potatoes at that meal, but have haricots and other vegetables stewed or dressed in other ways for supper. Their supper generally is bread and cheese and beer.

Children's Employment Commission, 2nd Report, page 102; PP. 1864, vol. 22.

12

Miss Bramwell's Revelations

Miss Bramwell, superintendent of The Home, Great Marlborough Street, London, 'where about 70 young women reside, nearly all of whom are employed as saleswomen in shops or as milliners and dressmakers in the work-rooms of fashionable establishments at the West End of London'.

There are two things above all which I wish employers would observe. One is, not to close their doors on a girl who comes back after hours. Let them dismiss her next morning if they please, but if they only knew how many falls are due to nothing more than missing a train or an omnibus they would alter this. The other is, to have a separate bed for each person [in their hostel]. Some I know have had to sleep with women of known bad character and even suffering from a loathsome disease. I cannot describe to you the sense of pollution which some of the young ones have shown in telling me of the character of their bedfellows.

In a large establishment, where a great deal of mourning is made, they work from 8 or 9 a.m. till 11 p.m. all the year round . . . One who works there has told me that her brain seems to get on fire before the time for clearing comes. She used to be a bright good-tempered girl, but now she has grown so irritable that I sometimes fear for her brain . . .

In several of these places, where you are shown a nice and comfortable sitting-room, you will find that it is only for the young men of the establishment. Even the show-rooms, where the girls, who serve there, are allowed to sit after their business is over, are locked on Sundays, so that they have only their own bedrooms to spend the day in, if it rains . . .

In the more outlying districts, such as Knightsbridge, Paddington, &c. they often are not expected to be in the house on Sundays. One poor girl, the daughter of a professional man who lived in the country—a curate I think he was—told me that on her first Sunday in London she asked her employer, in whose house she resided, what she was to do, as she had no friends to go to in London, and he only said, 'Go to the devil if you like; I can't be bothered all day with you'. So for that day she went to Church, and wandered about the park all day. The next two Sundays were wet; she had no money, as her salary was paid quarterly;

so she went without food from breakfast to tea-time, and had to sit under the trees in the park to keep herself dry during the interval between the morning and the afternoon services. After that she was taken on Sundays by some of her companions to a room where infidel doctrines were discussed, and was led away by them. She is dead now.

Many of the day-workers are nice, respectable, and virtuous girls, but they are surrounded by temptations; even those who live in the houses are far from being exempt, and some houses are really disreputable; there are some, where it is well-known that the young ladies always spend their holidays in the country with gentlemen.

The show-room and shop girls are especially to be pitied; they are always chosen for their brightness, their good figure, good manner, and pretty face. Then the tricks encouraged in some houses to get off an article out of date, for which some are allowed 'tinge money', a small percentage, and even to substitute an inferior article for one selected from the window, are painfully degrading . . .

At some houses all in the show-room are expected to wear black glacé silk. A dress does not often last them more than six weeks or two months; in the season especially the wear and tear is very great. I know of houses where the terms offered are, that the girls should provide themselves with silk dresses on 16s a week, living out of the house. If they wear their dress, until it begins to look shabby, one of the young men will ask to be allowed to serve them with a new dress. The hint is generally understood, and the new dress ordered. That has to my certain knowledge happened in a first-rate establishment to a lady whose salary was £40 a year. Nearly £20 a year must go in that one way . . .

I do not wish it to be thought that all employers are unkind and covetous; far from it. There is one house in Regent Street where they make a present of a new silk dress once and even twice to persons whom they are paying £1 a week and more . . .

Children's Employment Commission, 2nd Report, pp. 118–119; P.P. 1864, vol. 22.

13

The Girls Who Were Told to Leave

The Superintendent of a 'home' [for young women employed in the dress trades]: We have more than sixty young women resident here, most of them between the ages of 18 and 30. Of course, all are day workers. Nearly two-thirds are dress-makers; some few are milliners, and others artificial flower makers and fine shirt makers. We require two references with each girl, and are always obliged to keep a very strict watch over them all. Many are very respectable quiet girls; some are not so steady as they might be.

I have unfortunately had to dismiss two or three; they were receiving notes from gentlemen, and making appointments to meet them. It might be all innocent, but for the sake of the rest we had to send them away. [They] were particularly pretty and well-mannered girls. I had great doubts what I ought to do, for to dismiss them was perhaps to take away their last chance; but the example to the others was too dangerous. The fondness for dress and admiration in young girls in their class of life is a terrible temptation . . .

Children's Employment Commission, 2nd Report, page 119, P.P. 1864, vol. 22.

14

'They chuck the bottles over the roof'

Mr Trelawney, Marlborough Mews, Regent Street, London.—I have the entire management of this work-room for Mr Nicholl [of Regent Street]. You must not, however, take us here . . . as fair average specimens of the trade, for, in the first place, there is not another room like it—not so good, I mean—in the whole of London; in the next place, we work on a different plan to most . . . The usual way of business is to have the work done on the premises where the shop is, or else taken home by the men to their own homes . . . Females always make the waistcoats, and often the trousers; the coats are made by men . . .

I think tailors of both sexes have improved in moral character. There is not the drunkenness there was among them. The Monday and Tuesday used to be always spent on the 'spree'. Still I have had here even my best workwomen, fine handsome girls, and decently educated, bring bottles full of drink in their pockets, and chuck them over the roof when they had emptied them.

I spoke before of the badness of workrooms generally; even in coming here from Regent Street the difference is extraordinary, and yet we had rooms there in the front looking into the street. The health of the people is certainly better . . .

There was a flower which, from it having belonged to one who died, we took especial pains to rear, but we had always to keep it outside the window, and it seemed to dwindle away; but it has been in this room ever since we have, and has shot up more than a foot quite vigorously . . .

The great thing is, that we have a lofty room and good ventilation. There are also water-closets, washing apparatus, and a small place with a stove for tea and cooking their dinners, if they like, not on a large scale, but a great comfort. There is nothing of that kind in the private rooms where they usually work, seldom even pure water.

Children's Employment Commission, 2nd Report, page 148; P.P. 1864, vol. 22.

15

Wonderful stuff, cod-liver oil

I am engaged as the regular medical attendant of the persons employed in several shirt factories here [London], amounting to from 800 to 1000, nearly all females, a greater number, I am sure, than are attended by any other doctor in the town.

I attribute the diseases from which they suffer entirely to their poor living and insufficient clothing, and the bad air of their homes, not to the nature or place of their employment. They get up, dress, and take their cup of tea and a little bit of bread and butter, all in not more than a quarter of an hour, sometimes less. They take tea again for dinner, with a potato, and perhaps a herring, and tea again in the evening. This constant living on tea weakens the digestion, and produces what I call 'languid dyspepsia'. They cannot afford better living, and the wages, at any rate of the younger, all go to the parents, and are low at best. Many even who are grown up tell me that they do not get more than 4s a week.

This poor living, which is much poorer than what is usual in England, lowers the vital power, and produces a great disposition to scrofula and consumptive diseases, and I am obliged to keep them up with quinine and cod-liver oil, of which great quantities are used. These do keep them alive, and do a great deal of good, particularly the cod-liver oil, which is a wonderful cure.

I do not find that standing at work produces swelled legs. Indeed, considering their general condition, I am astonished at their freedom from this complaint. I consider the care of the sewing machine more healthy than needlework. It gives them more general exercise, and moves the muscles of respiration more, and thus more atmospheric air is introduced into the system.

Dr Bernard, Great James St., London; Children's Employment Commission, 2nd Report, page 62; P.P. 1864, vol. 22.

16

Penal Shirt-making

———————

Can anyone have forgotten the *Song of the Shirt*, which—as everybody should know—was first printed in these columns? Here is a case to bring that canticle to mind: a case brought the other day before the Hammersmith Police Court:—

'Emily Dawes, an attenuated and sickly-looking woman, living at Key's Terrace, Hammersmith, was placed in the dock before Mr Paynter charged with illegally pawning several soldiers' shirts which had been given to her to make up.

'Mr Martin said he appeared on behalf of the prosecutor, who was the sub-contractor for the making of military clothing under the contractor to the Government, and he did so with great pain, as he believed that the offence had been committed through the paltry pittance which was allowed for making up of shirts for soldiers and sailors. His client received 5s. 6d. a dozen for the making up of the shirts, and he employed women, who worked at them for 4s. 6d. a dozen, so that he had only a profit of 1s. a dozen. During the last few weeks his client had lost 20 dozen of shirts which had been given him to be made up, and according to his contract he was compelled to make them all good. He was therefore obliged, though reluctantly, to press the charge against the prisoner.'

A profit of 'only' one shilling on an outlay of four and sixpence, is at the rate of more than 25 per cent. Tradespeople whose business brings them 'only' this per-centage, can afford to lose a part of it by the pilferings and losses which are and ever will be incidental to such trades. We, therefore, cannot pump much sympathy up for any sub-contractor who may chance to have been robbed of twenty dozen of his shirts. The sympathy we feel is for the victims of this system of sub-sub-sub-contracting, which so 'sicklies' and 'attenuates' the poor folk who do the work. As the Magistrate remarked:—'These contracts often passed through many more hands than Mr Martin had mentioned in this case.' He then asked if the women had to find their own thread in making up the shirts at 4s. 6d. a dozen. Mr. Martin said they had. He also said that the shirts were made for the Government at 1s. 10d. each.

The thread which women have to find, when making shirts at the starvation price of four-and-sixpence per dozen, is not alone the thread which the linen-draper sells them. Life hangs by a thread, and 'tis the thread of their own lives which they so often use quite up, or cut short in the process. But it is no good talking sentiment. The question is if something can't be done, and that at once, to stop the strain upon this thread which in so many sicklied shirt-stitchers is so fast wearing out. On this point hear a man who is entitled to a hearing:—

'Mr. Paynter said it was a melancholy case, and he was afraid there was no cure for it. They could not think of regulating the labour market to prevent what was called "sweating", but he thought the public would be much benefited if that kind of work was made up in prisons. It was the right employment, and succeeded very well in the German prisons and the other parts of the Continent. He had pressed those views upon the authorities, but they met with strong objections. He sentenced the prisoner to pay 1s. 10d., the value of the shirt, and a fine of 20s., or 14 days' imprisonment. The prisoner was locked up in default.'

What the 'strong objections' were, we are curious to know. Very possibly the knowledge might convince us of their strength; but we own that in our ignorance we think that penal shirtmaking would prove a most effective and deterring form of punishment. We cannot help opining that our gaols would be less popular, were our criminals to be sentenced to learn sewing and make shirts; being dieted the while with the same amount of food as our poor starving sempstresses are able to afford themselves. Perhaps this might not wholly 'cure', but it would certainly, we think, reduce the sweating system, which the Government should do its best to throw cold water on, instead of fostering and fomenting, as seems now to be the case. Penal shirt-making would be more useful work than crank-turning; and if worthy Mr. Paynter's views were rightly carried out, our soldiers would no longer be of those of whom 'tis said—

> 'it is not linen you're wearing out,
> But human creatures' lives.'

Punch, September 24, 1859

A million and more women and girls were employed in 1851 in domestic
service of various kinds, some 520,000 in the textile manufacturers, and
340,000 in the 'dress trades', as dressmakers, milliners, and seamstresses,
and a further 18,000 described as tailors. Hosiery manufacture, based
on Leicester, employed 30,000, and in the 'warehouses' and other
establishments of the lace manufacture, centred upon Nottingham, there
were some 54,000. Victorian ladies (and not only ladies) wore gloves,
and so we find that there were 25,000 gloverers, or gloveresses as we
shall find them described in one of our documents. They also wore
straw bonnets, and as a consequence we find in the list 28,000 straw-
plait workers. Over 11,000 females were employed in the Potteries. It is
surprising to find 3,000 women coal-miners, but doubtless they were
workers above ground at the pit-head. The 10,000 female nailers were
chiefly in the Black Country. So we may go on, but we must not omit to
mention the 54 women railway workers and the 19 female commercial
clerks (and not a stenographer or shorthand-typist among them).

There were also getting on for a hundred thousand women and girls
employed in agriculture, whose conditions of employment are described
under a later heading in this chapter.

Added together, these make a formidable total, but there is still a vast
mass of female labour unaccounted for. The remainder found employment in a great variety of occupations, in which the work was done in
factories and workshops of one kind or another. Some of these are
represented in the documents that follow, but it should be appreciated
that many volumes would be required to do justice to the contribution
made by women and girls to the productive powers and proceesss of the
time. There will be no complaints, however, on the score of lack of
human interest. Here we are shown the good side and the bad of female
labour, in factory and workshop.

First on the list of places we are to visit is Messrs Fry's cocoa and
chocolate factory at Bristol, and we may join in the inspector's tribute to

the kindly administration of the benevolent Quakers. At Birmingham we are shown over the patent-screw factory that provided a solid base for Joseph Chamberlain's political ambitions. Nottingham provides us with some interesting contrasts among lace manufacturers. A Sheffield employer calls the girl workers 'soft, giddy things', and a Liverpool tobacco manufacturer grumbles that he can't persuade *his* girls to invest in a serviceable umbrella. Henry Mayhew introduces us to the pickle-girls at Messrs Crosse & Blackwell's Soho factory, and Mr Bennett of Cheapside, explains why he had to sack his young ladies. Dr Greenhow reports on the deplorable habits of married women in factories, who keep their children quiet with heavy doses of laudanum. Then we are taken to see one or two of the cottage industries which were still flourishing in the middle of the last century. Were Evesham's gloveresses really such an abandoned lot of hussies as the curate made them out to be?

17

Messrs Fry's Factory a Pleasure to Visit

Messrs J. S. Fry & Sons, Chocolate and Cocoa Manufacturers, Union Street, Bristol.—The evident care bestowed on the comfort and welfare of the people employed here is such as befits the well-known family name which the firm bears, and makes it a pleasure to visit the place.

The younger girls whom I spoke to had all been to school and said that they can read, and some elder girls and young women, sent down to me by the forewoman, without selection, all read nicely from a magazine, except one who made mistakes, as it seemed from nervousness.

A room is set apart as a school-room and chapel, at which I attended by invitation the short morning service, at which the Scriptures and a hymn are read, with explanations where necessary. It was pleasing to see the orderly way in which they came in and sat down, one by one, the little girls in front, then the elder and women, then the boys, and at the back the men, each taking down their Bibles from the shelves as they entered. I was much struck with the general attention shown throughout the service. Though it was 8.45 a.m., and therefore after work had been going on for some time, all came in as bright and fresh looking as if at a Sunday school, except that the clean canvas jackets of the men and boys and aprons of girls showed that it was a working day.

It cannot be doubted that this daily meeting, apart from the religious benefit, must tend greatly to the other indirect good results referred to by Mr Fry.

Children's Employment Commission, 5th Report, page 66; P.P. 1866, vol. 24.

18

The Best Nottingham Could Show?

Messrs Thomas Adams & Co.'s Lace Warehouse, in Stoney Street, Nottingham, is a remarkable instance of the regard shown by many employers for the welfare and comfort of their people. The building is very large, and planned so as to give as large a frontage as possible to the outer air, a point of great importance. A large room is set apart as a dining-room for those who do not go home, and used for this purpose by about a hundred daily, and for tea by nearly all. A woman is employed to prepare and serve their meals, there being a steam oven and all proper appliances for the purpose, teacups, &c. being supplied. Close by is a room for washing before leaving work, as well as white delft washing-places, purposely left open to view, and a separate closet, in each workroom. There is another tea room for the men. During meals the work rooms are closed and the windows opened, for which the over-looker is responsible.

There is a chapel and a chaplain, and the work begins each day with a short service, which is attended by nearly all, and is understood to be part of the system of this place. There are also a school-room provided with books, maps, &c., in which the chaplain has classes for religious and other instruction in the evening; a book club; a sick club, a payment of 1d a week to which entitles to medical attendance; a sick fund for further purposes; and a savings bank.

Alterations have been made in parts of the building to increase its healthfulness ... It appears, however, from the statement of the girls that the windows cannot be, or are not, opened, and that the girls suffer from the heat and bad air. The establishment is commonly spoken of as one in which arrangements of all kinds for the welfare of those employed have been carried to their fullest extent.

Rev. Edward Davies, chaplain to the establishment. The moral character of the workpeople has improved in a remarkable manner in the last few years. Formerly girls often had to leave from being with child, but this is now very uncommon. There is also a good deal of kindness shown by them to one another. Whenever a girl is ill and without friends of her own to nurse her, her companions collect money and will give up their own work in turns to attend her day and night. Unhappily illness is not unfrequent. Consumption is unusually common amongst the girls here. In the last month I have attended four cases of this disease amongst them, of which two have ended fatally, and there are two or three other cases of a like character. Cases of weakness of chest and general debility are very common indeed. These do not, however, generally go to the hospital.

Annie Lawrence, aged 13. 'Rolls', i.e. turns a roller for pressing lace. It is very hard work if the lace is thick and wants a deal of pressing. Has rolled here for two years, doing other work sometimes, i.e. 'joining', i.e. fastening pieces of lace together, and at another place before. It tires her more than it used to do. Feels very tired at night when she has rolled all day, and it makes her side ache sometimes. Never was very strong, 'but there are a many weaker'. Went out to lace drawing when 7. Often is not late for chapel for many weeks together; forfeits 1d. if she is, and a young woman 2d. The proper hour for leaving work is 6½; if they have tea it is 8. It was 8 nearly all the summer, and sometimes, but not often, 9, and two or three times only 10. Has 5s. set wages and 1d. a night for working till 8. Mother lets her have her overtime. Has been to a methodist school and chapel on Sunday for eight or nine years, except when mother is not so well, and understands what she hears there. Went to a day school for three or four years, but did not like it because she wanted to come to work, so as to earn something. Mother is going to send her to the People's Hall (night school) in a week or two; she will have to pay 2d. Can read short words, write a little, and do some sorts of sums.

Children's Employment Commission, 1st Report (1863), pp. 195–196; P.P. 1863, vol. 18.

19

The Lace Girl's Letter

To the Editor of the *Nottingham Daily Guardian*.

Sir,—I have been a lace warehouse girl about 13 years, and should know a little about the regulations of warehouses. Is there not an Act which compels the masters of factories to let children leave their employment at six o'clock at night ? If there is, can any one tell me why this Act is not applied to lace warehouses, which are heated with steam, for children and young women are kept there at work from 8 in the morning till 7, 8, and 9 o'clock at night, for about 3s 6d to 8s per week, which, in my opinion, is worse than slavery in South America, for I do not think they work above 12 hours a day; and if they do, they are better off than a portion of the warehouse girls of Nottingham, who have to work in cellars not fit for pigstyes, much more for human beings.

When I use the word cellar I mean the lowest room of the warehouse, which is 8 or 9 feet below the foot-road; but to do justice to the lace-masters in general, there are only a few who make their girls work in these holes. In rainy weather you can rub the wet off the walls; in dry weather they smell fusty and unhealthy. When the hands complain of the damp, the master or man orders the work to be taken up stairs, where it is dry. He does not think of the constitutions he is ruining; the work is of more consequence than the lives of his work girls. It is a rare specimen of self being first nature. When they have caught the rheumatics or one cold on another, which is the cause of half the consumptions, they have a recommendation for the infirmary given them as a salve. Hoping, for the sake of humanity, you will publish the above, I remain, Yours, *A Well Wisher*.

P.S. If the Sanitary Inspector was to visit these places he would be of my opinion.

Quoted in Report of J. E. WHITE, Children's Employment Commission, 1st Report, page 243: P.P. 1863, vol. 18.

20

What Made Mr Chamberlain's Girls Scream

Messrs Nettlefold & Chamberlain's Patent Screw Works, Smethwick. This factory stands in an open space at some distance from Birmingham, and was built about ten years back for making screws by new patent machinery, which greatly reduces the proportion of hands required. The buildings are all on the ground floor, and the main workshop, in which nearly all the females are employed, is 200 feet square and 16 feet to the spring of the rough glass roof, supported on iron pillars, and with canvas beneath to keep out the glare. It is well ventilated and clean, and has much the appearance of a large railway station. A better work place could not be well imagined . . .

There is a nuisance highly objectionable where several hundred young women and girls are employed, which the police have been applied to, but say that they have no power, to stop. It consists in men and boys bathing in the canal which runs along the side of the yard, which the females pass through to their work or may spend their spare time in . . .

Mr George Boyce, manager. We have not had any fatal or serious accidents here, nothing beyond the loss of a finger or so. But there have been several losses of crinolines and dresses from being caught in the shafts, which run along just in front of the knees. Indeed this is very frequent; but the shafts are driven very lightly, partly for this reason and partly so as not to hurt the machines in case of stoppages, so that no great hurt is done. Still it is a very awkward thing, for the girl sets up a great screaming, and all the rest do the same. I have known three caught in one day, and then perhaps a month without any.

Finding that some check was necessary, I put on a fine for it, and no one was caught for three months afterwards. It might be thought, as was indeed said to me, that the fright and the loss of the dress were punishment enough, but it is clear that the fine was wanted.

Children's Employment Commission, 3rd Report (1864), page 110; P.P. 1864, vol. 22.

21

Matilda Davis's Crinoline

———

Mr Walker, acting in the temporary absence of the house surgeon at the General Hospital, Birmingham:—Matilda Davis, a strong young woman of 28, was admitted about a fortnight ago with a compound fracture of the left leg, and a fracture of her right leg, and died in three days. At the inquest, at which I was present, it appeared that she was reaching over the shaft to get a tool to alter the span of the machine, which was properly the work of a foreman, when she was caught in the lower part of the machinery, which was protected only down to a certain height. Her dress from her waist downwards had been pulled off at the same machine before.

Louisa Leake, 12 Court, Broad Street:—Matilda Davis had lived with us as a lodger, her husband having long left her. She had worked at two screw factories before that—Parkes'—in which she had lost her life, and had been caught several times in the machinery in the same way before, once at the same place. I know of three times since she lived in this yard, and one of the times the skirt of her dress was ripped off; and she said she had been caught once before besides, but I believe she had not been very much hurt. She was a strong but not a careful young woman, and wore a very large crinoline, which I think was a great deal the cause of her accident.

Children's Employment Commission, 3rd Report (1864), page III; P.P. 1864, vol. 22.

22

'Girls are soft, giddy things'

Mr Robert Shirtcliffe, son of the proprietor of Shirtcliffe's Ivory, Pearl, and Tortoise-shell Cutter factory, West Street, Sheffield:—We let off the greater part of our works to persons working in several different trades, e.g. grinders of different kinds, pearl-cutters and fluters, ivory carvers, turners, silver buffers, &c. A small master, occasionally a woman, will take one or more rooms, and employ the workers in it.

Sophia Cockin, adult.—I rent this room, and employ a few girls in it on cutlery. I began cutting work at 6 years old. They lifted me on a stool to reach my work, as I was not big enough to get up myself. My lass, now dead, began cutting when two weeks turned 6 years old. Bless you! you'll find little ones at it up and down now, some, I daresay, nearly as young as I was. The trade is up and down, so that people are obliged to put their children to it as soon as they can bring on anything. There's many a little nattling job that little ones can do in it.

When I first began, I and my sister worked for mother, and then in a shop like this for my uncle. Even then he would have us up at 5 and 6 in the morning, and keep us at work sometimes till 8, but many a time till 10, 9, and 11 at night. At first, when at work late, I have fallen asleep with the work in my hand, and my mother would hit me over the head to wake me up. When I were a lass I have many a time worked all night on Friday; and after I grew up and married, for years I never went to bed on Friday night, because I was slaving for my children. On other days I have often worked from 4 and 5 a.m. till 12 at night.

I have a cough (she had coughed several times), and a pain in my chest. It is from the dust made by the lathe. I am very tired of the work now, but am obliged to keep on at it. It is easier for the bones now that we use steam power, but it is worse for the chest, as so much more dust is made. Working the lathe with the foot I should sweat even at Christmas on the coldest day with frost and snow on the ground.

The girls don't get caught here in the shafting, though we hear of such things at some places. I have been very careful about machines ever since I was a girl of 9 or 10 years old. We girls in some works of this kind were playing at hiding, and one about 14 years old hid beside a drum in a wheel not then working, and it was started and crushed her to pieces. They had to pick up her bones in a basket as they found them, and that's how they buried her.

Girls are soft, giddy things. That one there, now about 14, is a dragon for getting into danger, and I have great trouble with her. If I was not looking she would be putting her foot on the shaft, very likely, and once she sat down upon it, just to see how it felt when it was set agate.

The master does not have the shop cleaned; we must do it ourselves. But after working so long we are too tired. That heap of bone dust (a bushel or two) in the corner has been gathering for many a week. It is three weeks since we swept the rest of the shop. The dust is swept into the corner.

From MR J. E. WHITE's report on the Metal Manufacturers of the Sheffield District; Children's Employment Commission, 4th Report (1865), page 42; P.P. 1865, vol. 20.

23

'Curse and swear like troopers'

Messrs S. & C. Bishop & Co., Glass Works, St Helens. *Charles Taylor.*— I am general manager of Messrs Bishop's Works. Our young hands are a very rough lot, male and female. I think the latter perhaps the worst; we employ girls from about 16 years old in the cutting-rooms; there are two small rooms, one above the other; no men work in them. I put the better sort of girls into the upper rooms to keep them from being made worse than they are; but I fear they are not much helped by that, there is very little to choose between the two rooms.

Many of them are the children of colliers, who are the worst class of any about, so that home is a very bad school for them to begin in. Many can neither read nor write. Most of their conversation is horrid to listen to, some curse and swear like troopers; not a few have had several illegitimate children; our rule is not to admit them to work again after that, but it often happens that those are amongst our best workers and we can't do without them. There is one there who sleeps with one man or another nearly every night of her life, so they say. There are married women in the same room with them, but I don't know that that does any good.

There is the girl H. for instance, the language that her mother uses before her and to her is positively shocking; that is a case of a collier's family. There is another, E., she is 17, her father also is a collier, and in work; she earns her 15s a week, but she can't read; the family is large, and they are in a state of sad destitution . . .

St Helens is not a very moral place; there are dancing saloons all over the town; nearly every public house has one; the young fellows take the girls there and make them half tipsy, and then there follows what might be expected. I know very well that language, which would show a coarse and depraved mind when used in one class of society, may be merely the result of roughness and a want of refinement in a lower grade; but when the language and facts, the habits and mode of life I mean, correspond, as they do unfortunately among these girls, the words give the character.

Children's Employment Commission, 4th Report (1865), pp. 271–272; P.P. 1865, vol. 20.

24

The Girls Who Make Cigars

———————

Mr Steel's Cigar Manufactory, Duke Street, Liverpool. *Mackay*, foreman.—There are 90 or 100 girls and young women here in this room now; when we are full we have about 120. There are no males beside myself and a lad. Very few of the girls are under 14. At that age we apprentice them for 7 years. Their hours are from 8 a.m. to 7 p.m., with one hour for dinner at 1 p.m. At that hour they leave on Saturdays. These hours are occasionally exceeded, but we never go on after 9. We give the learners about 2s a week at first; after the first year they are paid by the hundred; in the second year they have 6d for every 100, and rise

1d a hundred in each succeeding year of their apprenticeship. Of course their earnings vary with their skill and industry. Here you see those in their third year earned in this week some 3s, some 8s., and some even 10s. In the sixth year some of them earned 17s and even £1 a week.

They are below the class of dressmakers. Their parents are chiefly poor people, labourers and the like, to whom their earnings are very useful. There is not much education amongst them. One-half of those here perhaps are able to read; certainly not one-half can write. None, that I know of, ever went to a night school; they prefer walking about the streets, and going to places of amusement, to improving themselves.

We do not allow singing or talking; they are fined if they do so. Their health is generally good; at first they may be sicklish for a day or two, but it soon goes off. Indeed the trade is noted for being free from the plague and cholera, when others in the town were attacked. The girls have, some of them, fainting or hysterical fits now and then; I think they are in connexion with their monthly periods and not with an effect of the tobacco. This room is close at times, it is badly contrived for such purposes; there are windows in the sloping roof, they do not open, but are only for light. Indeed, on a hot summer day it is boiling nearly.

Mr Steel.—What my foreman has told you is generally correct . . . He should have pointed out to you that the shutters in the vertical part of the roof open, though the windows do not; the door at the further end of the room opens also to the street at the back; it is their own fault if they do not have air enough. But they complain of cold and draught, and put things over their heads, if the windows are open for ten minutes. They are a singularly careless, unreasoning set. I have talked time after time to them about the propriety of putting by a little of their earnings to buy a pair of boots or an umbrella. There is scarcely an umbrella among them, and they come to work in the morning or from dinner on a rainy day dripping wet sometimes, and so will sit and work. It is that, and not anything in the work-place, or the nature of the work, that is likely to make them ill.

I started a savings' bank for the express purpose of helping them to put by a few pence a week to buy some useful article of clothing or the like—got a ledger, and opened a regular account; but I never had more than 10 or 12 of them, and they never left their money for more than a few weeks; but they preferred to spend their earnings on ribbons and ear-rings and worthless trinkets, or in going to places of amusement where they had better not be.

For one or two winters I used to let them have woollen polka jackets to work in so as to be warm; but so many in a few days disappeared into the pawn shops, that I shall not repeat that.

We have a system of fines for being late and for misbehaviour; 2d is the usual sum; these accumulate, and are divided at the end of each month among those who have not been fined. Last month the fines amounted to £3 16s. and were divided among twenty.

We suffer very much from robbery. We lose several hundred pounds worth every year, but we can never detect any one. We have a female searcher, who now and then stops one, as they pass out; but before there is time to do more, several other girls are round them and a packet of tobacco or cigars is found on the floor beneath their dresses; but no one can say from which it fell . . .

(Of seven or eight girls whom I examined here, I found only one who did not know her letters. The youngest I saw was about 12 years of age. Some told me that they were very tired when 9 o'clock came, but did not mind the sitting for the ordinary day's work. One, however, of about 25, whose duty it was to weigh the cigars, told me that she had herself been obliged to give up making cigars, because the sitting so long at the table gave her a pain in her side. Others, she said, had suffered more or less in the same way, and most were sick at first beginning; still she did not think the business unhealthy . . . H. W. L.)

From MR LORD'S report on Tobacco Manufacture; *op. cit.*, pp. 91–92; P.P. 1865, vol. 20.

25

Night and Day in the Paper Mills

Persons of both sexes are employed in paper mills. Returns received from 25 show that out a total of 4,642 as many as 2,454 are females, of whom 624 are under eighteen, 104 being under thirteen years of age . . .

Females of all ages are employed in cutting and sorting rags, or cotton waste. They stand for this purpose at long, narrow tables, each having a separate pit of rags and space of the table for herself, part of the latter being hollow and covered with open wire so as to allow the dust to fall through, as the sorter picks or cuts the rags above it. A short strong knife, in some cases part of an old scythe, is fixed upright in the table, the edge being turned from the cutter, who reaches over with one end of the rag in each hand and drags it against the sharp edge. They seem to cut their fingers very often at first, but not very seriously.

Rags are in many cases dusted by means of steam power, before or after they are cut; where 'bagging' and old ropes are used, they are chopped by machinery. The 'duster' in the former case is like a large squirrel cage fitted with spikes inside and raised at one end; the 'chopper' is an open wheel, the outer felloe of which is armed with knives and revolves at the mouth of a small trough-like feeder. These are sometimes fed by boys and girls as young as 12 or 13. It is in this department that the worst dust arises; some wear a handkerchief over their mouth and nose, but many do not adopt even that precaution.

In some mills the youngest sweep up—a very dusty operation in a paper mill, and one in continual requisition. Children also sort refuse paper and shavings, the cuttings of stationers and book-binders, to be made up again. Women are likewise occupied in picking and chopping African or other grass; for the latter purpose a kind of chaff-cutter is used.

After the rags are cut and sorted, they are boiled in huge iron vessels; these are filled in some cases by women. The number of the subsequent processes, and the order in which they proceed, depend upon the nature of the article to be produced, and in different mills different modes prevail . . .

The ordinary hours of work in paper mills are different in different districts, but for all the processes through which the material passes night work is . . . the common practice. This work is continued by relays without cessation through the week, usually from twelve on Sunday night to twelve on the following Saturday night . . . Sometimes only one meal is taken during the twelve night hours . . . supper at 10 p.m. and 'a drop of tea and a wash' at 4 a.m. . . .

The Resident Surgeon at the West Kent Hospital, Maidstone, informed me that the accidents at paper mills which came before him were seldom more than cut fingers, the worst cases being those caused by the cutting-machine, when the top joints were taken off . . . Fingers are often nipped and 'broken', in feeding the rollers or in leading the sheets of paper through the cylinders. Sometimes serious accidents occur . . . Horizontal shafting along the floor and unfenced cog wheels are especially dangerous where women work. Crinoline is forbidden in several mills on this account. Cases have been mentioned to me of women being killed through being caught by the back of their dress as they stooped or stepped back for a temporary purpose . . .

The rate of wages varies with the district, the highest being probably that which prevails in Kent, and the lowest that in Buckinghamshire . . . Rag cutters are paid by the piece, the weekly earnings of a child from 11 to 13 may be taken at about 4s.; that of a young woman of sixteen, 8s. They often purchase their knives from their employers for 1s. 6d., which they pay back by deduction of 3d. a week from their wages. Some make their knives last six weeks, and some six months . . .

MR LORD'S report on Paper Mills; 4th Report, *op. cit.*, pp. 142–147; P.P. 1865, vol. 20.

26

Girls in Pickle

Messrs Crosse & Blackwell, Sauce and Pickle Manufacturers, 20 & 21 Soho Square, London: The next step in our investigation was to mount to the pickle-filling department of the establishment . . . Here square street-like lamps were burning in the middle of the day, for the room was large and low, and being built at the back part of the premises where but little light could enter, gas was a necessity for the work to be done . . . This gallery was crowded with a bevy of women, ranged in front of the long counters, whereat they were one and all busily engaged in packing up the mound of pickles before them into the well-known square bottles, ready to their hands, which, together with their arms, almost up to the elbows, were as yellow with the juice of the pickled vegetables they were handling as the legs of game-cocks.

On the board before each was either a hillock of primrose-coloured cauliflower-sprouts, or a mound of white onions like so many glass marbles, or a small heap of huge olive green caterpillar-like gherkins. One of the girls was busy packing these as carefully as possible, by means of what is called the 'pickle-stick', into the square bottle before her and arranging them so as to be neither too tightly nor yet too loosely stowed within it. The next young woman was filling in gherkins, and taking care to place a bright red Chili at either side of the bottle, so as to give a more showy and striking effect to the olive-green colour of the cucumber-sprouts. Others were filling in long narrow pods of French beans . . .

In this pickle-filling gallery some seventy women are employed. They each of them fill 100 bottles a day, even of such pickles as require more care in the arrangement; whereas those who are engaged in filling the bottles for mixed pickles for piccalilli can do as many as 288 daily . . .

From the pickle-gallery we were conducted to the labelling and packing rooms. At one end of the apartments were girls engaged in pasting on the bottles the labels descriptive of the several kinds of pickles which we had seen bottled below. Some here had a pail beside them on a stool, and were busily occupied in washing the outside of the bottles before the labels were affixed. The duty of others was to stick such labels on the bottles as corresponded with their contents, while others again were engaged in wrapping the washed and labelled vessels in whitey-brown paper, stamped with the imprint of the firm, and ready to be distributed all over the kingdom. These girls, we were assured, could wash and label more than 500 bottles *per diem.*

HENRY MAYHEW, *The Shops and Companies of London,* etc. (1865), page 182.

27

A Job behind the Counter?

Saleswomen in shops. This is a good employment for a strong young person. A tall figure is considered an advantage, and the power of standing for many hours is requisite. A good deal of fatigue has to be undergone at first, but a shop girl told me that after a few weeks, they get so used to standing it seems as natural as sitting. The life is far more healthy to most persons than that of a dressmaker.

The power of making out a bill with great rapidity and perfect accuracy is also necessary, and this is the point where women usually fail. A poor half-educated girl keeps a customer waiting while she is trying to add up the bill, or perhaps does it wrong, and in either case excites reasonable displeasure. This displeasure is expressed to the master of the establishment, who dismisses the offender and engages a well-educated man in her place. He pays him double wages, but then feels sure that his assistant will not drive away customers by his incapacity.

Parents who intend their daughters to become saleswomen should take care that they are thoroughly proficient in arithmetic. Good manners are also requisite . . . the higher the class of shop, the more obliging and polished the manners of the assistants are expected to be. The slightest want of politeness to customers, even if they are themselves unreasonable and rude, is a breach of honesty towards the owner of the establishment, for if customers are offended they are likely enough to withdraw to some other shop. No one, therefore, ought to enter on this employment who does not possess entire self-command.

Salaries from £20 to £50 a year, with board and lodging. These situations are usually obtained by private recommendation.

EMILY FAITHFULL, tract on *Choice of a Business for Girls* (1864)

28

Mr Bennett Had to Sack His Young Ladies

———

Mr Bennett [of Cheapside, London], who has laboured so earnestly to open the manufacture of watches to women, told us an anecdote the other day, which illustrates at once the difficulties women have to contend with (from the other sex, we are sorry to say), in making their way into a sphere of labour hitherto considered sacred to the men, and the success that attended their courageous efforts.

Three young ladies, after a preliminary training at the Marlborough House School of Design, applied to him for occupation in engraving the backs of gold watches. Although perfect strangers to this kind of work, in six months, he tells us, they became as practised artists as a mere apprentice would have been in six years. At the end of this time, when they were making each three pounds a week by their labour, the men in the shop struck. These 'foreigners', as they were termed, must go, or *they* would; and Mr Bennett was obliged, sadly against his will, to comply with their wishes. These brave girls, however, were not to be beaten; they immediately turned their attention to engraving on glass, and are now employed at this delicate employment, and earn as much thereat as they did before at watch engraving. What these young girls did, thousands of well-educated young ladies may do also . . .

Mrs Grundy would doubtless turn up her nose at intelligent and educated Englishwomen directing their attention to a mechanical trade, forgetting that shirtmaking also is a mechanical trade, and that the needle and thimble are as much tools as the fine implements used in watch-making; nay, and much coarser tools too . . . It is in vain that we sing the *Song of the Shirt*, and get up annual subscriptions for down-stricken sempstresses. It is in vain that we hold midnight tea-meetings to tempt Lorettes from their evil courses; as long as we shut young women out from honourable means of employment, so long will their labour be a drug in the market, and their degradation but too facile a matter to the tempter.

ANDREW WYNTER, M.D.; *Our Social Bees; or, Pictures of Town and Country Life* (1869), pp. 269–272.

29

When Married Women Work in Factories

Factory women soon return to labour after their confinement. The longest time mentioned as the average period of their absence from work in consequence of childbearing was five or six weeks; many women amongst the highest class of operatives in Birmingham acknowledged to having generally returned to work at the expiration of a month; and it was stated by several medical men of great experience, and by other witnesses in Coventry and Blackburn, that the factory women even sometimes return to work as early as eight or ten days or a fortnight after their confinement . . .

Mothers employed in factories are, save during the dinner-hour, absent from home all day long, and the care of their infants during their absence is entrusted either to young children, to hired nurse-girls, sometimes not more than eight or ten years of age, or perhaps more commonly to elderly women, who eke out a livelihood by taking infants to nurse. Young girls, aged seven or eight years, are frequently removed from school for the purpose of taking charge of younger children while the mother is absent at work, and are sometimes said to return, on the death of the child, evidently rather pleased that this event has released them from their toil . . .

Children left by their mothers during so great a part of the day are fed in their absence on artificial food, which is for the most part unsuited to their digestive powers. The children are thus almost entirely spoon-fed, the mother being able to nurse them only at night, perhaps hastily early in the morning before setting out for the mill, again at dinner-time, and no more until evening . . .

Pap, made of bread and water, and sweetened with sugar or treacle, is the sort of nourishment usually given during the mother's absence, even to infants of a very tender age, and in several instances little children, not more than 6 or 7 years old, were seen preparing and feeding babies with this food, which in such cases consisted only of lumps of bread floating in sweetened water . . .

Illness is the natural consequence of this unnatural mode of feeding infants . . . Children who are healthy at birth rapidly dwindle under this system of mismanagement, fall into bad health, and become uneasy, restless, and fractious. To remedy the illness caused by mismanagement, various domestic medicines are administered, such as Godfrey's cordial, or laudanum. Wine, gin, peppermint, and other stimulants are likewise often given, for the purpose, as alleged, of relieving flatulence, their actual effect being, however, rather to stupefy the child. The quantity of opiates sold for the purpose of being administered to infants in some of the manufacturing towns is very large ... Women when remonstrated with on the subject of drugging their children with laudanum, say that they must keep their infants quiet, as their husbands and elder children, who have to work during the day, cannot do so if disturbed at night ...

Parents who thus entrust the management of their infants so largely to strangers become more or less careless and indifferent about them, and speak of the deaths of their children with a degree of nonchalance rarely met with among women who devote themselves mainly to the care of their offspring ...

DR GREENHOW; Privy Council Medical Reports, No. 4 (1861); P.P. 1861, vol. 16.

30

Cold Feet and Round Shoulders

————————

The women employed in the manufacture of lace in Towcester and Newport Pagnell work for 9, 10, or 12 hours per day, and occasionally even longer. The work is done in the cottage during the greater portion of the year ... During the winter, when the women work entirely within doors, every crevice or chink through which a draught of air could find entrance is carefully stopped. The women are said very rarely to leave the immediate vicinity of their dwellings and to take but little exercise in the open air, and that for the most part late in the evening, regardless of weather, and often very imperfectly clad.

The inmates of neighbouring cottages sometimes assemble in the same room to work in company, particularly at night, when artificial light is required, a single candle thus serving for several workers, each of whom has a globe filled with water, supported on a wooden stand, placed between the candle and her work, upon which it concentrates the light ...

Their sedentary mode of life renders the women liable to cold feet in the winter season; to obviate which annoyance many of them are accustomed to place a sort of chafing dish, filled with embers from the fire, or, it was said, with ignited charcoal, beneath their dress, a practice which, of course, tends to vitiate the atmosphere of their small, ill-ventilated cottages . . .

Lace is made upon circular pillows or cushions, stuffed with straw, which rest at one side upon a sort of wooden frame, and at the other upon the knees of the worker, who is thus compelled to maintain a more or less constrained position . . . The cushions are usually placed so low that the worker is compelled to stoop over her work, and the arms being continually brought forward, in order to enable the women to handle the bobbins, lacemakers are apt to become round-shouldered, and, their chests being contracted, the act of respiration, particularly when the cushion rests on the knee, is not freely and efficiently performed.

Privy Council Medical Reports, No. 4 (1861).

31

Evesham's Gloveresses

Rev. G. R. Dallas Walsh, Curate of Evesham and Chaplain to the Rt. Hon. Dowager Lady Vivian:—The trade of glove making is carried on to a very large extent in Evesham and the parishes roundabout, and it is followed by a large section of females, who are either too proud, or too lazy, to follow more arduous employments. I am of opinion, and it is the opinion of medical men, that it is by no means a healthy occupation; five or six, and often many more, living shut up in a small, badly ventilated room, stooping over their frames, and breathing an impure atmosphere for from 10 to 14 hours together; the consequence of this is, that they all appear most contracted in the chest, and generally complain of pain in the side and chest; in appearance they are deathly pale, or have a fixed high colour, which is not natural. The parents take their children away from school at a very early age, and compel them to work at gloving in the house, and in many cases they do not go to school after 8 years, but are at once put to gloving.

There is no doubt about it but that many evils arise out of the gloving. The women are allowed to take the work into their own houses, and consequently they are left free from anything like superintendence, or moral responsibility to their employers. Indeed, I imagine the employers look merely to the quality of the work, rather than anything connected with their moral conduct. The houses in which the gloving is carried on are generally gossip shops, and in many cases schools for scandal, and training places for immorality, from the tone of the language carried on there. They are also, as a rule, very dirty and untidy.

There is very little animal food consumed by the gloveresses; their meals consist chiefly of tea and bread and butter, and this arises from the sedentary life they lead, which naturally affects their appetite and digestion. They are in the habit of sitting close at the frames from 10 to 14 hours a day; the wages a first hand can earn is 4s per doz. pair for Dent's best gloves, and the ordinary gloveresses earn from 2s 6d to 3s per doz. pair. It is only a most expert first hand that can stitch three pairs in the day, but the average is one dozen per week, i.e. 3s or 4s per week per hand. If one of the gloveresses spoil a pair of gloves in any way, she is charged the full retail price, 3s 6d per pair, and the spoiled gloves are thrown on her hands.

In the schools we find that those girls, with whom we have the greatest difficulty in maintaining order and good discipline, are those who belong to gloving families. They leave school at much earlier age than in other cases; in fact, as soon as they can sit at the frames. I have heard of cases in which girls have been put to gloving as early as 7, but 8 is a common age to begin gloving. It is a very common thing to find numbers of girls here from 20 to 30, who cannot even write their names, and yet all these might have received a good education, and far superior to that of the older women, owing to the national schools having been built, when they were small, and of an age to attend school.

With regard to the effect the gloving trade has upon the morals of the young women in Evesham and the neighbourhood, I am sorry to be in a position to state that the far greater number of them lead very immoral lives; it is well known that many girls commence an early life of sin, being ruined as early as 14 or 15 years of age. This no doubt arises from the neglect of the parents, and from their improvident habits; and I believe the parents do not care what the girls do, as long as they can get anything to support themselves. And what they get from the gloving is not sufficient to support them, so that they will sin with anyone, who will give them the means of gratifying their inordinate love of dress.

There is very little open prostitution in the town. I am informed on reliable authority there are not more than three or four, who openly walk the streets to solicit prostitution. I find the number of illegitimate births remarkably few and on the decrease; but that proves nothing as to an increased state of morality: I think it rather tells the other way; indeed, I have no hesitation in saying that the young girls, from the age of 14, who are engaged in gardening and gloving, are highly immoral, and that a great amount of immorality ensues from the intermixture of the sexes during the seasons of asparagus tying, pea picking, and plum gathering.

I fear that the glove-making is to the young girls of Evesham and the neighbourhood, what the millinery is to the young women in London and the other large cities, a cloke for prostitution *sub rosa*. In consequence of this an inordinate love of dress is fostered, and they will do anything to get finery to make themselves attractive to the young men; besides, the young women having sat from 10 to 14 hours closely, go out about dusk, just at the time the young men are about after the gardening is over, and you will see in an evening all the streets and favourite places of resort crowded with gaily dressed girls; and this is seen especially on Sunday afternoons, and evenings, when they are walking about with young men, and I fear that by the conversation, that the younger ones hear in the cottages at work, their minds are very early polluted, so they fall an easy prey on the first opportunity.

As regards the morals of the older women, who are gloveresses and work in the gardens, many of them are of very drunken habits (worse, if possible, than the men), and dead to all sense of shame, and these, I fear, are a great cause of the immorality of the younger girls; they do not care anything about their children as long as they can indulge their propensity to drink ...

MR H. W. LORD; Children's Employment Commission, 2nd Report, pp. 179–180; P.P. 1864, vol. 22.

Of all the female workers whose conditions were examined by the assistant commissioners of the successive Government inquiries, those employed in the open air—on pit-banks and in iron workings and brickfields—seem to have aroused the deepest concern. Mixed with the concern was a good deal of surprise. They *ought* to have been utterly miserable, these women and girls who worked out of doors in all weathers, who were so inadequately clad, whose food was prepared and eaten anyhow. And yet, as often as not, they were not in the least depressed. On the contrary, they were remarkably jolly, they loved a joke—the rougher and ruder the better—and they were always singing the latest songs that had come their way.

32

'Degrading Employment of Females'

The employment of females upon the 'pit banks and cinder tips' has long been pointed out as one degrading to the female character. The kind of attire rendered necessary by the masculine nature of the employment, and the blackness and dirt with which these females cannot avoid being covered, can scarcely fail to undermine their modesty and self-respect, while it is notorious that their association with the coarse description of men employed in that branch of labour, exposes them to every deteriorating influence of language, manners, and habits. It has been constantly asserted by every well-wisher of the improvement of the working classes in those districts, that the continuance of this mode of employing females is most injurious to the progress of good morals, and to every domestic virtue and comfort; and that a general agreement among the employers to put an end to it is one of the steps most urgently required to be adopted by them.

To this masculine species of employment these females go as soon as they are old enough to be of any use, after having learnt at school scarcely anything calculated to be of service to them in the employments of domestic life, seeing in their homes very little by the example of which they are likely to profit. A woman of this class, so brought up, marries probably before she is twenty or soon after. What is she able to do towards the management of a house, and towards making her husband happy and comfortable? 1. She does not know how to keep a house clean and tidy. 2. She cannot cook. 3. She knows nothing of the management required to make her husband's earnings go as far as possible. 4. She is ignorant of the proper management of children.

So sensible are the men of the value of these qualities in a wife, that according to a gentleman who has been conversant with these districts for many years, 'they look out for wives among the girls who have been in domestic service; these are sure to find husbands, and nearly every tidy house is that of a woman who has been in service'.

MR H. S. TREMENHEERE; Report on South Wales mining district (1856), pp. 27–28; P.P. 1856, vol. 18.

33

Good-looking Welsh Women

Mr George Thomas Clark, a trustee of the Dowlais Ironworks, employing between 8,000 and 9,000 persons.—We employ a considerable number of women and children. I suppose we shall cease to employ them soon . . . and I am very glad of it. I think it a monstrous thing that a woman should be working on the hillside, and exposed, on a wet day . . .

Strange to say, the women so employed, do not become prematurely old. If you were to see on Sunday these Welsh women who work out in the open air you would find they look as healthy as possible. We have, or had until the last few months, a large industrial school, where 80 or 90 of the women came in the evening to sew. They come in their working dresses, and all we require is that they shall wash their hands and faces, and if you were to see them sitting round the table and singing as they work (the Welsh are very musical) I think you would feel convinced that they were in a very respectable state of health . . .

The Welsh women employed in out-of-door labour do not age nearly as much as I should have expected, but . . . it must be remembered that they are not women alone in the world; they are for the most part either the wives, or more generally still the daughters of the men employed, and the whole family earnings go together, and in that way the family do very well. The Welsh in the immediate neighbourhood of the iron-works do very well. If you go up the main street of a Merthyr Ironwork you see the fire, the chest of drawers, and the clock, and other signs of a great deal of comfort . . .

Trades Unions Commission, 5th Report (1868), page 85: P.P. 1867/8, vol. 39.

34
Jolly Breaks in the Pit-girls' Life

Of the groups engaged [at a colliery] above ground, the most remarkable are composed of the young women who work on the pit-mounds: they take charge of the 'skips', or baskets of coal and ironstone, when they are landed on the bank. They load the coal in trucks to be carried off to its destination. They separate the ironstone from the shale, which is wheeled off to the extremity of the gradually increasing mound, and they send off the ore to be stacked in large quadrangular heaps, where it is left to undergo, for a while, the cleansing influence of the atmosphere.

This is heavy and dirty work, and the pit-girls who are engaged in it, with their shabby dresses tied grotesquely about them, and their inverted bonnets stuck on the top of their heads, seem not less sordid. But before the philanthropist draws his conclusions, let him see them on Sunday (we wish it were an equivalent phrase to say at church), with clean persons, bright complexions, sparkling eyes, and dressed out in the cheap finery which now-a-days levels all distinctions of costume.

The labour of the pit-mound is severe, and is not regularly undertaken by those who are mothers; but the workwomen have an air of robust health, and the beauty and number of the children in the cottages prove that the constitution of the mothers has not been injured by over-work in early life. 'Huge women,' are they, 'blowsed with sun, and wind, and rain, and labour' (Tennyson's *Princess*). But strange to say, there are to be found among them forms of great refinement and delicacy . . .

The pit-girls are not less fond of holidays than their fathers, and much they enjoy the two days of saturnalia when, by immemorial custom, the field of labour is turned into a scene of general riot. On Easter Monday the men roam about the colliery in gangs, and claim the privilege of heaving, as they call it, every female whom they may meet,— that is to say, of lifting her up as high as they can, and saluting her in her descent. On Easter Tuesday the ladies have their revenge—and in their hands this strange horseplay acquires redoubled energy. Neither rank nor age are respected; not even the greatest of men, the manager himself, would be secure from attack; and those who will not enter into the fun must purchase exemption by a ransom proportionate to their station.

If the reader desires to see a specimen of the pit-girls he need not travel to the Black Country for the purpose. In the fruit season they come up in gangs to gather the contents of the suburban wilderness of summer fruits, which are grown for the consumption of voracious London. In the meantime they are much missed by the iron-master at home; but whether, if he could, he would have the cruelty to stop their expedition to the lands of verdure, can never be ascertained. For these fair heroines have a will of their own, and by that will alone they choose to be guided.

It is interesting to watch the departure of one of these parties as they troop down to the railway station, attended by their friends, relations, and sweethearts. Each errant damsel is accompanied by her swain to carry her bundle and offer her those little attentions which the fair ones of the Black Country can seldom command from the stronger sex. Her eyes sparkle with anticipated pleasure and present triumph, but the air of her attendant is humble and downcast. Perhaps his coquettish love has hinted she may find a more fitting mate in the south, and who can tell but she may keep her word? She would not be the first by a great many, who has been persuaded to do so by a smart policeman or some other great match in the great town. With melancholy and anxious gaze he follows the train as it whirls off. Perhaps some bystander, who himself is heart whole, ventures to joke with the disconsolate lover, but it is no joking matter. In moody silence he turns away to the nearest alehouse to find solid comfort in 'a glass of something', and of course not another stroke of work is done that day.

At the disembarkation of the party on their return, as the third-class train stops at the station the crowds jostling each other on the platform to greet them create a hubbub such as might be occasioned by a statute-fair or a horse-race. Each pit-girl carries on her head a huge bundle tied up in a sheet, like dirty linen for the washerwoman. It is not that she could not afford a trunk, and a handsome one, too, if she so pleased; but the sheet is more elastic, and more portable, and in it she has stowed all the investments which she has made of her earnings in foreign parts, and the commissions which she has executed for some of those who are so anxiously expecting her return . . .

Pit-mound labour is stigmatized by many well-meaning reformers as not only 'unfeminine', but also conducive to immorality. But to this we demur. The labour on the pit-mound in the open air is not degrading, it does not bring the workwomen into unseemly association with the men, nor does it expose them to the contamination of coarse language. They hear on the pit-mounds exactly the language they would hear at home, and much less of it, for work is not favourable to conversation. Regular occupation, and habits of independence and self-protection are not unfavourable to the preservation of female virtue among the working-classes; and in fact statistical returns prove that the morality of the colliery is quite equal to that of any rural district. Much may be done to improve the condition of the poor pit-girl, but it would be an ill beginning to deprive her of her bread.

From an article on 'The Black Country' in *The Edinburgh Review*, April 1863.

35

Clay-splashed Females in the Brickyards

I consider that in brickyards the degradation of the female character is most complete . . . One may, in fact, scarcely recognize, either in her person or the mind and manner of the female clay-worker, a feature of the sex to which she belongs . . . I have seen females of all ages, nineteen or twenty together (some of them mothers of families), undistinguishable from men, excepting by the occasional peeping out of an earring, sparsely clad, up to the bare knees in clay splashes, and evidently without a vestige of womanly delicacy, thus employed, until it makes one feel for the honour of a country that there should be such a condition of human labour existing in it.

I questioned one such group in a brickyard in South Staffordshire as to how many of them could read, and found that only one out of twenty was so qualified; and out of the whole number, she only had been to a place of worship on the Sunday previously, the whole of them being partially employed on Sundays, as well as week-days, in 'battening', 'turning bricks', or 'earthing the kiln'. But lest my evidence should seem partial, or as seen only through the medium of inspectorship, permit a master brick-maker to give his own version of the story.

'I am a brick and tile manufacturer and sanitary pipe maker, in the neighbourhood of Tipton, midway from Birmingham and Wolverhampton. I employ about fifty workpeople, about half of whom are women and children. I am opposed, however, to the employment of women and children in clay works and have made many efforts to dispense with their labour, but have always found insuperable obstacles in that direction . . .

'The moral evils consequent on the employment of women and young girls in clay works, are very serious, very general, and most disastrous to their well-being . . . A flippancy and familiarity of manners with boys and men, grows daily in the young girls. Then, the want of respect and delicacy towards females exhibits itself in every act, word, and look; for the lads are so precocious and the girls so coarse in their language and manners from close companionship at work, that in most cases, the modesty of female life gradually becomes a byeword instead of a reality, and they sing unblushingly before all, whilst at work, the lewdest and most disgusting songs, till oftentimes stopped short by the entrance of the master or foreman.

'The overtime work is still more objectionable, because boys and girls, men and women, are not then so much under the watchful eye of the master, nor looked upon by the eye of day.

'All these things, the immorality, levity and coarse pleasures, awful oaths, lewd gestures, and conduct of the adults and youths, exercise a terrible influence for evil on the young children. Hence, a generation full of evil phrases, manners, and thoughts is daily growing up in our midst, without the knowledge of better things.

'It is quite common for girls employed in brickyards to have illegitimate children. Of the thousands whom I have met with, or known as working, I should say that one in every four, who had arrived at the age of twenty, had had an illegitimate child. Several have had three or four, and it is a deplorable fact that, as a rule, brick manufacturers do not trouble themselves to inquire into the moral character of either women or children, when they employ them. I have found myself often looked upon as an oddity, when I have asked "Is she of good character?", and have been subjected to very sharp criticism when I have discharged a single woman, because she was palpably enceinte.'

ROBERT BAKER's report; Reports of Inspectors of Factories, half-year to October 31, 1864, pp. 120–124; P.P. 1865, vol. 20.

36

'Anything new in the way of a song'

Mr Thomas Wheat, yard-master at Messrs E. Baker & Co.'s Fire Brick Works, Moor Lane, Brierly Hill, Stourbridge.—My duty is to give orders, see that the work is done, give any that need it 'the sack', &c., and manage the work. The hours of work are from 6 a.m. till 6 p.m., and there is seldom any overtime for the girls, though the men who fire the kilns work at night. Some of the girls, most of about 15, carry off for the women who mould, one to each, and are paid by the 1,000, or about 10d a day. Others of about fourteen, 8d a day wenches, carry away bricks from the stoves; others, or young women, fill carts . . .

The 'pages', girls, come for about an hour every Sunday morning to turn the bricks. They would stay ever so long if I did not send them off. . . . It is pretty healthy work. They are all under cover, which is the great thing, and are always running about. They are always singing. If there is anything new in the way of a song they are bound to have it. They are generally pretty steady, but in such works as this, where the wenches are all in rucks together, they are cheeky. If any, however, misbehaved in any way with the chaps they would be dismissed. Some are butty colliers' daughters, and have got money in the bank. Those who are at the carts can read the numbers of the bricks on the cards, or if all cannot, some of the youngest can for them. I think that all the young go to Sunday schools. The clergyman is often down here.

Children's Employment Commission, 3rd Report (1864), page 139; P.P. 1864, vol. 22.

37

'Foul-mouthed boys before they are women'

Although the work is extremely laborious, it does not seem to be, generally speaking, unhealthy. The elder women speak of it as being 'mauling' work for girls, but it seems that the girls when inured to it prefer it much to the low kind of domestic service open to them.

The evil of the system of employing young girls at this work consists in its binding them from their infancy, as a general rule, to the most degraded lot in after life. They become rough, foul-mouthed boys before nature has taught them that they are women. Clad in a few dirty rags, their bare legs exposed far above the knees, their hair and faces covered with mud, they learn to treat with contempt all feelings of modesty and decency. During the dinner-hour they may be seen lying about the yards asleep, or watching the boys bathing in some adjoining canal. When their work is over they dress themselves in better clothes and accompany the men to the beershops ...

From MR F. D. LONGE'S report on the Brickfields of Staffordshire; 5th Report, Children's Employment Commission (1866), page 152; P.P. 1866, vol. 24.

38

'They have to stoop down ...'

A brickfield is certainly not the place for girls and young women to work in; a great deal of swearing goes on, and other improper language; the work they have to do too, at least those who are pug-bearers, often causes indecency; they have to stoop down to the ground to pick the pug up from the bottom of the mill; at all events they ought to have their clothes tied round them, indeed the respectable young women have.

Mr Dean, foreman at Mr Scott's brickfield, Sittingbourne, Kent; Report on Brickfields by MR H. W. LORD; Children's Employment Commission, 5th Report (1866), page 143; P.P. 1866, vol. 24.

39

'The girl's virtue is gone ...'

I am quite convinced that the employment of girls in brickfields has a very bad and demoralizing effect upon them; in the first place, they begin young, and work hard all their lives there, and never know how to cook, or wash, or mend clothes, and can never make good housewives; at the same time, as they grow up into young women, they are thrown into contact with young men, working, so to speak, side by side, —for the walk-flatter is often a young woman, and the off-bearer a young man of 17 or 18 and upwards.

Granting that they work perhaps under their parent's eye in the field—and the moulder's gang usually consists more or less of members of his family—still when there happens to be a fair or a race or any other amusement in the neighbourhood, they go off there together, or meet there, and too often the girl's virtue is gone before her holiday is over. I think, however, I can safely say that marriage follows in eight out of ten such cases.

MR H. W. LORD, reporting on Mr Smeed's brickfields, Sittingbourne; 5th Report, Children's Employment Commission, page 142; P.P. 1866, vol. 24.

(e) WOMEN IN AGRICULTURE

Ever since the English shires were marked out by the Saxon invaders, women have shared in the work of the fields. Whichever the century we may select, we must include these female drudges in the picture, bent double over the weeding, dressed in tatterdemalion garments, their heads and shoulders scantily covered against the wind and sleet by old sacks, their skirts sodden to the waist, their heavy boots clogged with mud.

No one took any particular notice of them: the legislature certainly didn't. They were so ordinary, and besides, since they worked alongside their men, any official concern with their welfare would have been resented as an unwarrantable interference with male prerogatives. A man should be left to look after his own ...

In the 1840s some attention was called to them when the manufacturers, anxious to deflect the limelight from their factories, sought to expose the shocking conditions in which the peasantry lived and worked. In particular the 'gang system' came in for some harsh criticism. But nothing was done to improve their lot until 1862 when Lord Shaftesbury moved in the House of Lords for a further inquiry into the conditions of labour of children, young persons, and women. This was agreed to, and a series of most informative reports were issued, from which we have drawn a number of 'documents' in earlier pages. In 1865 Shaftesbury moved that the 'gang system' should receive particular investigation, with the result that Tremenheere and Tufnell, the Royal Commissioners, devoted the whole of their 6th Report to it. Mr J. E. White carried out the special inquiry, and No. 40 is taken from his report.

Nor was this all. The state of the agricultural proletariat was now the subject of widespread concern, and in 1867 another Royal Commission was appointed, composed as before of Tremenheere and Tufnell, to inquire into the employment of children, young persons, and women in Agriculture. Four reports were published. The first two (1868 and 1869) were concerned with England, the third (1870) with Wales, and the fourth (1871) with Scotland. Worthy of special note is the fact that the Commissioners found it desirable to include men in their investigations, and so for the first time the condition of the whole body of agricultural labour came under official review. Referring to the extracts given here, the Rev. James Fraser (No. 44) was a country parson near Reading until 1870, when, because of the interest he had shown in public education, etc., he was appointed by Mr Gladstone bishop of Manchester; and in No. 46 we have an account of a very peculiar survival in our countryside.

Following upon these disclosures, the gang system was brought under control by the Gangs Act of 1868, and before the century was out it had become a thing of the past.

Perhaps it may be added that at the time these Reports were being published, Karl Marx was pursuing his studies in the Reading Room of the British Museum, and some of the most readable pages in *Das Kapital* are based on their revelations, particularly concerning the 'gang system'. Among the attractions of the gangs (he noted) were 'coarse freedom, jolly indiscipline, and obscene impudence', and he described the 'close' villages from which their members were drawn as so many 'Sodoms and Gomorrahs'.

40

Women and Girls of the 'Gangs'

By an agricultural gang is meant a number of persons, men, women, girls, lads, and boys, employed by and under the control of one person, who lets them out to different farmers in turn for certain kinds of work. In some of these gangs the males and females work together, in other gangs they work separately. The first of these systems is most common. A gang will number from twelve to thirty persons. The age of those employed will vary from eight years, and sometimes even younger, to grown up and married persons.

The gangs are employed in hoeing up or removing by hand-picking weeds of various kinds, especially twitch, red weed, docks, and thistles; stone picking, hoeing up and thinning out turnips, swedes, and mangolds, and topping and tailing them. The duration of labour [is] generally from 8 in the morning to 5 in the afternoon, but the gang may be kept later, as the gangman marks out in the morning a certain amount of land, which must be cleaned, hoed, or the crop thereon topped and tailed before he dismisses his gang. One hour is granted for dinner in the middle of the day.

The gang will often have to walk three, four, five, or even more miles before it commences its work, and will have in the evening to return the same distance. As the gang however is sometimes made up of persons from different villages, some of these may have even further to go.

The rate of wages [is] 4d. a day to children, 8d. to lads, girls, women, and even men. These latter however seldom belong to a gang, unless partially disabled by illness or some infirmity and incapable of performing the full amount of work required from an able-bodied man.

The advantage of the gang to the farmer or employer is that it enables him to dispense with a certain number of labourers ... he is able to procure assistance exactly at the time he requires it, and the work is quickly and expeditiously done. Another advantage is, the gangman acts as foreman or overlooker without receiving any extra pay for so doing ...

The gangman makes his profit in this way. Generally he takes a field at so much per acre for the work to be done; he then divides it according to the number of his gang into so many hours' or days' work, requiring from each person employed a full day's work, and paying a proportionally smaller day's wage than would otherwise be obtained. Thus, if a lad could earn 6d. a day, the gangman pays him only 4d., putting into his pocket 2d. a day, or 1s. a week. Thus the gangman over a gang of 15 or 20 persons can make an addition to his own week's wages from 15s. to £1. This comes entirely out of the earnings of those employed, and saves the employer the expense of a foreman or bailiff ...

From what I have stated it is clear that the persons employed are deprived of part of their fairly earned wages. Besides this, they have often, to use a Norfolk phrase, 'to play', that is, to remain unemployed on wet days, or when the weather is not altogether suitable for the kind of work required. Thus the amount of weekly wages earned is very precarious and differs greatly ...

As gangs can be most profitably employed on large farms, such as those in the marshland and fen districts, as those of Norfolk, Cambridgeshire, and Huntingdonshire, where the population is thin and where the villages lie at great distances from one another, the gang is constantly placed in situations where they can procure no shelter from rain or inclement weather ... The result of this is, that those so employed are subject to intermittent fever, rheumatism, scarlet fever, pleurisy, and may eventually become consumptive. The taking of the mid-day meal while seated on the ground, frequently damp, is another cause of illness. Now, if the strong are affected injuriously by labour under such circumstances, children, girls, and the more delicate among the women are even more liable to severe maladies arising from the causes mentioned . . .

As the gangman makes no inquiry as to the character of those he employs, the gang will sometimes include idle labourers who dislike regular and sustained employment, young women of immoral character, married women of slatternly, immodest, and idle habits, and young children . . .

In a gang of such a character it necessarily follows that even those who were steady and respectable when they joined it must become corrupted. When the gang is mixed, where I mean males and females work together, the evil becomes greater. The dress of the women is to a certain extent almost of necessity immodest. When the crops are wet they tuck up their dresses between their legs, often leaving the legs much exposed. The long absence and distance from home often render it necessary that the women should attend to the calls of nature, and this they frequently do in the presence of the lads, boys and men. Thus a girl who is when she joins these gangs modest and decent gradually loses her modesty.

This and the bad accommodation afforded in our labourers' cottages are two reasons, I believe, for the prevalence of fornication amongst the agricultural class of labourers, and the consequent numerous cases of bastardy.

As the women employed in these gangs are frequently of the character I have described, the conversations which take place in the meal hour, and whilst going to and returning from work, is of the worst character, and tends greatly to corrupt the character and feelings of others who were more moral and better disposed. Thus the gang system is the cause of a moral pestilence.

The conduct of the women and girls belonging to a gang, whilst travelling to and from the work, is often offensive even in the most public places to the passers by, and their remarks and coarse language distressing and annoying.

The character of women so employed in their own villages is generally indifferent. As mothers they are slatternly, careless about their domestic duties, indifferent as to the conduct of their children. Girls thus employed can seldom obtain employment afterwards as domestic servants. To say that a girl has been employed in the fields, in gangs or otherwise, is generally sufficient to cause anyone above the class of the smaller farmer and tradesman to reject her application for service.

With so many evil influences at work upon the character it is not to be supposed that persons thus employed will be religious. The clergy-man, however anxious to discharge his duties, has few, if any, opportunities of seeing them or conversing with them. They go out so early and return so late that he can seldom find them at home, and if he does so, they are not disposed to listen to any remarks he may make about their conduct or religious duties . . . Even if night schools for females were common in our country villages, it is doubtful whether they could or would attend them. Their impatience of restraint, their bodily weariness, and their want of application, would be all causes to prevent their attendance . . . With views of this kind they are not likely to attend places of worship, and they often spend the Lord's day in either utter idleness or in vicious pursuits. From inquiries I have made, I find the females will in the evening go to the meeting houses, not for spiritual edification and religious improvement, but, as one of them acknowledged to me, that they might meet the young men and walk home with them . . .

From MR J. E. WHITE'S report on Agricultural Gangs; Children's Employment Commission, 6th Report, pp. 83–84; P.P. 1867, vol. 16.

41

'*All dripping wet*'

Rachel Clackson Gibson, Castleacre. I can't speak up for the gangs; they ought all to be done away with . . . I don't think it proper that women-kind should go into the fields at all, in gangs or not, though I have done both. Harvest work is different: you are not under a gangmaster . . . and much more money can be made; a woman may make 2s 3d in a day, and that comes nice to any one.

But other work is different. I should have just liked you to have met that gang coming back this afternoon, with their great thick boots, and buskins on their legs, and petticoats pinned up; you might see the knees of some.

A girl whom I took in to live, because she has no home to go to, came back to-day from the gang all dripping wet from the turnips. If you don't feel any hurt from the wet when you are young, you do afterwards, when you are old and the rheumatism comes on . . .

Children's Employment Commission, 6th Report (1867), page 91; P.P. 1867, vol. 16.

42

'The girl was calling out'

Dr C. Morris, High Street, Spalding, Lincs.—I have been in practice in the town of Spalding for 25 years . . . I am convinced that the gang system is the cause of much immorality. The evil in the system is the mixture of the sexes in the case of boys and girls of 12 to 17 years of age under no proper control. The gangers . . . pay these children once a week at some beer house, and it is no uncommon thing for their children to be kept waiting at the place till 11 or 12 o'clock at night.

At the infirmary many girls of 14 years of age, and even girls of 13, up to 17 years of age, have been brought in pregnant to be confined here. The girls have acknowledged that their ruin has taken place in this gang work. The offence is committed in going or returning from their work. Girls and boys of this age go five, six, or even seven miles to work, walking in droves along the roads and by-lanes.

I have myself witnessed gross indecencies between boys and girls of 14 to 16 years of age. I saw once a young girl insulted by some five or six boys on the road side. Other older persons were about 20 or 30 yards off, but they took no notice. The girl was calling out, which caused me to stop. I have also seen boys bathing in the brooks, and girls between 13 and 19 looking on from the bank.

Children's Employment Commission, 6th Report (1867), page 34; P.P. 1867, vol. 16.

43

'The gangmaster pulled me down'

Case heard at the Downham Market Sessions, Aug. 6, 1866: assaulting a Female Child, named A. B. of —. *A. B.*, 13 years of age: 'I know C— (the defendant); he is the gangmaster. I remember last Monday week . . . Mr C. pulled me down and pulled up my clothes, only to my waist. I think there were a dozen in the gang, it was in the sight of the gang, we were sitting down to our dinners . . . The other boys and girls in the gang were round me. I called out, the others laughed. He said, 'Open your legs more.' He had a stick, and I had not run away with it. I told my mother (not directly I got home at night). I told her half an hour after. My mother spoke to me first.

'C— hurt my hand when I tried to get up, he was on me, and I could not get up, he was laying on me flat, I was on my back on the ground. I don't know how long he was on me. He did not say anything to any of the others, the others saw it. C— has threatened to flog us, if we told any tales . . .'

A boy, aged 10, brother of the girl: 'I saw C— pulling the girls about and showing their backsides. He did it to my sister, and (two other girls named).

A girl, 13 years (one of the girls named by the last witness): 'I work with C's gang. I was there one day last week. — (the girl assaulted) took his stick. He got on her and rubbed her face. He did not pull up her clothes.'

The document from which the above is taken appears to be a formal copy of the depositions, and was forwarded to me by a Member of Parliament, with the remark: 'I am afraid they (cases) would come oftener before the magistrates if children dared to speak.'

The farmer employing the gangmaster, an old man of 72, and who had employed him 30 years . . . had always found him 'a straightforward and upright man, and believed he would act as a father to the children.'

(The man was sentenced to two calendar months' hard labour.)

From MR J. E. WHITE'S report; 6th Report, *op. cit.* (1867), page 147; P.P. 1867, vol. 16.

44

What 8d. a Day Does to a Woman

It is universally admitted that such employment [the employment of females of whatever age or condition upon the labours of the farm], not so much from causes inherent in it as it is from circumstances by which it is surrounded, is to a great extent demoralizing.

Not only does it almost unsex a woman, in dress, gait, manners, character, making her rough, coarse, clumsy, masculine; but it generates a further very pregnant social mischief, by unfitting or indisposing her for a woman's proper duties at home.

Some of the work in which women are frequently employed, such as serving the threshing machine, weeding high wet corn, drawing turnips or mangolds, is work to which, on physical grounds, they never ought to be put at all. Exposure to wet or cold, from which no farm labour can claim exemption, is likely, owing to the greater susceptibility of the female constitution, to be specially injurious to them.

The farmers, almost to a man, complain of the difficulty of getting dairy maids and other domestic servants; and almost to a man again, express the opinion that the proper place for a young single girl is in the household, and not upon the land. It is admitted that the intermixture of the sexes is one great cause of demoralization; yet such is the nature of farm work that it would be difficult even by the best contrived arrangements—it would almost be impossible by legislation—to secure effective separation. It is said that a party of women almost necessitate the presence of a male superintendent to keep them steadily and methodically to their work; while even more corrupting than the intermixture of any number of men and women in their work is said to be the influence of two or three debased members of their own sex . . .

The evil is to some extent very mitigated by natural and spontaneous influences. Everywhere I heard the same story, that women are found to be less and less disposed to go out to work upon the land. They will refuse unsuitable work; they will stay at home on wet days. Whether from the easier circumstances in which they live, or from their having become intelligent enough to make a more accurate measure of loss and gain, there seems to be much less attraction for them in the farmer's 8d or 9d a day than there used to be.

REV. J. FRASER'S report; Employment of . . . Women in Agriculture, 1st Report (1867), pp. 16–17; P.P. 1867/8, vol. 17.

45

'Looked over like cattle'

The drunkenness at the 'statute' or 'mop' fairs is the main cause of the immorality which is said to prevail at them. There is something very degrading also in the fact of young men and women standing in the market-place to be looked over like cattle by the farmers who come to hire them. There is this further truth in the comparison that they are hired from their physical appearance, and very rarely from their previous character. And though in some places a room has been provided for the women to sit in under some respectable supervisor, it is not easy to induce them to relinquish the licence they have enjoyed at their only holiday in the year.

MR STANHOPE'S report; Employment of ... Women in Agriculture, 2nd Report, page 29; P.P. 1868/9, vol. 13.

46

Northumbria's Women Bondagers

As there are very few villages in this part of Northumberland [Glendale Union, extending in a southerly direction from Wark and Carham on the Tweed, over an area of 147,698 acres, with a population of 13,210], the farmers are almost entirely dependent on their cottagers for the labour of their farms ... To secure this, the hind [labourer] is bound to find the work of a suitable woman whenever she is needed.

The woman thus hired is called the 'bondager' or 'bound woman'. Her earnings are paid to the hind, who engages to give her wages, lodging, food, and washing. The usual payment to the hind for the bondager is 1s. a day, and 2s. 6d. or 3s. at harvest time for a certain number of days. The wages given by the hind to the woman would at the present time be about £12. 10s. a year, that is £8. 10s. for the summer half-year, and £4 for the winter. Her earnings would probably amount to £15, or under the most favourable circumstances to £17: 300 days at 1s. making £15, and £2 extra for harvest. This leaves a very small margin for her maintenance; but ... part of the hind's privileges of free house, coals, and potatoes are supposed to be compensation for this.

Of late years many objections have been raised to this system, mostly coming from the hinds themselves, principally on account of the loss entailed upon them if they are compelled to hire a stranger, not having any member of the family capable of working the bondage. They usually say, 'the woman only earns her wages. We meat and wash her for nothing' ... The system is also objected to ... on the ground of morality and decency, from the probable necessity of having to lodge the hired woman in the same room as the family. In the old description of cottages this was often unavoidable, and the practice may be justly censured as indecent; but there are many instances of a family dividing the one room by box beds, and making a separate place for the hired woman.

THE HAUNTED LADY, OR "THE GHOST" IN THE LOOKING-GLASS.

Madame La Modiste. "WE WOULD NOT HAVE DISAPPOINTED YOUR LADYSHIP, AT ANY SACRIFICE, AND THE ROBE IS FINISHED À MERVEILLE."

5. John Leech in *Punch*, 1863

WHAT WILL BECOME OF THE SERVANT-GALS?

Charming Lady (showing her House to Benevolent Old Gentleman). "THAT'S WHERE THE HOUSEMAID SLEEPS."
Benevolent Old Gentleman. "DEAR ME, YOU DON'T SAY SO! ISN'T IT VERY DAMP! I SEE THE WATER GLISTENING ON THE WALLS."
Charming Lady. "OH, IT'S NOT TOO DAMP FOR A SERVANT!"

George du Maurier in *Punch*, 1865

6. Dudley Street, Seven Dials, London.   Gustave Doré

A stranger clean from the country.   An inhabitant of Hyde-park.

Yokel (*in alarm*).—" *Thou beest wondrous grim, sure !*"
Londoner.—" *To this complexion ewe must come at last.*"

A stranger clean from
the country. An in-
habitant of Hyde-park

Yokel (*in alarm*).—
'Thou beest won-
drous grim, sure!'
Londoner.—'*To this*
complexion ewe
must come at last.'

Owing to the circumstances above stated, large families are in great request, as it is necessary to have female labour on a farm, particularly during the turnip season. Thus the bondage system is not universal and is gradually dying out; and the name 'bondager' is becoming unpopular, 'woman worker' being now substituted. Sometimes a spare cottage or 'bondage house', as it is called, is given to a single woman rent free, coals being led, and potatoes planted for her, in return for which she is bound to work on the farm at a certain rate. When there is an aged parent or relative for which the house is required this is an excellent arrangement; but when, as happens in rare instances, such houses are let to two single women, it cannot be said that the practice is conducive to morality.

Women are extensively employed throughout the whole year, and their labour is considered essential for the cultivation of the land. The work of two women is usually required for every 75 acres of the light land, and a larger proportion for that which is heavier . . . Their labour consists in the various operations of cleaning the land, picking stones, weeds, etc.; turnip hoeing, hay making, and harvest work, rooting and shawing, that is, cleaning turnips; barn work, with the thrashing and winnowing machines, filling dung carts, turning dung heaps, spreading the dung, and sowing artificial manure; turnip cutting in the winter for sheep, etc.; and occasionally driving carts or harrowing; in some instances forking (pitching) and loading hay or corn, though when such is the case two women are put to the work for one man.

The Northumbrian women who do these kinds of labour are physically a splendid race; their strength is such that they can vie with the men in carrying sacks of corn, and there seems to be no work which affects them injuriously, however hard it may appear . . . Reaping machines have generally put an end to the 'shearing' (reaping) which women considered laborious. They are now merely employed in putting the corn together for men to tie up and 'stooke', i.e. shock.

It has been frequently suggested to me by many gentlemen and occupiers of land . . . that the practice of women driving or leading horses, either on the road or the farm, is both dangerous and objectionable, unsuitable in every point of view . . . I have always found that such work was not forced upon the women. Their own words are, 'we fight to drive the carts, it is easier than the loading'. They are undoubtedly as fit to be trusted as those of the same sex, in a higher social position and of greater rank, who drive horses in the highest condition in every description of carriage; and with regard to the latter, few would be bold enough to suggest that they do not show as much science and nerve as many men, or to propose legislative interference.

It has also been represented to me that such work as turning manure

7. Northumbrian 'Bondagers'. (Cuthbert Bede, 1862)

heaps, filling dung carts, etc. is unsuitable for women . . . but it must be borne in mind that if such labour was not desired by the women and tendered by the farmers, these women would for many weeks be compelled to remain idle in their cottages for want of occupation, to their own and the hinds' loss.

There are many who hold the opinion that field work is degrading, but I should be glad if they would visit these women in their own homes after they have become wives and mothers. They would be received with a natural courtesy and good manners which would astonish them. Let the visitor ask to see the house; he will be 'taken over' it, with many apologies that he should have seen it not 'redd up'. He will then be offered a chair in front of a large fire, with the never-absent pot and oven, the mistress meanwhile continuing her unceasing family duties, baking, cooking, cleaning, etc.

Not one word of complaint will be heard; but he will be told that, though 'working people', they are not poor; and a glance at the substantial furniture, the ample supply of bacon over his head, the variety of cakes and bread on the board, and the stores of butter, cheese, and meal in the house, will convince him of the fact. When he inquires about the children, he will hear that though they have not much to give them, the parents feel it to be their sacred duty to secure them the best instruction in their power, and '*that* they are determined they shall have.'

The visitor will leave that cottage with the conviction that field work has had no degrading effect, but that he has been in the presence of a thoughtful, contented, and unselfish woman . . .

The dress of these north country women is admirably adapted for their work; being made to fit easily it does not encumber them, and being of strong materials it defies all weathers. Generally it consists of a pair of stout boots, a very short thick woollen petticoat, warm stockings, a jacket, etc.; over all a washing pinafore with sleeves (called a slip), which preserves their dress from dirt. Their faces are protected by a shade or 'ugly' of divers colours. Thus equipped, they present a great contrast to the draggled appearance of the women who only work in the fields occasionally, wearing some thin gown, with perhaps the addition of the husband's coat and boots . . .

From the report by MR JOSEPH J. HENLEY, assistant commissioner; 1st Report, Commission on the Employment of Children, Young Persons, and Women in Agriculture (1867), pp. 52–54; P.P. 1867/8, vol. 17.

47

Criminal Mothers of the Marshlands

It appears that the land in these [marsh] districts is generally light, and that the recently reclaimed 'black lands' are very light indeed, and may be submitted to women's work to a far greater extent than anywhere else in the kingdom ... The women's wages vary ... from 8d to 1s 8d a day, and for such work as they can do they are preferred to men, because of their superior industry and order. A party of women will often come from several miles off to work at a village in which numbers of men are unable to get work at all.

One source of profit in the employment of women is the superior management and consideration they show in combining their work with that of boys and girls, and this quality has led to the frequent formation of what are called 'gangs' of women and children, who work together for a stated sum paid by the farmer to a man called the undertaker, who contracts for the whole gang. These gangs will sometimes travel many miles from their own village; they are to be met morning and evening on the roads, dressed in short petticoats, with suitable coats, boots, and sometimes trousers, looking wonderfully strong and healthy, and heedless of the fatal results which their love of this busy and independent life is bringing on their unfortunate offspring who are pining at home ...

In looking over the register books of deaths in these districts the eye is immediately caught by the large number of baby deaths reported to have been caused by premature birth. A medical gentleman at Ely and others thought this term was used unduly and to a wide extent; that few children died in the first few months of life without it being said that they came before their time. There were, however, numerous cases related of labour coming on in the harvest field; and it may be fairly presumed that some of these premature births, succeeded by premature death, were the result of field work; for a search of the books revealed that by far the greater number of them took place in the summer quarter, and it is not difficult to suppose that the exposure of the pregnant mother to the heat of a twelve hours summer's day, without an inch of shelter from hedge or tree even at dinner time, and far away from her own home, will cause some part of the miscarriages which the books report to take place.

Less directly, but not less certainly, does field work induce premature birth through bastardy. The immorality caused by the gang system has caused it to be put an end to in many parishes, and it is invariably reprobated by those who are independent of its profits. It is said to account for the high number of illegitimate births in the counties involved. Attempts to produce premature birth on this account were reported, though they were not known to be very common. A French woman was said to have done a great deal of mischief in this way at Wisbeach; and a notion that the young women have that such drugs as savine or turpentine will induce miscarriages leads them to take large quantities, from which, although they are usually disappointed of their wishes, may be expected a diminished viability of the child . . .

The illegitimate births frequently occur in the workhouse, and here, until the child is taken out, it thrives as well as others, but within a few weeks after their discharge the mother will go to the registrar, to inform him that her child is dead, that it was always weakly and never 'likely for life'. The lawful child fares little better when the mother belongs to a gang, or even does ordinary field work in her own parish. In the agricultural population it may be roundly stated that of the illegitimates one third die under a year old, of the others one fourth part.

The diagnosis of infantile diseases seems to be considered difficult and unimportant. In the same village two practitioners recorded long lists of deaths of infants, the one almost exclusively certifying mesenteric disease as the cause of death, the other attributing nearly all his cases to cerebral disease. But, with hardly an exception, all stated, that under whatever late symptoms the death was recorded, the real cause of half of them was the mother's neglect. The degree of criminality attributed to the women varied, from a sympathizing excuse for their ignorance to a downright charge of wilful neglect with the hope of death—in fact, infanticide.

It may be easily understood that these degrees of criminality must be infinitely various. A poor girl, brought up in a gang, seduced in the field, and afterwards suddenly taken there in labour, will bring into the family a child for whom no provision has been made, and where it is most unwelcome. She is called away to work as soon as she is able, and it comes to her as a matter of course that she should leave the child to the old woman who professes to keep a school for such babes. The mother gives suck on depositing the child in the morning, and again on her return home. She, after carefully drawing and throwing away the first milk, gives the child its evening meal. She is too tired to fail to sleep through the night, and indeed she cannot afford to lose her rest. Both by day and night, therefore, is the child either deprived of food, or fed, not with a bottle but a spoon, and it soon acquires a taste for the unnaturally solid food given it. Cow's milk is dear, and often quite unattainable by these people, and sugar sop, a lumpy mass of bread, water, and sugar is given instead. This is either given cold, or is left on the fire hob in a cup, seldom or never changed or cleaned, whence the fermented and sooty mass is heaped into the infant's mouth by the nurse, who prefers this mess to cow's milk, under the notion that 'the two milks could never agree'.

A worse degree of criminality is found in older mothers. After losing a child or two, they begin to view the subject as one for ingenuity and speculation. It is related that on the birth of a second or third bastard baby, the neighbours will say, 'so and so has another baby; you'll see it won't live'; and that this becomes a sort of joke, in which the mother will join; public opinion expressing no condemnation of her cruelty. A medical man is called to the wasting infant ... The mother says the child is dying, and won't touch food. When *he* offers food, the child is ravenous, and 'fit to tear the spoon to pieces'. On some of the few occasions on which the surgeon in his disgust has insisted on opening the body, the stomach and bowels have been found quite empty. It was in many places reported that infant life had been saved ... by the threats of a determined surgeon or neighbour ...

Bad as is this starvation of infants, another practice is more common and more lethal: this is drugging with opium ... There can be no doubt of the truth of the horrid statement made by almost every surgeon in the marsh land, that there was not a labourer's house in which the bottle of opiate was not to be seen, and not a child but who got it in some form ... The favourite form for infants is called Godfrey's Cordial, a mixture of opium, treacle, and infusion of sassafras. This is thickish, and is often fetched in a teacup.

When the mother going to field work deposits her child with a nurse, she thinks it best to leave her own bottle of Godfrey, because the preparations of the different shops vary, and there is not a little village shop in the country that sells anything that does not sell its own Godfrey ... It has not unfrequently happened that a nurse has substituted her own Godfrey for her client's, and, frightened at its effects, has summoned the surgeon, who finds half-a-dozen babies, some snoring, some squinting, all pallid and eye-sunken, lying about the room, all poisoned ...

Cases of death from opium poisoning are supposed to be common; occasionally they are the subject of inquests; sometimes they are recorded as cases of 'Overlying'; but the medical practitioners are of opinion that by far the most common end of such cases is the simple registration and burial as cases of 'Debility from birth, no medical attendant', 'premature birth', and such like;—the public opinion of the neighbours seldom going beyond a sneer or sarcasm on the occurrence of a quarrel months or years after . . .

DR H. JULIAN HUNTER'S report on the Excessive Mortality of Infants in some Rural Districts of England; Medical Reports of the Privy Council, No. 6 (1863), Appendix 14; P.P. 1864, vol. 28.

CHAPTER 5

HOME SWEET HOME

Mid pleasures and palaces though we may roam,
Be it never so humble, there's no place like home.

When we see what sort of places some of the British people called 'home' we may well believe it . . . Of course, there were homes innumerable that were happy places for happy families, but we cannot get away from the evidence to the contrary afforded by such 'documents' as are included in this chapter. Nor shall we be greatly impressed by Mrs Felicia Dorothea Hemans' rapturous verses on *The Homes of England*.

The cottage Homes of England . . .
Through glowing orchards forth they peep,
Each from its nook of leaves,
And fearless there the lowly sleep,
As the bird beneath their eaves . . .

Only too clearly, that good lady just didn't know what she was talking about. Considerably nearer the truth would it be to assert that 'the lowly' slept in squalid hovels, crowded together in conditions that made common decency impossible and all too often led to disease and premature death.

But we must be fair. There were many fine and eager spirits who not only realized the evil but nerved themselves to meet it. One of the pioneers in the great work of improving the housing conditions of the masses was Prince Albert, whose 'model cottages' were one of the most prominent displays at the Great Exhibition. (After the Exhibition closed, they were taken down and re-erected in Kennington Park, where they may still be seen.) Then in the field of housing management, let us pay tribute to the work of that admirable Victorian lady, Miss Octavia Hill (1838–1912). She was the granddaughter of Dr Southwood Smith, one of the pioneer 'sanitarians' of the previous generation, and from him she heard of the terrible things he had found in the course of his explorations of the London slums. She had a vision of healthy and happy homes for the working people, and in 1864 John Ruskin lent her the money with which to start her first housing scheme. He urged upon her the necessity of making the books balance at the end of the year, and this fitted in well with her conviction that what the poor needed most was not 'charity' but guidance and encouragement. She took an active interest in other things besides housing, however, as when with Canon Rawnsley and Sir Robert Hunter she founded in 1905 the National Trust for Places of Historic Interest or Natural Beauty.

All the 'documents' in this chapter have to do with the homes of the working people. No excuse is offered or should be needed for that. The 'stately homes' have their special literature; the homes of the leisured and cultured are described in innumerable volumes of reminiscence in which yesterday is viewed through rose-coloured spectacles; and those of the middle and lower middle classes form the setting for most of the novels. But the 'cottages' of the poor—only too seldom are we allowed to penetrate into their stale and stuffy gloom. Very likely, after reading some of these we shall want to do what the doctor did in No. 13—throw the window open . . .

Much more pleasant is the account by a 'journeyman engineer' of a working-class family's week-end (No. 19), while from No. 20 we learn (not without surprise?) that there were 'detergents' in the 1860s and that Mr Harper Twelvetrees employed a copy-writer who might well hold his own in a modern advertisement agency.

I

'Every man's house is his castle'

It is so much the order of nature that a family should live in a separate house, that 'house' is often used for 'family' in many languages, and this isolation of families, in separate houses, it has been asserted, is carried to a greater extent in England than it is elsewhere.

A German naturalist, Dr Carus, the physician of the King of Saxony, in a description of the English people, has the following passage on English dwellings; which, although it bears the marks of hasty generalization, is not undeserving of consideration:—

'I cannot take leave of the subject without a remark on English dwelling-houses, which stand in close connection with that long-cherished principle of separation and retirement, lying as the very foundation of the national character. It appears to me, to be this principle which has given to the people that fixity in national character, and strict adherence to the historical usages of their country, by which they are so much distinguished; and up to the present moment, the Englishman still perseveres in striving after a certain individuality and personal independence, a certain separation of himself from others, which constitutes the very foundation of his freedom . . . it is that that gives the Englishmen that proud feeling of personal independence, which is stereotyped in the phrase, '*Every man's house is his castle.*' This is a feeling which cannot be entertained, and an expression which cannot be used in Germany or France, where ten or fifteen families often live together in the same large house.

'The expression, however, receives a true value, when by the mere closing of the house-door, the family is able, to a certain extent, to cut itself off from all communication with the outward world, even in the midst of great cities. In English towns or villages, therefore, one always meets either with small detached houses merely suited to one family, or apparently large buildings extending to the length of half a street, sometimes adorned like palaces on the exterior, but separated by partition walls internally, and thus divided into a great number of small high houses, for the most part three windows broad, within which, and on the various stories, the rooms are divided according to the wants or the convenience of the family; in short, therefore, it may be properly said, that the English divide their edifices perpendicularly into houses— whereas we Germans divide them horizontally into floors. In England, every man is master of his hall, stairs, and chambers—whereas we are obliged to use the two first in common with others, and are scarcely able to secure ourselves the privacy of our own chamber, if we are not fortunate enough to be able to secure a convenient house for ourselves alone.'

The possession of an entire house is, it is true, strongly desired by every Englishman; for it throws a sharp, well-defined circle round his family and hearth—the shrine of his sorrows, joys, and meditations. This feeling, as it is natural, is universal, but it is stronger in England than it is on the Continent . . . The towns and cities of the two northern English counties and of Scotland, however, are built in the continental style; and the families of the middle classes, as well as of the poor, live in large flats, which constitute separate tenements within the same party-walls.

From the Report of the Registrar-General (GEORGE GRAHAM) on the Census of 1851, pp. xxxv–xxxvi; P.P. 1852/3, vol. 85.

2

A Carpet in the Sitting-Room

If we look back to the condition of the people as it existed in this country, even so recently as the beginning of the present century, and then look around us at the indications of greater comfort and respectability that meet us on every side, it is hardly possible to doubt that here, in England at least, the elements of social improvement have been successfully at work, and that they have been and are producing an increased amount of comfort to the great bulk of the people.

This improvement is by no means confined to those who are called, by a somewhat arbitrary distinction, the working classes, but is enjoyed in some degree or other by tradesmen, shopkeepers, farmers—in short, by every class of men whose personal and family comforts admitted of material increase. Higher in the scale of society the same cause has been productive of increase of luxury, of increased encouragement to science, literature, and the fine arts, and of additions to the elegancies of life . . .

In nothing is the improvement here mentioned more apparent than in the condition of the dwellings of the middle classes. As one instance, it is not necessary to go back much beyond half a century to arrive at the time when prosperous shopkeepers in the leading thoroughfares of London were without that now necessary article of furniture, a carpet, in their ordinary sitting-rooms: luxury in this particular seldom went further with them than a well-scoured floor strewn with sand, and the furniture of the apartments was by no means inconsistent with this primitive, and, as we should now say, comfortless state of things. In the same houses we now see, not carpets merely, but many articles of furniture which were formerly in use only among the nobility and gentry: the walls are covered with paintings or engravings, and the apartments contain evidences that some among the inmates cultivate one or more of those elegant accomplishments which tend so delightfully to refine the minds of individuals, and to sweeten the intercourse of families.

G. R. PORTER, *The Progress of the Nation* (2nd ed., 1847), pp. 532–533.

3

A Londoner's Home

Let us penetrate some of the 'London Shadows', and show their distressing depths—their degrading results . . . In the outwardly respectable neighbourhood of the Marlborough-street Police Court, close to Berwick-street, exists a collection of houses . . . chiefly let in single rooms. The houses are mostly dilapidated, and dirty in the extreme . . . At the back of most of them, after passing through a long passage, are small, badly paved courts . . . The water stands here and there in deep puddles. In the courts we saw were conveniences, a dust-heap . . . and a water tank. These are all shared amongst the lodgers in the cellars, say eight persons. If only five persons occupy each of the eight rooms in front, and six the two rooms in the back court, this is all the accommodation of water, etc. provided for 54 persons.

On ascending some wooden steps, we find the room which we have engraved (*facing page 256*). We have not selected this as a harrowing example of London dwellings, although it is bad enough . . .

The room is little more than 7 feet long by 6 feet wide; the greatest height 6 feet 9 inches. The narrow bedstead, which is doubled up in the day time, reaches, when let down, close to the fireplace. The roof and part of the wall are mildewed with damp; through parts of the roof the sky is distinctly visible. Our engraving makes the room appear too large.

The room is occupied by a married couple of about 22 or 23 years of age, and a little girl about 2 years old. The young man had been brought up amongst poor persons in the neighbourhood; his education had been neglected, but he had been employed in various ways until he obtained a situation as light porter. He married a respectable young woman, a servant. A short time after marriage he lost his situation, and failed to obtain another. By some means he and his wife got into the method of cutting thin wooden splints, which are used in public-houses and cigar-shops. This, he says, is 'poor work; the price has become so much reduced, we are glad if we can manage to get two meals a day, and then but poor ones. We seldom can afford to get a fire except on Sunday, and perhaps in part of Monday; and this place is very cold, there are so many holes. I have spoken repeatedly to the landlord, but he has done nothing. I pay 1s. 6d. a week. I am 6s. 6d. back [in arrears] in my rent. The rain during the last wet weather poured into the room, sometimes upon the bed. In the morning, and during the wet days, we have a pool of water under the bed and on the floor. No one lives below; it is a kind of stable, and very dirty. The little child is often ill. I have parted with many of my things.'

The child was small, drooping, and bleached, like many of the plants which attempt to vegetate in such places. Yet this is not an example of the direst stage of London poverty. It is but a step in the story. Here are fire-irons, and various matters which would bring a price; there the neat hand of woman—the world's blessing, and who in her lowest degradation has a perception of the beautiful—has given a dash of taste to the arrangement. Above the fire-place are several little framed prints; one representing two lovers walking on a terrace, overlooking trees and gardens bright in the light of the clear sky; another shows a richly furnished chamber, with a couple of more mature years; there are also some unframed prints of the young royal family, and a row of small beads are festooned in the centre. On the mantelpiece are various little baskets, and other nicknacks of no great value, but evidently relics of a more prosperous time; a little key, perhaps of some prized workbox.

The cupboard without a door contains an odd collection of crockery; a candlestick with the extinguisher on the last snuff. No food visible, except a small crust on the shelf beside the teapot. Poor as this place is, it is *still a home* . . .

*   *   *

When we were in the Bishopsgate district, we made an examination of the houses occupied by the weavers of Spitalfields . . . The distress here is very great, and although the houses are for the most part in better condition than some we have described, for the weavers are a respectable class of persons, the close crowded rooms in which they work, with other local causes in operation, produce illness and shorten life. We give a sketch (*facing page 257*) of one of the rooms we entered, where the father and mother were continuing their midnight toil amidst the sleeping children spread about the apartment. They were at work on a white watered silk for wedding dresses!

GEORGE GODWIN (Editor of 'The Builder'): *London Shadows: A glance at the 'Homes' of the Thousands* (1854), pp. 3–6, 31.

4

Miss Octavia Hill's Housing Venture

About four years ago I was put in possession of three houses in one of the worst courts of Marylebone. Six other houses were bought subsequently. All were crowded with inmates.

The first thing to be done was to put them in decent tenantable order. The set last purchased was a row of cottages facing a bit of desolate ground, occupied with wretched, dilapidated cow-sheds, manure heaps, old timber, and rubbish of every description. The houses were in a most deplorable condition—the plaster was dropping from the walls; on one staircase a pail was placed to catch the rain that fell through the roof. All the staircases were perfectly dark; the banisters were gone, having been burnt as firewood by tenants. The grates, with large holes in them, were falling forward into the rooms. The washhouse, full of lumber belonging to the landlord, was locked up; thus the inhabitants had to wash clothes, as well as to cook, eat and sleep in their small rooms. The dust-bin, standing in the front part of the houses, was accessible to the whole neighbourhood, and boys often dragged from it quantities of unseemly objects and spread them over the court. The state of the drainage was in keeping with everything else. The pavement of the backyard was all broken up, and great puddles stood in it, so that the damp crept up the outer walls. One large but dirty water-butt received the water laid on for the houses; it leaked, and for such as did not fill their jugs when the water came in, or who had no jugs to fill, there was no water. The former landlord's reply to one of the tenants who asked him to have an iron hoop put round the butt to prevent leakage, was, that 'if he didn't like it,' (i.e. things as they were) 'he might leave' . . .

This landlord was a tradesman in a small way of business—not a cruel man, except in so far as variableness of dealing is cruelty; but he was a man without capital to spend on improvements, and lost an immense percentage of his rent by bad debts . . .

As soon as I entered into possession, each family had an opportunity of doing better: those who would not pay, or who led clearly immoral lives, were ejected. The rooms they vacated were cleansed; the tenants who showed signs of improvement moved into them, and thus, in turn, an opportunity was obtained for having each room distempered and papered. The drains were put in order, a large slate cistern was fixed, the wash-house was cleared of its lumber, and thrown open on stated days to each tenant in turn. The roof, the plaster, the woodwork was repaired; the staircase walls were distempered; new grates were fixed; the layers of paper and rag (black with age) were torn from the windows, and glass was put in; out of 192 panes only eight were found unbroken. The yard and footpath were paved.

The rooms, as a rule, were re-let at the same prices at which they had been let before; but tenants with large families were counselled to take two rooms, and for these much less was charged than if let singly: this plan I continue to pursue. In-coming tenants are not allowed to take a decidedly insufficient quantity of room, and no sub-letting is permitted. The elder girls are employed three times a week in scrubbing the passages in the houses, for the cleaning of which the landlady is responsible. For this work they are paid, and by it they learn habits of cleanliness. It is, of course, within the authority of the landlady also to insist on cleanliness of wash-houses, yards, staircases, and staircase-windows; and even to remonstrate concerning the rooms themselves if they are habitually dirty.

The pecuniary result has been very satisfactory. Five per cent has been paid on all the capital invested. A fund for the repayment of capital is accumulating. A liberal allowance has been made for repairs . . .

From the proceeds of the rent, also, interest has been paid on the capital spent in building a large room where the tenants can assemble. Classes are held there—for boys, twice weekly; for girls, once; a singing class has just been established. A large work-class for married women and elder girls meets once a week. A glad sight it is—the large room filled with the eager, merry faces of the girls, from which those of the older, careworn women catch a reflected light. It is a good time for quiet talk with them as they work, and many a neighbourly feeling is called out amongst the women as they sit together on the same bench, lend one another cotton or needles, are served by the same hand, and look to the same person for direction. The babies are a great bond of union: I have known the very women who not long before had been literally fighting, sit at the work-class busily and earnestly comparing notes of their babies' respective history. That a consciousness of corporate life is developed in them is shown by the not infrequent use of the expression 'One of us'.

Among the arrangements conducive to comfort and health, I may mention that instead of the clothes being hung, as formerly, out of front windows down against the wall, where they could not be properly purified, the piece of ground in front of the house is used as a drying ground during school hours. The same place is appropriated as a play-ground, not only for my younger tenants, but for the children from the neighbouring courts. It is a space walled round, where they can play in safety. Hitherto, games at trap, bat and ball, swinging, skipping, and singing a few Kinder-Garten songs with movements in unison, have been the main diversions. But I have just established drill for the boys, and a drum and fife band . . .

Mr Ruskin, to whom the whole undertaking owes its existence [he had at once come forward with all the money necessary, and took the whole risk of the undertaking upon himself] has had trees planted in the playground, and creepers against the houses. In May, we have a May-pole or a throne covered with flowers for the May-queen and her attendants. The sweet luxuriance of the spring flowers is more enjoyed in that court than could readily be believed. Some months after the first festival the children were seen sticking a few faded flowers into a crevice in the wall, saying they wanted to make it 'like it was the day we had the May-pole' . . .

Week by week, when the rents are collected, an opportunity of seeing each family separately occurs. There are a multitude of matters to attend to. First, there is the mere outside business—rent to be received, requests from the tenant respecting repairs to be considered; sometimes decisions touching the behaviour of other tenants to be made, sometimes rebukes for untidiness to be administered. Then comes the sad or joyful remarks about health or work, the little histories of the week. Sometimes grave questions arise about important changes in the life of the family—shall a daughter go to service? or shall the sick child be sent to hospital? etc. Sometimes violent quarrels must be allayed . . .

My tenants are mostly of a class far below that of mechanics. They are, indeed, of the very poor. And yet, although the gifts they have received have been next to nothing, none of the families who have passed under my care during the whole four years have continued in what is called 'distress', except such as have been unwilling to exert themselves. Those who will not exert the necessary self-control cannot avail themselves of the means of livelihood held out to them. But, for those who are willing, some small assistance in the form of work has, from time to time, been provided—not much, but sufficient to keep them from want or despair. The following will serve as an instance of the sort of help given, and its proportion to the results.

Alice, a single woman, of perhaps fifty-five years, lodged with a man and his wife—the three in one room—just before I obtained full possession of the houses. Alice, not being able to pay her rent, was turned into the street, where Mrs S. (my playground superintendent) met her, crying dreadfully.

It was Saturday, and I had left town till Monday, Alice had neither furniture to pawn nor friends to help her; the workhouse alone lay before her. Mrs S. knew that I esteemed her as a sober, respectable, industrious woman, and therefore she ventured to express to Alice's landlord that I would not let him lose money if he would let her go back to her lodging till Monday, when I should return home, thus risking for me a possible loss of fourpence—not very ruinous to me, and a sum not impossible for Alice to repay in the future.

I gave Alice two days' needlework, then found her employment in tending a bedridden cottager in the country, whose daughter (in service) paid for the nursing. Five weeks she was there, working, and saving her money. On her return I lent her what more she required to buy furniture and then she took a little room direct from me. Too blind to do much household work, but able to sew almost mechanically, she just earns her daily bread by making sailors' shirts, but her little home is her own, and she loves it dearly; and, having tided over that time of trial, Alice can live—has paid all her debts too, and is more grateful than she would have been for many gifts.

At one time I had a room to let which was ninepence a week cheaper than the one she occupied. I proposed to her to take it; it had, however, a different aspect, getting less of the southern and western sunlight. Alice hesitated long, and asked *me* to decide, which I declined to do; for, as I told her, her moving would suit my arrangements rather better. She, hearing that, wished to move; but I begged her to make her decision wholly irrespective of my plans. At last, she said, very wistfully, 'Well, you see, miss, it's between ninepence and the sun.' Sadly enough, ninepence had to outweigh the sun.

OCTAVIA HILL, *Homes of the London Poor* (1875), pp. 14–53.

5

Prince Albert's Model Cottages

Model houses for four families, at the Cavalry Barracks, Hyde Park, in connexion with the Exposition of the Works of Industry of All Nations, built by command of H.R.H. Prince Albert, President of the Society for Improving the Condition of the Labouring Classes. His Royal Highness has had this building raised on his own account, with a desire of conveying practical information calculated to promote the much-needed improvement of the dwellings of the working classes, and also of stimulating visitors to the Exhibition, whose position and circum-

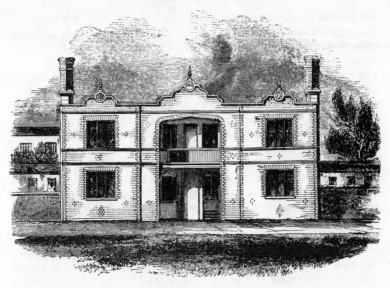

8. Prince Albert's Model Cottages. (Official Catalogue of the Great Exhibition)

stances may enable them to carry out similar undertakings, and thus, without pecuniary sacrifices, permanently to benefit those who are greatly dependent on others for their home and family comforts.

In its *general arrangement*, the building is adapted for the occupation of four families of the class of manufacturing and mechanical operatives, who usually reside in towns, or in their immediate vicinity . . .

The most prominent peculiarity of the design is that of the receding and protected central open staircase, with the connecting gallery on the first floor, formed of slate, and sheltered from the weather by the continuation of the main roof, which also screens the entrances to the dwellings.

The four tenements are arranged on precisely the same plan, two on each floor.

The entrance is through a small *lobby*, lighted from the upper part of the door.

The *living room* has a superficial area of about 150 feet, with a closet on one side of the fireplace, to which warm air may be introduced from the back of the range; over the fireplace is an iron rod for hanging pictures; and on the opposite side of the room a shelf is carried above the doors, with a rail fixed between them.

The scullery is fitted up with a sink, beneath which is a coal-bin of slate; a plate-rack at one end, drained by a slate slab into the sink, covers the entrance to the dust-shaft, which is enclosed by a balanced self-acting iron door. The dust-shaft leads into a closed depository under the stairs, and has a ventilating flue, carried up above the roof. The meat safe is ventilated through the hollow brickwork, and shelves are fixed over the doors. A dresser-flap may be fixed against the partition.

The *sleeping apartments*, being three in number, provide for that separation which, with a family, is so essential to morality and decency. Each has its distinct access, and a window into the open air; two have fireplaces.

The children's bedrooms contain 50 feet superficial each, and, opening out of the living room, an opportunity is afforded for the exercise of parental watchfulness, without the unwholesome crowding of the living room, by its use as a sleeping apartment.

The parents' bed-room, with a superficial area of about 100 feet, is entered through the scullery—an arrangement in many respects preferable to a direct approach from the living room, particularly in case of sickness. The recess in this room provides a closet for linen; and a shelf is carried over the door, with a rail fixed beneath it—a provision which is made in each of the other bed-rooms.

The water-closet is fitted up with a Staffordshire glazed basin, which is complete without any wood fittings, and supplied with water from a slate cistern in common of 160 gallons, placed on the roof over the party and staircase walls. The same pipes which carry away the rain-water from the roof serve for the use of the closets.

Constructive arrangement.—The peculiarities of the building in this respect are, the exclusive use of hollow bricks for the walls and partitions (excepting the foundations, which are of ordinary brickwork), and the entire absence of timber in the floors and roof, which are formed with flat arches of hollow brickwork, rising from 8 to 9 inches, set in cement, and tied in by wrought-iron rods connected with cast-iron springers, which rest on the external walls, and bind the whole structure together; the building is thus rendered fire-proof, and much less liable to decay than those of ordinary construction. The roof arching, which is levelled with concrete, and covered with patent metallic lava, secures the upper rooms from the liability to changes of temperature to which apartments next the roof are generally subject, and the transmission of sound, as well as the percolation of moisture, so common through ordinary floors, is effectually impeded by the hollow-brick arched floors . . . The floors, where not of Portland cement, are laid with Staffordshire tiles, excepting to the right-hand room first floor, which is of lava . . .

In most parts of England, the *cost* of four houses, built on the plan of this model structure, with ordinary materials, and finished similar to the ground-floor apartments, may be stated at £440 to £480, or from £110 to £120 for each tenement, contingent on the facilities for obtaining materials and the value of labour. Such dwellings, let at 3s. 6d. to 4s. a-week, would, after deducting ground-rent and taxes, afford a return of 7 per cent on the amount of outlay.

The Great Exhibition of 1851; Official Descriptive and Illustrated Catalogue, vol. I, pp. 111–112.

6

England's 'Show' Villages

One of the most powerful causes of insufficient cottage accommodation is the system of Close and Open villages, a system which prevails through all the Midlands and East of England, and which is doing much mischief by its operation on the quality, quantity, and locality of cottages. It is a hiding away of the cottage population in certain villages, and this is effected by unsparing destruction in others.

There are in all counties show villages where the cottages have been reduced to but a few, and where none but persons who are needed as shepherds, gardeners, or gamekeepers are allowed to live. In such nearly all the tenants are regular servants, and receive the good treatment usual to their class.

But the land requires cultivation, and it will be found that the labourers employed upon it are not the tenants of the owner, but that they come from a neighbouring open village perhaps three miles off, where a numerous small proprietary has received them, when their cottages were destroyed in the close villages around . . .

In the close village the scene is beautiful but unreal; without its open neighbour it could not exist. Turning to this latter, one sees miserable hovels, neglected cabbage gardens, the inhabitants seeking work many miles from home; abandoned by persons of competent means; the penal settlements for people of bad character from all the country round . . .

DR HUNTER'S report on the State of the Dwellings of Rural Labourers; 7th Report of the Medical Officer of the Privy Council, Appendix 6, page 135; P.P. 1865, vol. 26.

7

The Shame of 'Cottage Herding'

The majority of the cottages that exist in rural parishes are deficient in almost every requirement that should constitute a home for a Christian family in a civilized community. They are deficient in bedroom accommodation, very few having three chambers, and in some parishes the larger proportion only one; they are deficient in drainage and sanitary arrangements; they are imperfectly supplied with water; such conveniences as they have are often so situated as to become nuisances; they are full enough of drafts to generate any amount of rheumatism; and in many instances they are lamentably dilapidated and out of repair.

The natural history, so to call it, of these miserable, ruinous dwellings is very various. Some of the worst are parish cottages, either erected in the time of the old poor law or bequeathed to the parish as a last home for the aged paupers, which there are no funds to repair. Another almost uniformly bad class are the cottages run up by squatters on the waste, or held upon a lifehold or copyhold tenure, and which have not yet fallen in to the lord of the manor. Others have been put up by speculative builders of the flimsiest materials. Others are converted stables or farmhouses, attesting in the one case the conquest of the railway over the road, in the other the change in the phase of agricultural life which has merged half-a-dozen petty occupations into one large holding. Some belong to small proprietors too indigent to have anything to spare for their improvement; some to absentee or embarrassed landowners, the former of whom are unwilling to improve an area which they never see, the latter, in addition to being unable, are equally unwilling to improve a property from which they get no advantage.

It is impossible to exaggerate the ill effects of such a state of things in every aspect—physical, social, economical, moral, intellectual.

Physically, a ruinous, ill-drained cottage, 'cribbed, cabin'd, and confined', and overcrowded, generates any amount of disease—fevers of every type, catarrh, rheumatism—as well as intensifies to the utmost that tendency to scrofula and phthisis which, from their frequent intermarriages and their low diet, abounds so largely among the poor.

Socially, nothing can be more wretched than the condition of the 'open' parishes, like Docking, in Norfolk, and South Cerney, in

THE COTTAGE

Mr. Punch (to Landlord). "Your stable arrangements are
excellent! Suppose you try something of the sort here! Eh?"

9. John Leech in *Punch*, 1861

Gloucestershire, into which have been poured the scum and off-scour
of their 'close' neighbours.

Economically, the imperfect distribution of cottages deprives the
farmer of a large proportion of his effective labour power. The employer who has no cottages to offer those whom he employs must either
attract labourers by the offer of higher wages or must content himself
with refuse; and in either case when he gets his man gets him more or
less enfeebled by the distance he has had to travel to his work.

The moral consequences are painful to contemplate. 'I only wonder',
writes one clergyman to me, 'that our agricultural poor are as moral as
they are.' Modesty must be an unknown virtue, decency an unimagin-
able thing, where, in one small chamber, with the beds lying as thickly
as they can be packed, father, mother, young men, lads, grown and
growing up girls—two and sometimes three generations—are herded

247

promiscuously; where every operation of the toilette and of nature—dressings, undressings, births, deaths—is performed by each within the sight and hearing of all; where children of both sexes, to as high an age as 12 or 14, or even more, occupy the same bed; where the whole atmosphere is sensual, and human nature is degraded into something below the level of the swine. It is a hideous picture: and the picture is drawn from life.

Mr Clarke, of Norwich, can tell any one who will ask him tales of things he has himself seen, horrifying enough to make the very hair stand on end. The medical gentleman whose evidence I publish assures me that cases of incest are anything but uncommon. We complain of the ante-nuptial unchastity of our women, of the loose talk and conduct of the girls who work in the fields, of the light way in which maidens part with their honour, and how seldom either a parent's or a brother's blood boils with shame—*here*, in cottage herding, is the sufficient account and history of it all . . .

Report by REV. JAMES FRASER, assistant commissioner, on Norfolk, Essex, Sussex, Gloucestershire, &c; Employment of Children, Young Persons, and Women in Agriculture (1867), pp. 35–36; P.P. 1867–8, vol. 17.

8

The Leicestershire Lad's Bride

Something is perhaps lost to health when the bedroom, originally measuring its 12 feet by 10, is divided into sleeping cells by a plaster partition; but at the same time much is gained to decency.

To the Leicestershire lad who brings his bride to a home such as was seen at Lubenham, already filled with adult brothers and sisters, privacy is the first necessity. New married couples are no edifying study for grown up brothers and sisters; and, though instances must not be recorded, sufficient data are remembered to warrant the remark, that great depression and sometimes death are the lot of the female participator in the offence of incest. There is such crowding in private houses at Lubenham as would be prohibited by the police in a common lodging-house.

DR HUNTER on the State of the Dwellings of Rural Labourers; 7th Report of the Medical Officer of the Privy Council, Appendix 6, page 137; P.P. 1865, vol. 26.

9

The Home of a Somersetshire Peasant

Starting from Weston-super-Mare in the direction of Banwell, I met an old labourer trudging wearily along, and I stopped a few minutes to question him. I learnt that he was 77 years of age, and had worked in the district as a farm labourer nearly all his life. He had no wife or family, if I recollect rightly, but had only himself to support. At his age he could not, of course, do much active work. Still he was regularly employed by a farmer, working as well as he could during the day from about 6 in the morning to 6 at night. His wages were 7s. per week. He paid out of that sum for his cottage 1s. 6d. per week, thus leaving 5s. 6d. with which to find himself in food and clothes. No doubt, wretched as his circumstances were, he was comparatively well off in having so large a sum with which to support only himself. But it was pitiable to find such a result at the end of a long life of hard toil, and to think that a poor old creature of 77, who must at that advanced age have needed some comforts, was reduced to a sum per week which could only be sufficient to find the barest necessities. In the particular neighbourhood where this old man lived there had been just before my visit a slight rise in the wages in consequence of the Warwickshire 'strike'. Skilled labourers were receiving 11s., and in some cases 12s. a week.

A little further on I saw a strange sight. Lying a little way back from the road, I descried what I should have thought was a pigstye, but for the fact that a man was at a kind of door, cutting up a dead sheep. I called out and questioned him concerning himself and his cottage. I was then invited to visit the interior of the latter.

Unless I had seen it I could not have believed that such a place could exist in England. I had to stoop very low to get inside this habitation of an English agricultural labourer. The total length of this miserable hut was about seven yards, its width three yards, and its height, measured to the extreme point of the thatched roof, about ten feet; the height of the walls, however, not being so much as six feet. From the top of the walls was carried up to a point the thatched roof, there being no transverse beams or planks. In fact, had there been any, I could not have stood upright in this hovel.

There was, of course, no second floor to the place, and the one tiny floor was divided in the middle into two compartments, each being about three yards square, one used for a bedroom and the other for a sitting-room.

The ground was irregularly paved with large stones, with earth between them and in their crevices. On my remarking that the floor must be very damp, if not wet, in winter, the man said, 'Oh no, sir, it don't "heave" much'; by which he meant that the moisture did not come up through the stones.

From the thatch, in all directions, hung festoons of spiders' webs, intermingled with sprays of ivy, which, but for the terrible squalor of the place, would have given a romantic appearance to the hut.

John P. (the inhabitant of this 'cottage') was a short, thick-set man, sixty years of age. He had lived there, he told me, a quarter of a century. His predecessors were a man, his wife, and six children, all of whom, he said, had slept in the 'bedroom', nine feet square.

John told me that he could not work so well now as he used to do; but nevertheless he looked strong and healthy for his age; and his principal duty—a responsible one—was to look after his master's stock. His wages were 5s. a week. Out of that he paid his master £2. 10s. a year rent for his 'cottage', and 10s. more for the privilege of running his pig—for John had a pig, as well as some fowls—on his master's land. John also rented one-eighth of an acre of potato ground, for which—still out of his miserable wages—he paid 15s. a year. And yet this man was happy amidst it all. His wretched patched garments looked singularly inconsistent when viewed in connexion with his happy-looking face. He spoke well of his employer. His cottage walls were made of hardened mud, and some time since the rain had come through the old patched roof, and he thought it was good of his master to put a new roof and a new door to his 'cottage' when he asked him to do so.

John had been married, but had lost his wife. One daughter, however, was still living, and she had married a policeman in London. John said that when his cottage became no longer fit—according to John's idea of fitness—for a 'residence', the 'master' intended to pull down the mud walls and plough up the site.

FRANCIS GEORGE HEATH, *The English Peasantry* (1874), pp. 46–49.

10

As Bad as the Black Hole of Calcutta

The lodging which is obtained by the pitmen and other labourers connected with the collieries of Northumberland and Durham is perhaps on the whole the worst and the dearest of which any large specimens can be found in England, the similar parishes of Monmouthshire excepted . . . The extreme badness is in the high number of men found in one room, in the smallness of the ground plot on which a great number of houses are thrust, the want of water, the absence of privies, and the frequent placing of one house on the top of another, or distribution into 'flats', a form utterly unfit for working men, and only justified by the high price of land in large cities.

Prudhoe, in Northumberland, affords a remarkable example of the pressure of the mining population where work is plentiful . . . At Low Prudhoe, a coalowner had more than a hundred cots, all to be served with water by one small dribbling stream, little thicker than a pencil when I saw it. Twenty-one buckets were then formed *en queue* waiting for water, and a mob of women and children wrangling and lamenting over it. Some of the women professed to be terrified at the thought of the men coming home from the pit and being unable to wash or have tea. They related that at Mickley colliery the inhabitants of 'the Square' were even worse off for water, one woman having lately counted 100 buckets at the spring. Women get up in the middle of the night to get water, and even then find others waiting their turns at 2 or 3 o'clock.

For washing the house all can get, by carriage from the river, a sufficient supply of water, but it is hard and ferruginous, wasteful of soap, and every way unfit for use. The remedy for all this is obviously to form an underground rainwater tank, but the short tenures will always prevent such costly comfort.

The houses were 16 feet by 16, all one room, except that the four-post bed served as bed and bedroom too, and that there was a window in the roof loft which made it into a sort of children's bedroom. The houses were sometimes back to back, and sometimes 'single', but all of one size . . .

The whole colony of about 600 people, pitmen and their families, had not a single privy among them . . . In the walls opposite the housefronts bays or recesses are sunk a little below the usual level, and these are made, alternately, coal stores and cesspools. The women and children dung into pots, which are emptied into these bays, the men dunging away from home, valuing their dung and depositing it in the garden if they have one. And this possession of the dung is one of the absurd grievances which hinder the erection of privies. I have heard of privies being riotously destroyed, and often of their being only another speculation for making money out of the collier!

Great numbers of dogs were kept at Prudhoe; much of the furniture was even luxurious. The whole people was irritated about the want of water, but only one man had a word to say about the cesspools in front of his house door, or the want of privies . . .

Perhaps the pessimum of inhabitant misery is to be found at Birtley, near Gateshead. It would the multitudinous seas ensable to wash the outsides of Birtley, and were the Black Hole of Calcutta placed in the crater of Etna, it would but present the row of cots called the Red Row at Birtley. These eight houses are placed close to the iron works, although there is abundant land. The room measures 18 feet by 16 feet 8, by 7 feet high. The roof of the loft springs from walls only 2 feet high. Some although they pay £4 rent [a year] have no garden, no privy, no scullery, no middenstead, nor easy means of evacuation of filth but throwing it on the turnpike road.

In one of these cots lived six adults with four children, in another seven adults, in another five with one child, and in another three with four children. Had countless generations of gannets laid addled eggs instead of guano in the Chincha islands their odour would not have rivalled that of Red Row the day I visited it.

From DR HUNTER'S Inquiry into the state of the Dwellings of Rural Labourers, Durham and Northumberland; 7th Report of Medical Officer of the Privy Council, Appendix 6 (1864), pp. 180–186; P.P. 1865, vol. 26.

II

Duck and Green Peas

In estimating the present state of this important field of mining labour [South Staffs], it must not be forgotten how much has been altered for the better within living memory. The cruel and brutalizing sports to which the population were then addicted have greatly decreased, (and) with the decline of these exhibitions of cruelty [bull-baiting, cock-fighting, etc.] the manners and language of the lower classes have improved, and scenes of violence are less frequent. Even the external appearance of these large village-towns, and the means of cleanliness and comfort, though much yet remains to be accomplished in these respects, is far better than it was . . .

Nevertheless, in recognizing with satisfaction the advance already effected, and the more cheering prospects of the future, we must not be led away from a steady contemplation of the actual state of society in this district. Its distinguishing feature at the present moment unquestionably is, that as regards the labouring classes, the half-savage manners of the last generation have been exchanged for a deep and almost universally pervading sensuality . . .

The means of ministering abundantly to gratifications of this kind are seldom long out of the reach of the labouring classes in this district, especially those employed in the Iron-works, whose great earnings in good times (perhaps 50s. a week on an average) are well known. Even in times of depression, as of late, the colliers and miners seldom earn less than 16s., and might usually earn more if they would consent to work six days in the week . . .

The recklessness and extravagance with which these sums are spent have been commented upon in all the Reports on the habits of the mining population yet published. Poultry, especially geese and ducks; the earliest and choicest vegetables (e.g. asparagus, green peas, and new potatoes, when they first appear in the market); occasionally even port wine, drunk out of tumblers and basins; beer and spirits in great quantities; meat in abundance, extravagantly cooked; excursions in carts and cars, gambling, etc., are the well-known objects on which their money is squandered . . .

The causes that have encouraged this devotion to mere animal indulgences have been so often pointed out that they need scarcely be repeated. This vast crowd of men has been gathered together within a narrow space, without any adequate means being provided to arm them against the increased temptations which such agglomeration, accompanied by high wages, brought with it. The external circumstances with which they are surrounded,—the smoke that darkens the face of nature, the surface of the ground either occupied by or marked with the adjuncts of mining or manufacturing labour, the dirt of the streets and lanes, the frequent absence of drainage, the common want of a sufficient supply of water for purposes of cleanliness, personal and domestic, the crowded houses, the absence of privacy, the ignorance of the wife of household duties,—these causes, added to the vacancy of mind arising from want of culture, and the slight restraints imposed by their religious convictions, place every kind of recreation but those connected with the lowest appetites almost out of the question for the great majority, and combine to sink the labouring man below the level at which it is either safe or creditable that he should be.

H. SEYMOUR TREMENHEERE, report on South Staffs: Report of the Commission appointed to enquire into ... the state of the Mining Districts, P.P. 1850, vol. 23, pp. 8–10.

12

What the Miners Read

I asked a very respectable person (who is a Wesleyan local preacher, and who stated that it had been his habit for many years to visit constantly the colliers' houses) whether he had observed any material difference between the Scotch colliers and the English. His answer was:—

'When you go into some of the Scotchmen's houses you would be surprised to see the books they have—not many, but all choice books. Some of their favourite authors in divinity are very common among them. Many of them read such books as Adam Smith's *Wealth of Nations,* and are fond of discussing the subjects he treats of. They also read the lives of statesmen, and books of history; also works on logic, and sometimes mathematics. Such men can be reasoned with about anything appertaining to their calling, and they know very well why wages cannot be at particular times higher than a certain standard ... Such men will have nothing to do with the union ... They will also talk with great zest of many of their great men—their own countrymen, who have raised themselves by their industry. There are, undoubtedly, some men that come out of Scotland bad men, but these are not informed men ... There are a great many Scotch at all the collieries here, and most of them very respectable men, exceedingly so ...

'When a Scotchman comes here he earns English wages, but he does not spend them as an Englishman does. A Scotchman often, rather than lose buying a good book, will lose his dinner. The Scotchwomen begin to keep their houses cleaner after they get into England, and by degrees they come to keep them as clean as the Englishwomen ... They are generally very saving, and lay out the overplus of their earnings in books and furniture, or lay it by. They have a great disposition to have their children taught. Indeed, I have seen several lads that have been educated in the Scotch schools, and I find them very well taught; they can reason like men.'

I asked if he would state what difference he observed between the best specimens of the Northumbrian pitmen, and the best specimens of the Scotch which he had just described. Answer:—

'I don't think I ever saw Adam Smith's works in more than one or two English pitmen's houses. They are backward to attempt anything that requires steady thinking, such as that book, or any work on logic or mathematics. The Scotch often study both: they read Watts's *Logic* ... The English seldom attempt even English grammar or geometry; they always tell me they are obliged to give way when they have made a trial. They had rather read any popular work, such as *The Christian Philosopher*, the *Pilgrim's Progress*, or Walter Scott's novels. They love to read their country's history, and they like to talk of its renown in the ancient French wars of Edward III and Henry V. They are also great readers of Napoleon's and the Duke of Wellington's wars, and their soul seems to take fire when they talk of their country's victories. They are fond of biography, and especially that of men who rose from being poor men to be great characters.

'They are very generous in their dispositions, and will share their loaf with the poor, as all the trampers and beggars from Newcastle and all the country know. They are greatly improved in my time as to drinking habits; there is much less of it, and their money is chiefly spent in living well and making a great show on furniture and dress. The women, too, are improving, and manage their families much better than they used to ...'

H. SEYMOUR TREMENHEERE, *Report on Mining Districts* (1850); pp. 53-54; P.P. 1850, vol. 23.

13

The Nailers' Wash-basin

Thirty years experience amongst the nailers [of Sedgley parish, South Staffs] tells me they are the most immoral people in England ... Here men and women cohabit and propagate in unions connected by no marriage service; and, strange to say, the Poor Law seems partly to blame for this, for the unmarried receive 1s. 6d. a week for each child, and 2s. for himself, which is no inconsiderable boon to the unmarried father and mother. This is in many cases an insuperable bar to matrimony, and a premium for adultery . . .

The little nailer, reared in his earthen or quarry floor, promoted to the forges, prematurely elevated to the nail block, lives, when trade is good, what may be called a jolly sort of life, for he is never sad, though he grumbles much. Give him a little animal food, and a good deal of beer, and he is as happy as he can conceive it possible for him to be. No mechanics' institute reaches him; no lectures, however amusing; no concerts, fiddle they ever so sweetly, ever have him to spend his hard-earned pence on them. He will go if you promise him free beer; he will go to church or chapel, give him old clothes and a cup of beer; he will serve you like a dog, fight you, or for you, if you will but give him beer; wounds of his tenderest affections may be plastered up with beer; and all this applies to one [sex] just as much as the other. Indeed, the women have more manly qualities than their husbands; and in their free fights, the wife is often the victor.

Their homes are the worst, in whatever neighbourhood they settle. The broken panes where pieces of paper fill the place of glass, pilfered nail-bags keeping out the cold, the quarry or mud floor on which are three or four naked children sprawling unwashed, the ling fire in this land of coal, a round deal table with three rickety legs, a deal board smoothed on the upper side, and with four legs, acting as a chaise longue, a three-legged pot and a tin kettle, furnish many a living room.

Enter their sleeping rooms, as I did this morning, fresh from the summer air, and you must hold your breath and rush to the window and throw it open. There lie husband and wife and two sick children. A young man of 25 in the same bed with a daughter of 19, brother and sister. In a corner a truss of straw, covered by a bag or two, is the bed of two or more little ones; no blankets, no sheets, no washing apparatus —in fact, a certain article, more celebrated for its use than ornament, is the only washhand-basin they have ever known . . .

DR BALLENDEN; appendix to Factory Inspectors' Reports to 31 Oct. 1868, pp. 297–298; P.P. 1868/9, vol. 14.

7. The Dead and the Living: Bishopsgate-street District. Geo. Godwin, *London Shadows*, 1854

A Londoner's Home: Interior of House in Court

8. A Weaver's Garret in Spitalfields.   Geo. Godwin, *London Shadows*, 1854

John P—and his Cottage.   F. G. Heath, *The English Peasantry*, 1874

14

Halstead Weaver

In passing from cottage to cottage [at Halstead, Essex] to visit the sick, I often entered into conversation with the men who worked their looms at home. Frequently they were the husbands of women working in the factory all day. In 1847, Messrs. Courtauld's had 195 soft-silk looms at work in this town, besides about thirty-five persons employed in connexion with these. Most of the weavers work their hand-looms in their own houses; frequently the middle floor is entirely devoted to what they term the shop, the place of work.

A weaver's shop is sometimes a sad, dirty, and dismal place; but as often, to an artistic eye, it is quaint and picturesque, from the vast variety of its contents, symbolizing the lives of its inhabitants.

Not long ago I passed a night in one of these shops, a description of which would give a specimen of those belonging to the better class of our work-people. I passed through a neatly furnished parlour downstairs, into which the street door opened, then mounted stairs which led to one large room, the windows of which extended the whole of the two sides of the house, back and front. At the top of the stairs was also a very small bedroom, without any fireplace, in which the poor man I came to nurse was lying.

There were two looms, one at each window, in the shop, at which worked in the day-time the now heart-stricken parents of my dying friend; for a dear friend he had become, I having visited him for two years, since he had been suffering from consumption, and admiringly observed for that time his peculiarly gentle, intelligent, and refined mind. At the commencement of his illness he was a National schoolmaster, though, as a child, he had worked in the trade with his father.

As I sat in this room by the light of a wood and coal fire, made brighter than usual for my reception, with the addition of one dim candle, the shadows of the looms flickered strangely over the whitewashed wall and ceiling, whilst the many reminders scattered about me of the daily toil and thrift of the inmates, made me feel for the time as if reading the simple but earnest story of their struggling life. There were the looms, at once somewhat cumbrous and classic in form, with the costly fabrics they contained, contrasting with the old, threadbare, but well-kept greatcoat which 'Father', as the good woman always called her husband, had extended on the back of the arm-chair, to protect me from draught.

On the narrow mantelshelf were a few well-worn books of family devotion, besides some of the small tools used for their work. On one side was the ticking clock, with its swinging pendulum; on the other, the little safe, or cupboard, with all the etcetera of their small house-keepings; and around, were sundry articles of personal attire, such as you often seen hung up in cottage homes. Stowed up in another part of the room were gathered seeds tied up in bundles, and other matters, telling that 'Father' had an allotment garden, and worked in it, for the benefit of the household. On the little table beside me, were all the restoratives provided for their poor, sick, son, arranged with the thoughtful care of their kind hearts, before they retired for the rest they so much needed after many nights of anxious watching. Silent and alone, the thought of the hundreds of lives which are spent almost entirely in nooks like this, came vividly before me, waking intense sympathy with them in their many trials.

A weaver's shop must usually be both his kitchen and his sitting-room, because he cannot afford a fire elsewhere, as well as a sufficient one there—warmth being very necessary for his work; and neither frequent cleansing, nor thorough ventilation, are very possible when delicate and expensive work is in the loom. Thus neatness and health often suffer.

In such shops are often to be seen the men sitting in the click-clacking loom, with half-a-dozen children toddling or trotting in and out. Sometimes one of these would creep away, and slily hide her face behind the large, rough stones, tied to the end of the 'harness' to keep it steady; sometimes a baby face would peep out of a high wicker-cradle, the infant almost lost in what looked like dirty rags; whilst sitting on a tiny stool, or kneeling at the side of the cradle, might be seen another little one, scarcely larger than the baby, but taught to rock it till mother came from the factory . . .

MARY MERRYWEATHER, *Experiences of Factory Life . . . at Mr Courtauld's Silk Mill at Halstead, in Essex* (1862), pp. 31–34.

15

'Diabolic odour' of Welsh Cottages

In Wales the farmer as well as the labourer must be taken to mean a person generally badly lodged, and insufficiently fed and clothed. The poverty of the soil and the damp climate have rendered agriculture a trade which offers little attraction to persons of capital, and in which nothing but the sternest frugality can hope to find a gain.

The evil effect of poverty upon the health is rather increased by the frugal habits of the Welsh farmers. Among them may recently have arisen a few whose means and whose manners have changed, but it may be truly said of this class that in many districts the farmer himself does not eat fresh meat once a month; that his only animal food is sparingly taken, and consists of the lean of cheese, and lean beef or ham salted and dried to the texture of mahogany, and hardly worth the difficult process of assimilation.

The farmer's labourers who board in his house live proportionately worse. A morsel of the salt beef or bacon is used to flavour a large quantity of broth, or gruel, of meal and leeks, and day after day this is the labourer's dinner. His keep is reckoned at about five pence a day, but in many districts it was said to be much less cost to the farmer.

Some of the labourers' wives earn a few pence by a day's work in picking up stones, and in a few cases landlords were reported to allow free pasturage on their land for a labourer's cow.

In Cardigan district a medical practitioner described the children as 'pining for want as soon as weaned', and thought that if the climate were cold the whole race would perish . . .

It has been a matter of common remark in this county that the women are by far more vigorous than the men, but persons well able to judge believe that both women and men are going down to the lowest point of strength at which it is possible to live. This decline is said to be due to the abandonment of the solid homespun clothing in favour of the cheap and showy cotton goods, and to the introduction of tea. These things may contribute to the poverty and weakness of the race, but in the main they are due to insufficient earnings, and the effect is seen in the nearly universal prevalence of tuberculosis or scrofula.

The agriculturist, after several hours exposure to wind and rain, gains his cottage to sit by a fire of peat or of balls of clay and small coal kneaded together, from which volumes of carbonic and sulphurous acids are poured forth. His walls are of mud and stones, his floor the bare earth which was there before the hut was built, his roof a mass of loose and sodden thatch. Every crevice is stopped to maintain warmth, and in an atmosphere of diabolic odour, with a mud floor, with his only clothes drying on his back, he often sups and sleeps with his wife and children.

Obstetricians who have passed parts of the night in such cabins have described how they found their feet sinking in the mud of the floor, and they were forced (easy task) to drill a hole through the wall to effect a little private respiration . . .

DR HUNTER'S report on the Death-rate of the Population in parts of South
    Wales; 7th report of the Medical Officer of the Privy Council, Appendix
    No. 9, pp. 498–499; P.P. 1865, vol. 26.

16

Cardiganshire's Wretched Hovels

The great blot upon this country (Cardiganshire, Montgomeryshire, and Merionethshire) is the condition of its cottages. The exteriors sometimes promise well, but are deceptive. There is an appearance of neatness in the thatched roof and whitewashed walls which creates at first a favourable impression. The practice of whitewashing the walls, and not unfrequently the roofs with lime, which is mentioned by a Welsh bard of the sixth century, is still very generally practised. In some places it is common to mix clay with the lime for colouring the walls yellow, and the slate roofs are washed white.

Nothing, however, can be conceived more wretched that the interior of most of these habitations. The cottage is often only one room, which is divided into two compartments, in one of which the cooking is done; the other is used for meals and contains the beds which are simply boxes, and five or six of these box beds are often packed together within the compass of a few square yards. The windows have no apertures; ventilation is supplied by the chimney and the door; the floor is of clay, and in this close, damp, dreary hovel are often housed a labourer, his wife, and six or eight children.

The very wretched cottages in Cardiganshire appear to have originated in two causes: 1,—in squatters building upon the wastes at a time when manorial rights were very little looked after, and any possessed of a few pounds might, unmolested, erect a hovel for his residence. 2,—in a long established custom of granting building leases for a long term of years, leaving the tenant to form his own plan and choose his own materials. The result is the existence of perhaps a greater number of cottages unfit for the habitation of human beings than is to be found within an equal area in any part of Great Britain . . .

The decencies of life are more thought of than they were, and although, from the general want of privies, the lane, the field, and even the church-yard, are still resorted to for the purposes of nature, it is occasionally with a feeling akin to shame, and a sentiment certainly not of respect for the owners of those hovels, whose parsimony or indifference have compelled them to resort to such practices . . .

Mr Loxdale, of Castle Hill, Llanilar, a gentleman who has taken much interest in the improvement of labourers' dwellings, informed me that a marked change for the better has taken place of late years in regard to the observance of some of the proprieties of life. This gentleman has built a considerable number of cottages in the place of the hovels which were a disgrace to his neighbourhood, and he assured me that the desire for better accommodation is becoming general among the labouring classes. He has been able to build a considerable number of excellent cottages, with 3 bedrooms above, and kitchen, pantry, etc. below, for £120 each, for which an agricultural labourer in receipt of fair wages is willing to pay £5 a year.

Few cottages in Cardiganshire have gardens. In villages the houses are generally built in rows with no frontage but the road, and without any garden behind. Where detached houses have small gardens they are generally neglected. In the immediate neighbourhood of towns cottage gardens are not uncommon, and are comparatively well cultivated, and the wives of the cottagers may be seen on market day carrying their baskets of vegetables and fruit to the market town, or hawking them about from house to house . . .

3rd Report, Commission . . . employment of Children, Young Persons, and Women in Agriculture (1870), pp. 53–54; P.P. 1870, vol. 13.

17

'But-and-Ben' Cottages of the Scotch Peasantry

The cottages in Scotland are all very similar in form. The ordinary type of cottage is that which is called the 'but-and-ben' cottage. This consists of one oblong room about twice the length of its breadth, and having the door in the centre; opposite the door two box beds are placed across the cottage, thus dividing it into two separate apartments. In cottages of rather better construction a permanent partition is put up to divide the cottage into two rooms, the 'but' and the 'ben'; and in the class of cottage next above this a third room is provided, looking out to the back immediately opposite the door, and entered from one of the other rooms. This third room is a most valuable addition as a sleeping apartment, and is almost universally provided in all new cottages.

The cottages are very seldom provided with an upper floor, and where they are it is but rarely used if the family can possibly be accommodated downstairs. The kitchen is always preferred as a sleeping room, and the other rooms are only used when the kitchen is full. Women like to have their 'bairns' close to them when at work, and don't like the trouble of going upstairs, and fuel is thus saved.

The cottages are substantially built of stone, with either slate or thatched roofs. In ventilation, properly so called, the cottages are very deficient. The windows in scarcely any of the old cottages are made to open; and when they are, the means of ventilation thus offered are but rarely taken advantage of. At the same time the inmates do not appear to suffer from want of air, for they, more particularly the children, presented almost invariably a robust and healthy appearance. Probably the large chimneys, which communicate directly with the outer air, and below which, in the living room at any rate, a fire is almost always kept burning, added to the fact that the door is constantly being opened and shut, obviates the necessity of ventilation. However this may be, I feel sure that I never found the small rooms in which the Scotch families lived both by night and day, nearly as offensive as I have found the bedrooms of magnificent model cottages in England, the windows of which are never opened and which are so well built as to exclude all draughts . . .

To say that the drainage of the cottages of Scotland is defective would be a gross exaggeration, because as a general rule no attempt is made at drainage at all. They very seldom have privies. The cottages on Lord Airlie's property at Cortashy in Forfarshire would probably compare favourably with the cottages belonging to most proprietors in this respect, and I found that on Lord Airlie's property there are only 79 privies to 401 cottages. Where this accommodation is supplied it is often not used by the occupiers. I recollect finding the privy attached to the entrance lodge of a gentleman's park fitted up as a hen house. This struck me as being a remarkable instance of the habits of the people, because the tenant of the lodge occupied a position rather above that of ordinary farm servants.

All the cottages which are situated in the country are provided with good-sized gardens; those in the villages or towns are either without gardens, or if they have then the garden is generally too small to be of any practical use . . . I saw no signs of the pretty cottage flower gardens which are so common in England, and more particularly in the southern counties; but the severity of the climate renders this almost impossible.

The furniture in the cottages struck me as being rather too good for the cottages. One room is generally provided with substantial chairs, a table, and a chest of drawers of polished deal or mahogany; while in the other room, which is more constantly used, the furniture is of rather a ruder description. Box beds are almost invariably used. When a marriage takes place it is customary for the man to purchase all the tables, chairs, etc. (i.e. the substantial furniture of the house), while the wife buys crockery and linen. The furniture thus purchased by the wife is termed 'her providing', and costs about £10. The articles purchased by the husband cost from £12 to £15.

From MR F. H. NORMAN'S report on Forfar, Kincardine, Aberdeen, Banff, Moray, and Nairn; Report of Commission on Employment of Children, Young Persons, and Women in Agriculture, 4th Report (1870), page 37; P.P. 1870, vol. 13.

18

Seen from a Bus top

There is a great deal of the world to be seen in the inside of an omnibus . . . but there is still more to be seen on the outside. The 'knife-board', that is, the longitudinal seat which stretches from end to end of the roof, is a very favourite position with a numerous class of the metropolitan world. It is sufficiently far above the noise of the wheels to allow of undisturbed conversation, and is a point of eminence from which everything going forward below and around can be plainly seen.

We ourselves were indebted to it, not long ago, for a series of gastronomical observations of the mode in which London tradesmen live—a view, by the way, which might have satisfied the most sceptical of the material prosperity enjoyed by that class, in spite of occasional cries of 'bad times'.

Our omnibus slowly proceeded down a narrow and obstructed street. It was a warm summer's evening, between the hours of 9 and 10, and the shopmen of the district, from want of back parlours, were taking their supper in the front floor, with the windows of their apartments open. We say nothing of the garnished sirloins, parsley-decked hams, pickled salmon and lobster salads, with cold gooseberry pies in profusion, of which we had a vision sufficiently distinct, as we were carried along—having no intention of carping at the dietary of John Bull. Our sole comment shall be the remark of a rather hungry-looking genius in fustian who shared the knife-board with us, whose eyes twinkled, and whose mouth visibly watered at the sight, as he exclaims spontaneously, 'Crikey! don't they do it up tidy up here—jest!'—wiping his mouth.

CHARLES MANBY SMITH, *Curiosities of London Life* (1853), pp. 230–231.

19

Saturday Afternoon to Sunday Dinner

The working half of Saturday is up at 1 o'clock. In a well-ordered workshop every man is allowed a certain time each Saturday for 'tidying-up', sweeping of the floor and benches, cleaning and laying out in order the tools. This is completed a minute or two before 1 o'clock; and when the workmen, with their newly washed hands and their shop jackets or slops rolled up under their arms, stand in groups waiting for the ringing of the bell, it is a sight well worth seeing, and one in which the working man is, all things considered, perhaps seen at his best ... When the bell rings the men leave the works in a leisurely way that contrasts rather strongly with the eagerness with which they leave at other times.

The first proceeding of the workmen upon reaching home is to get their dinner, which they eat upon Saturday and Sunday only in a leisurely manner; and after dinner the smokers charge, light, and smoke their pipes, still in a leisurely contemplative manner unknown to them at other times. By the time they have finished their pipes it is probably 2 o'clock, and they then proceed to clean themselves up—the phrase being equivalent among 'the great unwashed' to the society one of performing your toilet. The first part of the cleaning-up process consists in 'a good wash', and it is completed by an entire change of dress. A favourite plan of cleaning-up on Saturday afternoons is—among those who live within easy reach of public baths—to take their clean suits to the bath, and put them on after they have bathed, bringing away their working suits tied up in a bundle.

Some of the higher paid mechanics present a very different appearance when cleaned up from that which they presented an hour or two before, when sauntering out of the shop gates. Working-class swelldom breaks out for the short time in which it is permitted to do so in all the butterfly brilliance of 'fashionable' made clothes, with splendid accessories in collars, scarves, and cheap jewellery. But neither the will nor the means to 'come the swell' are given to all men, and a favourite Saturday evening costume with the mass of working men consists of the clean moleskin or cord trousers that are to be worn at work during the ensuing week, black coat and waistcoat, a cap of a somewhat sporting character, and a muffler more or less gaudy.

Of course, the manner in which working men spend their Saturday afternoon is dependent upon their temperaments, tastes, and domestic circumstances. The man who goes home on a Saturday only to find his house in disorder, with every article of furniture out of its place, the floor unwashed or sloppy from uncompleted washing, his wife slovenly, his children untidy, his dinner not yet ready, or spoilt in the cooking, is much more likely to 'go on the spree' than the man who finds his house in order, the furniture glistening from the recent polishing, the burnished steel fire-irons looking doubly resplendent from the bright glow of the cheerful fire, his well-cooked dinner ready laid on a snowy cloth, and his wife and children tidy and cheerful. If the man whose household work is neglected or mismanaged is of a meek character, and has been unfortunate enough to get for a wife one who is a termagant as well as a sloven, he will have to devote his Saturday afternoon to assisting in the woman's work of his own house. But when the husband is not of the requisite meekness of spirit, he hastens from the disorderly scene, and roams about in a frame of mind that predisposes him to seek the questionable comforts of the public-house, or to enter into some other form of dissipation . . .

Taking it for granted that the representative working men have tolerably comfortable homes, their methods of spending their Saturday afternoons will then depend upon their respective tastes and habits. The steady man who is 'thoroughly domesticated' will probably settle himself by the fireside, and having lit his pipe, devote himself to the perusal of the weekly newspaper. He will go through the police intelligence with a patience and perseverance worthy of a better cause, then through the murders of the week, proceed from them to the reviews of books, take a passing glance at the sporting intelligence, and finally learns from the leading articles that he is a cruelly 'ground down' and virtually enslaved individual . . . This is generally about the range of a first reading, the foreign intelligence, news from the provinces, answers to correspondents . . . being left for a future occasion. By the time such first reading has been got through tea-time is near—for an early tea, a tea to which all the members of the family sit down together, and at which the relishes of the season abound to an extent known only to a Saturday and a pay-day, is a stock part of a working-man's Saturday.

The family man, whom the wives of other working men describe to their husbands as 'something like a husband', but who is probably regarded by his own wife as a bore, and by his shop mates as a mollicot— will go marketing with or for his wife . . . Many of the unmarried, and some of the younger married men of the working classes, are now members of volunteer corps, workshop bands, or boat clubs, and devote part of their Saturday afternoons to drill, band practice, or rowing. When not engaged in any of the above pursuits, the men of this class go for an afternoon stroll . . . Those men who are bent upon improving their general education, or mastering those branches of learning— generally mathematics and mechanical drawing—which will be most useful to them, spend their Saturday afternoons in reading.

But whatever may be the nature of their Saturday afternoon proceeding, working men contrive to bring them to a conclusion in time for an early (about 5 o'clock) tea, so as to leave themselves a long evening. Burns's *Cotter's Saturday Night* would be in no respect applicable as a description of the Saturday nights of the present generation of working men and their families . . . The 'intelligent artisan' does not spend his Saturday night by his ain fireside, or devote it to family worship, and however 'halesome parritch'—'thick a dick' he would call it—may be, he would emphatically object to it as a Saturday night's supper.

The lover of the modern Jenny, when going courting on Saturday night, will *not* rap gently at the door, but will give an authoritative ran tan upon the knocker; and on being admitted will not be 'sae bashfu' and sae grave'. On the contrary, he will have a free-and-easy, almost patronizing manner, will greet Jenny in an off-handed style, and will tell her to look sharp and get her things on; and while she is dressing, he will enter into familiar conversation with her father, incidentally telling him to what place of amusement he is going to take Jenny . . .

After tea those men who have been out during the afternoon generally stay in for an hour's rest before setting forth on their evening ramble in search of amusement . . . The theatre is the most popular resort of pleasure-seeking workmen, and the gallery their favourite part of the house. Two or three males generally go together, taking with them a joint-stock bottle of drink and a suitable supply of eatables. Or sometimes two or three married couples who have 'no encumbrance', or who have got some neighbour to look after the children, make up a party, the women carrying a plentiful supply of provisions . . .

After the theatres the music-halls are the most popular places of Saturday night resort with working men, as at them they can combine the drinking of the Saturday night glass, and the smoking of the Saturday night pipe, with the seeing and hearing of a variety of entertainments, ranging from magnificent ballets and marvellous scenic illusions to inferior tumbling, and from well-given operatic selections to the most idiotic of the so-called comic songs of the Jolly Dogs class . . .

Next to the theatres and music-halls, the shilling, sixpenny, and threepenny 'hops' of the dancing academies and saloons which abound in manufacturing districts, are the amusements most affected by the younger and more spruce of unmarried working men. And it is at these cheap dancing *academies* (which, not being connected, as the *saloons* generally are, with public-houses, are looked upon as exclusive and genteel establishments) that unfortunate working men generally make the acquaintance of those young ladies of the millinery and dressmaking persuasion, who entertain secret hopes of one day marrying a gentleman; but who unhappily for society in general and the working classes in particular, become the slovenly mismanaging wives of working men.

Often men spend their Saturday nights at public-house 'free-and-easies'. Of course there are some of my class who prefer above all things to spend a quiet Saturday evening in a reading-room, or at a working-men's club. But however different working men may spend the bulk of their Saturday night, it is an almost invariable practice with those of them who are not teetotallers, to 'drop in' some time during the night at some house of call, in order to have a pipe and a glass in company with the friends or shopmates who frequent the house . . .

A 'long lie in' on Sunday

The opportunity of indulging without self-reproach in the luxury of 'a long lie in' is the earliest and most universal of the delights of a working man's Sunday. It is believed that there are working men who often, and especially in the summer months, rise as early on Sunday mornings as they do on other mornings, but such men are regarded as men of evil conscience or bad digestion. There are also well authenticated instances in which unfortunate men who have been brought entirely under 'the wife's dominion', are habitually compelled to rise at a comparatively early hour on Sunday mornings and make the fire and tidy up the place before their lazy and masterful or lazy and lackadaisical wives come down . . .

The Sunday dinner is by a long way the most important culinary affair of the week; although its preparation and cooking is to the managing and industrious housewife a labour of love, it is also a labour of time, and must be started soon after breakfast, if dinner is to be on the table at the fashionable working-class dinner-hour of half-past one. A good plate of meat and potatoes, with bread and cheese *ad libitum* to follow, is not a bad week-day dinner, even for so distinguished an individual as 'the intelligent artisan', but it must not be compared with his Sunday one. The bill of fare for a working man's Sunday dinner will often include a roast or a boil, three different dishes of vegetables, and two different puddings, or pudding and tart, with bread and cheese and celery, and plenty of beer.

Nor is it merely in the greater variety of meats that warmly furnish forth the dinner table, that the Sunday dinner is an important affair; it is eminently important as a social institution and as a means of beneficially influencing the manners and customs of the working classes generally, from the more or less elaborate and polite style in which it is laid out and conducted. It is set out in the best room, and on the best table, covered with the best table-cloth, and family plate, consisting of a plated cruet-stand, a gravy-ladle, and a pair of table-spoons, and a salt-cellar and salt-spoon, with, of course, the best set of knives and forks—the set which, save on Sundays and such high days as Christmas and Good Friday, are wrapped in a cloth and carefully put away among the family linen. The carving, the helping to the various dishes and passing round of the plates are gone through with all due forms and observances . . . Lastly, though by no means leastly, the Sunday dinner is, with the exception of 'Christmas time', the sole vehicle for special family or friendly re-unions, and express interchange of social rites and courtesies . . . In short, the Sunday dinner and the customs connected with it, are, socially considered, perhaps the most important features, not only of the working man's Sunday, but of his household life generally . . .

From *Some Habits and Customs of the Working Classes, written by a Journeyman Engineer* (THOMAS WRIGHT); (1867), pp. 188–216.

20

Chit-Chat over the Wash-tub

Mr Harper Twelvetrees' Manufactory, Imperial Works, Bromley-by-Bow, London, where are manufactured 'cheap materials for the laundry', including penny packets of soap-powder—one of the announcements concerning the 'abolition of the horrors of washing-day' by the use of his detergents:—

A Friendly Bit of Chit-Chat between Mrs Scrubwell and Mrs Thrifty.
Scrubwell. Good morning, Neighbour Thrifty. How are you and your family? But how is this? I understood you had your 'week's wash' today, and I expected to find you 'up to the elbows' in suds; instead of which, here is a clean dry house, and the dinner-table all in apple-pie order, ready for your husband on his coming from work. Are you going to put off your wash till next week?
Thrifty. Why, neighbour, *I have done my washing!* I began at a little before 9 o'clock this morning, have washed every rag of clothes, and look, there they are on the lines in the garden, nearly dry.
Scrubwell. Well, I *am* surprised. But do you mean to say that you have washed all that lot of clothes this morning? *Impossible, surely!*
Thrifty. Impossible or not, *it is quite true.*
Scrubwell. You amaze me, neighbour. How have you done it, and who have you had to help you?
Thrifty. Oh, it is easy enough to get rid of the slap-dash, steam, and dribbling-slops on a washing-day, in good time. I can always make quick work of *my* washing by using 'Harper Twelvetrees' Glycerine Soap-Powder', and it makes the clothes beautifully clean and white too, I assure you. I scarcely ever rub our clothes now, and you know how black my Jim's shirts get at the Foundry.
Scrubwell. But how do you get the clothes clean if you do not rub them well?
Thrifty. I mean that I don't often find it necessary to rub them after I take them out of the soaking water. Of course, I always soak the white clothes over night, and soap the collars and wristbands of shirts, and rub the part most soiled; but I don't stand rubbing the clothes to pieces, and rubbing the skin off my hands at the wash-tub all the next day, as some people do.
Scrubwell. Well, this is really wonderful! I had no idea that washing-day

could be got over with so little trouble and labour. I think I shall try this wonderful powder.

Thrifty. If you give it a *fair trial*, you will find even far greater advantages than quickly getting the clothes out of the way. For instance, my husband, though a good, quiet, sober man (a teetotaller) used to be but sadly out of the way on washing days; for our house you know is small, and we have no wash-house. But now he knows very little about the wash, except the pleasure of having clean linen when he requires it.

Scrubwell. That's capital! I'll certainly try Harper Twelvetrees' 'Glycerine' at once, for my husband has often been sadly out of temper on washing-days and has frequently gone to the public-house, because, he said, he had no comfort at home.

Thrifty. And just consider what you save, in time, trouble, and labour, by using this 'Glycerine Soap-powder'. Just consider the difference between slop, slop, slopping about all day, and having your house cleaned up before dinner, or nearly so.

Scrubwell. Thank you, neighbour, for your friendly advice and information. I will try Harper Twelvetrees' 'Glycerine Soap-Powder' for myself.

Thrifty. And I am sure you will continue to use it, or my name is not Jane Thrifty.

Scrubwell. Thank you, neighbour, Good morning. (Exit Scrubwell.) (Enter James Thrifty, smiling at his nice clean house, and well-spread dinner-table.)

Quoted by HENRY MAYHEW; *The Shops and Companies of London,* etc. (1865), page 199.

CHAPTER 6

THE SANITARY IDEA

(a) LONDON, THE INSANITARY CITY

Queen Victoria's long reign will be remembered for many things, and many of them were good. And of the most worthy of remembrance it may well be that historians of the future will put in the forefront of their record the beginnings of what came to be known as Public Health.

When William IV, the Queen's predecessor, came to the throne in 1830, the subject was hardly heard of, and if the term had been mentioned few people would have had the foggiest idea of what it meant. There was, as Dr John Simon wrote in his classic volume on *English Sanitary Institutions* (1890) 'no general law of sanitary intention on the Statute Book' unless an act providing for quarantine in the case of certain pestilences might be so regarded, and the voting of £2000 annually by Parliament to support a national vaccination board. Outside these two matters the Central Government had nothing to say about public health, and the local authorities, such as they were, had very little to do with it. Most of the big towns had a public water supply, although this was not laid on to anything like every house, and only a very go-ahead municipality had been awakened to the necessity of making some public provision for the disposal of the accumulations of excreta and other filth, the products of a close-packed and rapidly growing population. Rome in the first century A.D. was a far cleaner place than London eighteen hundred years later. Most British families of the middle and upper classes lived above their own cesspool, and the poor man had his own individual dung-hill just outside his door, on which he looked with a proprietary interest, since its contents might be periodically turned into hard cash. The rivers and other watercourses had been made into sewers, even though they provided the water required for drinking and other domestic purposes by the great majority of the people. Doctors might practise with a minimum of qualifications. Drugs and poisons were on sale without restriction. The adulteration of food and drink was accepted as a matter of course, and there was no law against it.

This was the state of things in 1830, and it was still the state of things in 1837. But then began ten years of extraordinary efforts by an extra-ordinary man, one of the most extraordinary men in a generation of men great in every walk of life. Edwin Chadwick has never had anything like justice done to him. He was a bold, tremendously energetic, fiercely opinionated, quarrelsome, hard-as-iron bureaucrat, but it was he above all others who became seized with what he called 'the sanitary idea', and it was he who, as chief executive of the Poor Law Commission and then of the General Board of Health, strove manfully to put Public Health 'on the map'. In 1854 he got the sack (but with the very comfortable pension of £1000 a year, which he enjoyed until his death in 1890). As *The Times* put it in a lively article, under the Chadwick régime it had been a 'perpetual Saturday night', in course of which Master John Bull had been 'scrubbed and rubbed and small-tooth-combed till the tears ran into his eyes, and his teeth chattered, and his fists clenched themselves with worry and pain'. Now it was ended, and it had been demonstrated that 'we prefer to take our chance of cholera and the rest, than to be bullied into health.'

But *The Times* had congratulated itself and its readers too soon. There was no going back to the pre-Chadwick days when 'John Bull' could be as dirty and disgusting as he pleased. Chadwick had laid the foundations of a national public health service, and his work was most ably continued and extended by one of his principal lieutenants, Dr (later Sir) John Simon.

Perhaps even less justice has been done to Simon than to Chadwick. He was born in London in 1816, and died there in 1904. After getting his medical training at St. Thomas's hospital he was appointed in 1848 medical officer of health to the City of London. The appointment was a startling one, even though Liverpool had appointed a M.O.H. a few months before—the first English municipality to do so. Why so traditionally conservative a body as the City Corporation should have taken this step is not clear, and we may be sure that they had not the slightest idea of what they had let themselves in for. They were not kept long in ignorance. Simon grasped the fact that he had been given the chance of a lifetime, and he seized it with both hands. Looking round and about him, he saw a City that was filled with disease and squalor, filth and stinks and abominations: he resolved to make it clean and healthful and sweet.

In the very first Report that he presented to his masters, he told them that 'sanitary neglect is a very grievous fact', and if they were slow to believe it, he provided them with an abundance of evidence that was as nauseous as it was incontrovertible. Year after year, as long as he held the appointment, he described in his reports the evils that made the lives of so many of London's citizens miserable and short. 'I know nothing which brings the epic quality of the early Victorian warfare against barbarism into such vivid relief', wrote Mr G. M. Young in his *Portrait of an Age*, 'as the reports, eloquent, impassioned, and precise, which from 1848 onwards Simon addressed to the Corporation of the City of London'. The quotations from those reports given in the pages that follow will show how thoroughly well deserved is the tribute.

With Chadwick out of the way, the Board of Health was reconstituted, but Simon had proved too good an officer to be let go. In 1858 he was appointed medical officer to the Privy Council—the key post so far as the nation's public health was concerned—and in 1871 Chief Medical Officer to the new Local Government Board, from which the Ministry of Health he had advocated eventually derived. His reports continued to be masterpieces of illuminating statement, e.g. on 'unfit habitations' (No. 13) and the Mr G. Cholera Case (No. 19). He retired from the public serivce in 1876.

Other documents in this chapter add to our knowledge of 'the insanitary city'. But it should be understood that London was not exceptionally dirty and unhealthy. What is disclosed here about the metropolis is all too surely typical of the nation-wide state of affairs that Chadwick and Simon and the rest had to encounter and overcome.

I

Sanitary Neglect

This national prevalence of sanitary neglect is a very grievous fact . . . I would beg any educated person to consider what are the conditions in which alone animal life can thrive; to learn, by personal inspection, how far those conditions are realized for the masses of our population; and to form for himself a conscientious judgment as to the need for great, if even almost revolutionary, reforms.

Let any such person devote an hour to visiting some very poor neighbourhood in the metropolis, or in almost any of our large towns. Let him breathe its air, taste its water, eat its bread. Let him think of human life struggling there for years. Let him fancy what it would be to himself to live there, in that beastly degradation of stink, fed with such bread, drinking such water. Let him enter some house there at hazard, and—heeding where he treads, follow the guidance of his outraged nose, to the yard (if there be one) or the cellar. Let him talk to the inmates; let him hear what is thought of the bone-boiler next door, or the slaughter-house behind; what of the sewer-grating before the door; what of the Irish basket-makers upstairs—twelve in a room, who came in after the hopping, and got fever; what of the artisan's dead body, stretched on his widow's one bed, beside her living children.

Let him, if he have a heart for the duties of manhood and patriotism, gravely reflect whether such sickening evils, as an hour's inquiry will have shown him, ought to be the habit of our labouring population; whether the Legislature, which his voice helps to constitute, is doing all that might be done to palliate these wrongs; whether it be not a jarring discord in the civilization we boast—a worse than pagan savageness in the Christianity we profess, that such things continue, in the midst of us, scandalously neglected; and that the interests of human life, except against wilful violence, are almost uncared for by the law.

DR JOHN SIMON; preface to volume of reprinted City of London Medical Reports (1854)

2

Social Condition of the Poor

Often, in discussion of sanitary subjects ... the filthy, or slovenly, or improvident, or destructive, or intemperate, or dishonest habits of the lower classes, are cited as an explanation of the inefficiency of measures designed for their advantage.

It is constantly urged, that to bring improved domestic arrangements within the reach of such persons is a waste and a folly; that if you give them a coal-scuttle, a washing-basin, and a water-closet, these several utensils will be applied indifferently to the purposes of each other, or one to the purposes of all; and that meanwhile the objects of your charitable solicitude will remain in the same unredeemed lowness and misery as before.

Now it is unquestionable, and I admit it,—that in houses containing all the sanitary evils which I have enumerated—undrained, and water-less, and unventilated—there do dwell whole hordes of persons, who struggle so little in self-defence against that which surrounds them, that they may be considered almost indifferent to its existence, or almost acclimated to endure its continuance. It is too true that, among these classes, there are swarms of men and women, who have yet to learn that human beings should dwell differently from cattle; swarms, to whom personal cleanliness is utterly unknown; swarms, by whom delicacy and decency in their social relations are quite unconceived. Men and women, boys and girls, in scores of each, using jointly one single common privy; grown persons of both sexes sleeping in common with their married parents; a woman suffering travail in the midst of the males and females of three several families of fellow-lodgers in a single room; an adult son sharing his mother's bed during her confinement;—such are instances recently within my knowledge (and I might easily adduce others) of the degree and of the manner in which a people may relapse into the habits of savage life, when their domestic condition is neglected, and when they are suffered to habituate themselves to the uttermost depths of physical obscenity and degradation . . .

I do not mean in any degree to suggest that the evils adverted to present themselves within the City to a greater extent than in sundry other parts of the metropolis . . . Let me likewise observe that I am far from insinuating, or suspecting, that the majority of the poorer population of the City has fallen to that extreme debasement which I have just illustrated as affecting some portion (perhaps not an inconsiderable portion) of the poorest; but I dare not suppress my knowledge that such instances exist, nor can I refrain from stating my belief, that ignorance and poverty will soon contribute to increase them, if sanitary and social improvement do not co-operate against their continuance . . .

Contemplating such cases, I feel the deepest conviction that no sanitary system can be adequate to the requirements of the time, or can cure those radical evils which infest the under-framework of society, unless the importance be distinctly recognized, and the duty manfully undertaken, of improving the social condition of the poor.

Those who suffer under the calamitous sanitary conditions which I have disclosed, have been led, perhaps, to consider them as inseparable from poverty; and after their long habituation to such influences, who can wonder if personal and moral degradation conform them more and more to the physical debasement of their abode ? In the midst of inevitable domestic filth, who can wonder that personal cleanliness should be neglected ? In an atmosphere which forbids the breath to be drawn freely, which maintains perpetual ill health, which depresses all the natural spring and buoyancy of life, who can wonder that frequent recourse should be had to stimulants, which, however pernicious in themselves, still for a moment dispel the malarious languor of the place, give temporary vigour to the brain, and cheer the flagging pulses of a poisoned circulation ? Who can wonder that habits of improvidence and recklessness should arise in a population, which not only has much ignorance and prejudice amongst it, but is likewise often unaccustomed to consideration and kindness ? Who can wonder that the laws of society should at times be forgotten by those whom the eye of society habitually overlooks, and whom the heart of society often appears to discard ?

I believe that now there is a very growing feeling abroad, that the poor of a Christian country can no longer, in their own ignorance and helplessness, be suffered to encounter all the chances which accompany destitution, and which link it often indissolubly to recklessness, profligacy, and perdition. The task of interfering in behalf of these classes, however insensible they may be of their own danger and frequent degradation, begins at length to be recognized as an obligation of society . . .

DR JOHN SIMON; City Medical Reports, No. 1 (1849).

3

'Pestilential heaping of human beings'

The inhabitants of open streets can hardly conceive the complicated turnings, the narrow inlets, the close parallels of houses, and the high barriers of light and air, which are the common characteristics of our courts and alleys, and which give an additional noxiousness even to their cesspools and their filth.

There are very few who, without personal verification, would credit an account that might be given of the worst of such dwelling-places. Let any one, however, who would do full justice to this frightful subject, visit the courts about Bishopsgate, Aldgate, and the upper portion of Cripplegate, which present some of the worst, though by no means the only instances of pestilential residence. A man of ordinary dimensions almost hesitates, lest he should immovably wedge himself, with whomsoever he may meet, in the low and narrow crevice which is called the entrance to some such court or alley; and, having passed that ordeal, he finds himself as in a well, with little light, with less ventilation, amid a dense mass of human beings, with an atmosphere hardly respirable from its closeness and pollution. The stranger, during his visits, feels his breathing constrained, as though he were in a diving-bell and experiences afterwards a sensible and immediate relief as he emerges again into the comparatively open street . . .

In habitations of this kind the death-rate would of necessity be high, even if the population were distributed thinly in the district. A single pair of persons, with their children, having such a court for their sole occupancy, would hardly be otherwise than unhealthy; the infants would die teething, or would live pallid and scrofulous; or a parent would

276

perish prematurely—the father, perhaps, with typhus, the mother with puerperal fever. Judge then, gentlemen, how the mortality of such courts must swell the aggregate death-rate of the City, when I tell you that their population is in many instances so excessive, as, in itself, and by its mere density, to breed disease . . .

Instances are innumerable, in which a single room is occupied by a whole family—whatever may be its number, and whatever the ages and sexes of the children; birth and death go on side by side; where the mother in travail, or the child with smallpox, or the corpse waiting interment, has no separation from the rest . . . It is no uncommon thing, in a room 12 feet square or less, to find three or four families *styed* together (perhaps with infectious disease among them), filling the same space night and day—men, women, and children in the promiscuous intimacy of cattle. Of these inmates it is nearly superfluous to observe, that in all offices of nature they are gregarious and public; that every instinct of personal or sexual decency is stifled; that every nakedness of life is uncovered there. Such an apartment is commonly hired in the first instance by a single pair, who sub-let a participation in the shelter, probably to as many others as apply. Sometimes an obnoxious occupation is carried on within the space: thus I have seen mud-larks sitting on the floor with baskets of filth before them, sorting out the occasional bit of coal or bone, from a heterogeneous collection made along the bed of the river, or in the mouths of sewers; and this in a small room, inhabited night and day by such a population as I have described.

Who can wonder at what becomes, physically and morally, of infants begotten and born in these bestial crowds?

In my former Report, I drew your attention to this pestilential heaping of human beings, and suggested to you its results; and on many occasions, during the past year, complaints have been before your Hon. Court which have had their real origin in this uncontrolled evil. I revert to it because of its infinite importance.

While it maintains physical filth that is indescribable, while it perpetuates fever and the allied disorders, while it creates mortality enough to mask the results of all your sanitary progress, its moral consequences are too dreadful to be related.

I have to deal with the matter only as it relates to physical health. Whatever is morally hideous and savage in the scene—whatever contrast it offers to the superficial magnificence of the metropolis—whatever profligacy it implies and continues—whatever recklessness and obscene brutality arises from it—whatever deep injury it inflicts on the community—whatever debasement or abolition of God's image in men's hearts is tokened by it—these matters belong not to my office, nor would it become me to dwell on them. Only because of the physical sufferings am I entitled to speak; only because pestilence is for ever within the circle; only because Death so largely comforts these poor orphans of civilization.

To my duty it alone belongs, in such respects, to tell you where disease ravages the people under your charge, and wherefore; but while I lift the curtain to show you this—a curtain which propriety might gladly leave unraised, you cannot but see that side by side with pestilence there stalks a deadlier presence; blighting the moral existence of a rising population; rendering their hearts hopeless, their acts ruffianly and incestuous; and scattering, while society averts her eyes, the retributive seeds of increase for crime, turbulence, and pauperism.

DR JOHN SIMON; City Medical Reports, Nos. 1 and 2 (1849, 1850).

4

The 'Cesspool city' beneath the City

So far as I can calculate from very imperfect materials, I should conjecture that some thousands of houses within the City still have cesspools connected with them. It requires little medical knowledge to understand that animals will scarcely thrive in an atmosphere of their own decomposing excrements; yet such strictly and literally speaking, is the air which a very large proportion of the inhabitants of the City are condemned to breathe. Sometimes, happily for the inmates, the cesspool in which their ordure accumulates, lies at some small distance from the basement-area of the house, occupying the subsoil of an adjoining yard, or if the privy be a public one, of some open space exterior to the private premises. But in a very large number of cases, it lies actually within the four walls of the inhabited house; the latter reared over it, as a bellglass over the beak of a retort, receiving and sucking up incessantly the unspeakable abomination of its volatile contents. In some such instances, where the basement story of the house is tenanted, the cesspool lies—perhaps merely boarded over—close beneath the feet of a family of human beings, whom it surrounds uninterruptedly, whether they wake or sleep, with its fetid pollution and poison.

Now, here is a remarkable cause of death. These gases, which so many people are daily inhaling, do not, it is true, in their diluted condition, suddenly extinguish life; but, though different in concentration, they are identically the same in nature with that confined sewer-gas which, on a recent occasion, killed those who were exposed to it with the rapidity of a lightning-stroke. In their diluted state, as they rise from so many cesspools, and taint the atmosphere of so many houses, they form a climate the most congenial for the multiplication of epidemic disorders, and operate beyond all known influences of their class in impairing the chances of life.

It may be taken as an axiom for the purposes of sanitary improvement, that every individual cesspool is hurtful to its vicinage; and it may hence be inferred how great an injury is done to public health by their existence in such numbers, that parts of the City might be described as having a cesspool-city excavated beneath it . . .

DR JOHN SIMON; City Medical Reports, No. 1 (1849).

5

Scuffling at a Standcock

I am sure that I do not exaggerate the sanitary importance of water, when I affirm that its unrestricted supply is the first essential of decency, of comfort, and of health; that no civilization of the poorer classes can exist without it; and that any limitation to its use in the metropolis is a barrier, which must maintain thousands in a state of the most unwholesome filth and degradation.

In the City of London the supply of water is but a fraction of what it should be. Thousands of the population have no supply of it to the houses where they dwell. For their possession of this first necessary of social life, such persons wholly depend on their power of attending at some fixed hour of the day, pail in hand, beside the nearest standcock; where, with their neighbours, they wait their turn—sometimes not without a struggle, during the tedious dribbling of a single small pipe.

Sometimes there is a partial improvement on this plan; a group of houses will have a butt or cistern for the common use of some scores of inmates, who thus are saved the necessity of waiting at a standcock, but who still remain most insufficiently supplied with water.

Next in the scale of improvement we find water-pipes laid on to the houses; but the water is turned on only for a few hours in the week, so that all who care to be adequately supplied with it must be provided with very spacious receptacles. Receptacles are sometimes provided: and in these, which are often of the most objectionable description, water is retained for the purposes of diet and washing, during a period which varies from twenty-four to seventy-two hours. One of the most important purposes of a water-supply seems almost wholly abandoned—that, namely, of having a large quantity daily devoted to cleanse and clear the house-drains and sewers; and in many cases where a waste-pipe has been conducted from the water-butt to the privy, the arrangement is one which gives to the drainage little advantage of water, while it communicates to the water a well-marked flavour of drainage . . .

In inspecting the courts and alleys of the City, one constantly sees butts, for the reception of water, either public, or in the open yards of houses, or sometimes in their cellars; and these butts, dirty, mouldering, and coverless; receiving soot and all other impurities from the air; absorbing stench from the adjacent cesspool; inviting filth from insects, vermin, sparrows, cats, and children; their contents often augmented through a rain water-pipe by the washings of the roof, and every hour becoming fustier and more offensive. Nothing can be less like what water should be than the fluid obtained under such circumstances; and one hardly knows whether this arrangement can be considered preferable to the precarious chance of scuffling or dawdling at a standcock.

It may be doubted, too, whether, even in a far better class of houses, the tenants' water supply can be pronounced good. The cisternage is better, and all arrangements connected with it are generally such as to protect it from the grosser impurities which defile the water-butts of the poor; but the long retention of water in leaden cisterns impairs its fitness for drinking; and the quantity which any moderate cistern will contain is very generally insufficient for the legitimate requirements of the house during the intervals of supply. Every one who is personally familiar with the working of this system of intermittent supply can testify to its inconvenience; and though its evils press with immeasurably greater severity on the poor than on the rich, yet the latter are by no means without experience on the subject . . .

DR JOHN SIMON; City Medical Reports, No. I (1849).

6

What's in London Water

The waters supplied to the City are conducted in open channels; they receive in large measure the surface-washing, the drainage, and even the sewage of the country through which they pass; they derive casual impurities from bathers and barges; they are liable to whatever pollutions mischievous or filthy persons may choose to inflict on them; and then on their arrival in the metropolis (after a short subsidence in reservoirs, which themselves are not unobjectionable) are distributed, without filtration, to the public.

Whatever chemistry may say on this subject . . . I cannot consider it matter of indifference, that we drink—with whatever dilution, or with whatever imperfect oxidation—the excremental and other impurities which mingle in these sources of our supply. Such admixtures, though in their *quantity* less, are in their *quality* identical with those which render Thames-water, as taken at London Bridge, inadmissible for domestic consumption, and which occasion it, when stored for sea-use, to undergo, before it becomes fit to drink, a succession of offensive changes strictly comparable to putrefaction.

In this slovenly method of conveyance and distribution there is a neglect of common precaution for the purity and healthfulness of the supply, which I must report to you as highly objectionable; and this—the method of supply to our great metropolis, strikes one the more with astonishment and disgust, as one reflects on the long experience and admirable models which past centuries in foreign countries have supplied; and especially, as one remembers those colossal works which, more than two thousand years ago, were constructed under the Roman government, for the cool and cleanly conduction of water . . .

Of other sources of water-supply existing within the City of London, there are many of small extent in the form of superficial springs . . . To the use of waters of this description, within a large city, there is always much objection. In addition to extreme hardness, which in London they universally possess, they are liable, in a dangerous degree, to become contaminated by the leakage of drains, and by other sources of impurity; as, for instance, where situated within the immediate vicinity of graveyards they derive products of animal decomposition from the soil. Very recently, a celebrated pump within the City of London, that adjoining St. Bride's church-yard, has been abandoned on

account of such impregnations. Or perhaps I should rather say . . .
that it was not abandoned—for till almost the last moment the neighbours adhered to it with fondness; but the parochial authorities—
alarmed by the proximity of cholera—caused its handle to be locked . . .

DR JOHN SIMON; City Medical Reports, No. 2 (1850).

7

'Gigantic poison bed'

———————

Probably in considerable parts of the metropolitan area, house-drainage
is extensively absent: probably in considerable parts, the sewers, from
the nature of their construction, are very doubtful advantages to the
districts they traverse: but the evil, before all others, to which I attach
special importance . . . is that habitual empoisonment of soil and air
which is inseparable from our tidal drainage. From this influence, I
doubt not, a large proportion of the metropolis has derived its liability
to cholera.

A moment's reflection is sufficient to show the immense distribution
of putrefactive dampness which belongs to this vicious system. There is
implied in it that the entire excrementation of the metropolis (with the
exception of such as, not less poisonously, lies pent beneath houses)
shall sooner or later be mingled in the stream of the river, there to be
rolled backward and forward amid the population; that, at low water, for
many hours, this material shall be trickling over broad belts of spongy
bank which then dry their contaminated mud in the sunshine, exhaling
faetor and poison; that at high water, for many hours, it shall be retained
or driven back within all low-level sewers and house-drains, soaking far
and wide into the soil, or leaving putrescent deposit along miles of
underground brickwork, as on a deeper pavement.

Sewers which, under better circumstances, should be benefactions
and appliances for health in their several districts, are thus rendered
inevitable sources of evil. During a large proportion of their time they
are occupied in retaining or re-distributing that which it is their office to
remove. They furnish chambers for an immense faecal evaporation; at
every breeze which strikes against their open mouths, at every tide
which encroaches on their inward space, their gases are breathed into
the open air—wherever outlet exists, into houses, foot-paths, and
carriage-way . . .

DIPHTHERIA.   SCROFULA.   CHOLERA

FATHER THAMES introducing his offspring to the Fair City
of London.

10. John Leech in *Punch*, 1858

To some individual householder, dwelling at a high level, all concern
in this subject may seem to terminate with the defluxion of his own
sewage. So that his own pipes remain clear, little cares he for the
ultimate outfall of his nuisance! Perhaps, if he knew better, he would
care more. His gift returns to him with increase. Down in the valley,
whither his refuse runs, converge innumerable kindred contributions.
From city and suburb—from an area of a hundred square miles
covered by a quarter of a million of houses, with their unprecedented
throng of metropolitan life, there pours into that single channel every
conceivable excrement, out-scouring, garbage, and refuse, from man
and beast, street and slum, shamble and factory, market and hospital.
From the polluted bosom of the river steam up, incessantly though
unseen, the vapours of a retributive poison; densest and most destructive, no doubt, along the sodden banks and stinking sewers of lowest
level; but spreading over miles of land—sometimes rolled high by wind,
sometimes blended low with mist, and baneful even to their margin that
curls over distant fields.

For, not alone in Rotherhithe and Newington—not alone along the Effra or the Fleet, are traced the evils of this great miasm. The deepest shadows of the cloud lie here, but its outskirts darken the distance. A fever hardly to be accounted for, an infantile sickness of undue malignity, a doctor's injunction for change of air, may at times suggest to the dweller in our healthiest suburbs that, while draining his refuse to the Thames, he receives for requital some partial workings of the gigantic poison-bed which he has contributed to maintain.

DR JOHN SIMON; City Medical Reports, No. 5 (1853).

8

London Smoke

Those members of the Court [of Common Council] who have visited foreign capitals where other fuel than coal is employed, will remember the contrast between their climate and ours—will remember (for instance even in Paris) the transparence of air, the comparative brightness of all colour, the visibility of distant objects, the cleanliness of faces and buildings, instead of our opaque atmosphere, deadened colours. obscured distance, smutted faces, and black architecture. Those, even, who have never left our metropolis, but who, by early rising or late going to rest, have had opportunities of seeing a London sunrise, can judge, as well as by any foreign comparison, the difference between London as it might be and London as it is.

Viewed at dawn and noon-day, the appearances contrast as though they were of different cities and in different latitudes. Soon after daybreak, the great factory shafts beside the river begin to discharge immense volumes of smoke; their clouds soon become confluent; the sky is overcast with a dingy veil; the house-chimneys presently add their contributions; and by ten o'clock, as one approaches London from any hill in the suburbs, one may observe the total result of this gigantic nuisance hanging over the City like a pall.

If its consequences were confined to rendering London (in spite of its advantages) the unsightliest metropolis in Europe, to defacing all works of art, and rendering domestic cleanliness expensive, I should have nothing officially to say on the subject; but inasmuch as it renders cleanliness more difficult, and creates a despair of cultivating it with success, people resign themselves to dirt, domestic and personal, which they could remove but so temporarily: or windows are kept shut, in spite of immeasurable fustiness, because the ventilation requisite to health would bring with it showers of soot, occasioning inconvenience and expense. Such is the tendency of many complaints that have reached me, and of their foundation in truth and reason I have thorough conviction and knowledge ... I ought likewise to tell you, that there are valid reasons for supposing that we do not with impunity inhale day by day so much air which leaves a palpable sediment; that many persons of irritable lungs find unquestionable inconvenience from these mechanical impurities of the atmosphere; and (gathering a hint from the pathology of vegetation) that few plants will flourish in the denser districts of London, unless the air which conduces to their nourishment be previously filtered from its dirt.

If the smoke of London were inseparably identified with its commercial greatness, one might willingly resign oneself to the inconvenience. But to every other reason against its continuance must be added as a last one, on the evidence of innumerable competent and disinterested witnesses, that the nuisance, where habitual, is, for the greater part or entirely, voluntary and preventable; that it indicates mismanagement and waste; that the adoption of measures for the universal consumption of smoke, while relieving the metropolis and its population from injury, would conduce to the immediate interest of the individual consumer, as well as to indirect and general economy. For all the smoke that hangs over us is wasted fuel ...

With the progress of knowledge on these subjects, a time will undoubtedly arrive, and at no distant period, when chimneys will cease to convey to the atmosphere their present immense freight of fuel that has not been burnt, and of heat that has not been utilized; when each entire house will be uniformly warmed with less expenditure of material than now suffices to its one kitchen fire; and our successors* will wonder at the ludicrous ingenuity with which we have so long managed to diffuse our caloric and waste our coal in the direct ions where they least conduce to the purposes of comfort and utility.

* To the philosophical thinker there would seem to exist no important difficulty which would prevent the collective warming of many houses in a district by the distribution of heat from a central furnace—perhaps even so, that each house might receive its *ad libitum* share of ventilation with warmed air. Ingenuity and enterprise, in this country, have accomplished far more arduous tasks; and I little doubt that our next successors will have heat-pipes laid on to their houses, with absence of smoke and immense economy of fuel, on some such general organization as we now enjoy for gas-lighting and water-supply.

DR JOHN SIMON; City Medical Reports, No. 2 (1850).

9

'Grievous nuisance' of Slaughter-houses

I consider slaughtering within the City as both directly and indirectly prejudicial to the health of the population;—*directly*, because it loads the air with effluvia of decomposing animal matter, not only in the vicinity of each slaughter-house, but likewise along the line of drainage which conveys away its washings and fluid filth; *indirectly*, because many very offensive and noxious trades are in close dependence on the slaughtering of cattle, and round about the original nuisance of the slaughter-house ... you invariably find established the concomitant and still more grievous nuisances of gut-spinning, tripe-dressing, bone-boiling, tallow-melting, paunch-cooking, etc.

Ready illustrations of this fact may be found in the gut-scraping sheds of Harrow Alley, adjoining Butchers' Row, Aldgate; or in the Leadenhall skin-market, contiguous to the slaughtering places, where the stinking hides of cattle lie for many hours together, spread out over a large area of ground, waiting for sale, to the great offence of the neighbourhood.

DR JOHN SIMON; City Medical Reports, No. 1 (1849).

10

The Corpse amid the Living

There is no part of the subject which I have considered with more anxiety than that which relates to delays in interment, and to the prolonged keeping of dead bodies in the rooms of their living kindred.

Evils arising in this source are unknown to the rich. Soldered in its leaden coffin, on tressels in some separate and spacious room, a corpse may await the convenience of survivors with little detriment to their atmosphere.

Not so in the poor man's dwelling. The sides of a wooden coffin, often imperfectly joined, are at best all that divides the decomposition of the dead from the respiration of the living. A room, tenanted night and day by the family of mourners, likewise contains the remains of the dead. For some days the coffin is unclosed. The bare corpse lies there amid the living; beside them in their sleep; before them at their meals.

The death perhaps has occurred on a Wednesday or Thursday; the next Sunday is thought too early for the funeral; the body remains unburied till the Sunday week. Summer or winter makes little difference to this detention: nor is there sufficient knowledge on the subject, among the poorer population, for alarm to be excited even by the concurrence of infectious disease in a room so hurtfully occupied ... On an average, there would probably be lying within the City at any moment, from thirty to forty dead bodies in rooms tenanted by living persons ...

Among the wealthier classes, as I have said, this delay is practically unimportant, except in so far as every repetition maintains the pernicious custom. Scarcely on account of any risk arising to themselves in emanations from the dead, but mainly for the sake of influence and example, would one wish the educated classes of the community to adopt the usage of earlier burial. Our present practice is upheld by no law of necessity; nor for the most part does it represent any extravagance of grief, or fond reluctance of separation. Chiefly it subsists by our indolent acquiescence in a habit, which former prejudices and former exigencies established. Fears of premature interment, which had much to do with it, are now seldom spoken of but with a smile. The longer interval, once rightly insisted on as necessary for the gathering of distant friends, has now, in the progress of events, become absurdly excessive: in a vast majority of cases, all those whose presence is needed, live within a narrow circle; and the more distant mourner, who, fifty years ago, would have spent several days in coming from Paris or Edinburgh, can now finish his journey in twelve hours. It is much to be wished that, under these changed circumstances, an altered practice might ensue in the upper classes of society, fixing their time of burial within three or four days of death. Such example of wealthier neighbours aided by greater enlightenment and education among themselves, would greatly tend to detach the poor from many observances and delays, in relation to the dead, which, in their narrow dwellings cannot continue with impunity.

DR JOHN SIMON; City of London Medical Reports, Special report on Intramural Interments, 1852.

II

The Horrors of the Graveyards

In all those larger parochial burial-grounds where the maintenance of a right to bury can be considered important—in all such, and in most others, too, the soil is saturated and super-saturated with animal matter undergoing slow decomposition. There are, indeed, few of the older burial-grounds in the City where the soil does not rise many feet above the original level, testifying to the large amount of animal matter which lies beneath the surface . . . For the most part, houses are seen to rise on all sides in immediate contiguity to the burial-ground, forbidding the possibility of even such ventilation as might diminish the evil; and the inhabitants of such houses complain bitterly, as they well may, of the inconvenience which they suffer from this confined and noxious atmosphere.

With respect to burial in vaults, which prevails to a very great and dangerous extent in this City, I may observe that, among persons who are ill-informed on the subject, there exist erroneous notions as to the preservation of bodies under these circumstances. They are supposed, from the complete closure of their coffins, to remain unchanged for ages, like the embalmed bodies of Egypt and Peru; or at least—if perhaps they undergo some interior and invisible change (as the chrysalis within its sheath) that there is no interference with the general arrangement, no breach in the compactness of its envelope. Nothing can be less correct than this supposition.

It is unnecessary that I should detail to you the process of decay, as it occurs within the charnel-house; nor need I inquire, for your information, whether indeed it be true, as alleged, that part of the duty of a sexton consists in tapping the recent coffins, so as to facilitate the escape of gases which otherwise would detonate from their confinement. It is sufficient to state, that—whether such be or be not the duty of the functionary in question, the time certainly comes, sooner or later, when every corpse buried in the vault of a church spreads the products of its decomposition through the air as freely as though no shell had enclosed it. It is matter of the utmost notoriety that, under all ordinary conditions of vault-sepulture, the wooden case of the coffin speedily decays and crumbles, while the interior leaden one, bending with the pressure of whatever may be above it (or often with its own weight), yields, bulges and bursts, as surely as would a paper hat-box under the weight of a laden portmanteau . . .

It is a very serious matter for consideration, that close beneath the feet of those who attend the services of their church, there often lies an almost solid pile of decomposing human remains, co-extensive with the area of the building, heaped as high as the vaulting will permit, and generally but very partially confined . . .

The atmosphere in which epidemic and infectious diseases most readily diffuse their poison and multiply their victims is one in which organic matters are undergoing decomposition. Whence these may be derived signifies little. Whether the matter passing into decay be an accumulation of soaking straw and cabbage leaves in some miserable cellar, or the garbage of a slaughter-house, or an overflowing cesspool, or dead dogs floated at high water into the mouth of a sewer, or stinking fish thrown overboard in Billingsgate dock, or remains of human corpses undergoing their last chemical changes in consecrated earth, the previous history of the decomposed material is of no moment whatever. The pathologist knows no difference of operation between one decaying substance and another; so soon as he recognizes organic matter under-going decomposition, so soon he recognizes the most fertile soil for the increase of epidemic diseases; and I may state with certainty, that there are many churchyards in the City of London where every spadeful of soil turned up in burial sensibly adds to the amount of animal decompo-sition which advances too often inevitably around us.

Nor can I refrain from adding, as a matter claiming attention, that, in the performance of intramural interment, there constantly occur disgusting incidents dependent on overcrowdedness of the burial ground; incidents which convert the extremest solemnity of religion into an occasion for sickness or horror; perhaps mingling with the ritual of the Church some clamour of grave-diggers who have miscalculated their space; perhaps diffusing among the mourners some nauseous evidence and conviction, that a prior tenant of the tomb has been prematurely displaced, or that the spade has impatiently anticipated the slower dismembering of decay. Cases of this nature are fresh in the memory of the public; cases of extreme nuisance and brutal desecration in place of decent and solemn interment; and it is unnecessary that I should revive the record of transactions inconsistent with even the dawn of civilization.

From the circumstances which I have mentioned, it can hardly fail to appear most desirable to you, that the use of some spacious and open cemetery at a distance from the City should be substituted for the present system of interment, and the urgency of this requirement will be demonstrated all the more cogently, when it is remembered that the annual amount of mortality in the City averages about 3,000, and that under the present arrangements every dead body buried within our walls receives its accommodation at the expense of the living, and to their great detriment.

DR JOHN SIMON; City Medical Reports, No. 1 (1849).

12

Dr Simon's Plea for a Ministry of Health

Against *adulterations of food*, here and there, obsolete powers exist, for our ancestors had an eye to those things; but, practically, they are of no avail. If we, who are educated, habitually submit to have copper in our preserves, red-lead in our cayenne, alum in our bread, pigments in our tea, and ineffable nastiness in our fish-sauce, what can we expect of the poor? Can they use galactometers [to detect the dilutions of milk]? Can they test their pickles with ammonia? Can they discover the tricks by which bread is made dropsical (a chief artifice in the cheapening of bread is to increase its weight by various means which render it retentive of water), or otherwise deteriorated in value, even faster than they can cheapen it in price? Without entering on details of what might be the best organization against such things, I may certainly assume it as greatly a *desideratum*, that local authorities should uniformly have power to deal with these frauds (as, of course, with every sale of decayed and corrupted food) and that they should be enabled to employ skilled officers, for detecting at least every adulteration of bread and every poisonous admixture in condiments and the like.

In some respects this sort of protection is even more necessary, as well as more deficient in regard to the *falsification of drugs*. The College of Physicians and the Apothecaries' Company are supposed to exercise supervision in the matter; so that at least its necessity is recognized by the law. The security thus afforded is, in practice, null. It is notorious in my profession that there are not many simple drugs, and still fewer compound preparations, on the standard strength of which we may reckon. It is notorious that some standard medicines are so often falsified in the market, and others so often mis-made in the laboratory, that we are robbed of all certainty in their employment. Iodide of potassium—an invaluable specific, may be shammed to half its weight with the carbonate of potash. Scammony, one of our best purgatives, is rare without chalk or starch, weakening it, perhaps, to half the intention of the giver. Cod-liver oil may have come from seals or from olives. The two or three drops of prussic acid that we should give for a dose may be nearly twice as strong at one chemist's as at another's . . .

Again, with the *promiscuous sale of poisons*, what incredible laxity of government! One poison, indeed, has its one law. Arsenic may not be sold otherwise then coloured, nor except with full registration of the sale, and in the presence of a witness known to both buyer and vender. Admirable, so far as it goes! but why should arsenic alone receive this dab of legislation? Is the principle right, that means of murder and suicide should be rendered difficult of access for criminal purposes? Does any one question it? Then, why not legislate equally against all poisons?—against oxalic acid and opium, corrosive sublimate, strychnine?

Nor can our past legislators be more boastful of their labours for the *medical profession*—either for its scientific interests, or for the public protection against ignorance and quackery. Nearly two dozen corporate bodies within the United Kingdom are said to grant licences for medical practice; and I hardly know whether it lessens or aggravates this confusion, that such licences are in many cases partial;—that one licentiate may practise north of the Tweed, but nowise to the south; that one may practise in London, another only seven miles beyond it. Not that the licence seems much to matter! for innumerable poachers in all directions trespass on what the law purports to sell as a secured preserve for qualified practitioners: their encroachments are made with almost certain impunity; and—as for the titles of the profession, any impostor may style himself *doctor* or *surgeon* at his will . . .

Having said so much on the defects and the wrongs of our existing sanitary condition, perhaps I may venture to speak of the almost obvious remedy. 'Almost obvious' I say; for surely no one will doubt that this great subject should be dealt with by comprehensive and scientific legislation; and I hardly see how otherwise, than that it should be submitted in its entirety to some single department of the executive, as a sole charge; that there should be some tangible head, responsible— not only for the *enforcement* of existing laws . . . but likewise for their *progress* from time to time to the level of contemporary science . . . As regards its constituted head, sitting in Parliament ('a minister of Public Health') his department should be, in the widest sense, to *care for the physical necessities of human life* . . .

DR JOHN SIMON, in the preface to the reprinted City of London Medical Reports (1854).

13

'Unfit for human habitation'

By places 'unfit for human habitation' I mean places in which by common consent even moderately healthy life is impossible to human dwellers,—places which therefore in themselves (independently of removable filth which may be about them) answer to the common conception of 'nuisances';—such, for instance, as those underground and other dwellings which permanently are almost or entirely dark and unventilable; and dwellings which are in such constructional partnership with public privies, or other depositaries of filth, that their very sources of ventilation are essentially offensive and injurious; and dwellings which have such relations to local drainage that they are habitually soaked into by water or sewage; and so forth.

But beyond these instances where the dwelling would, I think, even now be deemed by common consent 'unfit for human habitation', instances, varying in degree, are innumerable, where, in small closed courts, surrounded by high buildings, and approached by narrow and perhaps winding gangways, houses of the meanest sort stand, acre after acre of them, back to back, shut from all enjoyment of light and air, with but privies and dustbins to look upon; and surely such can only be counted 'fit for human habitation' while the standard of that humanity is low. Again, by 'overcrowded' dwellings I mean those where dwellers are in such proportion to dwelling-space that no obtainable quantity of ventilation will keep the air of the dwelling-space free from hurtfully large accumulations of animal effluvium,—cases, where the dwelling-space at its best stinks more or less with decomposing human excretions, and where, at its worst, this filthy atmosphere may (and often does) have, working and spreading within it, the taint of some contagious fever.

Though my official point of view is one exclusively physical, common humanity requires that the other aspect of this evil should not be ignored. For where 'overcrowding' exists in its sanitary sense, almost always it exists even more perniciously in certain moral senses. In its higher degrees it almost necessarily involves much negation of all delicacy, such unclean confusion of bodies and bodily functions, such mutual exposure of animal and sexual nakedness, as is rather bestial than human. To be subject to these influences is a degradation which must become deeper and deeper for those on whom it continues to work. To children who are born under its curse it must often be a very baptism into infamy. And beyond all measures hopeless is the wish that persons thus circumstanced should ever in other respects aspire to that atmosphere of civilization which has its essence in physical and moral cleanliness, and enhances the self-respect which it betokens.

And as a particular class of cases in which both evils are combined to one monstrous form of nuisance, I ought expressly to mention certain of the so-called 'tenement houses' of the poor; especially those large but ill-circumstanced houses, once perhaps wealthily inhabited, but now pauperized, and often without a span of court-yard either front or back; where in each house perhaps a dozen or more rooms are separately let to a dozen or more families—each family with but a room to itself and perhaps lodgers; and where in each house the entire large number of occupants (which even in England may be little short of a hundred) will necessarily have the use of but a single staircase, and of a privy which is perhaps placed in the cellar.

Mere scantiness of privy-accommodation leads, of course, to filthy habits among the lodgers of crowded tenement-houses. And when the pretended accommodation is given in the above-described form, often in utter darkness, the likelihood is that the basement of the house will be one indescribable quagmire of filth.

DR JOHN SIMON; Privy Council Medical Reports, No. 8 (1865).

14

The Shocking Truth about London Bakehouses

As a rule, the bread of London is made in what in houses in general is the coalhole and the front kitchen, the back kitchen being the place where the small store of flour is kept together with the other things in daily use . . .

The principal fact, for which I certainly was not prepared, was their extreme dirt, and in many places the almost total covering of the entire space between the rafters with masses of cobwebs, weighed down with the flour dust that had accumulated upon them, and hanging in strips just above your head. A heavy tread or a blow upon the floor above, brought down large fragments of them, as I witnessed on more than one occasion; and as the rafters immediately over the troughs in which the dough is made are as thickly hung with them as any other part of the bakehouse, masses of these cobwebs must be frequently falling into the dough. Other bakehouses of this description were less thickly hung with cobwebs, but they were in most cases numerous enough to afford a great probability of their being frequently incorporated with the dough. The rafters were usually so black with the sulphurous exhalations from the oven that it needed not the admission of the proprietor that the bakehouse was very seldom whitewashed.

Animals in considerable numbers crawled in and out of and upon the troughs where the bread was made, and upon the adjoining walls. The dust had accumulated upon the broken and uneven floors. The smells from the drains, etc. were very offensive, the draft of the oven continually drawing the effluvia through the bakehouse. The ventilation was generally so injudiciously contrived as to produce a strong current of cold air upon the men while at work, and as they are always heated by their work, and very susceptible of cold in consequence of the high temperature to which they are habitually confined for so many hours, they rarely avail themselves of both the openings for the admission of air. The result is, that the air of those small bakehouses is generally overloaded with foul gases from the drains, from the ovens, and from the fermentation of the bread, and with the emanations from their own bodies. The air thus contaminated is necessarily incorporated with the dough in the process of kneading, &c. . . .

There cannot be a doubt that the public has a right to insist that their bread shall not be made in such filthy places as these, and that means

11. Water in the Milk ... (George Cruikshank, *The Comic Almanack*,) 1845

shall be taken to put a stop to the injury that must be inflicted by them upon the health of the journeymen. It is, as it appears to me, fairly argued by those who desire to see bakehouses placed under a system of inspection, that if slaughterhouses are inspected and subjected to regulations on sanitary grounds, there is quite as much reason, not only on sanitary grounds, but for the satisfaction of the public, in such an important matter as that of the making of their daily bread, that bakehouses should be dealt with on a similar principle ...

H. SEYMOUR TREMENHEERE; Report addressed to H.M. Principal Secretary of State for the Home Department relative to the Grievances complained of by the Journeymen Bakers (1862); P.P. 1862, vol. 47.

15

Much Worse Things than Water in the Milk!

Arthur Hill Hassall, MD, called in and examined.—You are, I believe, a medical man ?—I am a Doctor of Medicine of the University of London, and a Member of the Royal College of Physicians of London.

Have you devoted a great deal of attention to the consideration of questions of adulteration not only of articles of food and drink, but of drugs and other things ?—I have.

Is it your opinion that adulteration is very prevalent ?—I find adulteration to be very prevalent; it may be stated generally that it prevails in nearly all articles which it will pay to adulterate, whether of food, drink, or drugs. There are but few exceptions to this rule, I think ... The adulterations practised are very numerous, and they are varied both in kind and degree. The majority consists in the addition of substances of greatly inferior nature, for the sake of weight and bulk. Other adulterations consist in the addition of various colouring matters; these are employed either to conceal other adulterations, or to heighten, and, as it is considered, to improve the appearance of articles. Lastly, a few adulterations are practised for the purpose of imparting smell, pungency, or taste to certain articles ...

Bread is adulterated with mashed potatoes, alum, 'hards', and sometimes, though rarely, with sulphate of copper. Butter, with water. Bottled fruits and vegetables, with certain salts of copper. Coloured confectionery, with East India arrowroot, wheat and potato flour, hydrated sulphate of lime; and it is coloured with cochineal, lake, indigo, Prussian blue, Antwerp blue, artificial ultramarine, carbonate of copper, carbonate of lead or white lead, red lead, vermilion, and chrome yellows, etc. . . . Coffee, with chicory, roasted wheat, rye and potato flours, roasted beans, mangel-wurzel, and a substance resembling acorns. Chicory, with roasted wheat and rye flours, burnt beans, sawdust, carrot, mangel-wurzel; and it is coloured with ferruginous earths. . . . Cocoa and chocolate, with Maranta, East India and Tacea or Tahiti arrowroots . . . and it is coloured with ferruginous earths. Custard egg powders contain wheat, potato, and rice flours . . . Flour, with alum. Gin, with water, sugar, cayenne, cassia, cinnamon, and flavourings of various kinds. Rum, with water and cayenne pepper. Lard, with potato flour, water, salt, carbonate of soda, and caustic lime. Mustard, with wheat flour and turmeric. Milk, with water and annatto [a fruit juice]. Marmalade, with pulp of apple or turnip. Oatmeal, with barley flour, and the integuments of barley, called rubble. Porter and Stout, with water, sugar treacle, and salt. Pickles, with salts of copper . . . Potted meats and fish, with flour, probably wheat flour boiled, coloured with bole armenian, and sometimes Venetian red. Preserves, with salts of copper. Pepper, with wheat and pea flour, ground rice, ground mustard seeds, linseed oil, P.D. or pepper dust . . . Tea, with exhausted tea leaves, leaves other than those of tea, British and foreign; among the former, those of sycamore, horse-chestnut, and plum . . . Tobacco, with water, sugar treacle, and salts of various kinds. Vinegar, with water, burnt sugar, and sulphuric acid . . . This list does not embrace nearly all the substances employed in the adulteration of articles of food, drink, and drugs . . . only those which have actually been discovered by myself in the various articles submitted to analysis up to this time.

Most of those articles are not simply adulterations of an innocuous character, but they are many of them injurious to health, and some of them even poisonous—I think that there can be no question but that that is the case . . .

Report of the Select Committee appointed to inquire into the Adulterations of Food, Drinks, and Drugs, 1st Report, pp. 1–3; P.P. 1854/5, vol. 8.

16

Deadly Gas at Westminster

Gaseous sewage. Noxious gases are rapidly formed in the sewers by the decomposition of putrid and other matters; and as there is no ventilation or means provided for withdrawing them, they escape under the laws of diffusion of gases into the streets and houses wherever there happens to be an opening. The sewers are the same in every respect now as they were before waterclosets were in use; no change has been made to meet the altered requirements. The sewage gases are discharged in large quantities from the open mouths of the sewers along the sides of the river, seriously affecting the atmosphere of the Houses of Parliament.

Gaseous sewage is a deadly poison, and many valuable lives have been lost by inhaling it, in this country and abroad . . . In London . . . I have witnessed several cases of death, and others in which men were taken out insensible, after only a few seconds of exposure. In Warwick-street, Pimlico, five men were killed in 1852 by gaseous sewage. I was requested to examine the case, and gave a long evidence at the inquest.

Three of these poor fellows had gone into a sewer early in the morning, and not returning in time for breakfast, an alarm was felt for their safety. A surgeon, anxious to render assistance, entered the sewer, and was killed on the spot. A young policeman followed to assist, and was also struck dead in a few seconds. On examination, after death, there was evidence sufficient to show me that he could not have made more than two inspirations before death, after entering the sewer . . . On making an opening downwards from the street into the sewer, to get these poor fellows out, the gases, as they escaped, were set on fire by a match; they burnt with a yellow flame, rising 20 feet high . . .

I have stated elsewhere that the atmosphere of the Houses of Parliament is impregnated with sewage gases mostly escaping from the open mouths of the sewers in the neighbourhood alongside of the river. For a long time offensive smells were complained of in the courts of law at Westminster, and on one occasion the judges were driven from their benches by a sudden outbreak of stench, which also reached the Houses of Parliament. I was requested to examine into the matter, and found the stench escaping from the open mouth of a sewer, at this end of West-minster Bridge: Bridge-street Sewer. I recommended the mouth of the sewer to be trapped, so as to allow the solid, and liquid sewage, to escape; but not the gaseous. This was done, and no further complaints were heard either in the courts of law, or the Houses of Parliament, until within a fortnight before the end of last Session ... when the stench suddenly returned. On examination it was found that the trapping of the Bridge-street Sewer had been suddenly washed away ...

From the Report made by MR GOLD^Y GURNEY to the 1st Commissioner of Works on the State of the Thames in the Neighbourhood of the Houses of Parliament, Dec. 11, 1857, page 6; P.P. 1857-8, vol. 48.

17

A Bed for the Night

Unfortunately I have been familiar with low lodging-houses, both in town and country, for more than ten years. I consider that as to the conduct of these places, it is worse in London than in the country ... The worst I am acquainted with ... is in the neighbourhood of Drury Lane—this is the worst, both for filth and for the character of the lodgers. In the room where I slept, which was like a barn in size, the tiles were off the roof, and as there was no ceiling, I could see the blue sky from where I lay ...

Here I slept in what was called the single men's room, and it was confined to men. In another part of the house was a room for married couples ... For the bed with the view of the blue sky I paid 3d. If it rained there was no shelter. I have slept in a room in Brick-lane, Whitechapel, in which were fourteen beds. In the next bed to me, on the one side, was a man, his wife, and three children, and a man and his wife on the other. They were Irish people, and I believe the women were the men's wives—as the Irish women generally are. Of all the women that resort to these places, the Irish are far the best for chastity.

All the beds were occupied, single men being mixed with the couples of the two sexes. The question is never asked, when a man and woman go to a lodging-house, if they are man and wife.

All must pay before they go to bed, or be turned into the street. These beds were made—as all the low lodging-house beds are—of the worst cotton flocks, stuffed in coarse, strong canvas. There is a pair of sheets, a blanket, and a rug. I have known the bedding to be unchanged for three months; but that is not general. The beds are an average size. Dirt is the rule with them, and cleanliness the exception. They are all infested with vermin. I never met with an exception. No one is required to wash before going to bed in any of these places (except at a very few, where a very dirty fellow would not be admitted), unless he has been walking on a wet day without shoes or stockings, and then he must bathe his feet.

The people who slept in the room I am describing, were chiefly young men, almost all accompanied by young females. I have seen girls of fifteen sleep with 'their chaps'—in some places, with youths of from sixteen to twenty. There is no objection to any boy or girl occupying a bed, even though the keeper knows that they were previously strangers to each other.

The accommodation for purposes of decency is very bad in some places. A pail in the middle of the room, to which both sexes may resort, is a frequent arrangement. No delicacy or decency is ever observed. The woman are, I think, worse than the men. If anyone, possessing a sense of shame, says a word of rebuke, he is at once assailed, by the women in particular, with the coarsest words in the language. The Irish women are as bad as the others with respect to language; but I have known them keep themselves covered in bed when the other women were outraging modesty or decency. The Irish will sleep anywhere to save a halfpenny a night, if they have ever so much money . . .

It is not uncommon for a boy or a man to take a girl of the streets to these apartments. Some are the same as common brothels, women being taken in at all hours of the day or night. In most, however, they must stay all night as a married couple. In dressing or undressing there is no regard to decency; while disgusting blackguardism is often carried on in the conversation of the inmates. I have known decent people, those that are driven to such places from destitution, perhaps for the first time, shocked and disgusted at what they saw. I have seen a decent married pair so shocked and disgusted, that they have insisted on leaving the place, and have left it.

From a statement made to HENRY MAYHEW by 'a man of superior education and station . . . reduced from affluence to beggary', reported in a 'Letter to the *Morning Chronicle*', reprinted in *The Westminster Review*, vol. 53, pp. 498–499 (1850).

18

Cleaning Up the Lodging Houses

The Act for the well-ordering of Common Lodging Houses has now been in operation since the year 1851, and has been attended by the most beneficial results.

Before this enactment, the evils existing in the Lodging Houses of the poor was beyond description. Crowded and filthy, without water or ventilation, without the least regard to cleanliness or decency, they were hotbeds of disease, misery, and crime. Under the operation of the Act, the evils attending such houses have been in great degree removed or abated ...

The following cases, dealt with under the Act, furnish examples of the nature and extent of the evils which arise in Lodging Houses not controlled by law.

At a house, No 17, Lincoln Court, St Giles, in one room 10 feet square, whereas three persons would be allowed by the regulations now enforced, seven men, nine women, and one child were found huddled together in a most filthy state; the bedding dirty beyond description, no partitions or ventilation; and a few minutes before the visit of the officer, one of the females had been confined. The keeper was summoned on the 24th October, 1854, to Bow Street Police Court, and fined £4 or six weeks imprisonment.

In a house, 93 High Street, Shadwell, whereas 25 persons would be allowed, 45 persons, chiefly Lascars, were found. From the filthy and crowded state of the house, and the fumes of opium, the place was intolerable. The keeper was summoned, on the 12th December, 1854, to the Thames Police Court, and fined 40s and costs, or 14 days imprisonment.

At the house No 117, Cock Hill, Ratcliff, in a room having space for 5 persons, 15 were found in a most deplorable condition, 11 sleeping on the floor, covered only by a few filthy rags. The keeper was summoned on the 24th February, 1858, to the Thames Police Court, and fined 20s and costs, or 14 days imprisonment.

In a house, No 31, Farmer Street, Shadwell, containing six small rooms, were found 29 persons (Lascars and low prostitutes). In one of the rooms was the dead body of a Lascar covered with an old rug, and in a room adjoining another Lascar, in a dying state, lying in a cupboard amongst a few rags; this room was destitute of bedding and furniture.

The keeper was summoned on the 9th February, 1855, to Thames Police Court, and fined £5 or one month's imprisonment.

In a room at No 25, Goulston Court, Whitechapel, having space for three persons under the regulations, 9 adults (men and women) and one child were found; the beds, bedding, and house in a filthy state, and no partitions. This case was summoned, 8th November, 1855, to Worship Street Police Court; the defendant did not appear, and a warrant was granted, but the parties had left the neighbourhood.

In a room at No 8, Lincoln Court, St Giles, where 5 persons would be allowed by the regulations, there were found to be 3 male adults and 9 females; the rooms, bed, bedding in a dirty state, and no partitions to secure the privacy of the sexes. The keeper was summoned, on the 13th September, 1856, to Bow Street Police Court, and fined 20s and costs.

A house known as the American Lodging House, Glasshouse Yard, Whitechapel, chiefly resorted to by emigrants while awaiting the departure of ships, was, before the enforcement of the provisions of the Common Lodging Houses Acts, an example of overcrowding and neglect of health and decency. As many as 250 persons were lodged in this house, with one closet only, and that in a most filthy state. The keeper was summoned and fined, and the house is now registered, and 99 persons were properly accommodated.

WILLIAM C. HARRIS, Asst. Commissioner of Police for the Metropolis: Report upon the Operation of the Common Lodging Houses Act within the Metropolitan Police District (1857), page 3; P.P. 1857, Sess. 2, vol. 16.

(b) KING CHOLERA

Although it must seem cruel to say it, there can be little doubt that the successive invasions of cholera did this country a power of good. But for its ravages, the medical profession, and the public at large, would have continued to remain even longer in ignorance of the intimate connection of Disease and Dirt, particularly human dirt.

From its principal breeding grounds in Asia, cholera advanced slowly but steadily westwards, until in 1831 it appeared for the first time in England. This was in October of that year, at Sunderland, and in the following January the first cases were reported in London. In 1846/9 there was a second visitation, and an even more deadly one. Two thousand persons are stated to have died from cholera in a single week in September 1849, and during the outbreak more than fifty thousand persons died in England and Wales as a whole. There was a return visit in 1853/4, which caused the deaths of over twenty thousand persons, and a fourth epidemic was widely prevalent in the British Isles in 1865/6, although this was not quite so destructive of human life. For by this time the 'sanitarians' had some very substantial achievements to their credit in the field of public health.

From the first they were gravely hampered by a lack of knowledge of the true nature of the disease, and of its predisposing causes. *We* know that cholera is caused by a germ, but the first cholera germ was not found until 1883, when the German doctor Robert Koch discovered it in the faecal discharges of cholera patients in Egypt and elsewhere. Until the early eighteen-fifties the very existence of germs was hardly thought of. Cholera was lumped together with typhus, typhoid, etc. as 'fever', a principal symptom of which was acute diarrhoea, and according to the generally accepted theory in medical circles 'fever' was caused by an 'unknown something in the atmosphere', to which the name 'miasma' was given. In their report published in August 1850, the General Board of Health, under the guidance of Chadwick, gave a list of ten 'localizing' or 'predisposing' causes of the cholera epidemic then prevailing, viz. overcrowding, filth, malaria from putrescent mud, dampness, want of drains and bad drains, graveyards, unwholesome water supplies, poor food, fatigue, and excessive use of purgatives. Chadwick scoffed at the idea of 'diseased germs', and Florence Nightingale did her magnificent work in complete ignorance of the real nature of the enemy she was up against. Not until 1890, we are told, did John Simon bring himself to accept Koch's germ theory of disease.

But if their theory was altogether false, in their practice the 'sanitarians' were on the right track. Dirt and the rest do not *cause* disease, but they provide the environmental conditions in which it is enabled to flourish. For Simon it may be claimed that he was more enlightened than his fellows, since, as will have been clear from the extracts from his reports given earlier, and even more from his account of the Mr G. Cholera Case (No. 119), he charged bad and insufficient water supplies with being the villain of the piece. Mayhew was right, too, in describing such a place as Jacob's Island as being the 'capital of cholera'. And that very practical-minded old statesman Lord Palmerston was absolutely right in enjoining upon the religious leaders and the people in general that they should look to their drains . . .

19

When Mr G. Got Cholera

The choleraic infection of Egypt in May last, with the return of Mohammedan pilgrims from Mecca where the disease was epidemic; followed soon afterwards by the spread of the same infection, along each of the several lines of steamboat communication which diverge from Alexandria as a centre, to all the most considerable ports of the Levant and of Southern Europe; whence again in many instances inland spreadings of the disease took place;—this constituted a succession of events which augured badly for the public health in England. And presently, in the quarter where it was looked for, a first wave of the infection had touched our shores, though happily not yet greatly to harm us. For the first time in our experience of cholera, the attack was on our south-east coast: not as on former occasions on our ports which look toward the Baltic: but on Southampton, distinguished among all our ports as the one of quickest Mediterranean traffic, and perhaps also (though this may have been secondarily) on Weymouth or Portland or Dorchester.

Into Southampton there came on July 10th, and at intervals afterwards, very suspicious arrivals from Alexandria, Malta, and Gibraltar. In the middle of August, a young woman in the town had a choleraic attack of doubtful nature; on the 22nd September a labourer had undoubted Asiatic cholera, of which afterwards he died; and from then, for about six weeks, cholera-cases continued to occur in small numbers in and about Southampton, so that on the 4th November (when the little epidemic might be considered at an end) there had been in all 60 such cases, of which 35 had terminated in death.

It is a question whether from Southampton, or in any more direct way, the morbific influence may in August or September have reached Weymouth or Portland or Dorchester ... but I am informed that a gentleman from a distance, who early in August was spending a week in Weymouth, and visiting both Portland and Dorchester, contracted during that week a diarrhoea which on his return home developed to severe cholera; and in September there occurred in the neighbourhood of London, the following events which give peculiar interest to the question.

Mr G. and his wife, inhabitants of Theydon-Bois near Epping, had been lodging at Weymouth for seventeen days from the 8th September, had visited Portland on the 22nd, and Dorchester on the 23rd, and returned home on the 25th. On the evening of the 23rd Mr G. had been seized with diarrhoea, sickness and cramps, which continued more or less through the next day, and left him still unwell on the morning of the 25th. He, however, performed his journey to Epping with his wife. She, during the journey, began also to complain of abdominal discomfort; and this, after her return, developed, with gradually increasing diarrhoea, to cholera, of which (in its secondary fever) she eventually died on the 11th October. On the 30th September (while the last-named patient was still in collapse) one of her daughters, aged eight, was seized with cholera, and in a few hours died. That same night, a serving-lad in the house was seized with cholera, and barely escaped with his life. On the 2nd October, the doctor who was attending them died of cholera, after ten hours' illness. On the 3rd, another daughter of the house, aged 16, passed into cholera, but eventually, after some consecutive fever, recovered. On the 5th, a maidservant got diarrhoea, which, though relieved for a time, relapsed and became choleraic on the 8th, and she, after some promise of recovery, fell into secondary fever, with which she eventually died. On the 5th also a labourer who worked on the premises, but lived apart, was taken with diarrhoea, which, passing on to cholera and collapse, killed him next day but one.

A COURT FOR KING CHOLERA.

12. John Leech in *Punch*, 1852

On the 6th, the head of the house, the Mr G. who had suffered at Weymouth, and had ever since had relaxed bowels, got a very acute new attack, and died after 15 hours. On the same day his son was attacked with diarrhoea, and next day was in collapse, but rallied and finally got well. Also on the 6th, the grandmother of the house was similarly attacked; and she, though she emerged from collapse, eventually died on the 14th. On the 10th a woman, living near by, whose only known connexion with the above cases was that on the 8th she had assisted in laying out the dead body of the above-mentioned labourer, was taken with choleraic purging, which soon led to collapse, and next day to death.

Thus, within a fortnight, in that little circle, eleven persons had been attacked with cholera—mother, father, grandmother, two daughters, son, doctor, serving-lad, servant-maid, labourer, and country-woman: and, of these eleven, only three survived—the son, a daughter, and the serving-lad. Later, in the country-woman's family, there was another fatal case.

It cannot well be doubted but that the exciting cause of this succession

305

of events was, in some way or other, the return of the parents from Weymouth—of the father with remains of choleraic diarrhoea still on him, the mother with apparently the beginnings of the same complaint. But this is only part of the case, and the remainder teaches an impressive lesson.

All drinking-water of the house came from a well beneath the floor of the scullery; and into that well there was habitual soakage from the water-closet. Whether, in intimate pathology, there are any essential differences between the cholera which kills on a large scale, and the cholera which kills single victims, is hitherto so entirely unknown, that it would be idle to discuss, as a separate question, whether the G. illness, contracted at Weymouth and carried to Epping, was 'epidemic' or 'sporadic', 'Asiatic' or 'English' cholera; and, as above stated, I cannot prove it to have been an offshoot of the Southampton epidemic, or otherwise of Mediterranean origin. Certain, therefore, only is this:— that, from the time when Mr and Mrs G. returned ailing to their home, the discharges which passed from their bowels gave an additional and peculiar taint to the already foul water-supply of their household, and that thenceforth every one who drank water in the house drank water which had in it the ferment of decomposing diarrhoeal matters.

DR JOHN SIMON, Privy Council Medical Reports, No. 8 (1865)

20

A Visit to the 'Capital of Cholera'

Out of the 12,000 and odd deaths which, within the short space of three months, had arisen from cholera in 1849, more than half occurred on the southern shores of the Thames; and to this awful number no localities contributed so largely as Lambeth, Southwark, and Bermondsey, each adding at the height of the disease its hundred victims a week to the fearful catalogue of mortality. And one who ventured a visit to the last-named district in particular, would not have wondered at the ravages of the pestilence in that malarious quarter, bounded as it was on the north and east by filth and fever, and on the south and west by want, squalor, rags, and pestilence. Here stood the very capital of cholera—Jacob's Island—a patch of ground insulated by the common sewer.

Spared by the fire of London, the houses and comforts of the people in this loathsome place had scarcely known any improvement since that time. In the days of Henry II the foul, stagnant ditch, that to this day makes an island of this pestilential spot, was a running stream ... and the trees, now black with mud, were bowers under which the citizens loved, on sultry summer evenings, to sit drinking their sack and ale. But at the date of this pen-and-ink sketch the running brook was changed into a tidal sewer ... and where the ancient summer-houses stood, nothing but hovels, sties, and muck-heaps were then to be seen ...

The striking peculiarity of Jacob's Island consisted in the wooden galleries and sleeping rooms at the back of the houses overhanging the turbid flood. These were built upon piles ... At some parts of the stream whole rooms had been built out, so that the houses on opposite sides nearly touched one another; and there, with the very stench of death arising through the boards, human being slept night after night, until the last sleep of all came upon them years before its time ...

At the back of every house that boasted a square foot or two of outlet—and the majority had none at all—were pig-sties. In front waddled ducks, while cocks and hens scratched at the cinder heaps beside them. Indeed, the creatures that fattened on offal were the only living things that seemed to flourish there.

*　　*　　*

On approaching the tidal ditch from the Neckinger Road, the shutters of the house at the corner were shut up from top to bottom. Our intelligent and obliging guide, Dr Martin, of the Registrar's Office, informed us that a girl was lying dead there from cholera, and that but very recently another victim had fallen in the house adjoining it ... As we walked down George Row, our informant told us that at the corner of London Street he could see a short time back as many as nine houses in which there were one or two persons lying dead of the cholera at the same time; and yet there could not have been more than a dozen tenements visible from the spot.

We crossed the bridge and spoke to one of the inmates. In answer to our question she told us that she was never well. Indeed, the signs of the deadly influence of the place were painted in the earthy complexion of the woman. 'Neither I nor my children know what health is', she said. 'But what is one to do? We must live where our bread is! I've tried to let the house, and put a bill up, but cannot get any one to take it.'

From this spot we were led to narrow close courts, where the sun never shone, and the air seemed almost as stagnant and putrid as the ditch we had left behind. The blanched cheeks of the people that now came out to stare at us were white as vegetables grown in the dark; and as we stopped to look down the alley our informant told us that the place teemed with children...

Continuing our course we reached 'The Folly', another street so narrow that the names and trades of the shopmen were painted on boards that stretched across the thoroughfare. We were here stopped by our companion in front of a house 'to let'. The building was as cramped and unlike a human habitation as the wooden houses in a child's box of toys.

'In this house,' said our friend, 'when the scarlet fever was raging in the neighbourhood, the barber who was living here suffered fearfully from it, and no sooner did the man get well of this than he was seized with typhus, and scarcely had he recovered from the first attack of that, than he was struck down a second time with the same terrible disease. Since then he has lost his child from cholera, and at this moment his wife is in the workhouse suffering from the same affliction. The only wonder was that they are not *all* dead; for as the barber sat at his meals in his small shop, if he put his hand against the wall behind him, it would be covered with the soil of his neighbour's privy, sopping through the wall.'...

As we now passed along the reeking banks of the sewer, the sun shone upon a narrow slip of the water. In the bright light it appeared the colour of strong green tea, and positively looked as solid as black marble in the shadow. Indeed, it was more like watery mud than muddy water, and yet we were assured this was the only water the wretched inhabitants had to drink.

As we gazed in horror at the pool, we saw drains and sewers emptying their filthy contents into it, we saw a whole tier of doorless privies in the open road, common to men and women, built over it, we heard bucket after bucket of filth splash into it, and the limbs of the vagrant boys bathing in it, seemed, by pure force of contrast, white as Parian marble. And yet, as we stood gazing in horror at the fluvial sewer, we saw a child from one of the galleries opposite lower a tin can with a rope, to fill a large bucket that stood beside her.

In each of the rude and rotten balconies, indeed, that hung over the stream, the self-same bucket was to be seen in which the inhabitants were wont to put the mucky liquid to stand, so that they might after it had been left to settle for a day or two, skim the fluid from the solid particles of filth and pollution which constituted the sediment.

In this wretched place we were taken to a house where an infant lay dead of the cholera. We asked if they *really did* drink the water? The answer was, 'They were obliged to drink the ditch unless they could beg or thieve a pailful of the real Thames.'...

From this spot we crossed a little shaky bridge in Providence

Buildings, a peninsula set in sewers. Here in front of the house were small gardens that a table-cloth would have covered. Still, the one dahlia that here raised its round red head made it a happier and brighter place. Never was colour so grateful to the eye. All we had looked at had been so dark and dingy, and had smelt so much of churchyard clay, that this little patch of beauty was brighter than even an oasis in the desert . . .

HENRY MAYHEW; *London Characters* (1874; ed. of 1881, pp. 445–455).

21

Lord Palmerston's Advice

In the year 1853, the cholera, after having committed serious ravages in many parts of Europe, visited Scotland. There, it was sure to find numerous victims among a badly fed, badly housed, and not over-cleanly people. For, if there is one thing better established than another respecting this disease, it is that it invariably attacks, with the greatest effect, those classes who, from poverty or from sloth, are imperfectly nourished, neglect their persons, and live in dirty, ill-drained, or ill-ventilated dwellings. In Scotland, such classes are very numerous. In Scotland, therefore, the cholera must needs be very fatal . . .

Under these circumstances, it must have been evident, not merely to men of science, but to all men of plain, sound understanding, who would apply their minds to the matter without prejudice, that the Scotch had only one way of successfully grappling with their terrible enemy. It behoved them to feed their poor, to cleanse their cesspools, and to ventilate their houses. If they had done this, and done it quickly thousands of lives would have been spared. But they neglected it, and the country was thrown into mourning. Nay, they not only neglected it, but, moved by that dire superstition which sits like an incubus upon them, they adopted a course which, if it had been carried into full operation, would have aggravated the calamity to a frightful extent . . . In the name of religion, whose offices they thus abused and perverted to the detriment of man, instead of employing them for his benefit they insisted on the propriety of ordering a national fast, which, in so superstitious a country, was sure to be rigidly kept, and, being rigidly kept, was sure to enfeeble thousands of delicate persons, and, before twenty-four hours were passed, prepare them to receive that deadly poison which was already lurking around them, and which, hitherto, they had just strength enough to resist. The public fast was also to be accompanied by a public humiliation, in order that nothing might be wanting to appal the mind and fill it with terror . . .

This was the scheme projected by the Scotch clergy, and they were determined to put it into execution. To give greater effect to it, they called upon England to help them, and, in the autumn of 1853, the Presbytery of Edinburgh, thinking that from their position they were bound to take the lead, caused their Moderator to address a letter, ostensibly to the English Minister, but in reality to the English nation. In this choice production . . . the Home Secretary is assured that the members of the Presbytery had delayed appointing a day for fasting and humiliation on their own ecclesiastical authority, because they thought it likely that one would be appointed by the royal authority. But as this had not been done, the Presbytery respectfully requested to be informed if . . . the appointment by the Queen of a national fast was in contemplation . . .

The minister to whom the letter was addressed was Lord Palmerston, a man of vast experience, and perhaps better acquainted with public opinion than any politician of his time. He, being well aware of the difference between Scotland and England, knew that what was suitable for one country was not suitable for the other, and that notions which the Scotch deemed religious, the English deemed fanatical . . . The Scotch clergy took for granted that the cholera was the result of the Divine anger, and was intended to chastize our sins. In the reply which they now received from the English Government, a doctrine was enunciated, which to Englishmen seemed right enough, but which to Scotchmen sounded very profane. The Presbytery were informed, that the affairs of this world are regulated by natural laws, on the observance or the neglect of which the weal or woe of mankind depends. One of those laws connects disease with the exhalations of bodies; and it is by virtue of this law that contagion spreads, either in crowded cities, or in places where vegetable decomposition is going on. Man, by exerting himself, can disperse or neutralize these noxious influences. The apperance of the cholera proves that he has not exerted himself. The towns have not been purified; hence the root of the evil. The Home Secretary, therefore, advised the Presbytery of Edinburgh, that it was better to cleanse than to fast. He thought that the plague being upon them, activity was preferable to humiliation. It was now autumn, and before the hot weather would return, a considerable period must elapse. That period should be employed in destroying the causes of disease, by improving the abodes of the poor.

'Lord Palmerston would, therefore, suggest that the best course which the people of this country can pursue to deserve that the further progress of the cholera should be stayed, will be to employ the interval that will elapse between the present time and the beginning of next spring in planning and executing measures by which those portions of their towns and cities which are inhabited by the poorest classes, and which, from the nature of things, the most need purification and improvement, may be freed from those causes and sources of contagion which, if allowed to remain, will infallibly breed pestilence, and be fruitful in death, in spite of all the prayers and fastings of a united, but inactive nation.'

H. T. BUCKLE; *History of Civilization in England* (1861); World's Classics edition, vol. iii, pp. 474–480.

CHAPTER 7

WORKERS UNITE!

(a) TRADE UNIONS

'Workers unite!' The injunction sounds like an echo of the *Communist Manifesto* that Marx and Engels drew up in 1848 as a blueprint for the revolutionary movement on the Continent. But so far as the British working classes were concerned, it was quite unnecessary. They needed no urge to unite: this in fact was what they had been doing ever since the Industrial Revolution had thrown together large masses of workers engaged in much the same kinds of labour and living in dense congregations of population in the new towns. Very early they had come to appreciate the necessity for joining hands, against rapacious landlords and grinding employers and catchpenny tradesmen, and also with a view to meeting 'the thousand natural shocks that flesh is heir to'. Trade unions, co-operative societies, friendly societies—it is not too much to claim that all these grew out of British soil, were fed and watered and brought to fruition by humble toilers in the British industrial scene, and they remain to this day as among the chief contributions made by our race to the welfare of mankind.

Whether or not the trade unions are the direct descendants of the medieval guilds, there is no doubt that there were 'trade societies' before the close of the 18th century. From 1799 to 1824 trade unionism was under the ban of the law, but when the Combination Acts were repealed in 1824 there was a tremendous resurgence of trade union activity. The wildest hopes were indulged in, and Robert Owen's Utopian Socialism captured the hearts and minds of thousands. In place of a host of tiny societies there came into existence a vast lumbering union of all working men—the Grand National Consolidated Trades Union, instituted in 1834 'for the purpose of the more effectually enabling the working classes to secure, protect, and establish the rights of industry'. After a few hectic weeks it collapsed, and the dream of a general strike which would bring the capitalist class to their knees died with it. What remained of working-class vigour was channelled into the Chartist movement, and the trade unions languished and many of them disappeared from off the scene.

But in the eighteen-forties there opened a fresh chapter. With the approach of the 'Golden Age of Capitalism' economic conditions took a marked turn for the better, and out of the working class there emerged leaders who were resolved that the men they represented should have a bigger share in the bigger product. A new form of trade unionism established itself. Numbers of the small, purely local unions were merged into national groupings, each with its nation-wide membership, paying regular subscriptions and kept together by benefits of one kind and another, its staff of salaried officers, and a head office usually in London.

Most prominent among this new generation were William Allan (Amalgamated Society of Engineers), Robert Applegarth (Amalgamated Society of Carpenters), Daniel Guile (Ironfounders), Edwin Coulson (London Bricklayers) and George Odger, member of a small union of makers of ladies' shoes and a prominent London Radical. Together they constituted what was known as the 'Junta', and they set the tone for the movement as a whole. They were not in the least inclined to revolution, and would have scorned Marx's contention, that 'you have nothing to lose but your chains'. Whatever was the case with the working men on the Continent, they were fully persuaded that the British worker had a great deal to lose—and a great deal that he might gain, by strictly constitutional methods, by parliamentary agitation. They 'accepted' the capitalist system, and were fully prepared to co-operate in making it work. They were orthodox believers in the political economy taught by John Stuart Mill. They welcomed the support of such middle-class well-wishers as Thomas Hughes (author of *Tom Brown's Schooldays* and an early associate of Charles Kingsley and F. D. Maurice in the Christian Socialist movement) and Frederic Harrison ('Positivist' philosopher in religion and advanced Liberal in politics).

Under the guidance of these hard-headed, practical-minded, and very capable men, trade unionism made great strides in the middle of the century, with the result that it aroused intense suspicion and hostility among members of the governing class. In 1866 a series of outrages in Sheffield, directed by unionists against non-unionists and involving serious injuries and even death, aroused public feeling still more, and there was a widespread demand for an inquiry into the trade unions. The Junta hastened to dissociate themselves and the men they represented from the Sheffield activities, and joined whole-heartedly in the demand for a Government inquiry. The demand was granted. A Royal Commission was appointed in 1867 by the Conservative government. No Trade Unionist was included in its members, but Hughes secured a seat and the Junta obtained permission to nominate a special representative. Their choice fell on Frederic Harrison, and an excellent one it proved. Robert Applegarth was the first witness to be examined (No. 2), and he and his associates made a deep impression.

Between 1867 and 1869 the Commission issued no fewer than eleven Reports, and appended to the eleventh and final report was a valuable statement drawn up by Hughes and Harrison on Trade Unions in general (No. 1). On the whole, the Commission's conclusions were favourable to the unions.

The extension of the parliamentary franchise to the working-men of the towns in 1868 enormously strengthened the power of trade unionists, and the Trade Union Act followed in 1871. By this Act trade unions were legally recognized, and trade unions funds were fully protected. A further Act passed in 1875 put the legality of peaceful picketing beyond a doubt. Well might the Junta claim that their policy of reasonable moderation had been justified by its fruits.

I

Trade Unionism in the 1860s

The first impression which the results of this protracted Inquiry produces is one which it is of importance never to lose sight of—the great extent to which 'Unionism' has been carried. There is no industry in the country, with some very doubtful exceptions (e.g. millers and tanners) into which it has not entered, and very few parts of the country where it is not prevalent. The various estimates of the number of the different unions and of that of their members differ very widely, but all of them agree in making the numbers very high. One estimate that was given to us put the total number of unionists at 860,000. Mr Mault estimates the number of unionists as about 10·3 of the operatives in the building trade: Mr Applegarth, from his own experience, considers it to be rather 50 per cent . . .

But although in the absence of any official cognizance of their existence, no satisfactory estimate of the extent of unionism can be formed, there remains ample proof that it embraces every branch of skilled labour and a very large proportion of the working men of the kingdom. Opinions differ widely as to whether this proportion contains in all cases the higher class of workmen. It varies greatly, no doubt, in the different trades. It is probable that in many trades some of the best and most educated men stand aloof. It has not, however, been suggested by anyone that the union is ever composed of the inferior order of workmen, though it may not invariably be composed of the superior. In some trades, and those perhaps requiring the greatest skill, it seems to be admitted that the union contains the great bulk of the most skilled men—as the engineers, the iron-founders, the painters, glass-makers, printers, shipbuilders, and others.

All legislation, and all discussion with a view to legislation, must therefore take as its basis this general fact—viz., that a very great proportion of the skilled workmen of the country have for many years shown a strong and increasing disposition to unite themselves in these trade societies. The evidence leaves no doubt on our minds that the union as a rule consists of the superior class of workmen; and we can see no indications whatever that it is ever regarded as injurious by any body of workmen deserving attention from either their numbers or their character.

This very great extent is also accompanied by another fact, that or striking and steady increase. Taking a period of 10 or 20 years, this growth is very remarkable, as is shown in the following tables of the engineers, carpenters (*Amalgamated Society*), and iron founders.

	Numbers of members		
Year	*Engineers*	*Iron Founders*	*Carpenters*
1858	15,194	6,637	—
....			
1862	24,234	8,458	947
....			
1867	33,325	10,839	8,022

Improved character of Unionism since previous inquiries

Without disguising from ourselves the shocking character of certain atrocities which have been clearly brought home to unionists in various parts of the country ... it is some satisfaction to feel that a very great improvement in the general character of unionism is shown as con-trasted with the results of earlier Inquiries. The Blue Books which contain the evidence taken by the Parliamentary Committees of 1824, 1825, and 1838, before and after the repeal of the old combination laws, teem with stories of violence and outrage which are happily without any parallel in the evidence obtained by this Commission. Outside the area of the two Inquiries at Sheffield and Manchester ... instances of actual attempts on life and limb rarely occur. The peculiarly atrocious crime of vitriol throwing, with which the former Reports are full, has not been mentioned here. Nothing has been heard of either incendiar-ism or machine breaking. There has not been given in evidence, outside the two areas just mentioned, any single case of taking of life, and few definite acts of injury to the person ... Whilst, therefore, the course of the last quarter of a century exhibits an immense increase of unionism, and an advance of the unions to a much more highly organized and powerful position, the criminal element appears to be totally extinct in the more regular and developed form of unionism, and, with the exception just named, to have lost its dangerous form—i.e., organized outrage, even in the ruder types of unionism and the least educated trades ...

High character of the principal Unions

No question can exist in any mind that the best types of the union are to be found in the older, richer, and best established societies. The general organization, for instance, of the *Amalgamated Society of Engineers*, must strike everyone as a thoroughly efficient and complete system. As a mere administrative machine, it appears quite the equal of a high-class trading company. The secretary of that society must impress all who have the opportunity of knowing him as a man of ability and character. Exception may be taken on economic grounds to certain rules and practices of the society, and it would be strange if occasional instances of wrong-headed or unjust conduct were not heard of in a body of 30,000 working men; but no one can suppose that as an association the general management is less efficient or more prone to illegal conduct than that of any trading concern of repute ... But this is not a singular case. The same thing might be said of the officials of the *Amalgamated Carpenters*, of the *Manchester House Painters*, of the miners', the glassworkers', the shipwrights', the printers', and many other societies of great extent and influence. The great amalgamated societies—that is, those which extend over a large area and embrace many local societies—may be said to show as a rule the most unexceptionable central direction.

Those societies, again, which possess very large funds and great power over their respective trades are those against which there exists the least cause for complaint; whilst it may be said that those societies which offer the greatest amount of assurance benefits to their subscribers are just those which are least disposed to expend their accumulations in labour contests. Over a period of 10 years the engineers, with 33,000 members, have expended in benefits £459,000, in disputes £26,000, or about 6 per cent of their funds; and the iron founders, with 10,000 members, have expended in benefits £210,000, and in disputes £5,300, or about $2\frac{1}{2}$ per cent of their funds ... The shipwrights, over a period of 12 years, have hardly expended anything in strikes. The glassworkers have had no strike expenditure for 10 years.

We thus see that in proportion as the unions acquire extent in area, regularity, and publicity in their transactions, and become properly constituted associations, they gain in character and usefulness. In proportion as they are irregular in organization, and approach the form of the old secret trades union, without 'benefits', they preserve some criminal features of the surreptitious unions under the old law . . .

Influence of Unions on strikes and wages

It does not appear to be borne out by the evidence that the disposition to strike on the part of workmen is in itself the creation of unionism, or that this disposition increases in proportion to the strength of the union. It appears in fact that the relation of unions to strikes is rather the converse, and that many unions are hastily formed when the spirit of demanding a rise is rife; but that the effect of the established societies is to diminish the frequency and certainly the disorder of strikes, and to guarantee a regularity of wages and hours rather than to engage in constant endeavours to improve them . . .

It appears that the strongest, richest, and most extended of all the unions are to be found in those trades in which the wages and the hours of labour show the greatest permanence, and in which on the whole the fewest disputes occur. This, by itself, proves that any description of unionism as a struggle for the best price is incomplete . . . So that, taken broadly, the effect is this—that the frequency of disputes coincides with a weak, fluctuating, and poor union, and not with the reverse . . . On the other hand, the strikes are shown to be most frequent, and certainly the least orderly, where the union has acquired no real command over the workmen, or is struggling into existence . . . The tailors' and ironworkers' unions never possessed the power or the permanent character of such societies as the *Amalgamated Engineers* and *Amalgamated Carpenters*, and have had but small benefit purposes; and these trades are those in which the greatest complaints occur of the frequency of strikes . . .

Piecework

. . . The common notion that it is a fundamental principle of unionism in general to resist piecework is very far from being borne out by the evidence before us. In some of the largest industries in the kingdom, in which the conduct of the unions has been most strongly attacked, piecework is found to be the custom, and the unquestioned custom, of the trade . . . In fact, in the trades which have come before us, piecework and not day work, is the accepted rule, except in the case of the engineers, the iron-founders, and certain classes of the building trades; and in these piecework is not altogether excluded . . .

Equalization of wages

The evidence, as a whole, leaves no doubt that it is the general policy of the unions to establish a *minimum* or standard of wages, but there is not the slightest evidence that there is any attempt to fix a *maximum* ...
There is no foundation whatever for the impression that there is any attempt to establish a uniform rate of wages throughout various parts of the country ...

Non-unionists

It is clear that it is a very general practice for unionists, wherever their numbers are sufficiently great, to refuse work in company with non-unionists. It is, however, far from being universal. The evidence shows that in many trades no such practice exists—e.g. carpenters, bricklayers, engineers, ironworkers, colliers, printers, tailors. There can, however, be little doubt that it is constantly enforced whenever the union is strong enough to insist upon it. The practice is no doubt unsocial, and is often carried out in a vexatious and arbitrary spirit, but it is one too common amongst other classes of the community to require any special treatment. It is common to corporations, confraternities, and parties of all kinds; and, as it would be plainly unjust for the State to compel workmen to work with those to whom they objected, and even to punish them directly or indirectly for this refusal, it seems to us one of those things which must be left to gradual improvement of tone.

We are, on the whole, convinced by the evidence that the union is usually felt by the great body of workmen to be working for their benefit and with their adhesion; and we are inclined to think that the workmen who, under the influence of agencies without ... place themselves in antagonism to it, represent a very small and for the most part a wholly inferior minority ...

General purpose and origin of Trades Unions

It is common to take for granted that the objects of unionism are to raise the wages and to shorten the hours of labour, the means to this end being the threat of or resort to a strike. It is supposed to follow from this that whatever tends to increase the machinery and power of a union tends to increase the frequency and magnitude of strikes. This is a proposition, as we have seen, that is far from being borne out by the evidence before us. Little would be gained by attempting to give any precise formula for the objects aimed at by unionism, where the nature and spirit of the actual unions differ so widely. But the most general description which appears to us to correspond with the facts is this: that unions are associations of workmen for mutual assistance in securing generally the most favourable conditions of labour ...

It may very well be allowed that if not the principal, at any rate one of the most constant, objects of the unions is to obtain for the workmen the best rate of wages which their services will command, and then to reduce the number of hours in which the wages are to be earned . . .

Under a system which professes the right or rather the duty of all men peacefully to pursue their own interests for themselves, unionism appears to us the exact correlative to competition. The stronger prefer to pursue their ends by means of competition, the weaker by means of combination. But for the capitalist to deny the workman unlimited freedom to combine, is for the stronger to object to the weaker pursuing his interests by the most obvious resource in his reach . . . THOMAS HUGHES. FREDERIC HARRISON.

Trades Unions Commission, 11th and final Report (1869); statement referred to in the 3rd Dissent, pp. XXXII–XLII; P.P. 1868/9, vol. 31.

2

Joining the Union

Mr *Robert Applegarth*, general secretary of The Amalgamated Society of Carpenters and Joiners, giving evidence (as the first witness) before the Royal Commission on Trades Unions.—As stated in the preamble of the rules I hold in my hand . . . 'The object of this society is to raise funds for the mutual support of its members in case of sickness, accident, superannuation, for the burial of members and their wives, emigration, loss of tools by fire, water, or theft, and for assistance to members out of work; also for granting assistance in cases of extreme distress not otherwise provided for by the rules, for which purpose a contingent and benevolent fund shall be formed.'

To become a member of the association a person . . . is proposed on a regular meeting night of the branch by a member who knows him to be a qualified workman, to be in good health, and who knows that he can comply with the conditions which are laid down in the rules for his admission. They are as follows:—He must be in good health, have worked for five years at the trade, be a good workman, of steady habits, of good moral character, and not more than 45 years of age. He is seconded by some member who also knows him well. He then fills in the following form (and pays 3d for a copy of the rules). He says (after stating his name and address), 'I hereby certify that I am in good health, and, so far as I know, I am not afflicted with any bodily ailment or constitutional disease, and consider myself a proper person to become a member of this society.' Then he states his age in years and months, and how long he has worked at the trade, and says, 'I hereby give my concurrence in the rules' (which he has been furnished with previously), 'and should these statements be proved to be untrue, I shall be willing to submit to the penalties contained therein.' He is then asked several questions, whether he has belonged to the society before, for the purpose of ascertaining whether he has left in a disgraceful manner or not. He pays 2s 6d, which is called 'proposition money', and stands over for inquiries to be made respecting his character and abilities. The second time that he puts in an appearance, which must be within three months of the night when he was proposed, he answers all questions put to him, and is admitted or rejected by a majority of those present. If he is rejected his money is handed back to him; if he is accepted he pays his second 2s 6d and is furnished with his member's card, and he pays a shilling a week from that time, and 3d per quarter to a benevolent and contingent fund.

The benefits are as follows:—Donation benefit for 12 weeks, 10s per week; and for another 12 weeks, 6s per week. For leaving employment satisfactory to branch or executive council, 15s per week; tool benefit to any amount of loss, or when a man has been a member for only six months, £5; sick benefit for 26 weeks, 12s per week, and then 6s per week so long as his illness continues; funeral benefit £12, or £3 10s when a six months' member dies; accident benefit, £100; super-annuation benefit for life, if a member 25 years, 8s per week; if a member 18 years, 7s per week; if a member for 12 years, 5s per week. The emigration benefit is £6, and there are benevolent grants, according to circumstances, in cases of distress.

Trades Unions Commission, 1st Report (1867), pp. 1–2; P.P. 1867, vol. 32.

3

'Rattening' Explained

Robert Applegarth, when asked if it had come to his knowledge 'that any practice analogous to that of rattening at Sheffield' had been practised in his trade, replied:

As far as my experience of trade matters goes, the rattening that we have heard of only in reference to the Sheffield trades is common to every trade, and what is meant by rattening is that if a man renders himself objectionable to those he is working with they try to make it unpleasant to him in some way or other. I will mention an instance of rattening that took place at a large job at Trollope's, in Pimlico. Two men were discussing over their breakfast, and one struck the other. On that occasion the other men agreed amongst themselves to 'Put the man in Coventry' for a month who had struck the other—that is to say, not to speak to him at all. Every man on the job pledged himself under the penalty of a fine not to speak to him, and they did not speak to him during that month. They faithfully carried out their decision. That is the mildest form of rattening, and that is common to all trades. Again, it is the practice in many trades to remove a man's working tools, not to steal them. Now, that is a thing which I do not sanction or believe in at all, and it is a thing that is very fast dying out, but it is only fair to the Sheffield trades to say that it is not peculiar to them. I believe these practices are to be found amongst the trades that may be considered the most highly educated trades . . .

Mr. Roebuck. You spoke of rattening, and made use of the mild phrase of 'removing' not 'stealing' tools. Now removing tools from a man I suppose takes away his power of doing his work ?—Yes. And therefore deprives him of his wages ?—Yes. And therefore reduces him to starvation ?—Yes, it may be carried out to that extent.

That is rather a heavy result, is it not ?—It is, but you will remember I said that I did not agree with the practice . . . My society does not officially recognize the practice . . . They discourage it.

Trades Union Commission, 1st Report (1867), page 11; P.P. 1867, vol. 32.

4

Pickets on the Gate

I *do* justify picketing . . . I say that it is perfectly justifiable for men to appoint other men to wait at a shop door and to say to those who come, 'The men were dissatisfied with the terms upon which they were working at that place, and if you go in you will go in and undersell us; now we beg that you will not do that.' That is as far as I would justify men in going. If they use threats and coerce or intimidate that is beyond

13. 'Black-leg!' (*The Leisure Hour*, 1862)

the instructions ... If they did not do what I have justified it would
be absolute folly to strike in many instances.

ROBERT APPLEGARTH; R.C. on Trades Unions, 4th Report, p. 12; P.P. 1867,
vol. 32.

* * *

In 1859 our works were picketed morning, noon, and night. Several of
the men who came up from the country came to us, and said, 'I am
sorry I cannot stop; but when I go out, the men follow me, my wife is
annoyed, and my children get hooted at in the street, and therefore I
really cannot stop.'

MR G. F. TROLLOPE London building contractor; R.C. on Trades Unions,
1st Report, page 108; P.P. 1867, vol. 32.

5

'*Stinking hussies !*'

3 June 1867.—*Ellen Meade*, convicted of threatening and molesting a non-unionist workwoman to prevent her from working for her employer. The following statement is extracted from the evidence of the prosecutrix:—

'On Saturday last I met the prisoner in Wardour Street, when she said to me, "Well, Mrs Mills, you are doing the dirty work, are you?" I asked her what she meant, and she said, "Why, you are fetching work from shops that are on strike." I asked here if that had anything to do with her, and she replied, "Yes, it's all to do with me; it's all such stinking hussies as you who are keeping men out of their work, you stinking cow, and when the strike is over you'll be off, and there will be no work for you. You are a ...... When the strike is over I will do for you." '

The prisoner's brother was a journeyman tailor, and a sort of corporal of pickets.

From a Chronological Statement of some of the Commitments and Trials incident to the Strike of London Tailors in 1867; Trades Unions Commission, Appendix to 11th and Final report (1869), page 123, P.P. 1868/9, vol. 31.

6

The Strike at Trollope's

Mr George Francis Trollope, London builder, examined:—There had been for a considerable period an agitation amongst the men for what was called the nine hours' movement, and after a time it resulted in this, that on 18th July, 1859, we and three other London builders, received the following notice: 'Gentlemen, We, the men in your employ, consider that the time has arrived when some alteration in the hours of labour is necessary, and having determined that the reduction of the present working day to nine hours at the present rate of wages ...

EFFECTS OF A STRIKE

UPON THE CAPITALIST   AND   UPON THE WORKING MAN.

14. John Leech, in *Punch*, 1852

would meet our present requirement, we respectfully solicit you to concede the nine hours as a day's work. A definite answer to our request is solicited by the 22nd day of July, 1859.'

That was the first notice which the masters received, and on the 23rd of July our men struck. Now . . . at that time we had a great number of men who had been in our employ for a long time, and we saw many of them on the subject . . . I said, 'Really, I cannot see anything at all reasonable in your demand. The master builders for many years past have been very desirous to adopt the nine hours in the winter, that is, from November to February. You have resisted it, and have insisted on working ten hours, and now you say that you want nine hours all the year round . . . You next say that a reduction of the working hours to nine hours per day will meet "our present requirements". What do you mean by "our present requirements"?' They said, 'Well, sir, it is no use disguising the fact, if we get nine hours now we mean to get eight next summer; eight hours is all that they work in the colonies, Australia, and so on, and there is no reason why we should work longer.' I said, 'Do you mean that this nine hours or eight hours is to be restricted to the building trade? Because you cannot tell me for a moment that there is anything injurious to your health, or anything else connected with the trade that should cause your labour to be reduced to nine hours or eight hours per day any more than any other class of labourers, say agricultural labourers, or factory men for instance.' They replied, 'We have nothing to do with that; they can look after themselves; we think that we can force the master builders to give in to the nine hours per day, and we mean to try it.' That was the only answer I got. I said, 'I am very sorry that you have struck against us; nobody likes to stand in the front of the battle for nothing; but we cannot stand alone, we must act in concert with the whole body of the trade.'

The master builders conferred with one another as to what was the best thing to be done. Of course, everyone saw that it was not a question which affected Messrs Trollope only. If we had succumbed and conceded the nine hours, the next man to be taken was Mr Kelk, I believe, and we should have been knocked over one after the other like ninepins ... Then the master builders said to us, 'You must try what you can do for the next fortnight to get your works filled, and if at the end of a fortnight you cannot get your works filled, then we must take measures to support you.'

During that fortnight we endeavoured to get men, but ineffectually. The place was picketed, many men came and offered their services, but they were insulted, and so were afraid to continue.

At the end of the fortnight the masters met again, and ... they then agreed as follows:—'We will issue a notice that we will close our shops until yours (Trollope's) are filled', and they further required that there should be hung up in the shops, and be handed to every man who came in, a memorandum to this effect, "I declare that I am not now, nor will I during the continuance of my engagement with you, become a member of or support any society which, directly or indirectly, interferes with the arrangement of this or any other establishment, or the hours or terms of labour; and that I recognize the right of employers and employed individually to make any trade engagements on which they may choose to agree," and they added, 'Every workman shall be distinctly required to pledge his word to the observance of these conditions, and on his name being entered on the file of the engagement book ... he may resume his employment.' The thing went on for several weeks; the masters all stood loyally by us. Of course, we had to incur a great deal of loss, and a great deal of difficulty, because we took in a number of men who were perfect strangers to us, and we could not tell whether they really were good workmen or not ... At last the men said that they gave up the nine hours movement altogether, and that they only required this declaration to be taken down out of the shops.

After three or four weeks the thing gradually subsided, and the declaration was taken down, and the matter ended . . .

Earl of Lichfield: What are the hours now, are they the same as they were?—We made an alteration last year when we raised the wages (very unnecessarily as we thought) to 8d per hour . . . The hours before that strike were 10 hours per day all the year round, except on the Saturday when they left off earlier, and now they are 10 hours from the 14th of February to the 10th of November, and nine hours from the 10th of November to the 14th of February . . .

Comparing the day wages of 1859 and the hour wages at 8d, what were the two rates?—In 1859, if I recollect right, the wages were 5s 6d per day, that is to say, 33s per week, now the wages are 8d per hour, and the men on an average work 56½ hours, which makes about 38s per week . . .

In your opinion, have the unions operated to raise wages more than they would have risen if there had not been the action of unions?— I have no doubt at all that the operation of unions has been during the last few years to force up the rate of wages, quicker at all events . . . but it is a very unjust arrangement to fix a minimum rate of wages for all men. There are a great many men who have been perhaps years in our employment, and those men are not permitted, although incapable of doing as much work as a man in full health and strength, to receive less wages than such a man. It cannot be denied, I think, that this is tyranny, and that it injures those men, because directly we have a slackness of work we have to turn off a number of men, and under the present rule we cannot pay respect to a man's character beyond a certain extent, but we must immediately tell our foreman to turn off every man who is not up to the mark. Of course advanced age prevents a man being up to the mark . . . As far as I and my partners are concerned, and I believe the generality of the masters, we are very desirous to consult the comfort and the advantage of our workmen. But that feeling has unfortunately changed of late years. In my younger days there used to be some sort of attachment between master and men, but that has entirely gone, and I say that it is the unions and nothing else that has brought about that result. In the strike of 1859 men came to us who had worked at the place for 30 or 40 years and said to us, 'This is the saddest day that ever happened to us in our lives, but we must go, we are bound to go.'

You believe that the effect of these unions is to loosen the tie between the workman and his employer?—That most decidedly has been so. Of course in a large establishment (and ours is a moderately large establishment) you cannot know a thousand men, but you may know a great many men who have been in your employ for many years, and you may feel an attachment to those men. But when you find that you cannot come to those men and talk to them as friends, that in fact their individuality is lost because they are members of a union, it seems to me a most distressing thing . . .

Trades Unions Commission, 1st Report (1867), pp. 104–107; P.P. 1867, vol. 32.

7

Letters from America

To the Editor of The Beehive.—I shall feel obliged if you will insert these few remarks in your next edition. They will no doubt prove of great value to many ironworkers, who, we know, are fixing their minds on emigration to America. Moreover, we hope that it may have another desired effect, viz. of arousing practical sympathy in behalf of the wives and children of those men who have gone from our branch during our strike against a reduction of prices, which has lasted now for twenty weeks . . . Fourteen of them went at some £5 per head from the association, leaving their families entirely dependent upon the subscriptions we could get from the public and our fellow-workmen, till they could help themselves. The reports of America were of the most favourable description; thus they were confident that they would soon be able to send for their wives and families, again establish their homes, and enjoy its comforts, with something like a magnificent remuneration for their labour. What is the news? The following letters will show:—

'Dear wife,—I take the present opportunity of writing to you, hoping to find you all well, as it leaves me well in health—thank God for it. I hope you won't put yourself out about me, for I am safe; but the men are all on strike, and they are all a —— sight worse off than ever. We got a good passage, and I thought you would have come over in the spring. But if I don't get above £1 a day I shall come back to the old country, for it costs 50 cents for a breakfast and 30 cents for a bed. So as soon as I can get the money I shall come back to you for it is no good here at all. Take this to Sam and Will, and tell them not to be gulled from home for nobody. It's a pity for people not to tell the truth about the place, and stop other people from coming from their home. But cheer up, I am young yet . . . Tell the children I have not forgot them; I have them in my heart. From your loving husband, Benjamin Raybold. Pittsburg, Feb. 27th, 1866.

'Dear wife, child, and friends ... We have been sadly gulled by coming to America. Tell all my friends to content themselves in England, and not ruin themselves and families by coming to America. The works are all stopped for the last six weeks with no signs of commencing, as the men refused to work at the reduction of wages. Dear wife, 10s. in England is as good as nine dollars here; besides, there is a surplus of men, and they seldom work more than half time ... Give my respects to your father and mother; tell them I am well, but without money, and no prospects of earning any for some time; but when I am lucky enough to have any money I will take care to bring it to England myself, instead of sending it ... Dear wife, be of good cheer, as I am. Your devoted husband, William Hudson.'

'Dear wife,—It is with a trembling hand and an aching heart that I write to you. I am happy to say I arrived safe in New York, and had a good voyage. But I am sorry to say that we are deceived, for the men were all on strike when we got to Pittsburg ... Cheer up; I will do my best. God bless you and the children. All things work together for good. We have no money, but we have good hearts, and we hope you have. If we start to walk to New York we must die on the road, it is so cold. Cheer up, for I shall to the last. Your affectionate husband, John Cherrington.'

The above letters are copies of the originals that have come to hand this week. They slightly show the destitute condition of the men ... Eleven out of the fourteen have left families behind; some have left six children, some four, and three, and two. The least family is one child and wife. In most of these cases nearly all their goods were sold previous to the men going to America ... No money in the pocket, no food on the shelf, a sorrowful heart, and eyes swollen with grief have I seen ... Subscriptions will be thankfully received by John Bradley, secretary, Wheelock Branch, Associated Ironworkers, Sandbach, Cheshire.

Quoted in 5th Report, Trades Unions Commission (1868), pp. 59–60; P.P. 1867/8, vol. 39.

(b) CO-OPERATION

Like trade unions, there were co-operative societies of a sort in England before the end of the 18th century, and during the Owenite agitation they multiplied exceedingly. But almost without exception they soon came to grief and disappeared from off the scene. By general consent the modern Co-operative movement dates from 1844, when twenty-eight poor weavers, nearly all of them Owenite Socialists and Chartists, opened a co-operative store in Toad Lane, Rochdale, under the name of the 'Equitable Pioneers'.

Among those who gave them a helping hand was George Jacob Holyoake, son of a Birmingham mechanic, who throughout his long life—he did not die until 1906, at the age of 88—was never slow in giving his support to every movement that had for its aim the improvement of the condition of the working classes. Owenite lecturer, Radical journalist, prominent secularist—as a young man he served six months in gaol for having suggested that, when there was so much distress about it might be a good idea to put the Deity (i.e. the parsons) on half-pay—he was first and foremost a co-operator, believing to the end of his days that Co-operation would eventually supersede Competition as the guiding principle in economic affairs. He was the first to tell the world of what the Rochdale Pioneers were striving after and accomplishing, and here we may read something of that story in his own words. It is a typically Victorian story in its emphasis on Self-help. But then Holyoake *was* a typical Victorian, specially typical of that by no means inconsiderable class of people who, born in humble circumstances, by their grit and intelligence rose to positions of honourable distinction in public service.

8

Rochdale's 'Equitable Pioneers'

At the close of the year 1843, on one of those damp, dark, dense, dismal, disagreeable days which no Frenchman can be got to admire ... a few poor weavers out of employ, and nearly out of food and quite out of heart with the social state, met together to discover what they could do to better their industrial conditions. Manufacturers had capital, and shopkeepers the advantage of stock; how could they succeed without either? Should they avail themselves of the poor law? that were dependence; of emigration? that seemed like transportation for the crime of having been born poor. What should they do?

They would commence the battle of life on their own account. They would, as far as they were concerned, supersede tradesmen, millowners, and capitalists; without experience, or knowledge, or funds, they would turn merchants and manufacturers. The subscription list was handed round ... A dozen of these Lilliputian capitalists put down a weekly subscription of twopence each—a sum which these Rochdale Rothschilds did not know how to pay ...

From the Rational Sick and Burial Society's laws, a Manchester communistic production, they borrowed all the features applicable to their project, and ... their Society was registered, October 24th, 1844, under the title of the 'Rochdale Equitable Pioneers'.

Our Pioneers set forth their designs in the following amusing language, to which designs the Society has mainly adhered ... These Pioneers, in 1844, declared thus:—'The objects and plans of this Society are to form arrangements for the pecuniary benefit and the improvement of the social and domestic condition of its members, by raising a sufficient amount of capital in shares of one pound each, to bring into operation the following plans and arrangements:—The establishment of a Store for the sale of provisions, clothing, etc. The building, purchasing, or erecting a number of houses, in which those members desiring to assist each other in improving their domestic and social condition, may reside. To commence the manufacture of such articles as the Society may determine upon, for the employment of such members as may be without employment, or who may be suffering in consequence of repeated reductions in their wages. As a further benefit and security to the members of this Society, the Society shall purchase or rent an estate or estates of land, which shall be cultivated by the members who may be out of employment, or whose labour may be badly remunerated.'

Then follows a project which no nation has ever attempted, and no enthusiasts yet carried out:—'That, as soon as practicable, this Society shall proceed to arrange the powers of production, distribution, education, and government; or, in other words, to establish a self-supporting home-colony of united interests, or assist other societies in establishing such colonies . . .'

Then follows a minor but characteristic proposition:—'That, for the promotion of sobriety, a Temperance Hotel be opened in one of the Society's houses as soon as convenient.'

If these grand projects were to take effect sooner than universal Teetotalism or universal Chartism, it was quite clear that some activity must take place in the collection of the twopences. The difficulty in all working-class movements is the collection of means. At this time the members of the 'Equitable Pioneer Society' numbered about forty, living in various parts of the town, and many of them in the suburbs. The collector of the forty twopences would probably have to travel twenty miles; only a man with the devotion of a missionary could be expected to undertake this task . . . But irksome as it was, some indeed took it, and, to their honour, performed what they undertook. Three collectors were appointed, who visited the members at their residences every Sunday . . . To accelerate proceedings an innovation was made, which must at the time have created considerable excitement. The ancient twopence was departed from, and the subscription raised to threepence. The co-operators were evidently growing ambitious. At length the formidable sum of £28 was accumulated, and, with this capital, the new world, that was to be, was commenced . . .

Fifteen years ago, Toad Lane, Rochdale, was not a very inviting street. Its name did it no injustice. The ground floor of a warehouse in Toad Lane was the place selected in which to commence operations. Lancashire warehouses were not then the grand things that they have since become, and the ground floor of 'Mr Dunlop's premises', here employed, was obtained upon a lease of three years at £10 per annum. Mr William Cooper was appointed 'cashier'; his duties were very light at first. Samuel Ashworth was dignified with the title of 'salesman'; his commodities consisted of infinitesimal quantities of flour, butter, sugar, and oatmeal. The entire quantity would hardly stock a homeopathic grocer's shop, for after purchasing and consistently paying for the necessary fixtures, £14 or £15 was all they had to invest in stock. And on one desperate evening—it was the longest evening of the year—the 21st of December, 1844, the 'Equitable Pioneers' commenced business . . .

A few of the co-operators had clandestinely assembled to witness their own *dénouement*; and there they stood, in that dismal lower room of the warehouse, like the conspirators under Guy Fawkes in the Parliamentary cellar, debating on whom should devolve the temerity of taking down the shutters, and displaying their humble preparations... At length one bold fellow, utterly reckless of consequences, rushed at the shutters, and in a few minutes Toad Lane was in a titter.

Lancashire has its *gamins* as well as Paris... The 'doffers' are the *gamins* of Rochdale. The doffers are lads from ten to fifteen, who take off full bobbins from the spindles, and put them on empty ones. ... On the night when our Store was opened, the 'doffers' came out strong in Toad Lane—peeping with ridiculous impertinence round the corners, ventilating their opinion at the top of their voices, or standing before the door, inspecting, with pertinacious insolence, the scanty arrangements of butter and oatmeal; at length they exclaimed in a chorus, 'Ah! the owd weaver's shop is opened at last.'

Since that time two generations of 'doffers' have bought their butter and oatmeal at the 'owd weaver's shop', and many a bountiful and wholesome meal, and many a warm jacket, have they had from that Store, which articles would never have reached their stomachs or their shoulders, had it not been for the provident temerity of the co-operative weavers...

The founders of the Store were opposed to capital absorbing all profit from trade; and to hit upon a plan which should give proportionately the gain to the persons who make it, was a problem they had to solve. After meeting several times for the purpose of agreeing to laws, Mr Charles Howarth proposed the plan of dividing profits on purchase—that is, after paying expenses of management, interest on capital invested, at a rate of 5 per cent, the remaining profits to be divided quarterly among the members in proportion to their purchases or dealings with the Society...

At the end of the first quarter the Rochdale Society did pay a dividend of 3d. in the pound... The second dividend was 4d., the fourth, 7d., the fifth 9d., the 6th, 11d., the 7th. 1s. 2d., the 8th. 1s. 4d., the ninth 1s. 6d.; 1s. 8d. was the largest dividend they ever calculated upon getting, but for many years afterwards it ranged from 2s. to 2s. 6d. ...

The 'owd weyvur's shop', or rather the entire building, was in 1849 taken on lease by the Store... One room is now pleasantly fitted up as a newsroom. Another is neatly fitted up as a library... In 1844 the number of members was 28, amount of capital £28; in 1857, the number of members was 1850, the amount of capital £15,142. 1. 2., amount of cash sales in store annually £79,788, and amount of annual profit £5470. 6. 8½....

Saturday night at the 'Co-op'

The industrial districts of England have not such another sight as the Rochdale Co-operative Store on Saturday night.

At seven o'clock there are five persons serving busily at the counter, others are weighing up goods ready for delivery. A boy is drawing treacle. There are two sides of counters in the grocer's shop, twelve yards long. Members' wives, children of members, as many as the shop will hold, are being served; others are waiting at the door, in social conversation, waiting to go in. On the opposite side of the lane, three members serving in the drapery department, and nine or ten customers, mostly females, are selecting articles. In the large shop, on the same side of the street, three men are chopping and serving meat in the butcher's department, with from twelve to fifteen customers waiting. Two other officers are weighing flour, potatoes, preparing butter, etc. for other groups of claimants. In other premises adjoining, shoemakers, cloggers, and tailors are at work, or attending customers in their respective departments. The clerk is in his office, attending to members' individual accounts, or the general business of the Society.

The newsroom over the grocery has twenty or more men and youths perusing the newspapers and periodicals. Adjoining, the watch club, which has fifty-eight members, is collecting its weekly payments, and drawing lots as to who shall have the repeaters [watches] (manufactured by Charles Freeman, of Coventry) which the night's subscriptions will pay for. The library is open, and the librarian has his hands full in exchanging, renewing, and delivering books to about fifty members, among whom are sons, wives, and daughters of members. The premises are closed at 10 o'clock, when there has been received during the day, for goods £420, and the librarian has lent out two hundred books . . .

But it is not the brilliance of commercial activity in which either writer or reader will take the deepest interest; it is in the new and improved spirit animating this intercourse of trade. Buyer and seller meet as friends; there is no overreaching on one side, and no suspicion on the other; and Toad Lane on Saturday night, while as gay as the Lowther Arcade in London, is ten times more moral. These crowds of humble working men, who never knew before when they put good food in their mouths, whose every dinner was adulterated, whose shoes let in the water a month too soon, whose waistcoats shone with devil's dust [i.e. were shoddy], and whose wives wore calico that would not wash, now buy like millionaires, and, as far as purchasers of food goes, live like lords. They are weaving their own stuffs, making their own shoes, sewing their own garments, and grinding their own corn. They buy the purest sugar, and the best tea, and grind their own coffee. They slaughter their own cattle, and the finest beasts of the land waddle down the streets of Rochdale for the consumption of flannel weavers and cobblers . . .

The teetotallers of Rochdale acknowledge that the Store has made more sober men since it commenced than all their efforts have been able to make in the same time. Husbands who never knew what it was to be out of debt, and poor wives, who, during forty years, never had sixpence uncondemned in their pockets, now possess money sufficient to buy their cottages, and go every week into their own market with coins jingling in their pockets; and in that market there is no distrust, and no deception; there is no adulteration, and no second prices. The whole atmosphere is honest. Those who serve neither hurry, finesse, nor flatter. They have no interest in chicanery. They have but one duty to perform—that of giving fair measure, full weight, and a pure article . . .

GEORGE JACOB HOLYOAKE, *Self-Help by the People: the History of the Rochdale Pioneers* (1857); 10th edition, 1893, pp. 2-40.

9

Even the Cocks Crowed 'Co-operation'!

———————

The effect of this patient and obscure success [of the Toad Lane Store] was diffused about, as we might say in apostolical language, 'noised abroad'. There needed no advertisement to spread it. When profits—a new name among workpeople—were found to be really made, and known to be really had by members quarter by quarter, they were copiously heard of. The co-operator, who had never had any encouragement from his neighbour, felt a natural pride in making him sensible that he was succeeding. As he had never had any success to boast of before, he was not likely to make little of this. Besides, his animated face suggested that his projects were answering with him. He appeared better fed, which was not likely to escape notice among hungry weavers. He was better dressed than formerly, which gave him distinction among his shabby comrades in the mill. The wife . . . had a new gown, and she was not likely to be silent about that; nor was it likely to remain much in concealment. It became a walking and graceful advertisement of co-operation in every part of the town. Her neighbours were not slow to notice the change in her attire . . . and husbands received hints they might as well belong to the store. The children had cleaner faces, and new pinafores or new jackets, and they propagated the source of their new comforts in their little way, and other little children communicated to their parents what they had seen. Some old hen coops were furbished up, and new pullets were observed in them—the cocks seemed to crow of co-operation. Here and there a pig, which was known to belong to a co-operator, was seen to be fattening, and seemed to squeal in favour of the store. After a while a pianoforte was reported to have been seen in a co-operative cottage, on which it was said the daughters played co-operative airs, as the like of which had never been heard in that quarter . . .

The store was talked about in the mills. It was canvassed in the weaving shed. The farm labourer heard of it in the fields. The coal miner carried the news down the pit. The blacksmith circulated the news at his forge. It was the gossip of the barber's chair . . . The 'Toad Lane store' was the subject of conversation in the public-houses. It was discussed in the temperance coffee-shops . . . The landlord found his rent paid more regularly, and whispered the fact about. The shop-keeper told his neighbour that customers who had been in his debt for years had paid up their accounts . . . Politicians began to think there was something in it. Wandering lecturers visiting the town . . . were invited to houses where tables were better spread than formerly, and were taken to see the Store, as one of the new objects of interest in the town . . . News of it got into the periodicals in London . . . Professors and students of social philosophy from abroad heard of it, and sent news of it home to their country. And thus it spread far and wide that the shrewd men of Rochdale were doing a notable thing in the way of Co-operation. It was all true, and honour will long be accorded them therefore . . .

G. J. HOLYOAKE, *History of Co-operation in England* (3rd ed., 1885), vol. 2, pp. 34–43.

CHAPTER 8

'SEX' AND THE VICTORIANS

What the Victorians referred to as 'The Great Social Evil' was very much in the public eye in the middle years of the last century. That is about the only euphemism they allowed themselves in the matter. On the whole, they discussed Prostitution with marked plainness of speech.

Turning the pages of the newspapers and periodicals and books of the time, we may discern two ways of approach. The first is what may be called the orthodox view, the one most generally adopted perhaps. According to this, prostitutes were poor unhappy creatures who, whether by their own fault or the pressure of circumstances, had embarked on a career of vice which would inevitably bring them to a bad end. It is shown in such verses as Tom Hood's *The Bridge of Sighs* (1846), and in such novels as Mrs Gaskell's *Mary Barton* (1848), in which Esther is made to say, 'Don't speak to me of leading a better life—I must have drink ... You can do nothing for me. I am past hope ...' This is what the severe moralists believed it to be, and perhaps it is not too much to say, what they *wanted* it to be ...

But the second view is very different. According to this, prostitutes did not invariably come to grief. Their trade was not bound to reach a sticky end. On the contrary, there were prostitutes who managed somehow to retain their self-respect, conducted themselves with a decent circumspection, and were able to return to the paths of respectability. It was one of this class of successful harlots who wrote the letter to *The Times* which is quoted in full in No. 1. The letter, it will be gathered, was part of a correspondence, and the Editor not only gave it more than a column but the next day made it the subject of a 'leader' (No. 2).

Next we have substantial selections from Dr William Acton's factual account of London prostitution (No. 3), and this, too, supports the contention that by no means all harlots were the abandoned creatures of the 'orthodox' view. But No. 4 brings us back to the traditional picture, and since it comes from Henry Mayhew's notebook, there is no reason to question its authenticity. Another contribution to *The Times* correspondence columns forms No. 5, and then we have some sidelights on the moral behaviour of the Welsh and Lowland Scotch. Nos. 8 and 9 have for their background the Contagious Diseases Acts of 1864-69, which provided for the registration and police supervision of prostitutes operating in a number of military and naval stations, their periodical medical examination for the detection of venereal disease, and their compulsory detention in special hospitals if they were so found. Mrs Josephine Butler (1828–1906), wife of a Liverpool clergyman, took the lead in opposing these Acts as a violation of the dignity of woman-hood and indeed of human rights in general, and, thanks largely to the agitation she aroused and led, the Acts were repealed in 1885.

Perhaps the most surprising of the documents in this chapter may seem to be No. 10. Family Limitation, birth control, contraception . . . was not an invention of the twentieth century, as some people would seem to suppose. As early as 1776 sheaths made of animal gut were on sale in London, and in the 1820s Robert Owen, Francis Place, and Richard Carlile were pioneering birth-control activities. 'Neo-Mal-thusianism', as it was called, won considerable support throughout Victorian times. In 1854 there was published the book from which our final extract is taken. Its original title was *Physical, Sexual and Natural Religion*, and it was stated to be by a 'Doctor of Medicine'. The author was in fact a young Scotch doctor, George Drysdale (1825–1904)—his father was Sir William Drysdale, City Treasurer of Edinburgh—who wrote it soon after he had qualified at Glasgow University. Later his name was put on the title-page; a large number of editions appeared, and it was translated into the principal European languages. Of its several hundred closely printed pages in small type most deal with the Malthusian doctrine of Population, while many others are concerned with medical matters. Only a few describe the methods by which the pleasures of Love might be enjoyed without adding to the burdens of over-population, but these are explicit enough. Even more startling, perhaps, is Drysdale's advocacy of something akin to 'Free Love'. 'It is absolutely impossible', he writes, 'to have a free, sincere, and dignified sexual morality in our society, as long as marriage continues to be the only honourable provision for the union of the sexes, and as long as the marriage bond is so indissoluble as at present.' Before the end of the century more than 80,000 copies of the little book had gone into circula-tion, and in quite considerable measure it must have been responsible for the sudden dive in the birth-rate that started in the early eighteen-seventies.

I

The London Prostitute Who Wrote to The Times

To the Editor of The Times.—Sir, Another 'Unfortunate', but of a class entirely different from the one who has already instructed the public in your columns, presumes to address you. I am a stranger to all the fine sentiments which still linger in the bosom of your correspondent. I have none of those youthful recollections which, contrasting her early days with her present life, aggravate the misery of the latter.

My parents did not give me any education; they did not instil into my mind virtuous precepts nor set me a good example. All my experiences in early life were gleaned among associates who knew nothing of the laws of God but by dim tradition and faint report, and whose chiefest triumphs of wisdom consisted in picking their way through the paths of destitution in which they were cast by cunning evasion or in open defiance of the laws of man.

I do not think of my parents (long in their graves) with any such compunctions as your correspondent describes. They gave me in their lifetime, according to their means and knowledge, and as they had probably received from their parents, shelter and protection, mixed with curses and caresses. I received all as a matter of course, and, knowing nothing better, was content in that kind of contentedness which springs from insensibility; I returned their affection in like kind as they gave it to me. As long as they lived, I looked up to them as my parents. I assisted them in their poverty, and made them comfortable. They looked on me and I on them with pride, for I was proud to be able to minister to their wants; and as for shame, although they knew perfectly well the means by which I obtained money, I do assure you, Sir, that by them, as by myself, my success was regarded as the reward of a proper ambition, and was a source of real pleasure and gratification.

Let me tell you something of my parents. My father's most profitable occupation was brickmaking. When not employed at this, he did anything he could get to do. My mother worked with him in the brickfield, and so did I and a progeny of brothers and sisters; for somehow or other, although my parents occupied a very unimportant space in the world, it pleased God to make them fruitful. We all slept in the same room. There were few privacies, few family secrets in our house.

Father and mother both loved drink. In the household expenses, had accounts been kept, gin or beer would have been the heaviest items. We, the children, were indulged occasionally with a drop, but my honoured parents reserved to themselves the exclusive privilege of getting drunk, 'and they were the same as their parents had been'. I give you a chapter of the history of common life which may be stereotyped as the history of generation upon generation.

We knew not anything of religion. Sometimes when a neighbour died we went to the burial, and thus got within a few steps of the church. If a grand funeral chanced to fall in our way we went to see that, too—the fine black horses and nodding plumes—as we went to see the soldiers when we could for a lark. No parson ever came near us. The place where we lived was too dirty for nicely-shod gentlemen. 'The Publicans and Sinners' of our circumscribed, but thickly populated locality had no 'friend' among them.

Our neighbourhood furnished many subjects to the treadmill, the hulks, and the colonies, and some to the gallows. We lived with the fear of those things, and not with the fear of God before our eyes.

I was a very pretty child, and had a sweet voice; of course I used to sing. Most London boys and girls of the lower classes sing. 'My face is my fortune, kind sir, she said', was the ditty on which I bestowed most pains, and my father and mother would wink knowingly as I sang it. The latter would also tell me how pretty she was when young, and how she sang, and what a fool she had been, and how well she might have done had she been wise.

Frequently we had quite a stir in our colony. Some young lady who had quitted the paternal restraints, or perhaps, had started off, none knew whither or how, to seek her fortune, would reappear among us with a profusion of ribands, fine clothes, and lots of cash. Visiting the neighbours, treating indiscriminately, was the order of the day on such occasions, without any more definite information of the means by which the dazzling transformation had been effected than could be conveyed by knowing winks and the words 'luck' and 'friends'. Then she would disappear and leave us in our dirt, penury, and obscurity. You cannot conceive, Sir, how our ambition was stirred by these visitations.

'I lost, what?—not my virtue . . .'

Now commences an important era in my life. I was a fine, robust, healthy girl, 13 years of age. I had larked with the boys of my own age. I had huddled with them, boys and girls together, all night long in our common haunts. I had seen much and heard abundantly of the mysteries of the sexes. To me such things had been matters of common sight and common talk. For some time I had coquetted on the verge of a strong curiosity, and a natural desire, and without a particle of affection, scarce a partiality, I lost—what? not my virtue, for I never had any.

THE GREAT SOCIAL EVIL.

TIME:—Midnight. A Sketch not a Hundred Miles from the Haymarket.

Bella. "AH! FANNY! HOW LONG HAVE YOU BEEN *GAY?*"

15. John Leech, in *Punch*, 1857

That which is commonly, but untruly called virtue, I gave away. You reverend Mr Philanthropist—what call you virtue? Is it not the principle, the essence, which keeps watch and ward over the conduct, the substance, the materiality? No such principle ever kept watch and ward over me, and I repeat that I never lost that which I never had— my virtue.

According to my own ideas at the time I only extended my rightful enjoyments. Opportunity was not long wanting to put my newly-acquired knowledge to profitable use. In the commencement of my fifteenth year one of our be-ribanded visitors took me off, and introduced me to the great world, and thus commenced my career as what you better classes call a prostitute. I cannot say that I felt any other shame than the bashfulness of a noviciate introduced to strange society. Remarkable for good looks, and no less so for good temper, I gained money, dressed gaily, and soon agreeably astonished my parents and old neighbours by making a descent upon them.

Passing over the vicissitudes of my course, alternating between reckless gaiety and extreme destitution, I improved myself greatly; and at the age of 18 was living partly under the protection of one who thought he discovered that I had talent, and some good qualities as well as beauty, who treated me more kindly and considerately than I had ever before been treated, and thus drew from me something like a feeling of regard, but not sufficiently strong to lift me to that sense of my position which the so-called virtuous and respectable members of society seem to entertain. Under the protection of this gentleman, and encouraged by him, I commenced the work of my education; that portion of education which is comprised in some knowledge of my own language and the ordinary accomplishments of my sex;—moral science, as I believe it is called, has always been an enigma to me, and is so to this day. I suppose it is because I am one of those who, as Rousseau says, are 'born to be prostitutes'.

Common honesty I believe in rigidly. I have always paid my debts, and, though I say it, I have always been charitable to my fellow creatures. I have not neglected my duty to my family. I supported my parents while they lived, and buried them decently when they died. I paid a celebrated lawyer heavily for defending unsuccessfully my eldest brother, who had the folly to be caught in the commission of a robbery. I forgave him the offence against the law in the theft, and the offence against discretion in being caught. This cost me some effort, for I always abhorred stealing. I apprenticed my younger brother to a good trade, and helped him into a little business. Drink frustrated my efforts in his behalf. Through the influence of a very influential gentleman, a very particular *friend* of mine, he is now a well-conducted member of the police. My sisters, whose early life was in all respects the counterpart of my own, I brought out and started in the world. The elder of the two is kept by a nobleman, the next by an officer in the army; the third has not yet come to years of discretion, and is 'having her fling' before she settles down.

'What if I am a prostitute?'

Now, what if I am a prostitute, what business has society to abuse me? Have I received any favours at the hands of society? If I am a hideous cancer in society, are not the causes of the disease to be sought in the rottenness of the carcass? Am I not its legitimate child; no bastard, Sir? Why does my unnatural parent repudiate me, and what has society ever done for me, that I should do anything for it, and what have I ever done against society that it should drive me into a corner and crush me to the earth? I have neither stolen (at least since I was a child), nor murdered, nor defrauded. I earn my money and pay my way, and try to do good with it, according to my ideas of good. I do not get drunk, nor fight, nor create uproar in the streets or out of them. I do not use bad language. I do not offend the public eye by open indecencies. I go to the Opera, I go to Almack's, I go to the theatres, I go to quiet, well-conducted casinos, I go to all the places of public amusement, behaving myself with as much propriety as society can exact. I pay business visits to my trades-people, the most fashionable of the West-end. My milliners, my silk-mercers, my bootmakers, know, all of them, who I am and how I live, and they solicit my patronage as earnestly and cringingly as if I were Madam, the Lady of the right rev. patron of the Society for the Suppression of Vice. They find my money as good and my pay better (for we are robbed on every hand) than that of Madam, my Lady; and, if all the circumstances and conditions of our lives had been reversed, would Madam, my Lady, have done better or been better than I?

I speak of others as well as for myself, for the very great majority, nearly all the real undisguised prostitutes in London, spring from my class, and are made by and under pretty much such conditions of life as I have narrated, and particularly by untutored and unrestrained intercourse of the sexes in early life. We come from the dregs of society, as our so-called betters term it. What business has society to have dregs—such dregs as we? You railers of the Society for the Suppression of Vice, you the pious, the moral, the respectable, as you call yourselves, who stand on your smooth and pleasant side of the great gulf you have dug and keep between yourselves and the dregs, why don't you bridge it over, or fill it up, and by some humane and generous process absorb us into your leavened mass, until we become interpenetrated with goodness like yourselves? What have we to be ashamed of, we who do not know what shame is—the shame you mean?

I conduct myself prudently, and defy you and your policemen too. Why stand you there mouthing with sleek face about morality? What is morality? Will you make us responsible for what we never knew? Teach us what is right and tutor us in what is good before you punish us for doing wrong. We who are the real prostitutes of the true natural growth of society, and no impostors, will not be judged by 'One more unfortunate', nor measured by any standard of her setting up. She is a mere chance intruder in our ranks, and has no business there. She does understand what shame means and knows all about it, at least so it seems, and if she has a particle left, let her accept 'Amicus's' kind offer as soon as possible.

'Victims of seduction'?

Like 'One more unfortunate' there are other intruders among us—a few, very few, 'victims of seduction'. But seduction is not the root of the evil—scarcely a fibre of the root. A rigorous law should be passed and rigorously carried out to punish seduction, but it will not perceptibly thin the ranks of prostitution. Seduction is the common story of numbers of well brought up, who never were seduced, and who are voluntary and inexcusable profligates. Vanity and idleness send us a large body of recruits. Servant girls, who wish to ape their mistress' finery, and whose wages won't permit them to do so honestly—these set up seduction as their excuse. Married women, who have no respect for their husbands, and are not content with their lawful earnings, these are the worst among us, and it is a pity they cannot be picked out and punished. They have no principle of any kind and are a disgrace to us. If I were a married woman I would be true to my husband. I speak for my class, the regular standing army of the force.

Gentlemen of philanthropic societies and members of the Society for the Suppression of Vice may build reformatories and open houses of refuge and Magdalen asylums, and 'Amicus' may save occasionally a 'fallen sister' who can prevail on herself to be saved; but we who never were sisters—who never had any relationship, part, interest, or communion with the large family of this world's virtues, moralities, and proprieties—we, who are not fallen, but were always down—who never had any virtue to lose—we who are the natural growth of things, and are constantly ripening for the harvest—who, interspersed in our little, but swarming colonies throughout the kingdom at large, hold the source of supply and keep it fruitful—what do they propose to do with us? Cannot society devise some plan to reach us?

'One more unfortunate' proposes a 'skimming' progress. But what of the great bubbling cauldron? Remove from the streets a score or two of 'foreign women', and 'double as many English', and you diminish the competition of those that remain; the quiet, clever, cunning cajolers described by 'One more unfortunate'. You hide a prurient pimple of the 'great sin' with a patch of that plaster known as the 'observance of propriety', and nothing more. You 'miss' the evil, but it is existent still. After all it is something to save the eye from offence, so remove them; and not only a score or two, but something like two hundred foreign women, whose open and disgusting indecencies and practices have contributed more than anything else to bring on our heads the present storm of indignation. It is rare that English women, even prostitutes, give cause of gross public offence. Cannot they be packed off to their own countries with their base, filthy and filthy-living men, whom they maintain, and clothe, and feed, to superintend their fortunes, and who are a still greater disgrace to London than these women are?

Hurling big figures at us, it is said that there are 80,000 of us in London alone—which is a monstrous falsehood—and of those 80,000, poor hardworking sewing girls, sewing women, are numbered in by thousands, and called indiscriminately prostitutes; writing, preaching, speechifying, that they have lost their virtue too.

'A cruel calumny'

It is a cruel calumny to call them in mass prostitutes; and, as for their virtue, they lose it as one loses his watch who is robbed by the highway thief. Their virtue is the watch, and society is the thief. These poor women toiling on starvation wages, while penury, misery, and famine clutch them by the throat and say, 'Render up your body or die'.

Admire this magnificent shop in this fashionable street; its front, fittings, and decorations cost no less than a thousand pounds. The respectable master of the establishment keeps his carriage and lives in his country-house. He has daughters too; his patronesses are fine ladies, the choicest impersonations of society. Do they think, as they admire the taste and elegance of that tradesman's show, of the poor creatures who wrought it, and what they were paid for it? Do they reflect on the weary toiling fingers, on the eyes dim with watching, on the bowels yearning with hunger, on the bended frames, on the broken constitutions, on poor human nature driven to its coldest corner and reduced to its narrowest means in the production of these luxuries and adornments? This is an old story! Would it not be truer and more charitable to call these poor souls 'victims'?—some gentler, some more humane name than prostitute—to soften by some Christian expression if you cannot better the un-Christian system, the opprobrium of a fate to which society has driven them by the direst straits? What business has society to point its finger in scorn, to raise its voice in reprobation of them? Are they not its children, born of the cold indifference, of its callous selfishness, of its cruel pride?

Sir, I have trespassed on your patience beyond limit, and yet much remains to be said . . . The difficulty of dealing with the evil is not so great as society considers it. Setting aside 'the sin', we are not so bad as we are thought to be. The difficulty is for society to set itself, with the necessary earnestness, self-humiliation, and self-denial, to the work. To deprive us of proper and harmless amusements, to subject us in mass to the pressure of force—of force wielded, for the most part, by ignorant, and often by brutal men—is only to add the cruelty of active persecution to the cruelty of passive indifference which made us as we are. I remain, your humble servant, Another Unfortunate.

Letter published in *The Times*, London, February 24, 1858, under the heading 'The Great Social Evil'.

2

'A revelation', says the Editor

The letter is, to the best of our belief, a revelation of the feelings of the class to which the writer openly declares that she belongs. Now, the singularity of the communication consists in this,—that the writer, who must be supposed to be tolerably well acquainted with the feelings of her associates and friends—bids us, in considering the subject, to dismiss from our apprehension all the crudities with which divines, and philanthropists, and romance-writers have surrounded it. The great bulk of the London prostitutes are not Magdalens either in *esse* or *posse*, nor specimens of humanity in agony, nor Clarissa Harlowes. They are not—the bulk of them—cowering under gateways, nor preparing to throw themselves from Waterloo Bridge, but are comfortably practising their trade, either as the entire or partial means of their subsistence. To attribute to them the sentimental delicacies of a heroine of romance would be equally proposterous. They have no remorse or misgivings about the nature of their pursuit; on the contrary, they consider the calling an advantageous one, and they look upon their success in it with satisfaction. They have their virtues, like others; they are good daughters, good sisters, and friends, at least proportionately so with other classes of the community.

From a leading article in *The Times*, London, February 25, 1858.

3

A Plain Guide to London's Harlotry

The number of prostitutes in London has been variously estimated, according to the opportunities, credulity, or religious fervour of observers, and the width of interpretation they have put upon the word . . . I am indebted to the good offices of Captain Harris, Assistant Commissioner of Police, for a Return of the Number of Brothels and Prostitutes in each division . . .

Number of Brothels and Places—

Where Prostitutes are kept	2	
Where Prostitutes lodge	1756	
Where Prostitutes resort	132	
Coffee Houses or other Places where Business is ostensibly carried on, but which are known to the Police to be used as Brothels or places of accommodation for Prostitutes	229	2119

Number of Prostitutes—

Well-dressed, living in Brothels	11	
Well-dressed, living in private lodgings	2155	
In low Neighbourhoods	4349	6515

I must observe that these returns give but a faint idea of the grand total of prostitution by which we are oppressed. The police have not attempted to include—in fact, could not have justly included, I might almost say,—the unnumbered prostitutes, whose appearance in the streets as such never takes place—who are not seen abroad at unseemly hours—who are reserved in manners, quiet and unobtrusive in their houses or lodgings, and whose general conduct is such that the most vigilant of constables could have no pretence for claiming to be officially aware of their existence or pursuits. . . . For the sake of clearness, I shall briefly notice under separate heads:—(1) Homes, viz. dress houses; houses in which prostitutes lodge. (2) Haunts, viz. introducing houses; accommodation houses; casinos and pleasure gardens; the public streets.

Dress Houses

The description of brothels called dress houses was much more prevalent a few years ago than is the case at present. It appears from the police returns for 1868, that there are now only two such houses in the Metropolis, containing between them 11 inmates. They were maintained to some extent by persons who furnished board, lodging, and clothes to a number of prostitutes whom they sent out into the streets under guard of servants, or kept at home to receive visitors. The girls, who, it is needless to say, were of the most utterly degraded class, received but a small share of the wages of their sin . . .

The rouged and whitewashed creatures, with painted lips and eyebrows, and false hair, accustomed to haunt Langham Place, portions of the New Road, the Quadrant, the Peristyle of the Haymarket Theatre, the City Road, and the purlieus of the Lyceum, were the most prominent gangs of this description in London. They were watched by persons of their own sex, employed purposely to prevent their abstraction of the lodging-house finery, and clandestine traffic with men. These wretched women, virtually slaves, though nominally free, with bodies and time no longer their own, were restricted, for the convenience of the real proprietors, to certain parades or beats, and from year's end to year's end might be observed on the same side of one particular street, and within a few hundred yards of one particular spot. If their solicitations proved unsuccessful, their exertions were stimulated by the proprietor in person, who would sally forth from her den to aid the canvass, to admonish and to swear; and sometimes by the sentinel in charge, who assumed for the time being these functions of authority.

Women under like sad conditions may still be observed in some of the principal streets of London, but I am happy to say a great improvement has taken place in this respect during the last twelve years. There still exist establishments in which the women live with their landlady, by whom they are provided with food, dress, and lodging, all which are charged to the women at an exorbitant price, and the landlady usually contrives to keep them in her debt; they have, however, the right of receiving and retaining their own money, and the privilege of accepting or declining, at their own discretion, the attentions offered by their visitors.

Houses in which prostitutes lodge

If we enter the house, or apartment, in a suburban neighbourhood—where, perhaps, the occupier of the shop below is non-resident—of the first-class prostitute, we find it neat or slovenly, plain or elegant, according to its mistress's income, the manners and tastes of her admirers, and her tendency to sobriety or the reverse. We have cheap and respectable lodgings, in reputable quarters of the town, wherein young and pleasing women of unambitious temperament will reside for years, receiving no visitors at home, anxiously guarding their characters there, and from choice involving themselves in no more sin than will serve to eke out their modest earnings, or provide a slender maintenance, which they may have been precluded from earning in their normal walk of life by the first false step . . .

These present us with the least degraded aspect of prostitution; but both in the western and eastern districts, especially in the latter, are to be found a great number of lodging-houses crowded together, in certain neighbourhoods of no fair fame, and called generically, in police reports, 'notorious brothels', devoted especially to the reception of prostitutes. They are clean or dirty—comparatively well or ill-furnished, according to the capital embarked in them. From houses in St John's Wood, Brompton, and Pimlico, to the atrocious slums of Blackfriars and Whitechapel, there are, of course, many steps, and with the rent at which the proprietors offer their apartments varies, of course, the style of the sub-tenants.

In point of morality, there is, naturally, no difference; and in the general internal propriety, little enough. The most decently-minded woman who takes up her quarters in a circle of prostitutes, and, though she has a private apartment in which to receive visitors, betakes herself for society and distraction (as do always the inmates of such houses) to the common kitchen, must speedily fall to the common level. She finds that modesty and propriety are considered offensive hypocrisy. Liquor, in the intervals of business, is insisted upon by her companions and by the Landlady, who makes a profit on the supply. Her company is sought for novelty's sake when she is a new comer, and her absence or reserve is considered insulting when she is fairly settled; so, if she had any previous idea of keeping herself to herself, it is very soon dissipated. She finds, when she has no male visitors, a sort of communism established in her rooms, which she can only avoid by resorting to the common hall in the dirty kitchen. There is no making head against this practice in lodging-houses generally, and hence the remarkable uniformity in the habits, manners, dress, and demeanour of their inhabitants.

They are usually during the day, unless called upon by their followers, or employed in dressing, to be found, dishevelled, dirty, slipshod and dressing-gowned, in this kitchen, where the mistress keeps her *table d'hôte*. Stupid from beer, or fractious from gin, they swear and chatter brainless stuff all day, about men and millinery, their own schemes and adventures, and the faults of others of the sisterhood . . . In such a household, all decency, modesty, propriety and conscience must, to preserve harmony and republican equality, be planed down, and the woman hammered out, not by the practice of her profession or the company of men, but by association with her own sex and class, to the dead level of harlotry.

From such houses issue the greater number of the dressy females with whom the public are familiar as the frequenters of the Haymarket and the night-houses. Here they seem to rally, the last thing, from other parts of the town, when general society, and the most decent as well as the lowest classes of prostitutes, are alike housed for the night. Here they throw the last allures of fascination to the prowler and the drunkard—hence wander to their lairs, disgusted and weary if alone—noisy and high-spirited if chance has lent them company . . .

Introducing Houses

The establishments of certain procuresses (brokers, go-betweens, match-makers), vulgarly called 'introducing houses' . . . are worth notice as the leading centres of the more select circles of prostitution . . . Their existence depends upon the co-operation and discretion of various subordinate accomplices, and on the patronage of some of the many wealthy, indolent, sensual men of London, who will pay any premium for assurance against social discredit and sanitary damage. Disease is therefore rarely traceable to such a source, and notoriety and scandal almost as seldom. [The gentleman] usually obtains for his money security, comfort, and a superior class of prostitute, who is, according to his knowledge of the world or desires, presented to him as maid, wife, or widow—British, or imported direct from foreign parts. The female obtains fairly liberal terms, either directly from the paramour, or from the *entrepreneuse* (who, of course, takes good care of herself); the company of a gentleman; and, when this is an object with her, unquestionable privacy. A number of the first-class prostitutes have relations with these houses, and are sent for as occasion and demand may arise . . .

Accommodation Houses

Accommodation houses for casual use only, wherein permanent lodgers are not received, are diffused throughout the capital . . . Within the last few years, numerous coffee-houses and legitimate taverns, at which in former days no casual lodgers would have been admitted, without scrutiny, now give accommodation of the kind, for the most part openly, or when not exactly so, on exhibition of a slight apology for travelling baggage ... In addition to these coffee-shops, there are many restaurants at which people can obtain private rooms by ordering refreshments. Many abandoned women are also occupiers of houses, and though they do not receive lodgers, will, for a consideration and by arrangement, permit their rooms to be made use of by other women for immoral purposes ...

The few accommodation houses of London are generally thronged with custom, and their proprietors are of the same order as, and perhaps make even more money than, those of the lodging-houses. Their tariffs are various, and the accommodation afforded ranges between luxury and the squalor of those ambiguous dens, half brothel and half lodging-house, whose inhabitants pay their twopences nightly ... At the date of the introduction of the former edition of this work, [1857], the average sum charged for the hire of a room was about five shillings, but now the sum exacted for similar accommodation is never less than ten shillings, in the West End of London. In the East End and over the water, the numbers and the tariff remain as small as they were twelve years ago.

The Garden at Cremorne

It might seem rather late in the day to argue, on the grounds of its entertaining prostitutes among others, against the most beautiful public garden London can boast for the amusement of her people ... No less than fifteen thousand people have been known to be present at Cremorne, on the occasion of the manager's benefit, and the nightly visitors during the fine season amount to between 1500 and 2000. As my present business is with the demeanour of London prostitution, I must unwillingly limit myself to the consideration of public out-door amusements with reference to that common feature only, and state some impressions of travel on a pleasant July evening from Charing-cross to Chelsea.

As calico and merry respectability tailed off eastward by penny steamers, the setting sun brought westward Hansoms freighted with demure immorality in silk and fine linen. By about ten o'clock, age and innocence, of whom there had been much in the place that day, had seemingly all retired, weary with a long and paid bill of amusements, leaving the massive elms, the grass-plots, and the geranium-beds, the kiosks, temples, 'monster platforms', and 'crystal circle' of Cremorne to flicker in the thousand gas-lights there for the gratification of the dancing public only. On and around that platform waltzed, strolled, and fed some thousand souls—perhaps seven hundred of them men of the upper and middle class, the remainder prostitutes more or less *prononcées*. There was now and then a bare recognition between passers-by—they seemed to touch and go, like ants in the hurry of business ... There was among the general company barely vivacity, much less disorder . . . Of the character of the female visitors—let me always say *with some exceptions*—I could have little moral doubt, but it was clear enough that self-proclamation by any great number of them was out of the question. It was open to the male visitors to invite attention and solicit acquaintance. No gentlemanly proposition of the kind would have been rebuffed, no courteous offer of refreshment, possibly, declined, but I am firmly of opinion, that had the most eligible men present tarried in hopes of overtures from the other side, they might have been there yet . . .

There are other pleasure gardens in or about the London district, such as the gardens at North Woolwich, Highbury Barn, and Rosherville, but they do not call for any special notice, as, except that their frequenters are drawn chiefly from a lower class, they differ in no material respect from Cremorne.

Dancing-rooms

The principal dancing-rooms of London are the two casinos known respectively as the Argyll Rooms and the Holborn . . . They are open for music and dancing every evening, except Sunday, from half-past eight o'clock to twelve. The visitor, on passing the doors, finds himself in a spacious room, the fittings of which are of the most costly description, while brilliant gas illumination, reflected by numerous mirrors, imparts a fairy-like aspect to the scene. The company is, of course, mixed. Many of the men resorting to such places seek no doubt the opportunity of indulging their vicious propensities; but the majority of the better class go merely to while away an idle hour, because, unblessed by home ties, and weary of the cold monotony of their club, they find it pleasant to consume the '*post prandial weed*' in some place where, while chatting with friends, they can hear good music and see pretty faces. The women are of course all prostitutes. They are for the most part pretty, and quietly, though expensively, dressed, while delicate complexions, unaccompanied by the pallor of ill-health, are neither few nor far between. This appearance is doubtless due in many cases to the artistic manner of the make-up by powder and cosmetics, on the employment of which extreme care is bestowed. Few of these women, probably, could write a decent letter, though some might be able to play a little on the piano, or to sing a simple song. Their behaviour is usually quiet, little solicitation is observable, and all the outward proprieties of demeanour and gesture are strictly observed . . .

The casinos, music-halls, and similar places are closed at twelve o'clock; after that hour the search for dissipation must be extended to other places, and loose persons of both sexes may be found congregated in the divans and night houses situate in the Haymarket and adjoining streets. These places are for the most part small, ill-ventilated rooms, at which wine and other liquor, and also solid refreshment, can be procured. Here there is no amusement except such as the visitors can provide for themselves. Much of the restraint on the part of the women observable at the other places to which I have referred is, therefore, laid aside, and a very general *abandon* in conversation and behaviour on the part of both men and women is freely indulged in, while the opportunity of soliciting custom is certainly not neglected . . .

WILLIAM ACTON, M.R.C.S., *Prostitution, considered in its Moral, Social, and Sanitary Aspects* (2nd ed., 1870), pp. 3–22.

4

The Sixteen-year-old Streetwalker

A good-looking girl of sixteen gave me the following awful statement. Her hands were swollen with cold:—

'I am an orphan. When I was ten I was sent to service as maid-of-all-work, in a small tradesman's family. It was a hard place, and my mistress used me very cruelly, beating me often. I stood my mistress's ill-treatment for about six months. She beat me with sticks as well as with her hands. I was black and blue, and at last I ran away. I got to Mrs ——, a low lodging-house. I didn't know before that there was such a place. I heard of it from some girls at the Glasshouse [baths and wash-houses], where I went for shelter. I went with them to have a half-pennyworth of coffee, and they took me to the lodging-house. I then had three shillings, and stayed about three months, and did nothing wrong, living on the three shillings and what I pawned my clothes for, as I got some pretty good things away with me. In the lodging-house I saw nothing but what was bad, and heard nothing but what was bad. I was laughed at, and told to swear. They said, 'Look at her for a d— modest fool'—sometimes worse than that, until by degrees I got to be as bad as they were.

'During this time I used to see boys and girls from ten and twelve years old sleeping together, but understood nothing wrong. I had never heard of such places before I ran away. I can neither read nor write. My mother was a good woman, and I wish I'd had her to run away to. I saw things between almost children that I can't describe to you— very often I saw them, and that shocked me.

'At the month's end, when I was beat out, I met with a young man of fifteen—I myself was going on for twelve years old—and he persuaded me to take up with him. I stayed with him three months in the same lodging-house, living with him as his wife, though we were mere children, and being true to him. At the three months' end he was taken up for picking pockets, and got six months. I was sorry, for he was kind to me; though I was made ill through him; so I broke some windows in St Paul's Churchyard to get into prison to get cured. I had a month in the Compter [prison], and came out well. I was scolded very much in the Compter, on account of the state I was in, being so young. I had 2s. 6d. given to me when I came out, and was forced to go into the streets for a living.

'I continued walking the streets for three years, sometimes making a good deal of money, sometimes none, feasting one day and starving the next. The bigger girls could persuade me to do anything they liked with my money. I was never happy all the time, but I could get no character and could not get out of the life. I lodged all this time at a lodging-house in Kent-street. They were all thieves and bad girls. I have known between three and four dozen boys and girls sleep in one room. The beds were horrid filthy and full of vermin.

'There was very wicked carryings on. The boys, if any difference, was the worst. We lay packed on a full night, a dozen boys and girls squeezed into one bed. That was very often the case—some at the foot and some at the top—boys and girls all mixed. I can't go into all the particulars, but whatever could take place in words or acts between boys and girls did take place, and in the midst of the others. I am sorry to say I took part in these bad ways myself, but I wasn't so bad as some of the others. There was only a candle burning all night, but in summer it was light great part of the night. Some boys and girls slept without any clothes, and would dance about the room that way. I have seen them, and, wicked as I was, felt ashamed . . .

At three years' end I stole a piece of beef from a butcher. I did it to get into prison. I was sick of the life I was leading, and didn't know how to get out of it. I had a month for stealing. When I got out I passed two days and a night in the streets doing nothing wrong, and then went and threatened to break Messrs. —— windows again. I did that to get into prison again; for when I lay quiet of a night in prison I thought things over, and considered what a shocking life I was leading, and how my health might be ruined completely, and I thought I would stick to prison rather than go back to such a life. I got six months for threatening. When I got out I broke a lamp next morning for the same purpose, and had a fortnight. That was the last time I was in prison. I have since been leading the same life as I told you of for three years, and lodging at the same houses, and seeing the same goings on. I hate such a life now more than ever. I am willing to do any work that I can in washing and cleaning . . .

HENRY MAYHEW, 'Letters to the Morning Chronicle', quoted in *The Westminster Review*, vol. 53, pp. 496–497 (1850).

5

'Kiss me quick' Bonnets

The application of a little knowledge of the world and common sense to the case of the angry parents who consider it shameful that their young daughters cannot frequent Oxford and Regent-streets without the risk of being spoken to by 'miscreants', may possibly relieve you and the public from future appeals of a similar nature. I fear that in London, as in all other great cities, young and good-looking girls will always require a companion in public places frequented by young and good-looking men if they desire to be secure from interruption.

All fathers of families are, like 'Paterfamilias from the Country', quite certain that their daughters are perfectly demure and well behaved, until they have conclusive proof to the contrary. They forget the private history of their own youth; they cannot believe that Blanche ever looked kindly at a strange *joli garçon* who appeared struck with her appearance; or that Isabel ever designedly showed rather more than her very neat ankle to a young officer in crossing a street. It never occurs to them that bonnets of the 'kiss me quick' build, loud stockings, exaggerated tournures, capes and crinolines; vagrant ringlets straying over the shoulder, better known by the name of 'follow me, lads', and such like decoys, are all unmistakably intended to attract the notice and atten tions of the male sex.

From a letter in *The Times*, London, January 21, 1862

6

Welsh 'Laxity'

The laxity of morals among the female peasantry of Wales is unhappily notorious. The inveterate custom of night courting has destroyed all delicacy of character, and although marriage often follows such irregular proceedings the rate of illegitimacy is high. In the face of the well-known Welsh custom of 'bundling', which is not confined to the agricultural population, I cannot charge to the employment of women in agriculture the immorality which undoubtedly prevails . . .

The farmhouses on the small farms are, generally speaking, very defective, not only in sanitary arrangements but in proper sleeping accommodation. An instance was mentioned to me by a county magistrate in which men and women servants all sleep in a loft together, separated only by a row of boxes: and by another magistrate I was informed that in a great many of the small farmhouses the male and female servants have only one room in common.

J. HENRY TREMENHEERE, assistant commissioner; Employment of Children, Young Persons, and Women in Agriculture: 3rd Report (1870), pp. 52–53; P.P. 1870, vol. 13.

7

Courting Customs of the Lowland Scotch

Before the publication of the Registrar General's Report in 1858, nine Scotchmen out of ten would have asserted, with perfect belief in the truth of the assertion, that the Lowland Scotch were moral people. Since 1858 not only the Registrar General's Annual Report, but the investigations of such men as Dr Strachan, of Dollar, and others equally anxious to arrive at the truth of the matter, have given a rude shock to this belief.

Taking the Annual Reports of the Registrar General and the investigations of Dr Strachan as a basis, we are brought to the inevitable conclusion that amongst the Lowland Scotch of the labouring class, a very small proportion of the women preserve their chastity up to the date of their marriage. Here, then, lies the weight of the whole charge of immorality brought against the labouring population of the south and north-east of Scotland, that they esteem lightly the purity of their unmarried woman.

Infidelity after marriage is almost unknown, nor is there any inter- ference with nature either before or after childbirth productive of crimes, better known in towns than in country parishes. There is indeed no pressure on the woman to commit any crime in order to conceal her lapse from virtue, as amongst her own class there is no feeling of indig- nation aroused in consequence of what they call her 'misfortune'.

There is sometimes a good deal in a name, and this very term 'misfortune', used by the Lowland Scotch to designate the result of a woman's unchastity, is an index to their feeling on the subject. It is 'a misfortune', because she is for a time incapacitated from earning her own daily bread, and if unable, as is often the case in Scotland, to affiliate the child, she is casting a burden on herself or her parents. As an impediment to her after marriage either with the father of her child or some other man, the misfortune is, unhappily, of very little conse- quence.

All sorts of excuses are alleged for the impurity of the Lowland Scotch labouring women. The difficulty of obtaining cottages and remunerative employment, for instance, in agricultural districts ... Want of separation between the sexes in cottages is another excuse. I would instantly grant that this defect must be remedied before you can effect a cure, but that it is not a sufficient excuse may be proved from the comparative chastity of the women bred up in Irish or Highland cabins.

Dr Strachan, while pointing to the purity and good manners of this Celtic population, seems inclined to attribute some part of the difference in conduct to stronger passions of the Lowlander. It may be a wise provision of nature that the physically stronger race should have more inclination to reproduce itself, but I think we could point to our experiences in Wales to show that the Celt too, under certain circum- stances, is open to the charge of impurity.

There is a custom common to the south of Scotland and South Wales leading in both districts to the exaggeration of a common evil. I mean the custom of night courting. Under this head Dr Strachan says: 'Working men will not believe that it is possible to court a wife without stolen interviews, with the woman sitting on the man's knee or enfolded in his arms for hours in the dark. Among the working classes those who are attached to each other never meet in public or in the social circle.' Then after quoting two well known Scottish songs illustrative of courting 'among the rigs of barley', and in the girl's bedroom, he continues, 'The back of a haystack or the barn or the coal house, although not so poetical as "among the rigs o' barley"' is the more frequent scene of courtship; the most frequent of all, however, is the girl's bedroom. Wherever the place, the meeting is by stealth in the middle of the night in darkness.'

I don't mean to say that 'night courting' is the chief cause of the impurity of women; but it certainly reacts as a continuing cause of a state of things of which it may be only one of the signs.

To put an end to night courting and at the same time discourage the somewhat coarse tastes of the labouring class, I can do no better than endorse the recommendation to all persons interested in the welfare of their poorer brethren, to encourage social gatherings where young men and women may meet under more favourable circumstances than in the 'barn or coal house'. To encourage, I would add, any refined amusement, bodily or mental, which may tend to raise a manly, honest, and God-fearing race to a higher position in the scale of social refinement.

MR G. CULLEY, assistant commissioner, reporting on South-East Scotland; Employment of Children, etc. in Agriculture, 4th Report, pp. 80–81; P.P. 1870, vol. 13.

8

Unpalatable Facts about the 'Concubinage Market'

The inquiry of the department into the prevalence of venereal diseases among the civil population was intended to contribute some of the elements necessary for judging a question which of late has been much agitated before the public: the question, whether it is expedient to have in this country a systematic superintendence of prostitutes.

During the last few years, under the provisions of special Acts of Parliament—the so-called Contagious Diseases Acts of 1864 and 1866, a system of this sort has been administered on a small scale, by the War Office and Admiralty, at certain military and naval stations; and recently, while these departments have been proposing to extend their own operations with respect to the two public services which they direct, the more general question has been raised by the advocacy of a voluntary association formed for the purpose of promoting the extension of the Contagious Diseases Act, 1866, to the civil population of the United

Kingdom. The Association contends 'that sufferers under any kind of [venereal] contagious disease are dangerous members of society, and should, so long as they are in this state, be prevented from communicating it to others; ... that common prostitutes should be subject to a compulsory medical examination, and to compulsory detention in hospital as often as they are found diseased, and so long as they continue so; ... that, for the reception of prostitutes suffering from venereal disease, hospital accommodation should be provided in all towns where such persons congregate'.

To give a notion of the quantity of hospital accommodation which would be requisite to satisfy this programme, I may observe, for instance, that London is conjectured to have some 18,000 women whose living is gained by prostitution; and that ... of any given number of prostitutes, always about one-third may be assumed to be diseased. If, instead of insisting on these colossal estimates, we take only half their total result, the plan would require for London alone the creation and maintenance of new hospital accommodation nearly equal to that which is now given by the twelve general hospitals of London for all bodily diseases put together, namely, for 3,000 patients. The charge of maintaining (independently of the cost of constructing) such lazarets as the above would probably be at least £100,000 per annum; and their construction would probably represent a first cost little short of half a million of money; besides all which there would be the considerable annual charges for police arrangements and medical inspections. This for London alone! And the requirements of other large towns would probably be of like proportions.

Demands like the above are evidently not likely to be met by voluntary contributions. The result, if it be got at all, can only be got under action of law; and any such law, whether empowering the central government to defray expenses out of proceeds of general taxation, or empowering municipalities to assign local funds for the purpose is, of course, in relation to minorities, compulsory.

Now, it is quite certain that, rightly or wrongly, the proposed appropriation of money would, in the eyes of very large numbers of persons, be in the last degree odious and immoral. In most municipal constituencies there are swarms of persons who already find it no easy matter to satisfy the collectors of rates and taxes; they would see the prostitute kept in hospital at their expense for weeks or months, not necessarily from the exigencies of severe illness of her own, but essentially that she might be made clean for hire; they would remember in contrast, that for themselves wonderfully little is done by authority to protect them against adulterations of food, or against false weights or measures; and they might regard it as a strange caprice of law which should oblige them to contribute to the cost of giving an artificial security to their neighbour's looseness of life . . .

I suppose it may be assumed that public policy is very decidely in favour of marriage as against promiscuous fornication; that the latter, however powerless may be laws to prevent it, is, at least, an order of things which no State would willingly foster; that, whereas it has some inherent inconveniences, among which is the liability to specific contagious maladies, such drawbacks from its attractions are not in their kind a matter for general social regret; that venereal diseases are, in principle, infections which a man contracts at his own option, and against which he cannot in any degree claim to be protected by action of others—the less so, of course, as his option is exercised in modes of life contrary to the common good; that thus, *prima facie*, the true policy of Government is to regard the prevention of venerel diseases as a matter of exclusively private concern. *Caveat emptor!* And though it must be admitted that to some extent the consequences of promiscuous fornication spread, the infections of the brothel being oftentimes carried into simultaneous or consequent wedlock, and in some cases fixing their obscene brand even on the offspring of such marriages; this horrid fact is only one of many which might be cited, where innocent wives and children participate more or less severely in consequences which husbands and fathers have earned. To be wife or child of a drunkard or gambler involves evils against which the State does not affect to give security; and *prima facie*, the dependent interest must be equally unprotected by the State against harms which that other sort of looseness may bring on it . . .

Whether the venereal diseases of the civil population are henceforth to be deemed matter of public concern, whether the civil fornicant may reasonably look to constituted authorities to protect him in his commerce with prostitutes, is the principle which I conceive to be at stake. And I would repeat my opinion that, if that principle is affirmed, the responsibilities implied in it cannot be adequately met without stringent compulsory general legislation . . .

I apprehend that the concubinage-market, like other markets, tends to be fed according to demand; and that, if prostitution is really to be diminished, the principles of those who would diminish it must be preventive rather than reformatory. Of the many roots of the evil some are practically immutable, but others will undoubtedly vary with the general moral sentiments of the time. Always, of course, there are certain large quantities of mere brute passion, forcing at any price to have their way; and always, in our present social state, there are large unintelligent masses of human life with little sense of right and wrong, and much of abject poverty ready to sell itself for food, and even more of uneducated frivolous temperament. But if these be regarded as in my present sense 'fixed' elements (though indeed all of them are happily susceptible of reduction) a comparatively very variable force is represented in the influence of public opinion. That parents of the educated classes regard with immeasurably different degrees of interest the chastity of their daughters, on the one hand, and the continence of their sons, or future sons-in-law, on the other, is a fact which probably has its basis in a doctrine of supposed general consequences; but knowledge which is supplied in studying the venereal diseases of the civil population—a knowledge of the mischief and misery which a young man's transient incontinence may be preparing for his whole future domestic life, certainly gives room for consideration whether these ingredients of the one case ought not to be more popularly understood. The only state of things which can be regarded as essentially antagonistic to prostitution is the system of early marriages: which, in this respect, commends itself equally on moral and physical grounds; for, in proportion as it is accepted, the promiscuous intercourse of the sexes ceases to excuse itself by circumstances, and the chances of venereal infection fall to the lowest level they can attain . . .

DR JOHN SIMON; Privy Council Medical Reports, No. 11 (1868).

9

Mrs Josephine Butler to the Rescue

Mrs Josephine Butler, wife of Rev. George Butler, Principal of Liverpool College, appeared before the Committee and was questioned by the Chairman, Rt. Hon. W. N. Massey, M.P.:—
You have taken great interest in the [Contagious Diseases] Acts which are the subject of this Commission? Before these Acts were passed had you turned your attention to the subject of these unhappy women?—
Yes, for 15 years before 1869 . . . in leisure moments which I could spare from my family.

Had you been connected with any reformatory or refuge for women?
—Not officially . . . but I have received numberless women into my own house . . . My husband and I have taken them in as friends, patients when ill, and keeping them until they died. We have had sometimes five living together in our house until I could find situations for them.

Then in fact your house itself was a small refuge for them ?—It was, and is to this day.

How did you find the women you received into your house?—I visited them in low parts of the town; I have gone to brothels occasionally, both at night and in the day time; I see them in the streets, and speak to them. I have gone to the workhouse, and the Lock hospital [hospital for V.D. patients]. They get to know me, and then when they do, I seek them no longer but they seek me.

What has been the result of your labours—have they been successful and encouraging ?—It is very difficult indeed for me to answer that question. What I consider successful perhaps may not be what you would think successful.

When I speak of your efforts being successful, have you succeeded in inducing these women permanently to adhere to a virtuous life after they have left your protection ?—I have not generally failed to do that; but this frequently happens, that I do not succeed in placing them in situations which they are fit for, on account of their not having had industrial training. They become virtuous women, but not satisfactory members of society in that sense. I have been the cause of several emigrating, and they do better in Canada and other places than in England; but to my mind the cases have been successful, inasmuch as I believe they have been brought back to womanly dignity and virtue . . .

Have you kept any record of the number of women who have passed under your care ?—Never . . .

Can you inform the Commission approximately of how many you have dealt with in that way ?—No; because I have rather desired to forget it myself . . .

Report of the Commission on the Administration, etc., of the Contagious Diseases Acts, page 437; P.P. 1871, vol. 19.

10

Victorian Methods of Family Limitation

The only means by which the virtue and the progress of mankind are rendered possible is, 'Preventive Sexual Intercourse'. By this is meant, sexual intercourse where precautions are used to prevent impregnation. In this way love could be obtained, without . . . overcrowding the population. Two questions arise here: (1) Is this possible, and in what way ? (2) Can it be done without causing moral and physical harm ?

16. Over Population: George Cruikshank's vision of 'things to come!'

Though Malthus cries, 'Celibacy',
McCulloch, 'Emigration',
Folks stay at home and wed, we see,
Then swell the population!

The Comic Almanack, 1851

In answering the first question, I will give an account of the different modes in which preventive sexual intercourse has been tried or proposed; for it must not be thought that these means of checking population are new or unusual; they are, on the contrary, I believe, very common, both in this country and still more in some parts of the continent. People have been driven to devise and adopt them in numberless instances, to prevent an increase in their families, or to avoid having offspring in an unmarried intimacy.

The method proposed by M. Raciborski is to adopt a certain order in sexual intercourse. 'It results from my investigations' [he writes], 'that though there may not be periods when conception is physically inhibited, there are nevertheless periods when it is infinitely less likely to happen than at others.' Mr Bischoff, the celebrated German physiologist, is nearly of the same opinion ... In accordance with the views of these distinguished men, it is only necessary for women to abstain from sexual intercourse during a certain part of the month; and this would leave them about the half of each month for the free indulgence of their sexual appetites, without the danger of adding to an overcrowded population.

This, if true, would be a boon of incomparable value; and if even this amount of sexual intercourse were available to all women, it would probably prevent in good measure the evils of sexual morbidity, repressed sexual desires, and unexercised sexual organs, as they are seen in the numberless cases of chlorosis, hysteria, and diseases of menstruation ...

But besides these preventive means, which may be called the 'natural' ones, and which are as yet scarcely at all known to the mass of mankind, there are others, which are much more widely known, and much more generally adopted ... The 'unnatural' or mechanical ones are of different kinds, but have all the same object, namely, to avoid impregnation, by preventing the seminal fluid from entering the womb, and thus preventing the meeting of the sperm and germ cell, which is the essential part of impregnation. In this way the accessory and sensational part of the venereal act is obtained, while the essential and unconscious part is avoided.

This is done either by the withdrawal of the penis immediately before ejaculation takes place (which is very frequently practised by married and unmarried men); by the use of the sheath (which is also very frequent, but more so on the continent than in this country); by the introduction of a piece of sponge into the vagina, so as to guard the mouth of the womb, which lies high up in the vagina; or by the injection of tepid water into the vagina immediately after coition.

The first of these modes is physically injurious, and is apt to produce nervous disorder and sexual enfeeblement and congestion, from the sudden interruption it gives to the venereal act, whose pleasure moreover it interferes with. The second, namely the sheath, dulls the enjoyment, and frequently produces impotence in the man and disgust in both parties, so that it also is injurious.

These objections do not, I believe, apply to the third, namely, the introduction of a sponge or some other substance, to guard the mouth of the womb. This could easily be done by the woman, and would scarcely, it appears to me, interfere at all in the sexual pleasures, nor have any prejudical effect on the health of either party. (Any preventive means, to be satisfactory, must be used by the *woman*, as it spoils the passion and impulsiveness of the venereal act, if the man has to think of them) . . . The injection of tepid water into the vagina, immediately after intercourse, would also be a very effectual means of preventing impregnation; as it would wash away the seminal fluid, and also . . . destroy the fecundating properties of the spermatozooids, whose movements speedily cease in pure water.

By far the best of these mechanical means I should take to be the sponge, and it might be used during that part of the month in which fecundation can take place . . .

The pleasures of love

The second question was, can these means be used without causing physical and moral evils ? I firmly believe that they can . . . If by these means . . . each woman in our society could have a due share of the pleasures of love, and also of the blessings of motherhood, it appears to me that this could be done, with little, if any, necessary injury to the health . . . Impregnation and childbirth are certainly of the very greatest importance to the health and happiness of woman, and hence every woman should produce her fair share of offspring; but it is probable that two or three children during life would be quite sufficient to secure these advantages . . .

As regards the moral side of the question of preventive sexual intercourse, many people have an objection to it, because, they say, it is *unnatural*. But sexual abstinence is infinitely more unnatural; in fact, it is so unnatural, and therefore sinful, that it is totally incompatible with health and happiness, and produces the most widespread and desolating diseases. It is granted that preventive intercourse is unnatural, but the circumstances of our life leave us no alternative. If we were to obey all the natural impulses, and follow our sexual desires like the inferior animals, which live a natural life, we should be forced to prey upon and check the growth of each other, just as they do . . .

Preventive sexual intercourse then, is the mode, and the only possible mode, of reconciling the opposing difficulties of the population problem; and is the *only possible solution* of the great social evil of this and other old countries. I stake my life, I would stake a thousand lives, on the truth of this . . .

DR GEORGE DRYSDALE, *The Elements of Social Science; or Physical, Sexual and Natural Religion. An Exposition of the true Cause and only Cure of the Three Primary Evils: Poverty, Prostitution, and Celibacy* (1st ed. 1854; quoted from 35th ed., 1905; pp. 346–352).

EPILOGUE

Now we have arrived at the last page, and the people whom we have retrieved from the towns and streets, homes and 'places of work', of the middle years of the last century, must make their way back to the place whence they came. But before we take leave of them, let us pay them the tribute of a cheer. They deserve it.

Not all the belittling screeds of latter-day sneerers can deface their record of unparalleled achievement. In whatever field of activity we care to choose, the advances had been tremendous. Cities more extensive and populous than the world had ever seen; railways extending to thousands of miles of track; factories pouring out goods of luxury and necessity in immense variety and volume; the savings of the people invested in the instruments of economic advance, not only in Britain but in all the undeveloped or underdeveloped countries of the world; schools attended for the first time by the great majority of boys and girls; women standing on their own feet and demanding to be accepted as human beings with individualities, rights and reason of their own; the homes of the common people more comfortable, a bit larger, a bit better furnished with the conveniences of civilized living.

All these things, and many, many more, must be put to the credit side of the Victorian balance-sheet. Of course, there is a debit side too, and a very considerable one. But when we recall the squalor and poverty and inequality, the insensate pride of class and the bumptiousness of riches, let us not forget that it was in the Victorian epoch that sanitary science challenged the age-old foes of disease and malnutrition and premature death, and that *we* have had the inestimable benefit of being able to profit from the Victorians' inexperienced experiments and shots in the dark.

In the chronological arrangement of the myth-makers, the Golden Age was followed at length by one of Iron. Something like this happened to Britain towards the end of the period we have had under review. The iron dug from out of Britain's hills made it possible for the continents to be crisscrossed with railways, and British coal belched smoke from the funnels of the vast navies of steamships that took the wind out of the clippers' sails. Before the seventies were out, steel was well on the way to supplanting iron, and the newly emerging industrial giants of Germany and the United States were making things increasingly difficult for the Britain that had taught them their lessons. English farmers, grumbling with better reason than usual about the weather, had to meet the competition of cattle and grain grown on the prairies of the Middle West and the ranches of Australia, of dairy produce from the farms of Denmark and New Zealand. Even the classic doctrine of Free Trade came to have the look of being fly-blown, as 'protectionist' policies enabled Britain's competitors to expand and flourish. In business organization the small family firm had to make way for vast combinations of capital, which were before long challenged by conglomerations of labour power, sullen, resentful, fiercely determined to secure their place in the sun.

The Crystal Palace still glittered on the heights of Norwood to which it had been transferred from Hyde Park, but often ominous clouds gathered above its roofs and towers, the lightning flashed and the thunder rolled.

But still those Victorian grandparents and great-grandparents of ours presented a bold and confident front, and with their mental dexterity and manual skill kept Britain in the forefront of the march of progress.

INDEX

Aberdeen, meat from, 59
Abram, W. A., on factory workers, 78
Accidents in factories, 89; in pits, 80, 81
Accommodation, living, insufficient, 245. *See also* Agricultural workers; Dwellings; London
Accommodation Houses, 350–1
Acton, Dr W., on prostitution, 347–57
Adulteration of food, 271, 290–1, 295–6
Agricultural workers: accommodation of, 219, 245–8, 249–50; bondager, life of, 225–6; case of assault, 221–2; children, 217; females: 187, 216–31, inspected by farmers, 223–4, on Marshlands, 228, North Country, 227; fornication among, 219; hours and wages of, 217–18; ill-health of, 218–19. *See also* Farm Labourers
Agriculture, 9. *See also* Agricultural workers; Female workers
Albert, Prince, of Saxe-Coburg, 24, 28, 155; and business, 37; and Great Exhibition, 24, 44; and model cottages, on 233, 242; servants, old, 162; speech at Guildhall, 43–5
Aldgate, conditions in, 276
America, voyage to, 39
Animals, cruelty to, 59; slaughtering of, 59, 60
Applegarth, R., 314, 315, 320, 321, 322–3
Apsley House, 29
Arsenic, sale of, 291
Ashley, Lord, 109. *See also* Shaftesbury, Earl
Ashworth, S., Co-operative Society salesman, 332

Bakehouses, filth in, 293–5; ill-drainage of, 294; London, criticized, 293–5; ventilation of, 294

Baker, R., 48; reports: on females in brickyards, 212; potters, life of, 95
Bakers, health of, 294–5
Ballenden, Dr, on nailers, 256
Beer, consumption of, 55, 64
'Bees' and 'Butterflies', 43
Bennett, Mr, of Cheapside, 201
Bermondsey, and cholera, 306
Bernard, Dr, on meals for shirt-workers, 184–5
Billingsgate, 57; behaviour in, 57–8
Birmingham, 48; 85–9; education in, 124–5; factory: accidents in, 89, conditions in, 86; hours of work at, 88, flint-glass manufacture, 135; ignorance of young in, 124–5; industries of, 85 f.
Birth-control, 338, 362
Bischoff, Mr, and 'safe period', 364
Bishop & Co., young workers at, 194–5
Bishopsgate, conditions in, 276
Black Country, 48; 78, 209–11
Blacklegs, 323, 324
Blake, W., 138
Blue Books, 316
Blue-coat boy, 32
Bommeree, 58
Bondage house, 225
Bondager women, 224
Boucherett, J., on domestic servants, 162–3
Boyce, G., on accidents in screw factory, 192
Brick Lane, Whitechapel, lodging-house, 298
Brickfields, 9; females in, 213–15
Bricklayers' Union, 314
Brickworks, children in, 131–2
Brickyards, females in, 211–12; workers, immorality among, 212
Bridge-stocker, 79
Brighton, 52

Britain, living conditions in (1800), 38, 39; population of, 47; prosperity of (1851), 36

British: business in Victorian times, 8; families, living conditions of, 271; supremacy at Great Exhibition, 22

Brothels, 348; notorious, 349

Bryant, Mr S., 110, 117

Bryant & May's match factory, 117 f.

Buckle, H. T., 309

Buffet, girls at station, 101

Builders, anti-union, 326; speculative, and rural dwellings, 246; strike negotiations and, 325-6

Building Societies, 91 f.;

Building workers, strike of, 324-5; wages of, 327

Burial, earlier, urged, 287; vaults, 288

But-and-Ben cottages, 202-3

Butler, Mrs Josephine, 338; and prostitutes, 361

Button factory, child labour in, 126-8; wages of, 127

Capitalism, Golden Age of, 313

Capitalists, British, and the Great Exhibition, 21

Carders, 75

Cardiganshire, hovels in, 260-1

Carlile, R., 338

Carpenters and Joiners, Amalgamated Society of, 314, 316, 317, 318, 320-1

Carus, Dr, on English dwellings, 234

Cemeteries, new ones advised, 289

Census statistics, females, 155-6; domestic servants, 158

Cesspools in London, 278-9

Chadwick, E., 9; and cholera, 302-3; and public health, 271-2

Chamberlain, Joseph, 188

Chaplain of County House of Correction, Lancs, evidence of, 148-9

Chartist agitation, 36, 313, 332

Cheapside, dining in, 51

Child labour in Birmingham, 88

Child slaves of factory system, 109

Children Act (1908), 146

Children, age of employment, 112; agriculture, in, 217; born in filth, 292; brickworks, in, 131-2; buttermaking, 126-8; chimney-sweeps, 138 ff.; condition of, 109; concern for, 109; crime, taught, 145-7;

employment of, 47, 111; factories, in, 109; feeding of young, 229-30; flint-glass works, in, 135; cruelty to, 135; grinding metal, in, 133; hours of work, 41; life of poor, 55; medical examination of, 47; millinery manufacture, in, 123; nail factory, in, 128-9; opium, and, 230; pottery trade, in, 91, 114; scarecrows, as, 137; steel yards, in, 133-4; straw-plaiting, in, morals and education of, 121-2; unwelcome, 229; wages of, 74, 111, 113, 136

Children's Employment Commission, 109, 110, 111, 139, 115-53, 170, 176, 178-9, 180, 188-9, 193-5, 205-6, 213-15, 218-21

Children's Saving Fund, 91

Chimney-sweeping, machines for, 143

Chimney-sweeps, summoned, 139-41; work of apprentices, 138 ff. See also Climbing-boys

Choke-damp, 81

Cholera, case of, 304-6; cause of, 303; clergy and, 310; deaths from, 304-5; deaths from, in London district, 306; history of, 302; Scotland, in, 309; signs and symptoms of, 304; victims of, 302; Lord Palmerston, and, 309

Churchgoing, 37

Cigar-makers, female, 195-6

City Arabs, 147

City Medical Reports, 217-20, 273-4, 276-8, 278-80, 281-2, 286-91

Clapham, Sir John, 48

Clergy, Scottish, and cholera, 310

Clerks in London, 50; journey to work, 50-1; women, 187

Climbing-boy, death of, 139

Climbing-boys, 9, 138, 143-4; diseases of, 143-4; hours and wages of, 142; scandal of, 138 f.; schools of, 142; suffering of, 139, 140-1; work of, 110, 140-1. See also Chimney-sweeps

Close and Open villages, 245

Coal, 64, 65; metropolis of, 65; industry at Newcastle, 64; quantities, 64-5; shafts, 67; smelting, for, 80; workers' allowance of, 80; Black Country, 80

Coal-mine, boys in, 68–9; descent of described, 67–9; females in, 187; life in, 67–8; ponies in, 68; work in, 68–9
Coal-miners, 67–8; dwellings of, 70–1; life and labour of, 67–71
Coffins, tapping of, 288
Coles, W. R., on children in millinery manufacture, 123
Collective security, need for, 313
College of Physicians and Apothecaries Co., 290
Collieries, behaviour of workers in, 210–11; females in, 209–10; pitmound, labour of: unfeminine, 211; conducive to immorality, 211
Collieries of North, 65
Communication, means of, 42
Communist Manifesto, 313
Complaints among workers, 87
Concubinage, 358–60
Conditions of workpeople, 9; et passim
Condom sheaths, 364; early, 338
Congregationalism, factory workers and, 77
Contagious Diseases Acts (1864–69), 337
Co-operative Movement; 10; aims of, 330; funds of, 332; history of, 331–5; reason for, 331; success of, 335–6
Corn Laws, 36
Cornhill Magazine, 9; articles from, 64, 102
Corpses, decomposing, 289; delay in burying, 286–7
Cost of living, 38, 39; improves, 39
Costermongers, 58
Cottages, Prince Albert model, 242–5; rural, deficiencies of, 246; Welsh, conditions in, 260–1; Scottish, 262
Covent Garden, life in market of, 62–3; supplies to, 62
Creeler, 73
Cremorne, Garden at, 35
Crime, punishment for, 38 f.
Criminal and Destitute Juveniles, House of Commons Select Committee on, 145–6, 147
Crinoline, cause of injury, 192–3
Cripplegate, conditions in, 276

Cruel sports, 252
Cruikshank, G., 294; on domestic servants, 164
Crystal Palace, 21, 23, 36; transferred from Hyde Park, 368. See also Great Exhibition of 1851
Culley, G., on prostitution in Scotland, 356–8

Dairies, 61
Dancing-room, prostitutes at, 352
Das Kapital and the 'gang system', 217
Decomposition of animal matter, 289
Dickens, Charles, 157; on chimney boys, 139; on dressmakers, 169
Disraeli, B., 8, 109
Docking, open parish, 246
Doctors, unqualified, 291; lack of qualifications, 271
Doffers of Rochdale, 333
Domestic Early Closing Movement, 164
Domestic servants, 157 ff.; hard work of, 162–3; health of, 173; holidays for, 172; life of, 159; training of, 158 ff.; treatment of, 160 f.; wages of, 161
Dorchester, cholera at, 304
Drainage, house, lack of, 282; slaughter-house, 286
Dress houses, 348
Dressmakers, 169–87; apprentices, 171 ff.; food of, 180; health of, 180; hours and wages of, 169, 171, 174; life of, 169–86; living conditions of, 181–2; London, 169 ff.; outdoor, 173–4; pressure of work, 179; sanitary conditions of, 170 ff.; tricks of employers, 182. See also Millinery
Dressmaking, French girls in, 180
Drovers at Smithfield, 59
Drugs and poisons, sale of, 271
Drunkenness, 83, 93
Drury Lane lodging-houses, 298
Drysdale, G., on preventive sexual intercourse, 362–6
Dwellings, overcrowded, 292; privies for, 292; unfit, 292

Economist, The, 9; articles from: 37, 38–43, 45

Edinburgh Review, 9, articles from, 157–62; 209–11

Education in 1800, 42

Education of children, 111, 122

Educational societies, 145

Edward, Prince, 24

Eggs, supply of, 60

Engels, F., 313

Engine drivers, work of, 98–9

Engineers, Amalgamated Society of, 314, 315, 317; benefits of, 317; finances of, 318; power of, 318

Englishwoman's Review, article from, 162–3

Equitable Pioneers, 330; subscription to, 331–2. *See also* Rochdale Equitable Pioneers

Euston Square Station, 95

Evesham gloveresses, 8, 204–6

Excrement, disposal of, 282

Excursions by rail, 41

Exhibition. *See* Great Exhibition, The

'Exhibition Journal', Queen Victoria on Exhibition, 22 f.

Explosions in pits, 81

Factories and workshops, 9

Factories, child labour in, 74; conditions of, 86; life in, 72 f. *See also* Children

Factory Act (1867), 111

Factory Acts Extension Act (1864), 110

Factory hand, career of, 72–8

Factory life, attraction of, 159; work, repugnance to, 76; workers: prospects of, 75 f., conditions of, 73, fines for, 77

Fairs, mop and statute, 223; women inspected at, 223

Faithfull, Emily, on saleswomen, 200–1

Family, limitation of, 363–6; necessity of, 225

Farm labourers, dwellings of, 104; education of, 103; expenses of, 106; income of, 106–7; life of, 102–8; old, wages and expenses of, 249–50; pleasures of, 104; subsistence of, 103 f. *See also* Agricultural workers.

Farms, equipment of, 105

Fashion, 52, 53; shops, 49

Female labour. *See* Female workers.

Female morals, 207–8

Female Servants Early Closing Movement, 164

Female workers, agricultural, 216–31; brickfields, in, 207–8; 213–15; factory and workshop, in, 86, 187–8; glovemaking, in, 187–8; 205–6; injury to, 192; pit-banks, in, 207–8; potteries, in, 91; premature birth in, 229; degrading employment, in, 207–15; watch-making, 201

Fillers, 79

Firebrick works, child labour in, 131–2

Fire-damp, 81

Fish-supplies to London, 57

Flatpressers in potteries, 113

Food, adulteration of, 290–6

Food at the Great Exhibition, 33

Foreign fruit in London, 63

Foreigners and prostitution, 345

Fortnightly Review, 72

Fraser, Rev. J., on rural cottages, 246–8; on women in agriculture, 222–3

Free love advocated, 338

Free Trade, 36

Fretters, 69

Fruit, gathering, gangs at, 210; sales in London, 62–3

Gang system in agriculture, 216 ff.; and immorality, 229

Gases, cesspools, from, 278; mine, in, 81; from sewers, 282; affecting Houses of Parliament, 297

Gaskell, Mrs, 337

Glassworkers' Union, 317

Glovemakers (Gloveresses), morals of, 205–6; females, 187; hours and wages of, 205

Godfrey's cordial, 230

Godwin, G., on housing, 237; London dwellings, 237–8

Golden Age, The, 8, 21–35, 36, 38; sequel to, 367; success of, 367

Grand National Consolidated Trades Union, 313

Grave-diggers, miscalculations of, 289

Graveyards, horrors of, 288–90; water contamination, and, 281

Great Exhibition of 1851, 9, 21, 26; admission to 24 f.; attendance at, 24; British supremacy at, 22; building of, 22; educational value of, 33; exhibitors at, 22; farm equipment at, 105; food at, 25, 33; machinery at, 30; model cottages at, 233; opening of, 22–4, 26–9; by Queen Victoria, 22, 26; poor people at, 33; Prince Albert and, 44; 'Shilling Day' at, 29–33; success of, 21 f.; *The Times* and, 26; waiting-rooms at, 34 f.; water-closets at, 34 f.

Great Northern Railway, 59

Great Social Evil, The, 337 ff.

Greatest Plague of Life, The, 157

Greenhow, Dr, on married women workers, 188, 202–3

Grouse, 60

Gurney, G., on sewers, 297–8

Hales Owen, 128

Halstead, Essex, weavers of, 257–8

Hanley, child labour at, 112

Hardy, Thomas, 9

Harlotry, statistics of, 347

Harrow Alley, gut-scraping sheds of, 286

Head, Sir F. B., 48; on railways, 95–102

Heath, F. G., on peasant dwellings, 249–50

Henley, Joseph J., on agricultural work, 224–7

Henry II, 307

Hemans, Felicia D., poem of, 233

Her Majesty's Theatre, 53 f.

Hill, Matthew Davenport, Q.C., 146

Hill, Octavia, housing venture of, 233, 239–42

Holidays of workers, 89

Holyoake, G. J., on Co-operative Societies, 331–6

Hood, Tom, poem of, 337

Horley, W., on children, in straw-plaiting, 120–2

'Horrible Conspirators and Assassins', 20, 24

Hosiery workers, 187

Hospitals, conditions in, 37

House of Correction, 148–9

House drainage, deficiencies of, 282

Houses of Parliament, and sewer gases, 297

Housing conditions, 233–70

Housing management, 233

Human moles, 68–9

Hungry forties, 36

Hunter, Dr H. J., on agricultural workers, mortality rates of, 231; dwellings of, 245, 251–2; 259–60

Hunter, Sir, R., 234

Hyde Park, 21, 23, 26, 368; Great Exhibition at, 21, 26

Illegitimate children and crime, 146

Immorality in agricultural workers, 216 ff., South Staffordshire, in, 255–6

Industrial scene, 48

Infanticide of agricultural workers, 229–30

Infantile diseases, 229

Interment, delays of, 286–7

'Introducing houses', 350

Iron mines, 80, 81; accidents in, 80

Iron trade, workers in, 78–81

Iron workers, American, letters from, 328–9

Ironworks, women in, 208–9

Italian opera, model of, 31

Jacob's Island, 'capital of cholera', 306–8; conditions of, 307–8; diseases on, 308

Jay, Messrs, dressmakers at, 177–8

Jewish commission agents, 50

Juvenile delinquents, 9, 146–7; crimes of, 146–6; home life of, 149–50; House of Commons Select Committee on, 145–6, 147; punishment of, 148–9; suspicious of kindness, 147

Kingsley, Charles, 314

'Kiss me quick' bonnets, 355

Koch, Dr, R., and cholera, 302

Labour, appreciation of, 43; hours, reform of, 72

Lace industry, 188; conditions in, 203–4; females in, 187; health of, 203; hours and wages in, 190–1

Ladies, fashion of, 52
Lancashire factories, 72 f.; operatives, morals and religion of, 77
Larks, trade in, 60
Lavatories, 25
Leadenhall skin market, 60; odour from, 286
Leifchild, J. R., on coalfields, 67–71
Lichfield, Earl of, on building strike, 327
Liverpool, model of, 31
Locke, W., on Ragged Schools, 150 f.
Locomotion, 41
Lodging-houses, 298–301; conditions of, 300–1; filth of, 298–9; improvement of, 300–1; indecency in, 299; lavatories of, 299; mixing of sexes in, 298–9; overcrowding of, 300; prostitutes, for, 348–9; summonses for, 300–1
London, accommodation in, 237; effects on health of, 238; rents of, 237; cesspools of, 278–9; dairies of, 61; house-drainage in, 282, importance of, 47; lunch-hour in, 51; prostitutes: haunts of, 348–9, number of, 389; restaurants in, 51; sanitation, lack of, 271–2; smoke, 284–5; waste, disposal of, 282–3; water, impurities of, 281; lack of, 281
London City Missions and Ragged Schools, 151
London Dress Trades, 9
London & North Western Railway, 48
Londoners' homes, 237–8
Longe, F. D., 110, 115; on labour in brickfields, 214
Longton, 93, 94
Loxdale, Mr, on labourers' cottages, 261

Macaulay, Thomas Babington, 24; on Great Exhibition, 26
Machines for chimney-sweeping, 143
Magna Carta, 55
Man, Horace, on child employment, 111–12
Manchester, 48; inquiry at, 316; warehousemen of, 50
Manchester house painters, 317
Married women in factories, 202–3

Marrowbone stage, 50
Marrows, 68
Marshall & Snelgrove, 175
Martin, Dr, 307
Marx, Karl, 9, 10, 217, 313, 314
Match factories, conditions in, 115–16
Match-box maker, 8, 119
Matches, varieties of, 115
Maurice, F. D., 314
May Day Ode, 21
Mayhew Brothers, on domestic servants, 164–8
Mayhew, Henry, 33, 157, 269–70, 337; on cholera, 303; Exhibition, on, 24, 29; on Jacob's Island, 306–9; on lodging-houses, 298–9; London Labour and London Poor, 25; on pickle factory, 199, 300; on pickle girls, 188; on prostitution, 353–5
Meat, tainted, disposal of, 60; trade, 58
Medical examination, children, 74; prostitutes, 359
Merryweather, Mary, on factory life, 257–8
Metal trades, children in, 111
Methodism and factory workers, 77
Milk, transport of, 61
Mill, John Stuart, 314
Mill life, 76, 77; child labour in, 124; conditions in, 123;
Millinery, females in, 187–8; indoor, 173. See also Dressmakers
Miners, cruel sports of, 252; drink, and, 83; extravagance of, 253; life of, 80–85; living conditions of, 253; pleasures of, 83; reading of, 254–5; Union of, 317; wages of, 253
Model Cottages at Exhibition, 233; Prince Albert and, 242–5; Kennington Park, at, 237
Mohammedan pilgrims and cholera, 303
Morals improved, 42–3
Morning rush-hour in London, 50
Morris, Dr C., on agricultural work, 221
Mortality, annual, 290; infants, of, 230–1

Nails, manufacture of, conditions in, 128–9

Nailworkers, female, 187; health of, 130; homes of, 256; immorality of, 255–6; life of, 255–6; work of, 129–30

National Church, 78

National income, 37

National Trust, 234

Neo-Malthusianism, 338

Newcastle and coal, 65

Newgate market, 60

Newington, insanitation of, 283

Nightingale, Florence, 303

Non-unionist and trade union members, 319

Northumberland female agricultural workers, 224

North-Western Railway, 59

Nottingham and lacework, 189–90

Nottingham Daily Guardian, letter on laceworkers in, 190–1

Occupations, 47; statistics of, 155–6

Old Curiosity Shop, 157

Oliver Twist, 45

Orphans and crime, 146

Overcrowded dwellings, London, 276–7; rural, 246–7

Owen, R., 313; and birth-control, 338

Owenite Socialists, 330

Palmer, Mr, on provident institutions, 9, 91 f.

Palmerston, Lord, 146; on cholera, 310

Paper-mills, 197–9

Parliament, unreformed, 39

Pennines, 48

Peterman, Augustus, 47

Phosphorus, effects of, 118

Physical, Sexual, and Natural Religion, 338, 362

Picketing, 322

Pickle-factory workers, 199

Pickpockets, charges for, 26; children as, 148

Piece-workers, 77, 318

Piecer, 75

Pit-banks, 9

Pit-girls, life of, 209–10

Pitman, 67; lodging conditions of, 251–2; wife of, 70

Pit-mound labour, 211

Pit-people, 64

Pit-ponies, 68

Pits, accidents in, 78–9; Black Country, 78; ponies in, 68; villages, 70

Place, Francis, and birth-control, 338

Pleasure gardens in London, 352

Pointsman, work of, 99 f.

Poor, social conditions of, 274–6

Poor Law criticized, 255

Porter, G., on consumption of bread, 63; on progress in conditions, 236

Postage rate (1850), 38

Potteries, employment in, 90 f. females in, 187

Potters, behaviour of, 93–4; education, and, 94; morals of, 96; needs of, 95; savings, and, 91 f.; social state of, 90 ff. spending of, 92; wages of, 90–1. *See also* Pottery

Pottery, child labour in: 110, 112, 113; injuries to, 113–4, painting of, 114; price of, 113; wages in, 113

Poultry and game trade, 60

Pound, John, 150

Power loom at Great Exhibition, 32

Preventive sexual intercourse, 362–5

Primrose Hill, 97

Privies, public, criticized, 292–3

Privy Council Medical Reports, 292–3, 303–6

Progress 1800–1850, 40–3

Prosperity, Prince Albert and, 44

Prostitute, letter of, 339–46

Prostitutes, class of, 349–50; disease, and, 360; drink and, 349; haunts of, 348–9; hospital accommodation for, 359; houses of, 348–9; medical examination of, 359; numbers of, 345; procuresses of, 350; supervision of, 337

Prostitution, London, 337; Wales, 337, 356; Scotland, 337

Provident institutions in potteries, 91–2

Public Health, Ministry of, duties suggested, 291

Punch, domestic servants, on, 170; penal shirtmaking, and, 185–6

'Punch', Mr, 'Own Report' of Great Exhibition, 27 f.

Pupil teachers, 160

Putters, 68

Quarterly Review, 9, 57–64
'Queen Victoria's Sister', 155

Raciborski, M., and 'safe period', 366
Ragged Schools, 145, 150–3; Union, 150; child, class of, admitted to, 151; evening classes at, 151; results of, 152; success of, 150 f.
Railways, 95–102; buffets, 101–2; personnel of, 101 f.; coal, and, 66; company and injured workmen, 100; growth of, 41; stations: life on, 95–6, cabs at, 97; workers: 95 ff., female, 187
Rational Sick and Burial Society, 331
Rattering, 331–2
Rawnsley, Canon, 234
Reading material for miners, 254–5
Regent Street, 52
Rochdale Co-operative, goods of, 334; library of, 334
Rochdale Equitable Pioneers, 331–6; aims of, 331–2; dividends, 333; growth of, 333; Saturday night at, 334; subscription to, 332
Roman Catholicism in factory towns, 78
Rotherhithe sewers, insanitation of, 283
Rotten Row, 52
Royal Victoria Theatre, 54 f.
Ruff, G., on climbing-boys, 140–2
Rural cottages, 246; immorality in, 248; overcrowding of, 247
Ruskin, John, 241; and housing, 233

'Safe period', 364
Saint Monday, 88
Saleswomen, living conditions of, 181–2; wages of, 201; work of, 200
Sandboys, Christopher and family, 25
Sanitation, improvement in, 40; lack of, 273, 292. *See also* London; Simon, Dr J.
Saturday Review, 54
Saving, means of, 91 f.
Scammony, 290
Scarecrows, children as, 137
Schools, 42
Scotland, cholera in, 309–4; condition of dwellings in, 262–3; prostitution in, 356–8

Seamstresses (Semptresses), 47, 187
Seduction, prostitute writes on, 344
Serpentine, 26
Servants, old, life of, 162; problem, 156. *See* Domestic;
Sewage, gaseous, 297–8
Sewers, inadequacy of, 297
Sex, 337
Sexton, duties of, 288
Sexual intercourse, preventive, 364–5; morals of, 365
Shaftesbury, Earl of, 109–10; climbing-boys, and, 139; gang system, and, 216
Shanks's mare, 50
Sheffield Trade Union outrages, 216
Shepherd's Bush, 59
Shilling Day at Exhibition, 29, 30; folk, dress of, on, 31, 32
Shilling Handbook of Etiquette, 54
Shirtmakers, 184–6
Shirtmaking, military and penal, 185–6
Signalmen, duties of, 97
Simon, Dr J., 10, 170, 272; on: adulteration of food, 290–1; cholera, 304; graveyards, 288–90; dwellings, unfit, 292–3; intramural interments, 286–7; London, Public Health, 272; poor people, living conditions of, 274–6; prostitution, 358–61; sanitation, lack of, 273–80, 283–5, 286–93; water supply, lack of, 279
Slaughter-houses, London, 286
Slaughtering, criticized, 59, 286
Sleeping black, 144
Smelting furnaces, work at, 79–80
Smithfield, 58–9
Smoke, London, 284
Snelgrove, Mr, 8
Soap, tax on, 39
'Social Evil', 341
Social improvement, 236
Socialists and The Great Exhibition, 26
Society for Improving the Condition of the Labouring Classes, 242
Song of the Shirt, 170, 185, 201
Sooty cancer, 142
South Cerney, 246–7
Southampton, cholera at, 303–4, 306
Spitalfields, dwellings of weavers in, 238

Squalor of new towns, 37
Stabbing in boot factory, 120
Stanhope, Mr, on female agricultural workers, 223–4
Stansfield, R., on climbing-boys, 143–4
Steamship, first passenger, 41
Steamships, growing use of, 41
Stephenson, George, 66
Stockbrokers, 50
Stock-taker, furnace, 79
Stourbridge, 85; flint-glass factory at, 135
Strachan, D., 356
Straw-plait country, education in, 120 f.
Straw-plaiting, children in, 110, 121; wages of, 122; females in, 187
Street-walker, story of, 353–5
Streets, insanitation of, 276–8
Strikes, 40; picketing, 322–3
Summerfield glass works, 136
Suppression of Vice, Society for, 343
Surgeon killed in sewer, 297
Sweeps' Association, 142

Tacklers, 75
Tailors' Union, 318
Tapping coffins, 288
Taxes in 1850, 38–9
Tees, river, 66
Teetotalism, 332
Tenement houses, deficiencies of, 293
Tennyson, 8
Tenter, 74
Textiles, females in, 187 f.
Thackeray, W. M., poem of, 21
Thames, river, steamboats on, 51
Times, The, 337; on closing of Exhibition, 26; prostitute's letter to, 339; editorial in, 346
Toad Lane, 334–5; Rochdale Co-operatives at, 332
Toddington, straw-plaiting at, 120–1
Trade Unionists, number of, 315
Trade Union Act (1871), 315
Trade Unions, 10, 313–29; ban on, 313; blacklegs, and, 324; finances of, 317; general purposes of, 319; growth of, 315–18; joining the, 320–1; origin of, 315–20; picketing and, 322; piece-work, and, 318; rattening, 321–2; reasons for, 313;

skilled men in, 316; strikes, and, 318; wages, and, 318–19; women in, 324
Training reformed children, 146–7
Trains, 95 ff. See also Railways
Trappers, 69
Travel, 41
Trelawney, Mr, on tailors, 183
Tremenheere, H. S., 84, 110, 139, 254–5, on: agriculture, 216; bakehouses, 293–5; female workers, 207–8; mining population, 254
Trollope, G. F., on picketing, 323; builders' strike and, 324–5
Tufnell, E. C., 39, 110; on agriculture, 216
Tyne, river, and coal, 64–5
Tyneside, 48

Underdown Cliff, 31
Utopian Socialism, 313

Vaults, church, corpses in, 288–9
Vegetables, supply of, 61–2
Venereal disease, 360
Victoria, Princess Royal, 24
Victoria, Queen, 8, 20, 24, 155; and Exhibition, 22, 28 f.; and National Fasting, 310; praise of Prince Albert, 24; at theatre, 53
Victorian Age, 8; British business in, 8; living conditions in, 38; improvement in 39–40; magazines in, 48; successes of, 367
Victorian London, 49–56
Victorian mamma, 7
Victorian women, life of, 155 ff.
Victorians, 7; churchgoing of, 37; and business of, 37; pride and optimism of, 37; and sex, 337–66

Wages, 40; factories, in, 74, 75; Trade Unions and, 319
Waiting-room at Exhibition, 25, 34 f.
Wash-tub, chit-chat over, 269
Watchmaking, females in, 201
Water, insanitation of, 279–80; lack of supply of, 278; mixed with waste, 280; pits, in, 82; springs of contaminated, 281
Watercourses, pollution of, 279–80

Water-closets, 10; at the Great Exhibition, 25

Watercress, 63

Wearing apparel, manufacture of, 110

Weavers, Co-operative Society and, 330–1; life of, 75–6; living conditions of, 257 f.; poor, at Rochdale, 8; shops, 257;

Welsh cottages, 259–60

Westminster sewers, 297

Weymouth and Portland, cholera at, 304

White, J. E., 48, 110, 115–16, 118–19, on: Agricultural gangs, 218–19; brickworks, 130–1; children grinding metal, 132–3; button factory, 126–7; match factory, 117–18; metal factories in Birmingham, 90, 124–5, 126–8; small factories, 193–4; laceworkers, 191; steel work, 133–4; steel-pen factories, 125–6

Williams, Captain W. J., on juvenile delinquents, 147–8

Wolverton, 99, 100

Women workers. *See* Female workers

Women on horseback, 52

Workers as house-owners, 91, 92

Working class, leisure of, 55, 264–8; conditions of, 37

Workshops Act, 111

Workshops, small, in Birmingham, 87

Wright, T., on workers' life, 264–8

Wynter, Dr A., on: female watch-makers, 201; food supplies to London, 57–64

Young England, 109–10